Unit Operations
in Food Processing

Second Edition

Other publications of relevant interest

BIRCH *et al*

    Food Science, 3rd Edition

BUCKETT

    An Introduction to Farm Organisation and Management, 2nd Edition

LAWRIE

    Meat Science, 4th Edition

OTT

    Applied Food Science Laboratory Manual

RAO

    Food, Agriculture & Education

TAMIME

    Yoghurt: Science & Technology

Unit Operations in Food Processing

Second Edition

By

R. L. EARLE

Massey University, New Zealand

PERGAMON PRESS

OXFORD · NEW YORK · BEIJING · FRANKFURT
SÃO PAULO · SYDNEY · TOKYO · TORONTO

U.K.	Pergamon Press, Headington Hill Hall, Oxford OX3 0BW, England
U.S.A.	Pergamon Press, Maxwell House, Fairview Park, Elmsford, New York 10523, U.S.A.
PEOPLE'S REPUBLIC OF CHINA	Pergamon Press, Room 4037, Qianmen Hotel, Beijing, People's Republic of China
FEDERAL REPUBLIC OF GERMANY	Pergamon Press, Hammerweg 6, D-6242 Kronberg, Federal Republic of Germany
BRAZIL	Pergamon Editora, Rua Eça de Queiros, 346, CEP 04011, Paraiso, São Paulo, Brazil
AUSTRALIA	Pergamon Press Australia, P.O. Box 544, Potts Point, N.S.W. 2011, Australia
JAPAN	Pergamon Press, 8th Floor, Matsuoka Central Building, 1-7-1 Nishishinjuku, Shinjuku-ku, Tokyo 160, Japan
CANADA	Pergamon Press Canada, Suite No 271, 253 College Street, Toronto, Ontario, Canada M5T 1R5

First edition 1966

Second edition 1983

Reprinted 1985

Reprinted 1988

British Library Cataloguing in Publication Data

Earle, R. L.
Unit operations in food processing.—2nd ed.—(Pergamon international library)
1. Food industry and trade—Quality control
I. Title
664'.07   TP372.5

ISBN 0-08-025537-X Hardcover
ISBN 0-08-025536-1 Flexicover

Filmset by Speedlith Photo Litho Ltd., Manchester
Printed in Great Britain by A. Wheaton & Co. Ltd., Exeter

PREFACE TO SECOND EDITION

THERE has been, over the last few years, a general movement towards the SI system of units and it is important that students of food process engineering are introduced to this system. This meant quite a major revision if the basis of the book was to be changed to SI units and so the opportunity was taken to up-date the text. Comments were made by a number of people from various parts of the world suggesting additions or alterations which they felt to be improvements. These have been carefully considered and the opportunity taken to incorporate many of them. The section on material and energy balances has been expanded as these are so important to the technologist. More has been included on refrigeration and on psychrometry. As examples are so important in achieving an understanding of unit operations some further worked examples have been added, and it is emphasised again that these should be seen as an integral part of the text. In addition, a number of problems have been added at the end of each chapter as exercises for the students.

The level of the book has been maintained at that which is considered a reasonable minimum for food technologists who are concerned with processing plants and equipment. The very wide use of the first edition indicated a need for books at about this level: otherwise there would have been no point in preparing another edition. Those wishing to become specialists in food engineering will need to study the subject more deeply, and fortunately there are now several books available for this.

A great debt of gratitude is due to all who have made comments, made suggestions and pointed out errors and shortcomings, and to those in university and industry who have helped with individual items. There are too many to mention them all, but in particular Dr. J. R. Rosenau made available his copy with marked passages in need of further consideration. Dr. Paul Jelen was most helpful in encouraging the revision, reading manuscript and commenting, and, in conjunction with the Food Science Department at the University of Alberta and the Canada Council, in making available facilities in which much of the revision was undertaken.

So far as the machinery of typing and editing and publishing is concerned, I am indebted to those in Canada and New Zealand who have helped with typing and to those at Pergamon Press who have been involved in the preparation and production; also to those who have made material available for reproduction.

As in the earlier edition my wife, Dr. Mary Earle, has helped most materially with comments and in the extensive correcting which is always attendant on writing, and contributing in every respect to this new edition. Most of all, her encouragement has led to the work being completed.

CONTENTS

ing: thermal death time–equivalent killing power at other temperatures–pasteurization. Refrigeration, chilling and freezing: refrigeration cycle–performance characteristics–refrigerants–mechanical equipment–evaporators–chilling–freezing–cold storage. Summary. Problems.

7. DRYING   85

Basic drying theory: three states of water–heat requirements for vaporization–heat transfer in drying–dryer efficiencies. Mass transfer in drying. Psychrometry–wet-bulb temperatures–psychrometric charts–measurement of humidity. Equilibrium moisture content. Air drying: calculation of constant drying rates–falling rate drying–calculation of drying time. Conduction drying. Drying equipment: tray dryers–tunnel dryers–roller or drum dryers–fluidized bed dryers–spray dryers–pneumatic dryers–rotary dryers–trough dryers–bin dryers–belt dryers–vacuum dryers–freeze dryers. Moisture loss in freezers and chillers. Summary. Problems.

8. EVAPORATION   105

The single-effect evaporator: vacuum evaporation–heat transfer in evaporators–condensers. Multiple-effect evaporation–feeding of multiple-effect evaporators–advantages of multiple-effect evaporators. Vapour recompression. Boiling-point elevation. Evaporation of heat-sensitive materials. Evaporation equipment–open pans–horizontal-tube evaporators–vertical-tube evaporators–plate evaporators–long tube evaporators–forced circulation evaporators–evaporators for heat-sensitive liquids. Summary. Problems.

9. CONTACT-EQUILIBRIUM SEPARATION PROCESSES   116

PART 1. THEORY. Concentrations. Gas–liquid equilibria. Solid–liquid equilibria. Equilibrium concentration relationships. Operating conditions. Calculation of separation in contact-equilibrium processes.

PART 2. APPLICATIONS. Gas absorption: rate of gas absorption–stage-equilibrium gas absorption–gas-absorption equipment. Extraction: rate of extraction–stage-equilibrium extraction–washing–extraction and washing equipment. Crystallization: crystallization equilibrium–rate of crystal growth–stage-equilibrium crystallization–crystallization equipment. Membrane separations: rate of flow through membranes–membrane equipment. Distillation: steam distillation–vacuum distillation–batch distillation–distillation equipment. Summary. Problems.

10. MECHANICAL SEPARATIONS   143

The velocity of particles moving in a fluid. Sedimentation: gravitational sedimentation of particles in a fluid–sedimentation of particles in a gas–settling under combined forces. Centrifugal separations: rate of separation–liquid separation–centrifuge equipment. Filtration: constant-rate filtration–constant-pressure filtration–filter cake compressibility–filtration equipment. Sieving. Summary. Problems.

11. SIZE REDUCTION   159

Grinding and cutting: energy used in grinding–new surface formed by grinding–grinding equipment. Emulsification: preparation of emulsions. Summary. Problems.

12. MIXING

Characteristics of mixtures. Measurement of mixing. Particle mixing: mixing of widely different quantities – rates of mixing – energy input in mixing. Liquid mixing. Mixing equipment – liquid mixers – powder and particle mixers – dough and paste mixers. Summary. Problems.

13. SOME ENGINEERING APPLICATIONS OF PROCESS ENGINEERING IN THE FOOD INDUSTRY

The meat industry: material and energy balances – fluid flow – heat transfer – evaporation – drying – equilibrium contact separations – mechanical separations – size reductions – mixing. The dairy industry: material and energy balances – fluid flow-heat transfer- drying – evaporation – equilibrium contact separations – mechanical separations – size reduction – mixing

APPENDICES

REFERENCES

BIBLIOGRAPHY

INDEX

CHAPTER 1

INTRODUCTION

This book is designed to give the food technologist an understanding of the engineering principles involved in the processing of his products. He may not have to design process equipment in detail but he should understand how the equipment operates. With an understanding of the basic principles of process engineering, he will be able to develop new food processes and modify existing ones. The food technologist must also be able to make himself clearly understood by design engineers and by the suppliers of the equipment he uses.

Only a thorough understanding of the basic sciences applied in the food industry – chemistry, biology and engineering – can prepare the student for working in the complex food industry of today. This book discusses the basic engineering principles and shows how they are important in, and applicable to, every food industry and every food process.

For the food-process engineering student, this book will serve as a useful introduction to more specialized studies.

METHOD OF STUDYING FOOD-PROCESS ENGINEERING

As an introduction to food-process engineering, this book describes the scientific principles on which food processing is based and gives some examples of the application of these principles in several food industries. When he has understood some of the basic theory, the student should study more detailed information about the individual industries and apply the basic principles to their processes. For

example, after studying heat transfer here the student should seek information on heat transfer in the canning and freezing industries.

To supplement the relatively few books on food-process engineering other sources of information must be found, for example:

(1) Specialist descriptions of particular food industries. These in general are written from a descriptive point of view and deal only briefly with engineering.
(2) Specialist works in chemical and biological process engineering. These are studies of processing operations but they seldom have any direct reference to food processing. However, the basic unit operations apply equally to all process industries, including the food industry.
(3) Engineering handbooks. These contain considerable data including some information on the properties of food materials.
(4) Periodicals. In these can often be found the most up-to-date information on specialized equipment and processes.

BASIC PRINCIPLES OF FOOD-PROCESS ENGINEERING

The study of process engineering is an attempt to analyse all forms of physical processing into a small number of basic operations, which are called unit operations. Food processes may seem bewildering in their diversity, but careful analysis will show that these complicated and differing processes can be broken down into a small number of unit operations.

For example, consider heating, of which innumerable instances occur in every food industry. There are many reasons for heating and cooling – for example, the baking of bread, the freezing of meat, the tempering of oils. But in process engineering the prime considerations are the extent of the heating or cooling that is required and the conditions under which this must be accomplished. Thus, this physical process qualifies to be called a unit operation. It is called "heat transfer".

The essential concept is therefore to divide physical food processes into basic unit operations each of which can stand alone and which depends on coherent physical principles. For example, heat transfer is a unit operation and the fundamental physical principle underlying it is that heat energy will be transferred spontaneously from hotter to colder bodies. Because of the dependence of the unit operation on a physical principle, or a small group of associated principles, quantitative relationships in the form of mathematical equations can be built up to describe them. The equations can be used to follow what is happening in the process and for control and modification of the process if required.

Important unit operations in the food industry are fluid flow, heat transfer, drying, evaporation, contact equilibrium processes (which include distillation, extraction, gas absorption, crystallization, and membrane processes), mechanical separations (which include filtration, centrifugation, sedimentation and sieving), size reduction and mixing. These unit operations, and in particular the basic concepts on which they depend rather than the equipment used or the materials being processed, are the subject of this book.

Two very important laws which all unit operations obey are the laws of conservation of mass and energy.

The Conservation of Mass and Energy

The law of conservation of mass states that mass cannot be created nor destroyed. Thus in a processing plant the total mass of material entering the plant must equal the total mass of material leaving the plant, less any accumulation left in the plant. If there is no accumulation, then the simple rule holds that "what goes in must come out". Similarly all material entering a unit operation must in due course leave.

For example, if milk is being fed into a centrifugal separator to separate it into skim milk and cream, under the law of conservation of mass the total number of kilograms of material (milk) entering the centrifuge per minute must equal the total number of kilograms of material (skim milk and cream) that leave the centrifuge per minute.

Similarly, the law of conservation of mass applies to each component in the entering materials. For example, considering the butter fat in the milk entering the separator, the weight of butter fat entering the centrifuge per minute must be equal to the weight of butter fat leaving the centrifuge per minute. A similar relationship will hold for the other components, proteins, milk sugars and so on.

The law of conservation of energy states that energy cannot be created nor destroyed. The total energy in the materials entering the processing plant, plus the energy added in the plant, must equal the total energy leaving the plant. This is a more complex concept than the conservation of mass, as energy can take various forms such as kinetic energy, potential energy, heat energy, chemical energy, electrical energy and so on. During processing, some of these forms of energy can be converted from one to another. Mechanical energy in a fluid can be converted through friction into heat energy. Chemical energy in food is converted by the body into mechanical energy. Note that it is the sum total of all these forms of energy that is conserved.

For example, consider the pasteurizing process for milk, in which milk is pumped through a heat exchanger and is first heated and then cooled. The energy can be considered either over the whole plant or only as it affects the milk. For total plant energy, the balance must include: the conversion in the pump of electrical energy to kinetic and heat energy, the kinetic and potential energies of the milk entering and leaving the plant and the various kinds of energy in the heating and cooling sections.

To the food technologist, the energies affecting the product are the most important. In the case of the pasteurizer the energy affecting the product is the heat energy in the milk. Heat energy is added to the milk by the pump and by the heating water in the heat exchanger. Cooling water then removes part of the heat energy and some of the heat energy is also lost to the surroundings.

The heat energy leaving in the milk must equal the heat energy in the milk entering the pasteurizer plus or minus any heat added or taken away in the plant.

Heat energy leaving in milk = initial heat energy + heat energy added by pump + heat energy added in heating section − heat energy taken out in cooling section − heat energy lost to surroundings.

The law of conservation of energy can also apply to part of a process. For example, considering the heating section of the heat exchanger in the pasteurizer, the heat lost by the heating water must be equal to the sum of the heat gained by the milk and the heat lost from the heat exchanger to its surroundings.

From these laws of conservation of mass and energy, a balance sheet for materials and for energy can be drawn up at all times for a unit operation. These are called material balances and energy balances.

Overall View of an Engineering Process

Using a material balance and an energy balance, a food engineering process can be viewed overall or as a series of units. Each unit is a unit operation. The unit operation can be represented by a box as shown in Fig. 1.1. Into the box go the raw materials and energy, out of the box come the desired products, undesired products and energy. The equipment within the box will enable the required changes to be made with as little waste of materials and energy as possible. In other words, the desired products are required to be maximized and the undesired products minimized. Control over the process is exercised by controlling the flow of energy, or of materials, or of both.

DIMENSIONS AND UNITS

All engineering deals with definite and measured quantities, and so depends on the making of measurements. We must be clear and precise in making these measurements.

To make a measurement is to compare the unknown with the known, for example, weighing a material compares it with a standard weight of one kilogram. The result of the comparison is expressed in terms of multiples of the known quantity, that is, as so many kilograms. Thus, the record of a measurement consists of three parts: the dimension of the quantity, the unit which represents a known or standard quantity and a number which is the ratio of the measured quantity to the standard quantity. For example, if a rod is 1.18 m long, this measurement can be analysed into a dimension, length; a standard unit, the metre; and a number 1.18 which is the ratio of the length of the rod to the standard length, 1 m.

To say that our rod is 1.18 m long is a commonplace statement and yet because measurement is the basis of all engineering, the statement deserves some closer attention. There are three aspects of our statement to consider: dimensions, units of measurement and the number itself.

Dimensions

It has been found from experience that everyday engineering quantities can all be expressed in terms of a relatively small number of dimensions. These dimensions are length, mass, time and temperature. For convenience, in engineering calculations force is added as another dimension. Force can be expressed in terms of the other dimensions, but it simplifies many engineering calculations to use force as a dimension.

Dimensions are represented symbolically by: length $[L]$, mass $[M]$, time $[\theta]$, temperature $[T]$

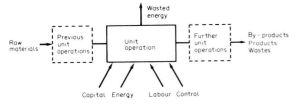

Fig. 1.1. Unit operation.

and force $[F]$. Note that these are enclosed in square brackets: this is the conventional way of expressing dimensions. Unfortunately, in English, time and temperature both begin with the letter t, so to avoid confusion the Greek letter θ (theta) is used for time.

All engineering quantities used in this book can be expressed in terms of these fundamental dimensions. For example:

Length $= [L]$, area $= [L]^2$, volume $= [L]^3$.

Velocity $=$ length travelled per unit time
$$= \frac{[L]}{[\theta]}.$$

Acceleration $=$ rate of change of velocity
$$= \frac{[L]}{[\theta]} \times \frac{[1]}{[\theta]} = \frac{[L]}{[\theta]^2}.$$

Pressure $=$ force per unit area $= \dfrac{[F]}{[L]^2}.$

Density $=$ mass per unit volume $= \dfrac{[M]}{[L]^3}.$

Energy $=$ force times length $= [F] \times [L]$.

Power $=$ energy per unit time
$$= \frac{[F] \times [L]}{[\theta]}.$$

As more complex quantities are found to be needed, these can be analysed in terms of the fundamental dimensions. For example in heat transfer, the heat-transfer coefficient, h, is defined as the quantity of heat energy transferred through unit area, in unit time and with unit temperature difference:

$$h = \frac{[F] \times [L]}{[L]^2 [\theta][T]} = [F][L]^{-1}[\theta]^{-1}[T]^{-1}.$$

Units

Dimensions are measured in terms of units. For example, the dimension of length is measured in terms of length units – the micrometre, millimetre, metre, kilometre, etc. So that the measurements can always be compared, the units have been defined in terms of physical quantities. For example, the metre

(m) is defined in terms of the wavelength of light. Similarly with mass, the standard kilogram (kg) is the weight of a standard lump of platinum-iridium; the second (s) is the time taken for light of a given wavelength to vibrate a given number of times; and the degree Celsius (°C) is a one-hundredth part of the temperature interval between the freezing point and the boiling point of water at standard pressure. The unit of force, the newton (N), is that force which will give an acceleration of 1 m sec^{-2} to a mass of 1 kg. The energy unit, the newton metre is called the joule (J) and the power unit, 1 J s^{-1}, is called the watt (W).

More complex units arise from equations in which several of these fundamental units are combined to define some new relationship. For example, volume has the dimensions $[L]^3$ and so the units are m³. Density, mass per unit volume, similarly has the dimensions $[M]/[L]^3$, and the units kg m^{-3}. A table of such relationships is given in Appendix 1.

When dealing with quantities which cannot conveniently be measured in m, kg, s, multiples of these units are used. For example, kilometres, tonnes and hours are useful for large quantities of metres, kilograms and seconds respectively. In general, multiples of 10^3 are preferred such as millimetres (m $\times 10^{-3}$) rather than centimetres (m $\times 10^{-2}$). Time is an exception: its multiples are not decimalized and so although we have micro (10^{-6}) and milli (10^{-3}) seconds, at the other end of the scale we still have minutes (min), hours (h), days (d), etc. Care must be taken to use appropriate multiplying factors when working with these units. The common secondary units then use the prefixes micro ($\mu, 10^{-6}$), milli (m, 10^{-3}), kilo (k, 10^3) and mega (M, 10^6).

Dimensional Consistency

All physical equations must be dimensionally consistent. This means that both sides of the equation must reduce to the same dimensions. For example, if on one side of the equation, the dimensions are $[M][L]/[T]^2$, the other side of the equation must also be $[M][L]/[T]^2$ with the same dimensions to the same powers. Dimensions can be handled algebraically and therefore they can be divided, multiplied, or cancelled. By remembering that an equation must be dimensionally consistent, the dimensions of otherwise unknown quantities can sometimes be calculated.

EXAMPLE 1.1. In the equation of motion of a particle travelling at a uniform velocity for a time θ, the distance travelled is given by $L = v\theta$. Verify the dimensions of velocity.

Knowing that length has dimensions $[L]$ and time has dimensions $[\theta]$ we have the dimensional equation

$$[v] = [L]/[\theta].$$

$\therefore$ the dimensions of velocity must be $[L][\theta]^{-1}$.

The test of dimensional homogeneity is sometimes useful as an aid to memory. If an equation is written down and on checking is not dimensionally homogeneous, then something has been forgotten.

Unit Consistency

Unit consistency implies that the units employed for the dimensions should be chosen from a consistent group, for example in this book we are using the SI (Système Internationale de Unites) system of units. This has been internationally accepted as being desirable and necessary for the standardization of physical measurements and although different countries are moving towards it at varying rates it seems quite clear that its complete adoption is only a relatively short matter of time. The other commonly used system is the fps (foot pound second) system and a table of conversion factors is given in Appendix 2.

Very often, quantities are specified or measured in mixed units. For example, if a liquid has been flowing at 1.3 l/min for 18.5 h, all the times have to be put into one only of minutes, hours or seconds before we can calculate the total quantity that has passed. Similarly where tabulated data are only available in non-standard units, conversion tables such as those in Appendix 2 have to be used to convert the units.

EXAMPLE 1.2. Convert 10 grams into pounds.

From Appendix 2, $1\,\text{lb} = 0.4536\,\text{kg}$ and $1000\,\text{g} = 1\,\text{kg}$.

$\therefore$ $(1\,\text{lb}/0.4536\,\text{kg}) = 1$ and $(1\,\text{kg}/1000\,\text{g}) = 1$.

$\therefore$ $10\,\text{g} = 10\,\text{g} \times (1\,\text{lb}/0.4536\,\text{kg}) \times (1\,\text{kg}/1000\,\text{g})$.

$= 2.2 \times 10^{-2}\,\text{lb}$

$\therefore$ $10\,\text{g} = 2.2 \times 10^{-2}\,\text{lb}$

The quantity in brackets in the above example is called a conversion factor. Notice that within the bracket, and before cancelling, the numerator and the denominator are equal. In equations, units can be cancelled in the same way as numbers.

EXAMPLE 1.3. Milk is flowing through a full pipe whose diameter is known to be 1.8 cm. The only measure available is a tank calibrated in cubic feet, and it is found that it takes 1 h to fill 12.4 ft³.

What is the velocity of flow of the liquid in the pipe?

Velocity is $[L]/[\theta]$ and the units in the SI system for velocity are therefore m s^{-1}:

$$v = L\theta^{-1} \text{ where } v \text{ is the velocity.}$$
Now $V = AL$ where V is the volume of a length of pipe L of cross-sectional area A

i.e. $L = V/A.$

$\therefore v = V/A\theta.$

Checking this dimensionally

$$[L][\theta]^{-1} = [L]^{3}[L]^{-2}[\theta]^{-1} = [L][\theta]^{-1}$$

which is correct.

Since the required velocity is in m s^{-1}, V must be in m^3, θ in s and A in m^2.

From the volume measurement

$$V/\theta = 12.4\,\text{ft}^3\,\text{h}^{-1}.$$

From Appendix 2, $1\,\text{ft}^3 = 0.0283\,\text{m}^3$.

$$1 = (0.0283 \, \text{m}^3/1 \, \text{ft}^3),$$
$$1 \, \text{h} = 60 \times 60 \, \text{s}.$$
$$\therefore \quad 1 = (3600 \, \text{s}/1 \, \text{h}) = (1 \, \text{h}/3600 \, \text{s}).$$
$$\therefore \quad V/\theta = 12.4 \, \text{ft}^3/\text{h} \times (0.0283 \, \text{m}^3/1 \, \text{ft}^3) \times$$
$$(1 \, \text{h}/3600 \, \text{s})$$
$$= 9.75 \times 10^{-5} \, \text{m}^3 \, \text{s}^{-1}.$$

Also the area of the pipe $A = \pi D^2/4$
$$= \pi(0.018)^2/4 \, \text{m}^2$$
$$= 2.54 \times 10^{-4} \, \text{m}^2.$$

$$\therefore \quad v = V/\theta \times 1/A$$
$$= 9.75 \times 10^{-5}/2.54 \times 10^{-4}$$
$$= 0.38 \, \text{m} \, \text{s}^{-1}.$$

EXAMPLE 1.4. The viscosity of water at 60°F is given as $7.8 \times 10^{-4} \, \text{lb} \, \text{ft}^{-1} \, \text{s}^{-1}$. Calculate this viscosity in $\text{N} \, \text{s} \, \text{m}^{-2}$.

From Appendix 2, $0.4536 \, \text{kg} = 1 \, \text{lb}$,
$$0.3048 \, \text{m} = 1 \, \text{ft}.$$
$$\therefore \quad 7.8 \times 10^{-4} \, \text{lb} \, \text{ft}^{-1} \, \text{s}^{-1} = 7.8 \times 10^{-4} \, \text{lb} \, \text{ft}^{-1} \, \text{s}^{-1}$$
$$\times \frac{0.4536 \, \text{kg}}{1 \, \text{lb}} \times \frac{1 \, \text{ft}}{0.3048 \, \text{m}}$$
$$= 1.16 \, 10^{-3} \, \text{kg} \, \text{m}^{-1} \, \text{s}^{-1}.$$
$$\text{But } 1 \, \text{N} = 1 \, \text{kg} \, \text{m} \, \text{s}^{-2}.$$
$$\therefore \quad 1 \, \text{N} \, \text{m}^{-2} \, \text{s} = 1 \, \text{kg} \, \text{m}^{-1} \, \text{s}^{-1}.$$
$$\therefore \quad \text{Required viscosity} = 1.16 \times 10^{-3} \, \text{N} \, \text{s} \, \text{m}^{-2}.$$

EXAMPLE 1.5. The thermal conductivity of aluminium is given as $120 \, \text{Btu} \, \text{ft}^{-1} \, \text{h}^{-1} \, °\text{F}^{-1}$. Calculate this thermal conductivity in $\text{J} \, \text{m}^{-1} \, \text{s}^{-1} \, °\text{C}^{-1}$.

From Appendix 2, $1 \, \text{Btu} = 1055 \, \text{J}$,
$$0.3048 \, \text{m} = 1 \, \text{ft},$$
$$°\text{F} = (5/9)°\text{C}.$$

$$\therefore \quad 120 \, \text{Btu} \, \text{ft}^{-1} \, \text{h}^{-1} \, °\text{F}^{-1} = 120 \, \text{Btu} \, \text{ft}^{-1} \, \text{h}^{-1} \, °\text{F}^{-1}$$
$$\times \frac{1055 \, \text{J}}{1 \, \text{Btu}} \times \frac{1 \, \text{ft}}{0.3048 \, \text{m}} \times \frac{1 \, \text{h}}{3600 \, \text{s}} \times \frac{1°\text{F}}{(5/9)°\text{C}}$$
$$= 208 \, \text{J} \, \text{m}^{-1} \, \text{s}^{-1} \, °\text{C}^{-1}.$$

Alternatively a conversion factor can be calculated:
$$1 \, \text{Btu} \, \text{ft}^{-1} \, \text{h}^{-1} \, °\text{F}^{-1} = 1 \, \text{Btu} \, \text{ft}^{-1} \, \text{h}^{-1} \, °\text{F}^{-1}$$
$$\times \frac{1055 \, \text{J}}{1 \, \text{Btu}} \times \frac{1 \, \text{ft}}{0.3048 \, \text{m}} \times$$
$$\frac{1 \, \text{h}}{3600 \, \text{s}} \times \frac{1°\text{F}}{(5/9)°\text{C}}$$
$$= 1.73 \, \text{J} \, \text{m}^{-1} \, \text{s}^{-1} \, °\text{C}^{-1}$$
$$\therefore \quad 120 \, \text{Btu} \, \text{ft}^{-1} \, \text{h}^{-1} \, °\text{F}^{-1} =$$
$$120 \times 1.73 \, \text{J} \, \text{m}^{-1} \, \text{s}^{-1} \, °\text{C}^{-1}$$
$$= 208 \, \text{J} \, \text{m}^{-1} \, \text{s}^{-1} \, °\text{C}^{-1}$$

Because engineering measurements are often made in convenient or conventional units, this question of consistency in equations is very important. Before making calculations always check that the units are the right ones and if not use the necessary conversion factors. The method given above, which can be applied even in very complicated cases, is a safe one if applied systematically.

A loose mode of expression that has arisen, which is sometimes confusing, follows from the use of the word per, or its equivalent the solidus, /. A common example is to give acceleration due to gravity as 9.81 metres per second per second. From this the units of g would seem to be m/s/s, that is $\text{m} \, \text{s} \, \text{s}^{-1}$ which is incorrect. A better way to write these units would be $g = 9.81 \, \text{m/s}^2$ which is clearly the same as $9.81 \, \text{m} \, \text{s}^{-2}$. Precision in writing down the units of measurement is a great help in solving problems.

Dimensionless Ratios

It is often easier to visualize quantities if they are expressed in ratio form and ratios have the great advantage of being dimensionless. If a car is said to be going at twice the speed limit, this is a dimensionless ratio which quickly draws attention to the speed of the car. These dimensionless ratios are often used in process engineering, comparing the unknown with some well-known material or factor.

For example, specific gravity is a simple way to express the relative masses or weights of equal volumes of various materials. The specific gravity may be defined as the ratio of the weight of a volume of the substance to the weight of an equal volume of water.

$$SG = \frac{\text{weight of a volume of the substance}}{\text{weight of an equal volume of water}}.$$

Dimensionally,

$$SG = \frac{[F]}{[L]^{-3}} \div \frac{[F]}{[L]^{-3}}$$
$$= 1.$$

If the density of water, that is the mass of unit volume of water, is known, then if the specific gravity of some substance is determined, its density can be calculated from the following relationship:

$$\rho = SG\rho_w$$

where ρ (rho) is the density of the substance, SG is the specific gravity of the substance and ρ_w is the density of water.

Perhaps the most important attribute of a dimensionless ratio, such as specific gravity, is that it gives an immediate sense of proportion. This sense of proportion is very important to an engineer as he is constantly making approximate mental calculations for which he must be able to maintain correct proportions. For example, if the specific gravity of a solid is known to be greater than 1 then that solid will sink in water. The fact that the specific gravity of iron is 7.88 makes the quantity more easily visualized than the equivalent statement that the density of iron is $7880 \, \text{kg m}^{-3}$. Another advantage of a dimensionless ratio is that it does not depend upon the units of measurement used, provided the units are consistent for each dimension.

Dimensionless ratios are employed frequently in the study of fluid flow and heat flow. They may sometimes appear to be more complicated than specific gravity, but they are in the same way expressing ratios of the unknown to the known material or fact. These dimensionless ratios are then called dimensionless numbers and are often called after a prominent person who was associated with them, for example Reynolds number, Prandtl number, and Nusselt number.

When evaluating dimensionless ratios, all units must be kept consistent. For this purpose, conversion factors must be used where necessary.

Precision of Measurement

Every measurement necessarily carries a degree of precision, and it is a great advantage if the statement of the result of the measurement shows this precision. The statement of quantity should either itself imply the tolerance, or else the tolerances should be explicitly specified. For example, a quoted weight of 10.1 kg should mean that the weight lies between 10.05 and 10.149 kg. Where there is doubt it is better to express the limits explicitly as 10.1 $\pm$ 0.05 kg.

The temptation to refine measurements by the use of arithmetic must be resisted. For example, if the surface of a tank is measured as 4.18 m × 2.22 m and its depth estimated at 3 m, it is obviously unjustified to calculate its volume as $27.8388 \, \text{m}^3$ which is what arithmetic or an electronic calculator will give. A more reasonable answer would be $28 \, \text{m}^3$. Multiplication of quantities in fact multiplies errors also.

In process engineering, the degree of precision of statements and calculations should always be borne in mind. Every set of data has its least precise member and no amount of mathematics can improve on it. Only better measurement can do this.

A large proportion of practical measurements are accurate only to about 1 part in 100. In some cases factors may well be no more accurate than 1 in 10, and in every calculation proper consideration must be given to the accuracy of the measurements. Electronic calculators may work to eight figures or so, but all figures after the first few may be physically meaningless. For much of process engineering three significant figures are all that are justifiable.

SUMMARY

1. Food processes can be analysed in terms of unit operations.
2. In all processes, mass and energy are conserved.
3. Material and energy balance can be written for every process.
4. All physical quantities used in this book can be expressed in terms of five fundamental dimensions $[M]$ $[L]$ $[\theta]$ $[F]$ $[T]$.
5. Equations must be dimensionally homogeneous.
6. Equations should be consistent in their units.
7. Dimensions and units can be treated algebraically in equations.
8. Dimensionless ratios are often a very graphic way of expressing physical relationships.
9. Calculations are based on measurement, and the precision of the calculation is no better than the precision of the measurements.

PROBLEMS

1. Show that the following heat transfer equation is consistent in its units:

$$q = UA\,\Delta t$$

where q is the heat flow rate $(J\,s^{-1})$, U is the overall heat transfer coefficient $(J\,m^{-2}\,s^{-1}\,°C^{-1})$, A is the area (m^2) and Δt is the temperature difference $(°C)$.

2. The specific heat of apples is given as $0.86\,Btu\,lb^{-1}\,°F^{-1}$. Calculate this specific heat in $J\,kg^{-1}\,°C^{-1}$.

3. If the viscosity of olive oil is given as $5.6 \times 10^{-2}\,lb/ft\,sec$, calculate the viscosity in SI units.

4. The Reynolds number for a fluid in a pipe is

$$\frac{Dv\rho}{\mu}$$

where D is the diameter of a pipe, v is the velocity of the fluid, ρ is the density of the fluid and μ is the viscosity of the fluid. Using the five fundamental dimensions $[M]$, $[L]$, $[\theta]$, $[F]$ and $[T]$ show that this is a dimensionless ratio.

5. Determine the protein content of the following mixture clearly showing the accuracy:

	% Protein	Weight in mixture
Maize starch	0.3	100 kg
Wheat flour	12.0	22.5 kg
Skim milk powder	30.0	4.31 kg

6. In determining the rate of heating of a tank of sugar syrup the temperature at the beginning was $20°C$ and it took 30 min to heat to $80°C$. The volume of the sugar syrup was $50\,ft^3$. The specific heat of the sugar syrup is $0.8\,Btu/lb°F$. Determine the rate of heating in SI units $(J\,s^{-1})$.

7. The gas equation is $PV = nRT$, if P the pressure is $2.0\,atm$, V the volume of the gas is $6\,m^3$, R the gas constant is $0.08206\,m^3$ atm mole^{-1} K^{-1} and T is 300 degrees Kelvin, what are the units of n and what is its numerical value?

8. The gas law constant R is given as $0.08206\,m^3$ atm mole^{-1} K^{-1}.
Find its value in: (a) mm Hg ft^3 lb-mole^{-1} K^{-1},
(b) m^3 Pa mole^{-1} K^{-1},
(c) Joules g-mole^{-1} K^{-1}.

9. The equation determining the liquid pressure in a tank is $z = P/\rho g$ where z is the depth, P is the pressure, ρ is the density and g is the acceleration due to gravity. Show that the two sides of the equation are dimensionally the same.

10. The Grashof number (Gr) arises in the study of natural convection heat flow. If the number is given as

$$\frac{D^3 \rho^2 \beta g\,\Delta t}{\mu^2},$$

verify the dimensions of β the coefficient of expansion of the fluid. The symbols are all defined in Appendix 1.

CHAPTER 2

MATERIAL AND ENERGY BALANCES

MATERIAL quantities, as they pass through food-processing operations, can be described by material balances. Such balances are statements on the conservation of mass. Similarly, energy quantities can be described by energy balances, which are statements on the conservation of energy. If there is no accumulation, what goes into a process must come out. This is true for batch operation. It is equally true for continuous operation over any chosen time interval.

Material and energy balances are very important in the food industry. Material balances are fundamental to the control of processing, particularly in the control of yields of the products. The first material balances are determined in the exploratory stages of a new process, improved during pilot plant experiments when the process is being planned and tested, checked out when the plant is commissioned and then refined and maintained as a control instrument as production continues. When any changes occur in the process, the material balances need to be determined again.

The increasing cost of energy has caused the food industry to examine means of reducing energy consumption in processing. Energy balances are used in the examination of the various stages of a process, over the whole process and even extending over the total food production system from the farm to the consumer's plate.

Material and energy balances can be simple, at times they can be very complicated, but the basic approach is general. Experience in working with the simpler systems such as individual unit operations will develop the facility to extend the methods to the more complicated situations which arise. The increasing availability of computers has meant that very complex mass and energy balances can be set up and manipulated quite readily and therefore used in everyday process management to maximize product yields and minimize costs.

BASIC PRINCIPLES

If the unit operation, whatever its nature, is seen as a whole it may be represented diagrammatically as a box, as shown in Fig. 2.1. The mass and energy going into the box must balance with the mass and energy coming out.

The law of conservation of mass leads to what is called a mass or a material balance.

$$\text{Mass In} = \text{Mass Out} + \text{Mass Stored.}$$

$$\text{Raw Materials} = \text{Products} + \text{Wastes} + \text{Stored Materials.}$$

$$\sum m_R = \sum m_p + \sum m_W + \sum m_S$$

(where $\sum$ (sigma) denotes the sum of all terms).

$$\sum m_R = m_{R1} + m_{R2} + m_{R3}$$
$$= \text{Total Raw Materials.}$$
$$\sum m_P = m_{P1} + m_{P2} + m_{P3}$$
$$= \text{Total Products.}$$
$$\sum m_W = m_{W1} + m_{W2} + m_{W3}$$
$$= \text{Total Waste Products.}$$
$$\sum m_S = m_{S1} + m_{S2} + m_{S3}$$
$$= \text{Total Stored Products.}$$

If there are no chemical changes occurring in the plant, the law of conservation of mass will apply also

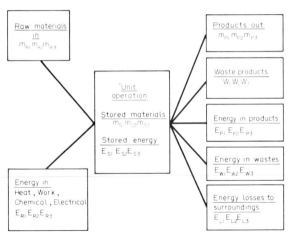

FIG. 2.1. Mass and energy balance

to each component, so that:

m_A in entering materials = m_A in the exit
materials + m_A stored in plant.

For example, in a plant that is producing sugar, if the total quantity of sugar going into the plant is not

where Losses are the unidentified materials.

Just as mass is conserved, so is energy conserved in food-processing operations. The energy coming into a unit operation can be balanced with the energy coming out and the energy stored.

$$\text{Energy In} = \text{Energy Out} + \text{Energy Stored}$$
$$\sum E_R = \sum E_P + \sum E_W + \sum E_L + \sum E_S$$

$$\text{where } \sum E_R = E_{R1} + E_{R2} + E_{R3} + \cdots = \text{Total Energy Entering}$$
$$\sum E_P = E_{P1} + E_{P2} + E_{P3} + \cdots = \text{Total Energy Leaving with Products}$$
$$\sum E_W = E_{W1} + E_{W2} + E_{W3} + \cdots = \text{Total Energy Leaving with Waste Materials}$$
$$\sum E_L = E_{L1} + E_{L2} + E_{L3} + \cdots = \text{Total Energy Lost to Surroundings}$$
$$\sum E_S = E_{S1} + E_{S2} + E_{S3} + \cdots = \text{Total Energy Stored}$$

equalled by the total of the purified sugar and the sugar in the waste liquors, then there is something wrong. Sugar is either being burned (chemically changed) or accumulating in the plant or else it is going unnoticed down the drain somewhere. In this case

$$(m_A) = (m_{AP} + m_{AW} + m_{AU})$$

where m_{AU} is the unknown loss and needs to be identified. So the material balance is now:

Raw Materials = Products
                + Waste Products
                + Stored Products
                + Losses

Energy balances are often complicated because forms of energy can be interconverted, for example mechanical energy to heat energy, but overall the quantities must balance.

MATERIAL BALANCES

The first step is to look at the three basic categories: materials in, materials out and materials stored. Then the materials in each category have to be considered whether they are to be treated as a whole, a gross mass balance, or whether various constituents should be treated separately and if so what constituents. To take a simple example, it might be to take dry solids as opposed to total material; this really means separating the two groups of constituents non-water and water. More complete dissection can separate out chemical types such as minerals, or chemical elements such as carbon. The choice and the detail depend on the reasons for making the balance and on the information that is required. A major factor in industry is, of course, the value of the materials and so expensive raw materials are more likely to be considered than cheaper ones, and products than waste materials.

Basis and Units

Having decided which constituents need consideration the basis for the calculations has to be decided. This might be some mass of raw material entering the process in a batch system, or some mass per hour in a continuous process. It could be some mass of a particular predominant constituent, for example mass balances in a bakery might be all related to 100 kg of flour entering, or it might be of some unchanging constituent such as in combustion calculations with air where it is helpful to relate everything to the inert nitrogen component, it could be carbon added in the nutrients in a fermentation system because the essential energy relationships of the growing microorganisms are related to the combined carbon in the feed, or the essentially inert non-oil constituents of the oilseeds in an oil-extraction process. Sometimes it is unimportant what basis is chosen and in such cases a convenient quantity such as the total raw materials into one batch, or passed in per hour to a continuous process are often selected. Having selected the basis, then the units may be chosen such as mass, or concentrations which can be by weight or can be molar if reactions are important.

Total mass and composition

Material balances can be based on total mass, mass of dry solids, or mass of particular components, for example protein.

EXAMPLE 2.1. Skim milk is prepared by the removal of some of the fat from whole milk. This skim milk is found to contain 90.5 % water, 3.5 % protein, 5.1 % carbohydrate, 0.1 % fat and 0.8 % ash. If the original milk contained 4.5 % fat, calculate its composition assuming that fat only was removed to make the skim milk and that there are no losses in processing.

Basis 100 kg of skim milk. This contains, therefore, 0.1 kg of fat. Let the fat which was removed from it to make skim milk be x kg.

$$\text{Total original fat} = (x + 0.1)\,\text{kg}$$
$$\text{Total original mass} = (100 + x)\,\text{kg}$$

and as it is known that the original fat content was 4.5 % so

$$\frac{x + 0.1}{100 + x} = 0.045$$

whence $\quad x + 0.1 = 0.045\,(100 + x).$

$$\therefore \quad x = 4.6\,\text{kg}.$$

So the composition of the whole milk is then

fat = 4.5 %, $\quad$ water = $\dfrac{90.5}{104.6} = 86.5\%$, $\quad$ protein

= $\dfrac{3.5}{104.6} = 3.3\%$, carbohydrate = $\dfrac{5.1}{104.6} = 4.9\%$

and ash = 0.8 %.

Concentrations

Concentrations can be expressed in many ways – weight/weight (w/w), weight/volume (w/v), molar concentration (M), mole fraction. The weight/weight concentration is the weight of the solute divided by the total weight of the solution and this is the fractional form of the percentage composition by weight. The weight/volume concentration is the weight of solute in the total volume of the solution. The molar concentration is the number of molecular weights of the solute expressed in kg in 1 m^3 of the solution. The mole fraction is the ratio of the number of moles of the solute to the total number of moles of all species present in the solution. Notice that in process engineering it is usual to consider kg moles and in this book the term mole means a mass of the material equal to its molecular weight in kilograms. In this book, percentage signifies percentage by weight (w/w) unless otherwise specified.

EXAMPLE 2.2. A solution of common salt in water is prepared by adding 20 kg of salt to 100 kg of water, to make a liquid of density 1323 kg m^{-3}. Calculate the concentration of salt in this solution as a (a) weight fraction, (b) weight/volume fraction, (c) mole fraction, (d) molal concentration.

(a) Weight fraction:

$$\frac{20}{100 + 20} = 0.167.$$

∴   % weight/weight = 16.7%.

(b) Weight/volume:

A density of 1323 kg m^{-3} means that 1 m^3 of solution weighs 1323 kg but 1323 kg of salt solution contains $\dfrac{20}{100 + 20} \times 1323$ kg salt = 220.5 kg salt m^{-3}.

∴   1 m^3 solution contains 220.5 kg salt.

∴   Weight/volume fraction = $\dfrac{220.5}{1000}$

$$= 0.2205.$$

∴   % weight/volume = 22.1%.

(c) Moles of water = $\dfrac{100}{18} = 5.56.$

Moles of salt = $\dfrac{20}{58.5} = 0.34.$

∴   Mole fraction of salt = $\dfrac{0.34}{5.56 + 0.34}$

$$= 0.058.$$

(d) The molar concentration (M) is 3.77 moles in 1 m^3.

Note that the mole fraction can be approximated by the (moles of salt/moles of water) as the number of moles of water are dominant, that is the mole fraction is close to 0.34/5.56 = 0.061. As the solution becomes more dilute this approximation improves and generally for dilute solutions the mole fraction of solute is a close approximation to the moles of solute/moles of solvent.

In solid/liquid mixtures of all these methods can be used but in solid mixtures the concentrations are normally expressed as simple weight fractions.

With gases, concentrations are primarily measured in weight concentrations or as partial pressures. These can be related through the gas laws. Using the gas law in the form:

$$pV = nRT$$

where p is the pressure, V the volume, n the number of moles, T the absolute temperature, and R the gas constant which is equal to 0.08206 m^3 atm mole^{-1} K^{-1}, the molar concentration of a gas is then

$$n/V = p/RT$$

and the weight concentration is then nM/V where M is the molecular weight of the gas.

The SI unit of pressure is the N m^{-2} called the Pascal (Pa). As this is of inconvenient size for many purposes, standard atmospheres (atm) are often used as pressure units, the conversion being 1 atm = 1.013 × 10^5 Pa,   or   very   nearly 1 atm = 100 kPa.

EXAMPLE 2.3. If air consists of 77% by weight of nitrogen and 23% by weight of oxygen calculate:

  (a)   the mean molecular weight of air,
  (b)   the mole fraction of oxygen,
  (c)   the concentration of oxygen in mole m^{-3} and kg m^{-3} if the total pressure is 1.5 atmospheres and the temperature is 25°C.

(a) Taking the basis of 100 g of air; it contains $\dfrac{77}{28}$ moles of N$_2$ and $\dfrac{23}{32}$ mole of O$_2$.

∴   Total number of moles = 2.75 + 0.72

$$= 3.47 \text{ moles.}$$

∴   Mean molecular weight = $\dfrac{100}{3.47} = 28.8.$

(b) The mole fraction of oxygen = $\dfrac{0.72}{2.75 + 0.72}$

$$= \dfrac{0.72}{3.47} = 0.21.$$

(c) In the gas equation, where n is the number of moles present: the value of R is 0.08206 m^3 atm mole^{-1} K^{-1} and at a temperature of 25°C = 25 + 273 = 298 K,   and   where $V = 1$ m^3

$$pV = nRT$$

and so $1.5 \times 1 = n \times 0.08206 \times 298$.

$\therefore \quad n = 0.061 \,\text{mole m}^{-3}$.

$\therefore \quad$ weight of air $= n \times$ mean molecular weight

$\quad\quad = 0.061 \times 28.8 = 1.76 \,\text{kg m}^{-3}$

and of this 23% is oxygen.

$\therefore \quad$ concentration of oxygen $= 0.4 \,\text{kg/m}^{-3}$

or $\dfrac{0.4}{32} = 0.013 \,\text{mole m}^{-3}$.

When a gas is dissolved in a liquid, the mole fraction of the gas in the liquid can be determined by first calculating the number of moles of gas using the gas laws, treating the volume as the volume of the liquid, and then calculating the number of moles of liquid directly.

EXAMPLE 2.4. In the carbonation of a soft drink, the total quantity of carbon dioxide required is the equivalent of 3 volumes of gas to one volume of water at 0°C and atmospheric pressure. Calculate (a) the mass fraction and (b) the mole fraction of the CO_2 in the drink ignoring all components other than CO_2 and water.

Basis 1 m^3 of water $= 1000 \,\text{kg}$.
Volume of carbon dioxide added $= 3 \,m^3$.
From the gas equation $pV = nRT$

$\quad\quad 1 \times 3 = n \times 0.08206 \times 273$.

$\quad\quad \therefore \quad n = 0.134 \,\text{mole}$.

Molecular weight of carbon dioxide $= 44$.

$\therefore \quad$ weight of carbon dioxide added $= 0.134 \times 44$

$\quad\quad\quad\quad\quad\quad\quad\quad\quad\quad = 5.9 \,\text{kg}$.

(a) Mass fraction of carbon dioxide in drink
$= 5.9/(1000 + 5.9) = 5.9 \times 10^{-3}$.

(b) Mole fraction $= 0.134/(1000/18 + 0.134)$

$\quad\quad\quad\quad\quad\quad = 2.41 \times 10^{-3}$.

Types of Process Situations

Continuous processes

In continuous processes, time also enters into consideration and the balances are related to unit time. Thus in considering a continuous centrifuge separating whole milk into skim milk and cream, if the material holdup in the centrifuge is constant both in mass and in composition, then the quantities of the components entering and leaving in the different streams in unit time are constant and a mass balance can be written on this basis. Such an analysis assumes that the process is in a steady state, that is flows and quantities held up in vessels do not change with time.

EXAMPLE 2.5. If 35,000 kg of whole milk containing 4% fat is to be separated in a 6-h period into skim milk with 0.45% fat and cream with 45% fat, what are the flow rates of the two output streams from a continuous centrifuge which accomplishes this separation?

Basis 1 hour's flow of whole milk

Mass in

Total mass $= \dfrac{35,000}{6} = 5833 \,\text{kg}$.

Fat $= 5833 \times 0.04$

$\quad\quad = 233 \,\text{kg}$.

$\therefore \quad$ Water plus solids – not-fat $= 5600 \,\text{kg}$.

Mass out

Let the mass of cream be x kg then its total fat content is $0.45x$. The mass of skim milk is $(5833 - x)$ and its total fat content is $0.0045(5833 - x)$.

Material balance on fat:

Fat in $=$ Fat out

$5833 \times 0.04 = 0.0045(5833 - x) + 0.45x$.

$\therefore \quad x = 465 \,\text{kg}$.

So that the flow of cream is $465 \,\text{kg h}^{-1}$ and skim milk $5833 - 465 = 5368 \,\text{kg h}^{-1}$.

The time unit has to be considered carefully in continuous processes as normally such processes operate continuously for only part of the total factory time. Usually there are three periods, start up, continuous processing (so-called steady state) and close down, and it is important to decide what material balance is being studied. Also the time interval over which any measurements are taken must be long enough to allow for any slight periodic or chance variation.

Chemical and biological changes

In some instances, a reaction takes place and the material balances have to be adjusted accordingly. Chemical changes can take place during a process, for example bacteria may be destroyed during heat processing, sugars may combine with amino acids, fats may be hydrolysed and these affect details of the material balance. The total mass of the system will remain the same but the constituent parts may change, for example in browning the sugars may reduce but browning compounds will increase. An example of the growth of microbial cells is given. Details of chemical and biological changes form a whole area for study in themselves, coming under the heading of unit processes.

EXAMPLE 2.6. Baker's yeast is to be grown in a continuous fermentation system using a fermenter volume of $20\,m^3$ in which the flow residence time is 16 h. A 2% inoculum containing 1.2% of yeast cells is included in the growth medium. This is then passed to the fermenter, in which the yeast grows with a steady doubling time of 2.9 h. The broth leaving the fermenter then passes to a continuous centrifuge which produces a yeast cream containing 7% of yeast which is 97% of the total yeast in the broth. Calculate the rate of flow of the yeast cream and of the residual broth from the centrifuge.

The volume of the fermenter is $20\,m^3$ and the residence time in this is 16 h so the flow rate through the fermenter must be

$$20/16 = 1.250\,m^3\,h^{-1}.$$

Assuming the broth to have a density substantially equal to that of water,

$$\therefore \quad \text{mass flow rate} = 1250\,kg\,h^{-1}.$$

Yeast concentration in the liquid flowing to the fermenter = (concentration in inoculum)/dilution of inoculum

$$= (1.2/100)/(100/2) = 2.4 \times 10^{-4}\,kg\,kg^{-1}.$$

Now the yeast mass doubles every 2.9 h

$$\therefore \quad \text{in 2.9 h, 1 kg becomes } 1 \times 2^1 = 2\,kg.$$

In 16 h there are $16/2.9 = 5.6$ doubling times

$$\therefore \quad 1\,kg \text{ yeast grows to } 1 \times 2^{5.6}\,kg$$

$$= 48.5\,kg.$$

$$\therefore \quad \text{Yeast leaving fermenter} = \text{initial concentration} \times \text{growth} \times \text{flow rate}$$

$$= 2.4 \times 10^{-4} \times 48.5 \times 1250$$

$$= 15\,kg\,h^{-1}.$$

$$\text{Yeast-free broth flow} = (1250 - 15)$$

$$= 1235\,kg\,h^{-1}.$$

From the centrifuge flows a (yeast rich) stream with 7% yeast, this being 97% of the total yeast:

$$\therefore \quad \text{stream is } (15 \times 0.97) \times \frac{100}{7} = 208\,kg\,h^{-1}$$

and the broth (yeast lean) stream is $(1250 - 208)$

$$= 1042\,kg\,h^{-1}$$

which contains $\left(15 \times \dfrac{3}{100}\right) = 0.45\,kg\,h^{-1}$ yeast and the yeast concentration in the residual broth = 0.45/1042

$$= 0.043\%.$$

A mass balance, such as in Example 2.6 for the manufacture of yeast, could be prepared in much greater detail if this were necessary and if the appropriate information were available. Not only broad constituents, such as the yeast, can be balanced as indicated but all the other constituents must also balance. One constituent is the element carbon: this comes with the yeast inoculum in the medium which must have a suitable fermentable carbon source, for example it might be sucrose in molasses. The input carbon must then balance the output carbon which will include the carbon in the outgoing yeast, carbon in the unused medium and also that which was converted to carbon dioxide and which came off as a gas or remained dissolved in the liquid. Similarly all of the other elements such as nitrogen and phosphorus can be balanced out and calculation of the balance can be used to determine what inputs are necessary knowing the final yeast production that is required and the expected yields. While a formal solution can be set out in terms of a number of simultaneous equations, it can often be easier both to visualize and to calculate if the data are tabulated and calculation proceeds step by step gradually filling out the whole detail.

Blending

Another class of situations which arise are blending problems in which various ingredients are combined in such proportions as to give a product of some desired composition. Complicated examples, in which an optimum or best achievable composition must be sought, need quite elaborate calculation methods, such as linear programming, but simple examples can be solved by straight-forward mass balances.

EXAMPLE 2.7. A processing plant is producing minced meat which must contain 15 % of fat. If this is to be made up from boneless cow beef with 23 % of fat and from boneless bull beef with 5 % of fat what are the proportions in which these should be mixed?

Let the proportions be A of cow beef to B of bull beef.
Then by a mass balance on the fat,
$A \times 0.23 + B \times 0.05 = (A + B) \times 0.15$,
that is $A(0.23 - 0.15) = B(0.15 - 0.05)$,
$A(0.08) = B(0.10)$,
$$A/B = \frac{10}{8}$$
or $A/(A + B) = 10/18 = 5/9$,
i.e. 100 kg of product will have 55.6 kg of cow beef to 44.4 kg of bull beef.

It is possible to solve such a problem formally using algebraic equations and indeed all material balance problems are amenable to algebraic treatment. They reduce to sets of simultaneous equations and if the number of independent equations equals the number of unknowns the equations can be solved. For example, the blending problem above can be solved in this way.

If the weights of the constituents are A, B and proportions of fat are a, b, blended to give C of composition c:

then for fat
$$Aa + Bb = Cc$$
and overall
$$A + B = C$$

of which A and B are unknown, and say we require these to make up 100 kg of C, then
$$A + B = 100$$

or
$$B = 100 - A$$
and substituting into the first equation
$$Aa + (100 - A)b = 100c$$
or
$$A(a - b) = 100(c - b)$$
or
$$A = 100 \frac{c - b}{a - b}$$

and taking the numbers from the example
$$A = 100 \left(\frac{0.15 - 0.05}{0.23 - 0.05} \right)$$
$$= 100 \frac{0.10}{0.18}$$
$$= 55.6 \, \text{kg}$$
and $B = 44.4 \, \text{kg}$

as before, but the algebraic solution has really added nothing beyond a formula which could be useful if a number of blending operations were under consideration.

Layout

In setting up a material balance for a process a series of equations can be written, for the various individual components and for the process as a whole. In some cases, where groups of materials maintain constant ratios, then the equations can include such groups rather than their individual constituents. For example in drying vegetables, the carbohydrates, minerals, proteins, etc., can be grouped together as "dry solids", and then only dry solids and water need be taken through the material balance.

EXAMPLE 2.8. Potatoes are dried from 14 % total solids to 93 % total solids. What is the product yield from each 1000 kg of raw potatoes assuming that 8 % by weight of the original potatoes are lost in peeling.

Basis 1000 kg potato entering

Mass in (kg)		Mass out (kg)	
		Dried product	
Potato solids	140 kg	Potato solids	$140 \times \dfrac{92}{100}$
Water	860 kg		$= 129$ kg
		Associated water	10 kg
		Total product	139 kg
		Losses	
		Peelings—potato	
		solids	11 kg
		—water	69 kg
		Water evaporated	781 kg
		Total losses	861 kg
Total	1000 kg	Total	1000 kg

Product yield $\dfrac{139}{1000} = 14\%$.

Often is is important to be able to follow particular constituents of the raw material through a process. This is just a matter of calculating each constituent.

EXAMPLE 2.9. 1000 kg of soya beans, of composition 18 % oil, 35 % protein, 27.1 % carbohydrate, 9.4 % fibre and ash, 10.5 % moisture, are:

(a) crushed and pressed, which reduces oil content in beans to 6 %;
(b) then extracted with hexane to produce a meal containing 0.5 % oil;
(c) finally dried to 8 % moisture.

Assuming that there is no loss of protein and water with the oil, set out a mass balance for the soya-bean constituents.

Mass in:

$$\text{Oil} \quad = 1000 \times 18/100 = 180 \text{ kg}$$
$$\text{Protein} = 1000 \times 35/100 = 350 \text{ kg}$$

Carbohydrate, ash, etc., are calculated in a similar manner to fat and protein.

Mass out:

(a) Expressed oil. In original beans, 820 kg of protein, water, etc., are associated with 180 kg of oil. In pressed material, 94 parts of protein, water, etc., are associated with 6 parts of oil. Total oil in expressed material $= 820 \times 6/94 = 52.3$ kg. Loss of oil in press $= 180 - 52.3 = 127.7$ kg.

(b) Extracted oil. In extracted meal, 99.5 parts of protein, water, etc., are associated with 0.5 parts of oil. Total oil in extracted meal $= 820 \times 0.5/99.5 = 4.1$ kg. Loss of oil to hexane $= 52.3 - 4.1 = 48.2$ kg.

(c) Water. In the extracted meal, 8 parts of water are associated with 92 parts of oil, protein, etc.

Weights of dry materials in final meal
$$= 350 + 271 + 94 + 4.1 = 719.1 \text{ kg}.$$
Total water in dried meal
$$= 719.1 \times 8/92 = 62.5 \text{ kg}.$$
Water loss in drying
$$= 105 - 62.5 = 42.5 \text{ kg}.$$

MASS BALANCE, BASIS 1000 KG SOYA BEANS ENTERING

Mass in (kg)		Mass out (kg)		
Oil	180	Expressed oil		127.7
Protein	350	Oil in hexane		48.2
Carbohydrate	271	Total meal		781.6
Ash and fibre	94	Consisting of:		
Water	105	Protein	350	
		Carbohydrate	271	
		Ash and fibre	94	
		Water	62.5	
		Oil	4.1	
		Water lost in drying		42.5
Total	1000	Total		1000

ENERGY BALANCES

Energy takes many forms such as heat, kinetic energy, chemical energy, potential energy but because of interconversions it is not always easy to isolate separate constituents of energy balances. However, under some circumstances certain aspects predominate, such as in many heat balances in which other forms of energy are insignificant; in some chemical situations mechanical energy is insignificant and in some mechanical energy situations, as in the flow of fluids in pipes, the frictional losses appear as heat but the details of the heating need not be considered. We are seldom concerned with internal energies. Therefore practical applications of energy balances tend to focus on particular dominant aspects and so a heat balance, for example, can be a useful description of important cost and quality aspects of a food-process situation. When unfamiliar with the relative magnitudes of the various forms of energy entering into a particular processing situation, it is wise to put them all down and then after some preliminary calculations the important ones emerge and other minor ones can be lumped together or even ignored without introducing substantial errors. With experience, the obviously minor ones can perhaps be left out completely though this always raises the possibility of error.

Energy balances can be calculated on the basis of external energy used per kilogram of product, or raw material processed, or on dry solids, or some key component. The energy consumed in food production includes direct energy which is fuel and electricity used on the farm, and in transport and in factories, and in storage, selling, etc., and indirect energy which is used to actually build the machines, to make the packaging, to produce the electricity and the oil and so on. Food itself is a major energy source, and energy balances can be determined for animal or human feeding; food energy input can be balanced against outputs in heat and mechanical energy and chemical synthesis.

In the SI system there is only one energy unit, the joule. However, kilocalories are still used by some nutritionists and British thermal units (Btu) in some heat-balance work.

The two applications used in this book are heat balances which are the basis for heat transfer and the energy balances used in analysing fluid flow.

Heat Balances

The most common important energy form is heat energy and the conservation of this can be illustrated by considering operations such as heating and drying. In these, enthalpy (total heat) is conserved and as with the mass balances so enthalpy balances can be written round the various items of equipment, or process stages, or the whole plant, and it is assumed that no appreciable heat is converted to other forms of energy such as work.

Enthalpy is always referred to some reference level or datum, so that the quantities are relative to

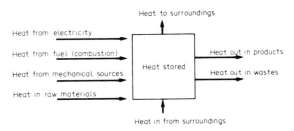

FIG. 2.2. Heat balance.

this datum. Working out energy balances is then just a matter of considering the various quantities of materials involved, their specific heats, and their changes in temperature or state (as quite frequently latent heats arising from phase changes are encountered). Fig. 2.2 illustrates the heat balance.

Heat is absorbed or evolved by some reactions in food processing but usually the quantities are small when compared with the other forms of energy entering into food processing such as sensible heat and latent heat. Latent heat is the heat required to change, at constant temperature, the physical state of materials from solid to liquid, liquid to gas, or solid to gas. Sensible heat is that heat which when added or subtracted from food materials changes their temperature and thus can be sensed. The units of specific heat are $J\,kg\,°C^{-1}$ and sensible heat is calculated by multiplying the mass by the specific heat by the change in temperature. The units of latent heat are $J\,kg^{-1}$ and total latent heat is calculated by multiplying the mass of the material which changes its phase by the latent heat. Having determined those factors which are significant in the overall energy balance, the simplified heat balance can then be used with confidence in industrial energy studies. Such calculations can be quite simple and straightforward but they give a quantitative feeling for the situation and can be of great use in design of equipment and process.

EXAMPLE 2.10. It is desired to freeze 10,000 loaves of bread each weighing 0.75 kg from an initial room temperature of 18°C to a final store temperature of −18°C. If this is to be carried out in such a way that the maximum heat demand for the freezing is twice the average demand, estimate this maximum demand, if the total freezing time is to be 6 h.

If data on the actual bread is unavailable, the following can be found in the literature:

(a) Tabulated data (Appendix 7) suggests specific heat above freezing $2.93\,\mathrm{kJ\,kg^{-1}\,°C}$, below freezing $1.42\,\mathrm{kJ\,kg^{-1}\,°C^{-1}}$, latent heat of freezing $115\,\mathrm{kJ\,kg^{-1}}$ and freezing temperature is $-2°C$.

$\therefore$ Total enthalpy change, (ΔH)

$= [18 - (-2)]2.93 + 115$

$\quad + [-2 - (-18)]1.42$

$= 196\,\mathrm{kJ\,kg^{-1}}.$

(b) Formula (Appendix 7) assuming the bread is 36% water gives

specific heat above freezing

$\quad 4.2 \times 0.36 + 0.82 \times 0.64$

$\quad = 2.04\,\mathrm{kJ\,kg^{-1}\,°C^{-1}},$

specific heat below freezing

$\quad 2.1 \times 0.36 + 0.82 \times 0.64$

$\quad = 1.28\,\mathrm{kJ\,kg^{-1}\,°C^{-1}},$

latent heat

$\quad 0.36 \times 335 = 121\,\mathrm{kJ\,kg^{-1}}.$

$\therefore$ Total enthalpy change, (ΔH)

$= [18 - (-2)]2.04 + 121$

$\quad + [-2 - (-18)]1.28$

$= 183\,\mathrm{kJ\,kg^{-1}}.$

(c) Enthalpy/temperature data for bread of 36% moisture (Mannheim *et al.*, 1957) suggests

$H_{18.3°C} = 210.36\,\mathrm{kJ\,kg^{-1}},$

$H_{17.8°C} = 65.35\,\mathrm{kJ\,kg^{-1}}.$

$\therefore$ from $+18°C$ to $-18°C$ total enthalpy change $\Delta H = 145\,\mathrm{kJ\,kg^{-1}}.$

(d) The above enthalpy/temperature table can also be used to estimate "apparent" specific heats as $\Delta H/\Delta t = c$ and so using the data

t, °C	$= -20.6$	-17.8	15.6	18.3
H, kJ kg^{-1}	$= 55.88$	65.35	203.4	210.4

giving $c_{-18} = \left(\dfrac{\Delta H}{\Delta t}\right) = \dfrac{65.35 - 55.88}{20.6 - 17.8}$

$\qquad = 3.4\,\mathrm{kJ\,kg^{-1}\,°C^{-1}},$

$c_{18} = \left(\dfrac{\Delta H}{\Delta t}\right) = \dfrac{210.4 - 203.4}{18.3 - 15.6}$

$\qquad = 2.6\,\mathrm{kJ\,kg^{-1}\,°C^{-1}}.$

Note that the "apparent" specific heat at $-18°C$ is higher than the specific heat below freezing in (a). The reason for the high apparent specific heat at -18 is due to some freezing still continuing at this temperature. It is suggested that at $-18°C$ only about two-thirds of the water is actually frozen to ice. This implies only two-thirds of the latent heat has been extracted at this temperature. Making this adjustment to the latent-heat terms, estimates (a) and (b) give $161\,\mathrm{kJ\,kg^{-1}}$ and $154\,\mathrm{kJ\,kg^{-1}}$ respectively, much improving the agreement with (c). Taking ΔH as $150\,\mathrm{kJ\,kg^{-1}}$ then the total,

$$\Delta H = 150 \times 10{,}000 \times 0.75$$

$$= 1.125 \times 10^6\,\mathrm{kJ}.$$

$$\text{Total time} = 6\,\mathrm{h} = 2.16 \times 10^4\,\mathrm{s}.$$

$$\therefore \quad \Delta H/\Delta\theta = 52\,\mathrm{kJ\,s^{-1}}$$

$$= 52\,\mathrm{kW\ on\ average.}$$

And if the maximum rate of heat removal is twice the average:

$$\therefore \quad (\Delta H/\Delta\theta)_{max} = 2 \times 52 = \underline{104\,\mathrm{kW}}.$$

Example 2.10 illustrates the application of heat balances, and it also illustrates the advisability of checking or obtaining corroborative data unless reliable experimental results are available for the particular system that is being considered. The straightforward application of the tabulated overall data would have produced a result about 30% higher than that finally calculated. On the other hand, for many engineering calculations to be within 30% is not too bad.

In some cases, it is convenient to make approximations to heat-energy balances by isolating dominant terms and ignoring less important ones. To make approximations with any confidence, it is necessary to be reasonably sure about the relative magnitudes of the quantities involved. Having once determined the factors that dominate the heat-energy balance, simplified balances can then be set up if appropriate to the circumstances and used with confidence in industrial energy studies. This simplification reduces the calculation effort, focuses attention on the most important terms, and helps to inculcate in the engineer a quantitative feeling for the situation.

EXAMPLE 2.11. A casein dryer is found to consume 4 m³/h of natural gas with a calorific value of 800 kJ/mole. If the throughput of the dryer is 60 kg of wet casein per hour, drying it from 55% moisture to 10% moisture, estimate the overall thermal efficiency of the dryer taking into account the latent heat of evaporation only.

60 kg of wet casein contains

$$60 \times 0.55 \text{ kg water} = 33 \text{ kg moisture}$$

and $60 \times (1 - 0.55) = 27$ kg bone dry casein.

As the final product contains 10% moisture, the moisture in the product is

$$\frac{27}{9} = 3 \text{ kg}.$$

$\therefore$ Moisture removed/hour
$$= (33 - 3) = 30 \text{ kg/h}.$$

Latent heat of evaporation $= 2257 \text{ kJ/kg}^{-1}$.

$\therefore$ Heat necessary to supply
$$= 30 \times 2257 = 6.8 \times 10^4 \text{ kJ/h}^{-1}.$$

Assuming the natural gas to be at standard temperature and pressure at which 1 mole occupies 22.4 litres

Rate of flow of natural gas $= 4 \text{ m}^3/\text{h}^{-1}$
$$= \frac{4 \times 1000}{22.4}$$
$$= 179 \text{ moles/h}^{-1}$$

$\therefore$ Heat available from combustion $= 179 \times 800 = 14.3 \times 10^4 \text{ kJ h}^{-1}$.

$\therefore$ Approximate thermal efficiency of dryer $= \dfrac{\text{heat needed}}{\text{heat used}}$
$$= 6.8 \times 10^4/14.3 \times 10^4$$
$$= 48\%.$$

To evaluate this efficiency more completely it would be necessary to take into account the sensible heat of the dry casein solids and the moisture, and the changes in temperature and humidity of the combustion air which would be combined with the natural gas. However, as the latent heat of evaporation is the dominant term, the above calculation gives a quick estimate and shows how a simple energy balance can give useful information.

Similarly energy balances can be carried out over thermal processing operations, and indeed any processing operations in which heat or other forms of energy are used.

EXAMPLE 2.12. An autoclave contains 1000 cans of pea soup. It is heated to an overall temperature of 100°C. If the cans are to be cooled to 40°C before leaving the autoclave, how much cooling water is required if it enters at 15°C and leaves at 35°C?

The specific heats of the pea soup and the can metal are respectively 4.1 kJ kg^{-1}°C^{-1} and 0.50 kJ kg^{-1}°C^{-1}. The weight of each can is 60 g and it contains 0.45 kg of pea soup. Assume that the heat content of the autoclave walls above 40°C is 1.6×10^4 kJ and that there is no heat loss through the walls.

Let w = the weight of cooling water required; and the datum temperature be 40°C, the temperature of the cans leaving the autoclave.

Heat entering

Heat in cans = weight of cans
$$\times \text{ specific heat}$$
$$\times \text{ temperature above datum}$$
$$= 1000 \times 0.06 \times 0.50$$
$$\times (100 - 40) \text{ kJ}$$
$$= 1.8 \times 10^3 \text{ kJ}.$$

Heat in can contents

$$= \text{ weight pea soup}$$
$$\times \text{ specific heat}$$
$$\times \text{ temperature above datum}$$

$$= 1000 \times 0.45 \times 4.1$$
$$\times (100 - 40)$$
$$= 1.1 \times 10^5 \text{ kJ.}$$

Heat in water = weight of water
$$\times \text{ specific heat}$$
$$\times \text{ temperature above datum}$$
$$= w \times 4.186 \times (15 - 40)$$
$$= -104.6w \text{ kJ.}$$

Heat leaving

Heat in cans $= 1000 \times 0.06 \times 0.50$
$$\times (40 - 40) \text{ (cans leave}$$
at datum temperature)
$$= 0.$$

Heat in can contents $= 1000 \times 0.45 \times 4.1$
$$\times (40 - 40)$$
$$= 0.$$

Heat in water $= w \times 4.186 \times (35 - 40)$
$$= -20.9w.$$

manufacturer, expresses the proportion (usually as a percentage) of the electrical input energy which emerges usefully at the motor shaft and so is available.

When considering movement, whether of fluids in pumping, of solids in solids handling, or of foodstuffs in mixers, the energy input is largely mechanical. The flow situations can be analysed by recognising the conservation of total energy whether as energy of motion, or potential energy such as pressure energy, or energy lost in friction. Similarly, chemical energy released in combustion can be calculated from the heats of combustion of the fuels and their rates of consumption. Eventually energy emerges in the form of heat and its quantity can be estimated by summing the various sources.

EXAMPLE 2.13. The bread-freezing operation of Example 2.10 is to be carried out in an air-blast freezing tunnel. It is found that the fan motors are rated at a total of 80 horsepower and measurements

HEAT-ENERGY BALANCE OF COOLING PROCESS 40°C AS DATUM LINE

Heat entering (kJ)		Heat leaving (kJ)	
Heat in cans	1800	Heat in cans	0
Heat in can contents	110,000	Heat in can contents	0
Heat in autoclave walls	16,000	Heat in autoclave walls	0
Heat in water	−104.6w	Heat in water	−20.9w
Total heat entering	127,800 − 104.6w	Total heat leaving	−20.9w

$$\text{Total heat entering} = \text{Total heat leaving}$$
$$127,800 - 104.6w = -20.9w$$
$$\therefore \quad w = 1527 \text{ kg}$$

∴ amount of cooling water required = 1527 kg.

Other Forms of Energy

Motor power is usually derived, in food factories, from electrical energy but it can be produced from steam engines or water power. The electrical energy input can be measured by a suitable wattmeter, and the power used in the drive estimated. There are always losses from the motors due to heating friction and windage; the motor efficiency, which can normally be obtained from the motor

suggest that they are operating at around 90% of their rating, under which conditions their manufacturer's data claims a motor efficiency of 86%. If 1 ton of refrigeration is 3.52 kW, estimate the maximum refrigeration load imposed by this freezing installation assuming (a) that fans and motors are all within the freezing tunnel insulation and (b) the fans but not their motors are in the tunnel. The heat-loss rate from the tunnel to the ambient air has been found to be 6.3 kW.

Extraction rate from freezing bread (maximum) = 104 kW.

Fan rated horsepower   = 80.

Now 0.746 kW = 1 horsepower
and the motor is operating at 90% of rating,

∴   (fan + motor) power   = (80 × 0.9) × 0.746
                                                 = 53.7 kW.

(a) With motors + fans in tunnel

     ∴   heat load from fans + motors   = 53.7 kW
         heat load from ambient   = 6.3 kW.

     ∴   Total heat load   = (104 + 53.7 + 6.3) kW
                                                 = 164 kW
                                                 = 46.6 tons refrigeration.

(b) with motors outside, the motor ineffi-
     ciency = (1 − 0.86) does not impose a load on
     the refrigeration.

     ∴   Total heat load   = (104 + [0.86 × 53.7] + 6.3)
                                                 = 156 kW
                                                 = 44.5 tons refrigeration.

In practice, material and energy balances are often combined as the same stoichiometric information is needed for both.

SUMMARY

1. Material and energy balances can be worked out quantitatively knowing the amounts of materials entering into a process, and the nature of the process.
2. Material and energy balances take the basic form Content of inputs = content of products + wastes/losses + changes in stored materials.
3. In continuous processes, a time balance must be established.
4. Energy includes heat energy (enthalpy), potential energy (energy of pressure or position), kinetic energy, work energy, chemical energy. It is the sum over all of these that is conserved.
5. Enthalpy balances, considering only heat, are useful in many food-processing situations.

PROBLEMS

1. If 5 kg of sucrose are dissolved in 20 kg of water estimate the concentration of the solution in (a) w/w, (b) w/v, (c) mole fraction, (d) molal concentration. The specific weight of a 20% sucrose solution is 1070 kg m^{-3}.
2. If 1 m^3 of air at a pressure of 1 atm is mixed with 0.1 m^3 of carbon dioxide at 1.5 atm and the mixture is compressed so that its total volume is 1 m^3, estimate the concentration of the carbon dioxide in the mixture in (a) w/w, (b) w/v, (c) mole fraction.
3. It is convenient to add salt to butter, produced in a continuous buttermaking machine, by adding a slurry of salt with water containing 60% of salt and 40% of water by weight. If the final composition of the butter is to be 15.8% moisture and 1.4% salt, estimate the original moisture content of the butter prior to salting.
4. In a flour mill, wheat is to be adjusted to a moisture content of 15% on a dry basis. If the whole grain received at the mill is found to contain 11.4% of water initially, how much water must the miller add per 100 kg of input grain as received, to produce the desired moisture content?
5. In an analysis, sugar beet is found to contain 75% of water and 17.5% of sugar. If of the remaining material, 25% is soluble and 75% insoluble, calculate the sugar content of the expressible juice assumed to' contain water and all soluble solids pro rata.

   If the beets are extracted by addition of a weight of water equal to their own weight and after a suitable period the soluble constituents are concentrated evenly throughout all the water present, calculate the percentage of the total sugar left in the drained beet and the percentage of the total sugar extracted, assuming that the beet cells (insoluble) after the extraction have the same quantity of water associated with them as they did in the original beet.

6. A sweet whey, following cheesemaking, has the following composition: 5.5% lactose, 0.8% protein, 0.5% ash. The equilibrium solubility of lactose in water is:

Temp. °C	0	15	25	39	49	64
Lactose solubility kg/100 kg water		11.9	16.9	21.6	31.5	42.4	65.8

Calculate the percentage yield of lactose when 1000 kg of whey is concentrated in a vacuum evaporator at 60°C to 60% solids and the concentrate is then cooled with crystallization of the lactose, down to 20°C over a period of weeks.

7. In an ultrafiltration plant in which whey is to be concentrated, 140,000 kg per day are to be processed to give a 12-fold concentration of 95% of the protein from an original whey concentration of 0.93% protein and 6% of other soluble solids. Assuming that all of the soluble solids other than protein remain with the stream which has the 5% of the protein in it, estimate the daily flows and concentrations of the two product stream.

8. It is desired to prepare a sweetened concentrated orange juice. The initial pressed juice contains 5% of total solids and it is desired to lift this to 10% of total solids by evaporation and then to add sugar to give 2% of added sugar in the concentrated juice. Calculate the quantity of water which must be removed and of sugar which must be added with respect to each 1000 kg of pressed juice.

9. In a casein factory, the entering coagulum containing casein and lactose is passed through two cookers and acidified to remove the casein. The casein separates as a curd. The curd is removed from the whey by screening, and then washed and dried. The casein fines are removed from the whey and the wash water by hydrocyclones, and mixed with the heated coagulum just before screening. The whey is used for heating in the first cooker and steam in the second cooker by indirect heating. Some of the more accessible streams have been sampled and analysed for casein and lactose. In addition, the moisture content of the final dried product has been determined:

	% Composition on Wet Weight Basis		
	Casein	Lactose	Moisture
Coagulum	2.76	3.68	
Whey (raw)	0.012	4.1	
Whey (cycloned)	0.007		
Wash water	0.026	0.8	
Waste wash water	0.008		
Dried product			11.9

From these data, calculate a complete mass balance for the process, using a simple step-by-step approach, starting with the hydrocyclones. Assume lactose completely soluble in all solutions, and concentrations in fines and wastes streams from hydrocyclones are the same.

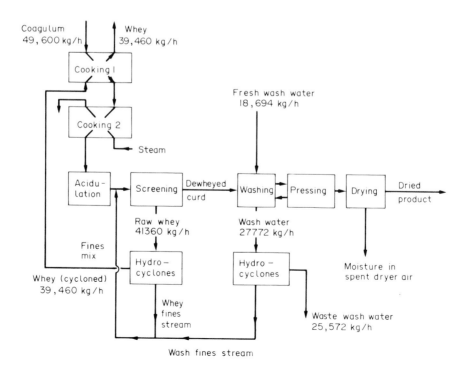

(a) Draw up and fill in the following table.

	Mass flows kg/h		
	Casein	Lactose	Total
Coagulum and fines mix			
Fines mix			
Dewheyed curd			
Raw whey			
Whey fines stream			
Spent wash water			
Wash water fines stream			
Pressed curd			
Final dried product			

(b) What percentage of the casein going to the first screen is recovered fines?

(c) What percentage recovery efficiencies do the two sets of hydrocyclones display?

(d) What are the percentage compositions of the pressed curd and dried product?

10. A tomato-juice evaporator takes in juice at the rate of $1200 \, kg \, h^{-1}$. If the concentrated juice contains 35% of solids and the hourly rate of removal of water is $960 \, kg$, calculate the moisture content of the original juice and the quantity of steam needed per hour for heating if the evaporator works at a pressure of $10 \, kPa$ and the heat available from the steam is $2200 \, kJ \, kg^{-1}$. Assume no heat losses.

11. Processing water is to be heated in a direct fired heater, which burns natural gas with a calorific value of $20.2 \, MJ \, m^{-3}$. If $5000 \, kg \, h^{-1}$ of this water has to be heated from $15°C$ to $80°C$ and the heater is estimated to be 45% efficient, estimate the hourly consumption of gas.

CHAPTER 3

FLUID-FLOW THEORY

MANY raw materials for foods and many finished foods are in the form of fluids. These fluids have to be transported and processed in the factory. Food technologists must be familiar with the principles which govern the flow of fluids, and with the machinery and equipment which is used to handle fluids. In addition, there is an increasing tendency to handle powdered and granular materials in a form in which they behave as fluids. Fluidization, as this is called, has been developed because of the relative simplicity of fluid handling compared with the handling of solids.

The engineering concept of a fluid is a wider one than that in general use, and it covers gases as well as liquids and fluidized solids. This is because liquids and gases obey many of the same laws so that it is convenient to group them together under the general heading of fluids.

The study of fluids can be divided into the study of fluids at rest – fluid statics, and the study of fluids in motion — fluid dynamics. For some purposes, further subdivision into compressible fluids such as gases, and incompressible fluids such as liquids, is necessary. Fluids in the food industry vary considerably in their properties. They include such materials as:

Thin liquids — milk, water, fruit juices,
Thick liquids — syrups, honey, oil, jam,
Gases — air, nitrogen, carbon dioxide,
Fluidized solids — grains, flour, peas.

FLUID STATICS

A very important property of a fluid at rest is the pressure exerted by that fluid on its surroundings.

Pressure is defined as force exerted on an area. Under the influence of gravity, a mass of any material exerts a force on whatever supports it. The magnitude of this force is equal to the mass of the material multiplied by the acceleration due to gravity. The mass of a fluid can be calculated by multiplying its volume by its density which is defined as its mass per unit volume. Thus the equation can be written:

$$F = mg = V\rho g$$

where F is the force exerted, m is the mass, g the acceleration due to gravity and ρ the density. The units of force are $\mathrm{kg\,m\,s^{-2}}$.

For a mass to remain in equilibrium, the force it exerts due to gravity must be resisted by some supporting medium. In the case of a weight resting on a table, the table provides the supporting reaction; in the case of a multistorey building, the upper floors must be supported by the lower ones so that as you descend the building the burden on the floors increases until the foundations support the whole building. In a fluid the same situation applies. Lower levels of the fluid must provide the support for the fluid that lies above them. The fluid at any point must support the fluid above. Also, since fluids at rest are not able to sustain shearing forces, which are forces tending to move adjacent layers in the fluid relative to one another, it can be shown that the forces at any point in a fluid at rest are equal in all directions. The force per unit area in a fluid is called the fluid pressure. It is exerted equally in all directions.

Consider a horizontal plane in a fluid at a depth Z below the surface, as illustrated in Fig. 3.1.

If the density of the fluid is ρ, then the volume of

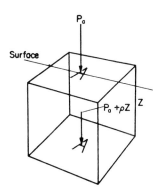

P_a

Surface

$P_a + \rho Z$

Z

FIG. 3.1. Pressure in a fluid.

fluid lying above an area A on the plane is ZA and the weight of this volume of fluid, which creates a force exerted by it on the area A which supports it, is $Z\rho Ag$. But the total force on the area A must also include any additional force on the surface of the liquid. If the force on the surface is P_a per unit area,

$$\therefore \quad F = AP_a + Z\rho Ag \qquad (3.1)$$

where F is the total force exerted on the area A and P_a is the pressure above the surface of the fluid (e.g. it might be atmospheric pressure). Further, since total pressure P is the total force per unit area,

$$P = \frac{F}{A} = P_a + Z\rho g \qquad (3.2)$$

In general, we are interested in pressures above or below atmospheric. If referred to zero pressure as datum, the pressure of the atmosphere must be taken into account. Otherwise the atmospheric pressure represents a datum or reference level from which pressures are measured. In these circumstances we can write

$$P = Z\rho g. \qquad (3.3)$$

This may be considered as the fundamental equation of fluid pressure. It states that the pressure at any depth in a fluid is given by the product of the density of the fluid and the depth.

EXAMPLE 3.1. Calculate the greatest pressure in a spherical tank, of 2 m diameter filled with peanut oil of specific gravity 0.92, if the pressure measured at the highest point in the tank is 70 kPa.

Density of water $= 1000\,\mathrm{kg\,m^{-3}}$.

$\therefore$ density of oil $= 0.92 \times 1000\,\mathrm{kg\,m^{-3}}$
$\qquad\qquad = 920\,\mathrm{kg\,m^{-3}}$

and $Z \qquad =$ greatest depth $= 2\,\mathrm{m}$.

Now $P \quad = Z\rho g$ and g is $9.81\,\mathrm{m\,s^{-2}}$.

$\therefore \qquad P = 2 \times 920 \times 9.81\,\mathrm{kg\,m\,s^{-2}}$
$\qquad\qquad = 18,050\,\mathrm{Pa} = 18.1\,\mathrm{kPa}.$

To this must be added the pressure at the surface of 70 kPa.

$\therefore \quad$ Total pressure $= 70 + 18.1 = 88.1\,\mathrm{kPa}.$

Note in Example 3.1 that the pressure depends upon the pressure at the top of the tank added to the pressure due to the depth of the liquid; the fact that the tank is spherical (or any other shape) makes no difference to the pressure at the bottom of the tank.

In the previous paragraph we have established that the pressure at a point in a liquid of a given density is solely dependent on the density of the liquid and on the height of the liquid above the point, plus any pressure which may exist at the surface of the liquid. When the depths of the fluid are substantial, fluid pressures can be considerable. For example, the pressure on a plate $1\,\mathrm{m^2}$ lying at a depth of $30\,\mathrm{m}$ will be the weight of $1\,\mathrm{m^3}$ of water multiplied by the depth of $30\,\mathrm{m}$ and this will amount to $30 \times 1000 \times 9.81 = 294.3\,\mathrm{kPa}$. As 1 tonne exerts a force on $1\,\mathrm{m^2}$ of $1000 \times 9.81 = 9810\,\mathrm{Pa} = 9.81\,\mathrm{kPa}$ the pressure on the plate is equal to that of a weight of $\dfrac{294.3}{9.81} = 30$ tonnes.

Pressures are sometimes quoted as absolute pressures and this means the total pressure including atmospheric pressure. More usually, pressures are given as "gauge" pressures which implies the pressure above atmospheric pressure as datum. For example, if the absolute pressure is given as 350 kPa, the gauge pressure is $(350 - 100) = 250\,\mathrm{kPa}$ assuming that the atmospheric pressure is 100 kPa. These pressure conversions are illustrated in Fig. 3.2.

Standard atmospheric pressure is actually 101.3 kPa but for our practical purposes 100 kPa is sufficiently close and most convenient to use. Any necessary adjustment can easily be made.

Another commonly used method of expressing pressures is in terms of "head" of a particular fluid.

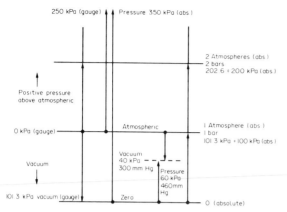

FIG. 3.2. Pressure conversions.

From eqn. (3.3) it can be seen that there is a definite relationship between pressure and depth in a fluid of given density. Thus pressures can be expressed in terms of depths, or heads as they are usually called, of a given fluid. The two fluids most commonly used, when expressing pressures in this way, are water and mercury. The main reason for this method of expressing pressures, is that the pressures themselves are often measured by observing the height of the column of liquid that the pressure can support. It is straightforward to convert pressures expressed in terms of liquid heads to equivalent values in kPa by the use of eqn. (3.3.).

EXAMPLE 3.2. Calculate the head of water equivalent to standard atmospheric pressure of 100 kPa.

$$\text{Density of water} = 1000 \, \text{kg m}^{-3},$$
$$g = 9.81 \, \text{m s}^{-2}$$
$$\text{and pressure} = 100 \, \text{kPa}$$
$$= 100 \times 10^3 \, \text{Pa}$$

but from eqn. (3.3) $Z = P/\rho g$,

$$\therefore \quad Z = \frac{100 \times 10^3}{1000 \times 9.81}$$
$$= 10.5 \, \text{m}.$$

EXAMPLE 3.3. Calculate the head of mercury equivalent to a pressure of two atmospheres.

$$\text{Density of mercury} = 13,600 \, \text{kg m}^{-3}$$
$$\therefore \quad Z = \frac{2 \times 100 \times 10^3}{13,600 \times 9.81}$$
$$= 1.5 \, \text{m}$$

FLUID DYNAMICS

In most processes fluids have to be moved so that the study of fluids in motion is important. Problems on the flow of fluids are solved by applying the principles of conservation of mass and energy. In any system, or in any part of any system, it must always be possible to write a mass balance and an energy balance. The motion of fluids can be described by writing appropriate mass and energy balances and these are the basis for the design of fluid handling equipment.

Mass Balance

Consider part of a flow system, such for example as that shown in Fig. 3.3. This consists of a continuous pipe which changes its diameter, passing into and out of a unit of processing plant which is represented by a tank. The processing equipment might be, for example, a pasteurizing heat exchanger. Also in the system is a pump to provide the energy to move the fluid.

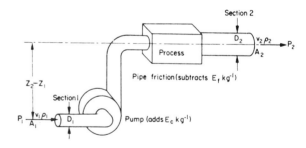

FIG. 3.3. Mass and energy balance in fluid flow.

In the flow system of Fig. 3.3 we can apply the law of conservation of mass to obtain a mass balance. Once the system is working steadily, and if there is no accumulation of fluid in any part the system, the quantity of fluid that goes in at section 1 must come out at section 2. If the area of the pipe at section 1 is A_1, the velocity at this section, v_1 and the fluid density ρ_1, and if the corresponding values at section 2 are A_2, v_2, ρ_2, the mass balance can be expressed as

$$\rho_1 A_1 v_1 = \rho_2 A_2 v_2. \tag{3.4}$$

If the fluid is incompressible $\rho_1 = \rho_2$, so that in this case

$$A_1 v_1 = A_2 v_2. \tag{3.5}$$

Equation (3.5) is known as the continuity equation for liquids and is frequently used in solving flow problems. It can also be used in many cases of gas flow in which the change in pressure is very small, such as in many air-ducting systems, without any serious error.

EXAMPLE 3.4. If whole milk is flowing into a centrifuge through a full 5-cm diameter pipe at a velocity of $0.22 \, \text{m s}^{-1}$ and if, in the centrifuge, it is separated into cream of specific gravity 1.01 and skim milk of specific gravity 1.04, calculate the velocities of flow of milk and of the cream if they are discharged through 2-cm diameter pipes. The specific gravity of whole milk of 1.035.

From eqn. (3.4)

$$\rho_1 A_1 v_1 = \rho_2 A_2 v_2 + \rho_3 A_3 v_3$$

where suffixes 1, 2, 3 denote respectively raw milk, skim milk and cream. Also, since volumes will be conserved, the total leaving volumes will equal the total entering volume and so

$$A_1 v_1 = A_2 v_2 + A_3 v_3$$

and from this equation

$$v_2 = (A_1 v_1 - A_3 v_3)/A_2. \tag{a}$$

This expression can be substituted for v_2 in the mass balance equation to give:

$$\rho_1 A_1 v_1 = \rho_2 A_2 (A_1 v_1 - pA_3 v_3)/A_2 + \rho_3 A_3 v_3.$$
$$_1 A_1 v_1 = \rho_2 A_1 v_1 - \rho_2 A_3 v_3 + \rho_3 A_3 v_3.$$
$$\therefore \quad A_1 v_1 (\rho_1 - \rho_2) = A_3 v_3 (\rho_3 - \rho_2). \tag{b}$$

From the known facts of the problem we have:

$$A_1 = (\pi/4) \times (0.05)^2 = 1.96 \times 10^{-3} \, \text{m}^2,$$
$$A_2 = A_3 = (\pi/4) \times (0.02)^2$$
$$= 3.14 \times 10^{-4} \, \text{m}^2,$$

$$v_1 = 0.22 \, \text{m s}^{-1},$$
$$\rho_1 = 1.035 \times \rho_w, \rho_2 = 1.04 \times \rho_w,$$
$$\rho_3 = 1.01 \times \rho_w$$

where ρ_w is the density of water.

Substituting these values in eqn. (b) above we obtain:

$$-1.96 \times 10^{-3} \times 0.22 \, (0.005) = -3.14 \times 10^{-4} \times v_3 \times (0.03)$$
$$\therefore \quad v_3 = 0.23 \, \text{m s}^{-1}.$$

Also from eqn. (a) we then have, substituting $0.23 \, \text{m s}^{-1}$ for v_3,

$$v_2 = [(1.96 \times 10^{-3} \times 0.22)$$
$$- (3.14 \times 10^{-4} \times 0.23)]/3.14 \times 10^{-4}$$
$$= 1.1 \, \text{m s}^{-1}.$$

Energy Balance

In addition to the mass balance, the other important quantity we must consider in the analysis of fluid flow, is the energy balance. Referring again to Fig. 3.3 on page 26 we shall consider the changes in the total energy of unit mass of fluid, one kilogram, between section 1 and section 2.

Firstly, there are the changes in the intrinsic energy of the fluid itself which include changes in:

(1) The potential energy.
(2) The kinetic energy.
(3) The pressure energy.

Secondly, there may be energy interchange with the surroundings including:

(4) Energy lost to the surroundings due to friction.

(5) Mechanical energy added by pumps.
(6) Heat energy in heating or cooling the fluid.

In the analysis of the energy balance, it must be remembered that energies are normally measured from a datum or reference level. Datum levels may be selected arbitrarily, but in most cases the choice of a convenient datum can be made readily with regard to the circumstances.

Potential energy

Fluid maintained above the datum level can perform work in returning to the datum level. The quantity of work it can perform is calculated from the product of the distance moved and the force-resisting movement; in this case the force of gravity. This quantity of work is called the potential energy of the fluid. Thus the potential energy of one kilogram of fluid at a height of Z(m) above its datum is given by E_p, where

$$E_p = Zg \, (\text{J}).$$

Kinetic energy

Fluid that is in motion can perform work in coming to rest. This is equal to the work required to bring a body from rest up to the same velocity which can be calculated from the basic equation

$$v^2 = 2as, \quad \therefore \quad s = v^2/2a,$$

where v (m s^{-1}) is the final velocity of the body, a (m s^{-2}) is the acceleration and s(m) is the distance the body has moved.

Also work done $= W = F \times s$, and from Newton's Second Law, for m kg of fluid

$$F = ma,$$

$$\therefore \quad E_k = W = mav^2/2a = mv^2/2.$$

The energy of motion, or kinetic energy, for 1 kg of fluid is therefore given by E_k where $E_k = v^2/2$ (J).

Pressure energy

Fluids exert a pressure on their surroundings. If the volume of a fluid is decreased, the pressure exerts a force which must be overcome and so work must be done in compressing the fluid. Conversely, fluids under pressure can do work as the pressure is released. If the fluid is considered as being in a cylinder of cross-sectional area A(m^2) and a piston is moved a distance L (m) by the fluid against the pressure P (Pa) the work done is PAL joules. The quantity of the fluid performing this work is $AL\rho$

(kg). Therefore the pressure energy which can be obtained from one kg of fluid (that is the work that can be done by this kg of fluid) is given by E_r, where

$$E_r = PAL/AL\rho$$
$$= P/\rho \, (\text{J}).$$

Friction loss

When a fluid moves through a pipe or through fittings, it encounters frictional resistance and energy can only come from energy contained in the fluid and so frictional losses provide a drain on the energy resources of the fluid. The actual magnitude of the losses depends upon the nature of the flow and of the system through which the flow takes place. In the system of Fig. 3.3 on page 26, let the energy lost by 1 kg fluid between section 1 and section 2, due to friction, be equal to E_f(J).

Mechanical energy

If there is a machine putting energy into the fluid stream, such as a pump as in the system of Fig. 3.3, the mechanical energy added by the pump per kg of fluid must be taken into account. Let the pump energy added to 1 kg fluid be E_c(J). In some cases a machine may extract energy from the fluid, such as in the case of a water turbine.

Other effects

Heat might be added or subtracted in heating or cooling processes, in which case the mechanical equivalent of this heat would require to be included in the balance. Compressibility terms might also occur, particularly with gases, but when dealing with low pressures only, they can usually be ignored.

For the present let us assume that the only energy terms to be considered are E_p, E_k, E_r, E_f, E_c.

Bernouilli's Equation

We are now in a position to write the energy balance for the fluid between section 1 and section 2 of Fig. 3.3. The total energy of one kg of fluid entering at section 1 is equal to the total energy of one kg of fluid leaving at section 2, less the energy added by the pump, plus friction energy lost in travelling between the two sections. Using the subscripts 1 and 2 to denote conditions at section 1 or section 2, respectively, we can write

$$E_{p1} + E_{k1} + E_{r1} = E_{p2} + E_{k2} + E_{r2}$$
$$+ E_f - E_c. \qquad (3.6.)$$

$$\therefore \quad Z_1 g + v_1^2/2 + P_1/\rho_1 = Z_2 g + v_2^2/2$$
$$+ P_2/\rho_2$$
$$+ E_f - E_c. \qquad (3.7)$$

In the special case where no mechanical energy is added and for a frictionless fluid, $E_c = E_f = 0$, and we have

$$Z_1 g + v_1^2/2 + P_1/\rho_1 = Z_2 g + v_2^2/2$$
$$+ P_2/\rho_2 \qquad (3.8)$$

and since this is true for any sections of the pipe the equation can also be written

$$Z g + v^2/2 + P/\rho = k \qquad (3.9)$$

where k is a constant.

Equation (3.9) is known as Bernouilli's equation. It was first discovered by the Swiss mathematician Bernouilli in 1738, and it is one of the foundations of fluid mechanics. It is a mathematical expression, for fluid flow, of the principle of conservation of energy and it covers many situations of practical importance.

Application of the equation of continuity, eqn. (3.4) or eqn. (3.5), which represents the mass balance, and eqn. (3.7) or eqn. (3.9), which represents the energy balance, is the basis for the solution of many flow problems for fluids. In fact much of the remainder of this chapter will be concerned with applying one or another aspect of these equations.

The Bernouilli equation is of sufficient importance to deserve some further discussion. In the form in which it has been written in eqn. (3.9) it will be noticed that the various quantities are in terms of energies per unit mass of the fluid flowing.

If both sides of the equation are multiplied by the density of the fluid flowing, then we have pressure terms and the equation becomes

$$\rho Z g + \rho v^2/2 + P = k'. \qquad (3.10)$$

and the respective terms are known as the potential head pressure, the velocity pressure and the static pressure.

On the other hand, if the equation is divided by the acceleration due to gravity, g, then we have an expression in terms of the head of the fluid flowing and the equation becomes:

$$Z + v^2/2g + P/\rho g = k'' \qquad (3.11)$$

and the respective terms are known as the potential head, the velocity head and the pressure head. The most convenient form for the equation is chosen for each particular case, but it is important to be consistent having made a choice.

If there is a constriction in a pipe and the static pressures are measured upstream or downstream of the constriction, and in the constriction itself, then the Bernouilli equation can be used to calculate the rate of flow of the fluid in the pipe. This assumes that the flow areas of the pipe and in the constriction are known. Consider the case in which a fluid is flowing through a horizontal pipe of cross-sectional area A_1 and then it passes to a section of the pipe in which the area is reduced to A_2. From the continuity equation [eqn. (3.5)] assuming that the fluid is incompressible:

$$A_1 v_1 = A_2 v_2$$

and so

$$v_2 = v_1 A_1/A_2.$$

Since the pipe is horizontal

$$Z_1 = Z_2.$$

Substituting in eqn. (3.8)

$$v_1^2/2 + P_1/\rho_1 = v_1^2 A_1^2/(2A_2^2) + P_2/\rho_2$$

and since $\rho_1 = \rho_2$, as it is the same fluid throughout and it is incompressible,

$$P_1 - P_2 = \rho_1 v_1^2 (A_1^2/A_2^2 - 1)/2. \qquad (3.12)$$

From eqn. (3.12), knowing $P_1, P_2, A_1, A_2, \rho_1$, the unknown velocity in the pipe, v_1, can be calculated.

Another application of the Bernouilli equation is to calculate the rate of discharge from a nozzle with a known pressure differential. Consider a nozzle placed in the side of a tank in which the surface of the fluid in the tank is H ft above the centre line of the nozzle as illustrated in Fig. 3.4.

Take the datum as the centre of the nozzle. The velocity of the fluid entering the nozzle is approximately zero as the tank is large compared

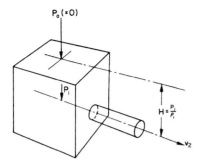

$P_0 (\approx 0)$

P_1

$H = \frac{P_1}{P_1}$

v_2

FIG. 3.4. Flow from a nozzle.

with the nozzle. The pressure of the fluid entering the nozzle is P_1 and the density of the fluid ρ_1. The velocity of the fluid flowing from the nozzle is v_2 and the pressure at the nozzle exit is 0 as the nozzle is discharging into air at the datum pressure. There is no change in potential energy as the fluid enters and leaves the nozzle at the same level. Writing the Bernouilli equation for fluid passing through the nozzle:

$$0 + 0 + P_1/\rho_1 = 0 + v_2^2/2 + 0$$
$$v_2^2 = 2P_1/\rho_1,$$

whence

$$v_2 = \sqrt{(2P_1/\rho_1)}$$

but

$$P_1/\rho_1 = gH$$

(where H is the head of fluid above the nozzle)

$$\therefore \quad v_2 = \sqrt{(2gH)}. \qquad (3.13)$$

EXAMPLE 3.5. Water flows at the rate of $0.4 \, \text{m}^3 \, \text{min}^{-1}$ in a 7.5-cm diameter pipe at a pressure of 70 kPa. If the pipe reduces to 5 cm diameter calculate the new pressure in the pipe. Density of water is $1000 \, \text{kg} \, \text{m}^{-3}$.

Flow rate of water $= 0.4 \, \text{m}^3 \, \text{min}^{-1}$
$$= 0.4/60 \, \text{m}^3 \, \text{s}^{-1}.$$

Area of 7.5-cm diameter pipe
$$= (\pi/4)D^2$$
$$= (\pi/4)(0.075)^2$$
$$= 4.42 \times 10^{-3} \, \text{m}^2.$$

$\therefore$ velocity of flow in 7.5-cm diameter pipe,
$$v_1 = (0.4/60)/(4.42 \times 10^{-3})$$
$$= 1.51 \, \text{m} \, \text{s}^{-1}.$$

Area of 5-cm diameter pipe
$$= (\pi/4)(0.05)^2$$
$$= 1.96 \times 10^{-3} \, \text{m}^2.$$

$\therefore$ velocity of flow in 5-cm diameter pipe,
$$v_2 = (0.4/60)/(1.96 \times 10^{-3})$$
$$= 3.4 \, \text{m} \, \text{s}^{-1}.$$

Now
$$Z_1 g + v_1^2/2 + P_1/\rho_1 = Z_2 g + v_2^2/2 + P_2/\rho_2$$

$\therefore \quad 0 + (1.51)^2/2 + 70 \times 10^3/1000 = 0 + (3.4)^2/2 + P_2/1000$
$\therefore \quad 0 + 1.1 + 70 = 0 + 5.8 + P_2/1000$
$\therefore \quad P_2/1000 = (71.1 - 5.8)$
$$= 65.3$$
$\therefore \quad P_2 = 65.3 \, \text{kPa}.$

EXAMPLE 3.6. Olive oil of specific gravity 0.92 is flowing in a pipe of 2 cm diameter. If a constriction is placed in the pipe such that the diameter of the pipe in the constriction is reduced to 1.2 cm and if the measured pressure difference between the clear pipe and the most constricted part of the pipe is 8 cm of water, calculate the flow rate of the olive oil.

Diameter of pipe, in clear section, equals 2 cm and at constriction equals 1.2 cm.

$$\therefore \quad A_1/A_2 = (D_1/D_2)^2 = (2/1.2)^2.$$

Differential head $= 8$ cm water.

$\therefore$ differential pressure $= \rho g H$
$$= 9.81 \times 1000 \times 0.08$$
$$= 785 \, \text{Pa}.$$

$\therefore$ substituting in eqn. (3.12)

$$785 = 0.92 \times 1000 \times v^2\,[(2/1.2)^4 - 1]/2$$
$$v^2 = 785/3091$$
$$\underline{v = 0.5\,\mathrm{m\,s^{-1}}.}$$

EXAMPLE 3.7. The level of water in a storage tank is 4.7 m above the exit pipe. The tank is at atmospheric pressure and the exit pipe discharges into the air. If the diameter of the exit pipe is 1.2 cm what is the mass rate of flow through this pipe?

From eqn. (3.13)

$$v = \sqrt{(2gH)}$$
$$= \sqrt{(2 \times 9.81 \times 4.7)}$$
$$= 9.6\,\mathrm{m\,s^{-1}}.$$

Now area of pipe

$$A = (\pi/4)D^2$$
$$= (\pi/4) \times (0.012)^2$$
$$= 1.13 \times 10^{-4}\,\mathrm{m^2}.$$

$\therefore$ volumetric flow rate, Av

$$= 1.13 \times 10^{-4}\,\mathrm{m^2} \times 9.6\,\mathrm{m^3\,s^{-1}}$$
$$= 1.13 \times 10^{-4} \times 9.6 \times 10^3\,\mathrm{kg\,s^{-1}}$$
$$= \underline{1.08\,\mathrm{kg\,s^{-1}}.}$$

EXAMPLE 3.8. Water is raised from a reservoir up 35 m to a storage tank through a 7.5-cm diameter pipe. If it is required to raise 1.6 cubic metres of water per minute, calculate the horsepower input to a pump assuming that the pump is 100% efficient and that there is no friction loss in the pipe. 1 Horsepower = 0.746 kW.

Volume of flow

$$V = 1.6\,\mathrm{m^3\,min^{-1}} = 1.6/60\,\mathrm{m^3\,s^{-1}}$$
$$= 2.7 \times 10^{-2}\,\mathrm{m^3\,s^{-1}}.$$

Area of pipe,

$$A = (\pi/4) \times (0.075)^2$$
$$= 4.42 \times 10^{-3}\,\mathrm{m^2},$$

$\therefore$ velocity in pipe $= 2.7 \times 10^{-2}/(4.42 \times 10^{-3})$
$$= 6\,\mathrm{m\,s^{-1}},$$

$\therefore$ applying eqn. (3.7)

$$E_c = 35 \times 9.81 + 6^2/2$$
$$= 343.4 + 18$$
$$= 361.4\,\mathrm{J},$$

$\therefore$ total power required $= E_c \times$ mass rate of flow
$$= E_c V\rho$$
$$= 361.4 \times 2.7 \times 10^{-2} \times 1000\,\mathrm{J\,s^{-1}}$$

and, since 1 h.p. $= 7.46 \times 10^2\,\mathrm{J\,s^{-1}}$,

required power $= 13\,\mathrm{h.p.}$

VISCOSITY

Viscosity is that property of a fluid which gives rise to forces which resist the relative movement of adjacent layers in the fluid. Viscous forces are of the same character as shear forces in solids and they arise from forces which exist between the molecules.

If two parallel plane elements in a fluid are moving relative to one another, it is found that a steady force must be applied to maintain a constant relative speed. This force is called the viscous drag because it arises from the action of viscous forces. Consider the system shown in Fig. 3.5.

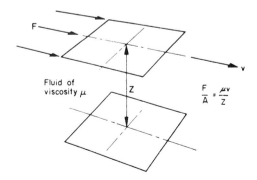

FIG. 3.5. Viscous forces in a fluid.

If the plane elements are at a distance Z apart, and if their relative velocity is v, then the force F required to maintain the motion has been found, experimentally, to be proportional to v and inversely proportional to Z for many fluids. The coefficient of proportionality is called the viscosity of the fluid, and it is denoted by the symbol μ (mu).

From the definition of viscosity we can write

$$F/A = \mu v/Z \qquad (3.14)$$

where F is the force applied, A is the area over which force is applied, Z is the distance between planes, v is the velocity of the planes relative to one another, and μ is the viscosity.

By rearranging the eqn. (3.14) the dimensions of viscosity can be found.

$$[\mu] = \frac{FZ}{Av} = \frac{[F][L][\theta]}{[L^2][L]} = \frac{[F][\theta]}{[L]^2}.$$

There is some uncertainty about the writing and the naming of the unit of viscosity; there is no doubt about the unit itself which is the $N\,s\,m^{-2}$ but it can be expressed in poises, $Pa\,s$, converting to mass units and using the basic mass/force equation, $kg\,s^{-1}\,m^{-1}$. The older units, the poise and its sub-unit the centipoise seem to be obsolete, although the conversion is simple with 10 poises or 1000 centipoises being equal to $1\,N\,s\,m^{-2}$. The new unit is rather large for many liquids, the viscosity of water at room temperature being around $1 \times 10^{-3}\,N\,s\,m^{-2}$ and for comparison, at the same temperature, the viscosities of other liquids are acetone, 0.3×10^{-3}; a tomato pulp, 3×10^{-3}; olive oil, 100×10^{-3}; and molasses $7000\,N\,s\,m^{-2}$. Viscosity is very dependent on temperature decreasing sharply as the temperature rises. For example, the viscosity of golden syrup is about $100\,N\,s\,m^{-2}$ at $16°C$, 40 at $22°C$ and 20 at $25°C$. Care should be taken not to confuse viscosity μ, as defined in eqn. (3.14) which strictly is called the dynamic or absolute viscosity, with μ/ρ which is called the kinematic viscosity and given another symbol. In technical literature, viscosities are often given in terms of units which are derived from the equipment used to measure the viscosities experimentally. The fluid is passed through some form of capillary tube or constriction and the time for a given quantity to pass through is taken and can be related to the viscosity of the fluid. Tables are available to convert these arbitrary units, such as "Saybolt Seconds" or "Redwood Seconds", to poises.

The viscous properties of many of the fluids and plastic materials which must be handled in food-processing operations are more complex than can be expressed in terms of one simple number such as a coefficient of viscosity.

Newtonian and Non-Newtonian Fluids

From the fundamental definition of viscosity in eqn. (3.14) we can write:

$$F/A = \mu v/Z = \mu \left(\frac{dv}{dz}\right) = \tau$$

where τ (tau) is called the shear stress in the fluid. This is an equation originally proposed by Newton and which is obeyed by fluids such as water. However, for many of the actual fluids encountered in the food industry, measurements show deviations from this simple relationship, and lead towards a more general equation:

$$\tau = k \left(\frac{dv}{dz}\right)^n \qquad (3.15)$$

which can be called the power-law equation, and k is a constant of proportionality.

Where $n = 1$ the fluids are called Newtonian because they conform to Newton's equation (3.14) and $k = \mu$, and all other fluids may therefore be called non-Newtonian. Non-Newtonian fluids are varied and are studied under the heading of rheology which is a substantial subject in itself and the subject of many books. Broadly, the non-Newtonian fluids can be divided into:

(1) Those in which $n < 1$. As shown in Fig. 3.6 these produce a concave downward curve and for them the viscosity is apparently high under low shear forces decreasing as the shear force increases. Such fluids are called pseudoplastic, an example being tomato purée. In more extreme cases, where the shear forces are low, there is no flow at all until a yield stress is reached after which flow occurs, and these fluids are called thixotropic.

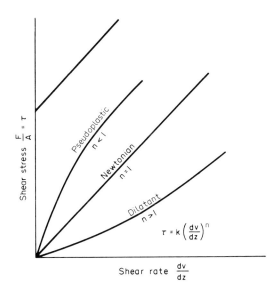

Fig. 3.6. Shear stress/shear rate relationships in liquids.

(2) Those in which $n > 1$, with a low apparent viscosity under low shear stresses becoming more viscous as the shear rises. This is called dilatancy and examples are gritty slurries such as crystallized sugar solutions. Again there is a more extreme condition with a zero apparent viscosity under low shear and such materials are called rheopectic.

In many instances in practice non-Newtonian characteristics are important, and they become obvious when materials which it is thought ought to pump quite easily just do not. They get stuck in the pipes, or overload the pumps, or need specially designed fittings before they can be moved. Sometimes it is sufficient just to be aware of the general classes of behaviour of such materials. In other cases it may be necessary to determine experimentally the rheological properties of the material so that equipment and processes can be adequately designed. For further details see, for example, Charm (1963).

STREAMLINE AND TURBULENT FLOW

When a liquid flowing in a pipe is observed carefully, it will be seen that the pattern of flow becomes more disturbed as the velocity of flow increases. Perhaps this phenomenon is more commonly seen in a river or stream. When the flow is slow the pattern is smooth, but when the flow is more rapid eddies develop and swirl in all directions and at all angles to the general line of flow.

At the low velocities, flow is calm. In a series of experiments Reynolds showed this by injecting a thin stream of dye into the fluid and finding that it ran in a smooth stream in the direction of the flow. As the velocity of flow increased, he found that the smooth line of dye was broken up until finally, at high velocities, the dye was rapidly mixed into the disturbed flow of the surrounding fluid.

From analysis, which was based on these observations, Reynolds concluded that this instability of flow could be predicted in terms of the velocity and the viscous forces which act on the fluid. In fact the instability which leads to disturbed, or what is called "turbulent" flow, is determined by the ratio of the kinetic and the viscous forces in the fluid stream. The kinetic forces tend to maintain the flow in its general direction, whereas the viscous forces tend to retard this motion and introduce eddies.

The inertial force is proportional to the velocity pressure of the fluid ρv^2 and the viscous drag is proportional to $\mu v/D$ where D is the diameter of the pipe. The ratio of these forces is

$$\rho v^2 D/v\mu = Dv\rho/\mu.$$

This ratio is very important in the study of fluid flow. As it is a ratio, it is dimensionless and so it is independent of the units of measurement so long as these are consistent. It is called the Reynolds number and is denoted by the symbol (Re).

From a host of experimental measurements on fluid flow in pipes, it has been found that the flow remains calm or "streamline" for values of the Reynolds number up to about 2100. For values above 4000 the flow has been found to be turbulent. Between above 2100 and about 4000 the flow pattern is unstable; any slight disturbance tends to upset the pattern but if there is no disturbance, streamline flow can be maintained in this region.

To summarize for flow in pipes:

for (Re) < 2100	streamline flow,
for 2100 < (Re) < 4000	transition,
for (Re) > 4000	turbulent flow.

EXAMPLE 3.9. Milk is flowing at $0.12\,\mathrm{m^3\,min^{-1}}$ in a 2.5-cm diameter pipe. If the temperature of the milk is 21°C, is the flow turbulent or streamline?

Viscosity of milk at 21°C $\quad = 2.1\,\mathrm{cP} = 2.10 \times 10^{-3}\,\mathrm{Pa\,s}.$

Density of milk at 21°C $\quad = 1029\,\mathrm{kg\,m^{-3}}.$

Diameter of pipe $\quad = 0.025\,\mathrm{m}.$

Cross-sectional area of pipe $= (\pi/4)D^2$

$\qquad\qquad\qquad\qquad\quad = \pi/4 \times (0.025)^2$

$\qquad\qquad\qquad\qquad\quad = 4.9 \times 10^{-4}\,\mathrm{m^2}.$

Rate of flow $\qquad\qquad = 0.12\,\mathrm{m^3\,min^{-1}},$

$\therefore\quad$ velocity of flow $\qquad = \dfrac{0.12}{60} \times \dfrac{1}{4.9 \times 10^{-4}}$

$\qquad\qquad\qquad\qquad\quad = 4.1 \times \mathrm{m\,s^{-1}},$

$\therefore\quad (Re) = (Dv\rho/\mu) \qquad = 0.025 \times 4.1 \times$

$\qquad\qquad\qquad\qquad\quad 1029/2.1 \times 10^{-3}$

$\qquad\qquad\qquad\qquad\quad = 50{,}230$

and this is greater than 4000 so that the flow is turbulent.

As (Re) is a dimensionless ratio, its numerical value will be the same whatever units are used. However, it is important that consistent units be used throughout, for example the SI system of units as are used in this book. If, for example, cm were used instead of m just in the diameter (or length) term only, then the value of (Re) so calculated would be greater by a factor of 10. This would make nonsense of any deductions from a particular numerical value of (Re). On the other hand, if all of the length terms in (Re) and this includes not only D but also $v\,(\mathrm{m\,s^{-1}})$, $\rho\,(\mathrm{kg\,m^{-3}})$ and $\mu\,(\mathrm{N\,s\,m^{-2}})$ are in cm then the correct value of (Re) will be obtained. It is convenient, but not necessary to have one system of units such as SI. It is necessary, however, to be consistent throughout.

ENERGY LOSSES IN FLOW

Energy losses can occur through friction in pipes, bends and fittings and in equipment.

Friction in Pipes

In Bernouilli's equation the symbol E_f was used to denote the energy loss due to friction in the pipe. This loss of energy due to friction has been shown, both theoretically and experimentally, to be related to the Reynolds number for the flow. It has also been found to be proportional to the velocity pressure of the fluid and to a factor related to the smoothness of the surface over which the fluid is flowing.

If we define the wall friction in terms of velocity pressure of the fluid flowing we can write:

$$F/A = f\rho v^2/2 \qquad (3.16)$$

where F is the friction force, A is the area over which the friction force acts, ρ is the density of the fluid, v is the velocity of the fluid, and f is a coefficient called the friction factor.

Consider an energy balance over a differential length, dL, of a straight horizontal pipe of diameter D, as in Fig. 3.7.

FIG. 3.7. Energy balance over a length of pipe.

Consider the equilibrium of the element of fluid in the length dL. The total force required to overcome friction drag must be supplied by a pressure force giving rise to a pressure drop dP along the length dL.

The pressure drop force is

$$dP \times \text{Area of pipe} = dP \cdot \frac{\pi D^2}{4}.$$

The friction force is

$$\text{(force/unit area)} \times \text{wall area of pipe} = \frac{F}{A} \cdot \pi D \cdot dL$$

from eqn. (3.16)

$$= (f\rho v^2/2) \times \pi D \cdot L,$$

$\therefore$ equating

$$(\pi D^2/4)\,dP = (f\rho v^2/2)\pi D \cdot dL,$$

$$\therefore \quad dP = 4(f\rho v^2/2) \times dL/D,$$

$$\therefore \quad \int dP = \int 4(f\rho v^2/2) \times dL/D.$$

Integrating between L_1 and L_2, in which interval P goes from P_1 to P_2 we have:

$$P_1 - P_2 = (4g\rho v^2/2)(L_1 - L_2)/D,$$

i.e.

$$\Delta P_f = (4f\rho v^2/2) \times (L/D)$$

or

$$E_f = \Delta P_f/\rho = (4fv^2/2)(L/D) \qquad (3.17)$$

where $L = L_1 - L_2 = $ length of pipe in which the pressure drops, $\Delta P_f = P_1 - P_2$ is the frictional pressure drop, and E_f is the frictional loss of energy.

Equation (3.17) is an important equation; it is known as the Fanning equation, or sometimes the D'Arcy or the Fanning–D'Arcy equation. It is used to calculate the pressure drop which occurs when liquids flow in pipes.

The factor f in eqn. (3.17) depends upon the Reynolds number for the flow, and upon the roughness of the pipe. In Fig. 3.8 experimental results are plotted, showing the relationship of these factors. If the Reynolds number and the roughness factor are known then f can be read off from the graph.

It has not been found possible to find a simple expression which gives analytical equations for the curve of Fig. 3.8, although the curve can be approximated by straight lines covering portions of the range. Equations can be written for these lines. Some writers use values for f which differ from that defined in eqn. (3.16) by numerical factors of 2 or 4. The same symbol, f, is used so that when reading off values for f its definition in the particular context should always be checked. For example, a new $f' = 4f$ removes the numerical factor from eqn. (3.17).

Inspection of Fig. 3.8 shows that for low values of (Re) there appears to be a simple relationship between f and (Re) independent of the roughness of the pipe. This is perhaps not surprising, as in streamline flow there is assumed to be a stationary boundary layer at the wall and if this is stationary there would be no liquid movement over any roughness that might appear at the wall. Actually, the friction factor f in stream-line flow can be predicted theoretically from the Hagen–Poiseuille equation, which gives:

$$f = 16/(\text{Re}) \qquad (3.18)$$

and this applies in the region $0 < (\text{Re}) < 2100$.

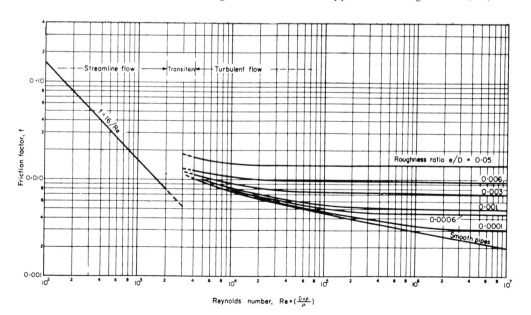

FIG. 3.8. Friction factors in pipe flow [from Moody (1944) by permission].

In a similar way, theoretical work has led to equations which fit other regions of the experimental curve, for example the Blasius equation which applies to smooth pipes in the range $3000 < (Re) < 100{,}000$ and in which:

$$f = \frac{0.316}{4}(Re)^{-0.25} \qquad (3.19)$$

In the turbulent region a number of curves are shown in Fig. 3.8. It would be expected that in this region the smooth pipes would give rise to lower friction factors than rough ones. The roughness can be expressed in terms of a roughness ratio which is defined as the ratio of average height of the projections, which make up the "roughness" on the wall of the pipe, to the pipe diameter. Tabulated values are given showing the roughness factors for the various types of pipe, based on the results of Moody (1944). These factors ε are then divided by the pipe diameter D to give the roughness ratio to be used with the Moody graph. The question of relative roughness of the pipe is under some circumstances a difficult one to resolve, but in most cases reasonable accuracy can be obtained by applying Table 3.1 and Fig. 3.8.

TABLE 3.1
RELATIVE ROUGHNESS FACTORS FOR PIPES

Material	Roughness factor (ε)	Material	Roughness factor (ε)
Riveted steel	0.001–0.01	Galvanized iron	0.0002
Concrete	0.0003–0.003	Asphalted cast iron	0.001
Wood staves	0.0002–0.003	Commercial steel	0.00005
Cast iron	0.0003	Drawn tubing	Smooth

EXAMPLE 3.10. Calculate the pressure drop along 170 m of 5-cm diameter steel pipe through which olive oil at 20°C is flowing at the rate of 0.1 m³ min⁻¹.

Diameter of pipe $= 0.05\,\text{m}$,

$\therefore$ area of cross-section $A = (\pi/4)D^2$

$= \pi/4 \times (0.05)^2$

$= 1.96 \times 10^{-3}\,\text{m}^2$.

From Appendix 4 the viscosity of olive oil at $20°\text{C} = 84 \times 10^{-3}\,\text{Pa s}$ and the density $= 910\,\text{kg m}^{-3}$,

$\therefore$ velocity $= (0.1 \times 1/60)/(1.96 \times 10^{-3})$

$= 0.85\,\text{m s}^{-1}$,

$\therefore$ $(Re) = (Dv\rho/\mu)$

$= (0.05 \times 0.85 \times 910/84 \times 10^{-3})$

$= 460$

so that the flow is streamline, and from Fig. 3.8, for $(Re) = 460$

$$f = 0.03.$$

Alternatively for streamline flow $f = 16/(Re)$ $= 16/460 = 0.03$ as before.

Pressure drop in 170 m, from eqn. (3.17)

$= 4 \times 0.03 \times 910 \times (0.85)^2 \times \dfrac{1}{2} \times 170$

$\times \dfrac{1}{0.05}$

$= 1.34 \times 10^5\,\text{Pa}$

$= 134\,\text{kPa}.$

Energy Losses in Bends and Fittings

When the direction of flow is altered or distorted, as when the fluid is flowing round bends in the pipe or through fittings of varying cross-section, energy losses occur which are not recovered. This energy is dissipated in eddies and additional turbulence and finally lost in the form of heat. However, this energy must be supplied if the fluid is to be maintained in motion, in the same way as energy must be provided to overcome friction. Losses in fittings have been found, as might be expected, to be proportional to the velocity head of the fluid flowing. In some cases the magnitude of the losses can be calculated but more often they are best found from tabulated values based largely on experimental results. The energy loss is expressed in the general form,

$$E_f = kv^2/2 \qquad (3.20)$$

where k has to be found for the particular fitting. Values of this constant k for some fittings are given in Table 3.2.

Energy is lost at sudden changes in pipe cross-section. At a sudden enlargement the loss has been

TABLE 3.2
FRICTION LOSS FACTORS IN FITTINGS

	k
Valves, fully open: gate	0.13
globe	6.0
angle	3.0
Elbows: 90°standard	0.74
medium sweep	0.5
long radius	0.25
square	1.5
Tee, used as elbow	1.5
Tee, straight through	0.5
Entrance, large tank to pipe: sharp	0.5
rounded	0.05

shown to be equal to:

$$E_f = (v_1 - v_2)^2/2. \qquad (3.21)$$

For a sudden contraction

$$E_f = kv_2^2/2 \qquad (3.22)$$

where v_1 is the velocity upstream of the change in section and v_2 is the velocity downstream of the change in pipe diameter from D_1 to D_2.

The coefficient k in eqn. (3.22) depends upon the ratio of the pipe diameters (D_2/D_1) as given in Table 3.3.

TABLE 3.3
LOSS FACTORS IN CONTRACTIONS

D_1/D_2	0.1	0.3	0.5	0.7	0.9
k	0.36	0.31	0.22	0.11	0.02

Pressure Drop through Equipment

Fluids sometimes have to be passed through beds of packed solids, for example in the air drying of granular materials hot air may be passed upward through a bed of the material. The pressure drop resulting is not easy to calculate, even if the properties of the solids in the bed are well known. It is generally necessary, for accurate pressure-drop information, to make experimental measurements.

A similar difficulty arises in the calculation of pressure drops through equipment such as banks of tubes in heat exchangers. An equation of the general form of eqn. (3.20) will hold in most cases, but values

for k will have to be obtained from experimental results. Useful correlations for particular cases may be found in books on fluid flow and from works such as Perry (1973) and McAdams (1954).

Equivalent Lengths of Pipe

In some applications it is convenient to express pressure drops in terms of equivalent lengths of straight pipe, rather than in terms of velocity heads or velocity pressures when making pipe-flow calculations. This means that a fictitious length of straight pipe is added to the actual length, such that friction due to the fictitious pipe is the same as that which would arise from the fitting under consideration. In this way various fittings, for example bends and elbows, are simply equated to equivalent lengths of pipe and the total friction losses computed from the total pipe length, actual plus fictitious. As E_f in eqn. (3.20) is equal to E_f in eqn. (3.17), k can therefore be replaced by $4fL/D$ where L is the length of pipe (of diameter D) equivalent to the fitting.

Compressibility Effects for Gases

The equations so far have all been applied on the assumption that the fluid flowing was incompressible, that is its density remained unchanged through the flow process. This is true for liquids under normal circumstances and it is also frequently true for gases. Where gases are passed through equipment such as dryers, ducting, etc., the pressures and the pressure drops are generally only of the order of a few centimetres of water and under these conditions compressibility effects can normally be ignored.

Calculation of Pressure Drops in Flow Systems

From the previous discussion, it can be seen that in many practical cases of flow through equipment, the calculation of pressure drops and of power requirements is not simple, nor is it amenable to analytical solutions. Estimates can, however, be made and useful generalizations are:

(1) Pressure drops through equipment are in general proportional to velocity heads, or pressures; in other words, they are proportional to the square of the velocity.

(2) Power requirements are proportional to the product of the pressure drop and the mass rate of flow, that is to the cube of the velocity, $v^2 \times \rho A v = \rho A v^3$.

SUMMARY

1. The static pressure in a fluid, at a depth Z, is given by:

$$P = \rho g Z$$

taking the pressure at the fluid surface as datum.

2. Fluid flow problems can often be solved by application of mass and energy balances.

3. The continuity equation, which expresses the mass balance for flow of incompressible fluids, is:

$$A_1 v_1 = A_2 v_2.$$

4. The Bernouilli equation expresses the energy balance for fluid flow:

$$Z_1 + v_1^2/2 + P_1/\rho_1 = Z_2 + v_2^2/2 + P_2/\rho_2.$$

Friction and other energy terms can be inserted where necessary.

5. The dimensionless Reynolds number (Re) characterizes fluid flow, where

$$(\text{Re}) = (Dv\rho/\mu)$$

For (Re) < 2100, flow is streamline, for (Re) > 4000 is turbulent, between 2100 and 4000 the flow is transitional.

6. Energy loss in pipes is expressed by the equation:

$$E_f = (4fv^2/2) \times (L/D)$$

and pressure drop in pipes:

$$\Delta p = (4f\rho v^2/2) \times (L/D).$$

PROBLEMS

1. In an evaporator, the internal pressure is read by means of a U-tube containing a liquid hydrocarbon of specific gravity 0.74. If on such a manometer the pressure is found to be below atmospheric by 83 cm, calculate the vacuum in the evaporator and estimate the boiling temperature of water in the evaporator by using the steam tables in Appendix 8.

2. Estimate the power required to pump milk at 20°C at 2.7 m s^{-1} through a 4-mm diameter steel tube that is 3 m long.

3. A 22% sodium chloride solution is to be pumped up from a feed tank into a header tank at the top of a building. If the feed tank is 40 m lower than the header and the pipe is 1.5 cm in diameter, find the velocity head of the solution flowing in the pipe, and the power required to pump the solution at a rate of 0.81 cubic metres per hour. Assume that the solution is at 10°C, pipe line losses can be ignored, the pump is 68% efficient, and that the density of the sodium chloride solution is 1160 kg m^{-3}.

4. It is desired to design a cooler in which the tubes are 4 mm diameter, to handle 10,000 kg of milk per hour. Calculate how many tubes would be needed in parallel to give a Reynolds number of 4000.

5. Soyabean oil is to be pumped from a storage tank to a processing vessel. The distance is 148 m and included in the pipeline are six right-angle bends, two gate valves and one globe valve. If the processing vessel is 3 m lower than the storage tank, estimate the power required to pump the oil at 20°C, at the rate of 20 tonnes per hour through the 5-cm diameter pipe assuming the pump is 70% efficient.

6. In the design of an air dryer to operate at 80°C, the fan is required to deliver 100 cubic metres per minute in a ring duct of constant cross-section 0.6 m by 1.4 m. The fan characteristic is such that this delivery will be achieved so long as the pressure drop round the circuit is not greater than 2 cm of water. Determine whether the fan will be suitable if the circuit consists essentially of four right-angle bends of long radius, a pressure drop equivalent to four velocity heads in the bed of material and one equivalent to 1.2 velocity heads in the coil heater.

CHAPTER 4

FLUID-FLOW APPLICATIONS

Two practical aspects of fluid flow are: measurements in fluids including pressures and flow rates and the production of fluid flow by means of pumps and fans. When dealing with fluids, it is important to be able to make and to understand measurements of pressures and velocities in the equipment. Only by measuring appropriate variables such as the pressure and the velocity can the flow of the fluid be controlled. When the fluid is a gas it is usually moved by a fan, and when a liquid by a pump. Pumps and fans are very similar and usually have a centrifugal or rotating action, although some pumps use longitudinal or vertical displacement.

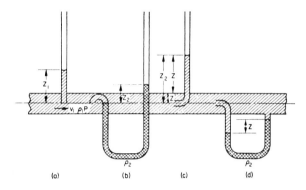

FIG. 4.1. Pressure measurements in pipes.

MEASUREMENT OF PRESSURE IN A FLUID

The simplest method of measuring pressure is to use the piezometer ("pressure measuring") tube. This is a tube containing the fluid which is under pressure and in which the fluid is allowed to rise to a height that corresponds to the excess of the pressure of the fluid over its surroundings. In most cases the surroundings are ambient air, so that we have the circumstances shown in Fig. 4.1(a). The pressure to be measured is that in the pipe and by allowing the fluid to rise in the vertical tube until it reaches equilibrium with the surrounding air pressure, the height to which it rises is the pressure head existing in the pipe. This tube is called the manometer tube.

This head can be related to the pressure in the pipe by use of eqn. (3.3) and so we have:

$$P = \rho_1 Z_1 g$$

where P is the pressure, Z_1 is the height to which the

fluid rises in the tube and ρ_1 is the density of the fluid.

A development of the piezometer is the U-tube, in which another fluid is introduced which must be immiscible with that fluid whose pressure is being measured. The fluid at the unknown pressure is connected to one arm of the manometer tube and this pressure then causes the measuring fluid to be displaced as shown in Fig. 4.1(b). The unknown pressure is then equal to the difference between the levels of the measuring fluid in the two arms of the U-tube. The differential pressure is given directly as a head of the measuring fluid and this can be converted to a head of the fluid in the system, or to a pressure difference, by eqn. (3.3).

EXAMPLE 4.1. The pressure in a vacuum evaporator was measured and was found to be less than atmospheric pressure by 25 cm of mercury as measured in a U-tube. Calculate the extent by which the pressure in the evaporator is below atmospheric pressure (i.e. the vacuum in the evaporator) in kPa and the absolute pressure in the evaporator. The atmospheric pressure is 75.4 cm of mercury and the specific gravity of mercury is 13.6.

We have $P = \rho Z g$

$$= 13.6 \times 1000 \times 25$$
$$\times 10^{-2} \times 9.81$$
$$= 33.4 \, kPa$$

and this is the vacuum in the evaporator.

For atmospheric pressure

$$P = 13.6 \times 1000 \times 75.4 \times 10^{-2} \times 9.81$$
$$= 100.6 \, kPa,$$

∴   the absolute pressure in the evaporator

$$= 100.6 - 33.4$$
$$= 77.2 \, kPa.$$

Although manometer tubes are used quite extensively to measure pressures, the most common pressure-measuring instrument is the Bourdon-tube pressure gauge. In this, use is made of the fact that a coiled tube tends to straighten itself when subjected to internal pressure and the degree of straightening is directly related to the difference between the pressure inside the tube and the pressure outside it. In practice, the inside of the tube is generally connected to the unknown system and the outside is generally in air at atmospheric pressure. The tube is connected by a rack and pinion system to a pointer and the pointer can then be calibrated to read pressure directly. A similar principle is used with a bellows gauge where unknown pressure, in a closed bellows, acts against a spring and the extent of expansion of the bellows against the spring gives a measure of the pressure. Bellows-type gauges sometimes use the bellows itself as the spring.

MEASUREMENT OF VELOCITY

If a tube, bent as shown in Fig. 4.1(c), is inserted into a flowing stream of fluid and orientated so that the mouth of the tube faces directly into the flow as in the diagram, the pressure in the tube will give a measure of velocity head due to the flow. Such a tube is called Pitot tube. The pressure exerted by the flowing fluid on the mouth of the tube is balanced by

the manometric head of fluid in the tube itself so that in equilibrium, when there is no flow in the tube, Bernouilli's equation can be applied. For the Pitot tube and manometer we can write

$$Z_1 g + v_1^2/2 + P_1/\rho_1 = Z_2 g + v_2^2/2 + P_2/\rho_1$$

in which subscript 1 refers to conditions at the entrance to the tube and subscript 2 refers to conditions at the top of the column of fluid which rises in the tube.

Now,

$Z_2 = Z + Z'$, taking the datum level at the mouth of the tube and letting Z' be the height of the upper liquid surface in the pipe above the datum, and Z be the additional height of the fluid level in the tube, above the upper liquid surface in the pipe; Z' may be neglected if P_1 is measured at the upper surface of the liquid in the pipe, or if Z' is small compared with Z.
$v_2 = 0$ as there is no flow in the tube.
$P_2 = 0$ if atmospheric pressure is taken as datum and if the top of the tube is open to the atmosphere.
$Z_1 = 0$ because the datum level is at the mouth of the tube.

The equation then simplifies to

$$v_1^2/2 + P_1/\rho_1 = (Z + Z')g \doteqdot Zg. \qquad (4.1)$$

This analysis shows that the differential head on the manometer measures the sum of the velocity and the pressure heads in the flowing liquid.

The Pitot tube can be combined with a piezometer tube, and connected across a common manometer as shown in Fig. 4.1(d). The differential head across the manometer is the velocity head plus the static head of the Pitot tube, less the static head of the piezometer tube. In other words, the differential head measures directly the velocity head of the flowing liquid or gas. This differential arrangement is known as a Pitot-static tube and it is extensively used in the measurement of flow velocities.

We can write for the Pitot-static tube,

$$Zg = v_1^2/2. \qquad (4.2)$$

EXAMPLE 4.2. Air at 0°C is flowing through a duct in a chilling system. A Pitot-static tube is inserted into the flow line and the differential pressure head measured is 0.8 mm of water. Calculate the velocity of the air in the duct. The density of air at 0°C is $1.3 \, \text{kg m}^{-3}$.

From eqn. (4.2) we have

$$Zg = v_1^2/2.$$

In working with Pitot-static tubes it is convenient to convert pressure heads into equivalent heads of the flowing fluid, in this case air, using the relationship $\rho_1 Z_1 = \rho_2 Z_2$

$$\text{Now } 0.8 \, \text{mm water} = 0.8 \times 10^{-3} \times \frac{1000}{1.3}$$

$$= 0.62 \, \text{m of air,}$$

$$\therefore \quad v_1^2 = 2Zg$$

$$= 2 \times 0.62 \times 9.81,$$

$$\therefore \quad v_1 = 3.5 \, \text{m s}^{-1}.$$

Another method of using pressure differentials to measure fluid flow rates is used in Venturi and orifice meters. If flow is constricted, there is a rise in velocity and a fall in static pressure in accordance with Bernouilli's equation. Consider the system shown in Fig. 4.2.

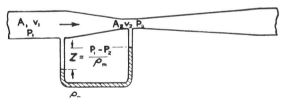

FIG. 4.2. Venturi meter.

A gradual constriction has been interposed in a pipe decreasing the area of flow from A_1 to A_2. If the fluid is assumed to be incompressible and the respective velocities and static pressure are v_1 and v_2, and P_1 and P_2, then we can write Bernouilli's equation for the section of horizontal pipe:

$$v_1^2/2 + P_1/\rho_1 = v_2^2/2 + P_2/\rho_2.$$

Furthermore, from the mass balance, eqn. (3.5)

$$A_1 v_1 = A_2 v_2,$$

also as it is the same fluid

$$\rho_1 = \rho_2 = \rho,$$

so that we have

$$v_1^2/2 + P_1/\rho = (v_1 A_1/A_2)^2/2 + P_2/\rho$$

$$v_1^2 = [2(P_1 - P_2)/\rho] \times A_2^2/(A_1^2 - A_2^2).$$

By joining the two sections of a pipe to a U-manometer, as shown in Fig. 4.2, the differential head $(P_1 - P_2)/\rho$ can be measured directly. A manometric fluid of density ρ_m must be introduced, and the head measured is converted to the equivalent head of the fluid flowing by the relationship

$$(P_1 - P_2)/\rho = gZ\rho_m/\rho.$$

If A_1 and A_2 are measured, the velocity in the pipe, v_1, can be calculated. This device is called a venturi meter. In actual practice energy losses do occur in the pipe between the two measuring points and the coefficient C is introduced to allow for this:

$$v_1 = C \sqrt{\left\{ \frac{2(P_1 - P_2)}{\rho} \cdot \frac{A_2^2}{A_1^2 - A_2^2} \right\}}$$

In a properly designed venturi meter, C lies between 0.95 and 1.0.

The orifice meter operates on the same principle as the venturi meter, constricting the flow and measuring the corresponding static pressure drop. Instead of a tapered tube, a plate with a hole in the centre is inserted in the pipe to cause the pressure difference. The same equations hold as for the venturi meter, but in the case of the orifice meter the coefficient, called the orifice discharge coefficient, is smaller. Values are obtained from standard tables, for example British Standard Specification 1042. Orifices have much greater pressure losses than venturi meters, but they are easier to construct and to insert in pipes.

Various other types of meters are used; propeller meters where all or part of the flow passes through a propeller, and the rate of rotation of the propeller can be related to the velocity of flow; impact meters where the velocity of flow is related to the pressure developed on a vane placed in the flow path; rotameters in which a rotor disc is supported against gravity in a tapered vertical tube and the rotor disc rises to a height in the tube which depends on the flow velocity.

PUMPS AND FANS

In pumps and fans, mechanical energy from some other source is converted into pressure or velocity energy in a fluid. Whilst the food technologist is not concerned with details of pumps he should know what classes of pump are used and something about their characteristics.

The efficiency of a pump is the ratio of the energy supplied by the motor to the increase in velocity and pressure energy given to the fluid.

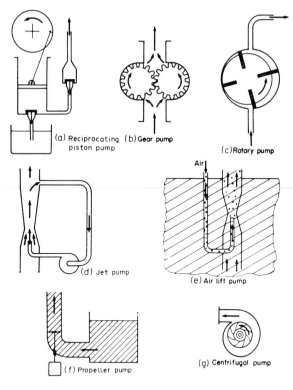

FIG. 4.3. Liquid pumps.

Positive Displacement Pumps

In a positive displacement pump, the fluid is drawn into the pump and is then forced through the outlet. Types of positive displacement pumps include, reciprocating piston pumps; gear pumps in which the fluid is enmeshed in rotating gears and forced through the pump; rotary pumps in which rotating vanes draw in and discharge fluid through a system of valves. Positive displacement pumps can develop high-pressure heads but they cannot tolerate throttling or blockages in the discharge. These types of pumps are illustrated in Fig. 4.3 (a), (b) and (c).

Jet Pumps

In jet pumps, a high-velocity jet is produced in a venturi nozzle, converting the energy of the fluid into velocity energy. This produces a low-pressure area causing the surrounding fluid to be drawn into the throat as shown diagrammatically in Fig. 4.3(d) and the combined fluids are then discharged. Jet pumps are used for difficult materials which cannot be satisfactorily handled in a mechanical pump. They are also used as vacuum pumps. Jet pumps have relatively low efficiencies but they have no moving parts and therefore have a low initial cost. They can develop only low heads per stage.

Air-lift Pumps

If air or gas is introduced into a liquid it can be used to impart energy to the liquid as illustrated in Fig. 4.3 (e). The air or gas can be provided from external sources or if it can be produced by boiling within the liquid. Examples of the air-lift principle are:

(1) Air introduced into the fluid as shown in Fig. 4.3 (e) to pump water from an artesian well.

(2) Air introduced above a liquid in a pressure vessel and the pressure used to discharge the liquid.

(3) Vapours produced in the column of a climbing film evaporator.

(4) In the case of powdered solids, air blown up through a bed of powder to convey it in a "fluidized" form.

A special case of this is in the evaporator where the gas is generated by boiling of the liquid and it is used to promote circulation. Air or gas can be used directly to provide pressure to blow a liquid from a container out to a region of lower pressure. Air-lift pumps and air blowing are inefficient, but they are convenient for materials which will not pass easily through the ports, valves and passages of other types of pumps.

Propeller Pumps and Fans

Propellers can be used to impart energy to fluids as shown in Fig. 4.3 (f). They are used extensively to mix the contents of tanks and in pipe lines to mix and convey the fluid. Propeller fans are common and have high efficiencies. They can only be used for low heads, in the case of fans only a few centimetres or so of water.

Centrifugal Pumps and Fans

The centrifugal pump converts rotational energy into velocity and pressure energy and is illustrated in Fig. 4.3 (g). The fluid to be pumped is taken in at the centre of a bladed rotor and it then passes out along the spinning rotor, acquiring energy of rotation. This rotational energy is then converted into velocity and pressure energy at the periphery of the disc. Centrifugal fans work on the same principles. These machines are very extensively used and centrifugal pumps can develop moderate heads of up to 20 m of water. They can deliver very large quantities of fluids with high efficiency. The theory of the centrifugal pump is rather complicated and will not be discussed. However, when considering a pump for a given application, the manufacturers will generally supply characteristic curves showing how the pump performs under various conditions of loading. These curves should be studied in order to match the pump to the duty required. Figure 4.4 shows a characteristic curve for a centrifugal pump.

For a given centrifugal pump, the capacity of the pump varies with its rotational speed; the pressure developed by the pump varies as the square of the rotational speed; and the power required by the pump varies as the cube of the rotational speed. The same proportional relationships apply to centrifugal fans and these relationships are often called the "fan laws" in this context.

EXAMPLE 4.3. Water for a processing plant is required to be stored in a reservoir to supply sufficient working head for washers. It is believed

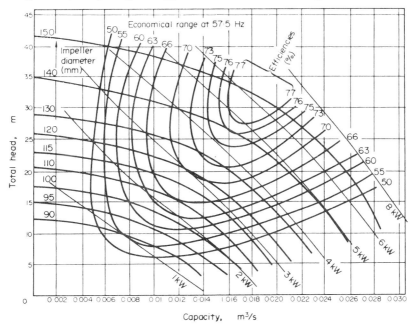

FIG. 4.4. Characteristic curves for a centrifugal pump. Reproduced with permission from J. M. Coulson and J. F. Richardson, *Chemical Engineering*, 2nd edition, fig. 6.15

that a constant supply of $1.2\,\text{m}^3\,\text{min}^{-1}$ pumped to the reservoir which is 22 m above the water intake would be sufficient. The length of the pipe is about 120 m and there is available galvanized iron piping 15 cm diameter. The line would need to include eight right-angle bends. There is a centrifugal pump whose characteristics are shown in Fig. 4.4. Would this pump be sufficient for the duty and what size of electric drive motor would be required?

Properties of water at 20°C are density $998\,\text{kg}\,\text{m}^{-3}$, and viscosity $0.001\,\text{N}\,\text{s}\,\text{m}^{-2}$.

Cross-sectional area of pipe $A = (\pi/4)D^2$
$$= \pi/4 \times (0.15)^2$$
$$= 0.0177\,\text{m}^{-2}.$$

Volume of flow $V = 1.2\,\text{m}^3\,\text{min}^{-1}$
$$= 1.2/60\,\text{m}^3\,\text{s}^{-1}$$
$$= 0.02\,\text{m}^3\,\text{s}^{-1}.$$
$\therefore$ Velocity in the pipe $= V/A$
$$= (0.02)/(0.0177)$$
$$= 1.13\,\text{m}\,\text{s}^{-1}.$$
$\therefore$ $(\text{Re}) = (Dv\rho/\mu)$
$$= (0.15 \times 1.13 \times 998)/0.001$$
$$= 1.7 \times 10^5,$$
$\therefore$ flow is clearly turbulent.

From Table 3.1 the roughness factor ε is 0.0002 for galvanized iron

and so
$$\varepsilon/D = 0.0002/0.15$$
$$= 0.001$$
So from Fig. 3.8,
$$f = 0.0053,$$

$\therefore$ the friction loss of energy $= (4fv^2/2) \times (L/D)$
$$= [4 \times 0.0053 \times (1.13)^2 \times 120]/(2 \times 0.15)$$
$$= 10.8\,\text{J}.$$

For the eight right-angled bends from Table 3.2 we would expect a loss of 0.74 velocity energies at each making $(8 \times 0.74) = 6$ in all. There would be one additional velocity energy loss because of the

unrecovered flow energy discharged into the reservoir.

Velocity energy $= v^2/2$
$$= (1.13)^2/2$$
$$= 0.64\,\text{J},$$
$\therefore$ total loss from bends and discharge energy
$$= (6 + 1) \times 0.64$$
$$= 4.5\,\text{J}.$$

Energy to move 1 kg water against a head of 22 m of water is $E_p = Zg$,
$$= 22 \times 9.81$$
$$= 215.8\,\text{J}.$$
$\therefore$ total energy requirement per kg
$$E_{\text{tot}} = 10.8 + 4.5 + 215.8$$
$$= 231.1\,\text{J}$$
and theoretical power requirement
$$= (\text{Energy/kg}) \times \text{kg}\,\text{s}^{-1}$$
$$= 231.1 \times 1.2/60 \times 998$$
$$= 4613\,\text{J}\,\text{s}^{-1}.$$

Now the head equivalent to the energy requirement
$$= E_{\text{tot}}/g$$
$$= 231.1/9.81$$
$$= 23.5\,\text{m of water},$$
and from Fig. 4.4 this would require the 150-mm impeller to be safe at the speed of 57.5 cycles s^{-1}, and the *pump would probably be fitted with a 7.5-kW motor*.

SUMMARY

1. Pressure in fluids can be measured by instruments such as the piezometer tube, the U-tube and the Bourdon tube.

2. Velocity can be measured by instruments such as the Pitot tubes – static tubes where:
$$v^2 = 2gZ$$
and Venturi meters where:
$$v^2 = 2(P_1 - P_2)A_2^2/\rho(A_1^2 - A_2^2).$$

3. Basic pumps for liquids include reciprocating, gear, vane and centrifugal types.
   Fans for air and gases are usually either centrifugal or axial flow (propeller) types.

PROBLEMS

1. The difference in levels between a fluid in the two legs of a U-tube is 4.3 cm. What differential pressure is there between the surfaces of the fluid in the two legs if the fluid in the tube is (a) water, (b) soyabean oil and (c) mercury?

2. A Pitot tube is to be used for measurement of the rate of flow of steam at a pressure of 300 kPa above atmospheric pressure, flowing in a 10-cm diameter pipe. If it is desired to measure flow rates in this pipe of between 300 and 600 kg h^{-1}, what would be the differential pressures across the tube, in mm of water?

3. If across a 2-cm diameter orifice measuring the flow of brine of density 1080 kg m^{-3} in a 5-cm diameter pipe, the differential pressure is 1.82 Pa estimate the mass rate of flow of the brine. Take the orifice discharge coefficient as 0.97.

4. A venturi meter is being used to determine the flow of soyabean oil at 65°C in a pipe. The particular pipe is 15 cm in diameter which decreased to 6 cm in the throat of the venturi. If the differential pressure is measured as 14 cm of water estimate the flow rate of the soyabean oil.

5. A volume of 0.5 m^3 h^{-1} of water is being pumped at a velocity of 1.1 m s^{-1} from the bottom of a header tank, 3 m deep, down three floors (a total fall of 10 m from the bottom of the header tank) into the top of a water pressure tank which is maintained at a pressure of 600 kPa above atmospheric. Estimate the theoretical pump power required, ignoring pipe friction.

6. In the pumping system of worked Example 4.3, the actual pump selected for the duty would pump more water than the 1.2 m^3 min^{-1} needed for the duty. By plotting a capacity curve for the system, varying the flow rate and determining the total head for each selected rate, determine from the interaction of this curve and the pump characteristic curve, the expected flow rate.

7. Using the same flow rate as in worked Example 4.3 and the same piping system, determine the total head against which a pump would have to operate if the pipeline diameter were halved to 7.5 cm diameter.

CHAPTER 5

HEAT-TRANSFER THEORY

HEAT transfer is an operation that occurs repeatedly in the food industry. Whether it is called cooking, baking, drying, sterilizing, or freezing, heat transfer is part of the processing of almost every food. An understanding of the principles which govern heat transfer is essential to an understanding of food processing.

Heat transfer is a dynamic process in which heat is transferred spontaneously from one body to another cooler body. The rate of heat transfer depends upon the differences in temperature between the bodies, the greater the difference in temperature, the greater the rate of heat transfer.

Temperature difference between the source of heat and the receiver of heat is therefore the driving force in heat transfer. An increase in the temperature difference increases the driving force and therefore increases the rate of heat transfer. The heat passing from one body to another travels through some medium which in general offers resistance to the heat flow. Both these factors, the temperature difference and the resistance to heat flow, affect the rate of heat transfer. As with other rate processes, these factors are connected by the general equation:

$$\text{rate of transfer} = \text{driving force} / \text{resistance}.$$

For heat transfer:

$$\text{rate of heat transfer} = \text{temperature difference} / \text{heat flow resistance of medium}.$$

During processing temperatures may change and therefore the rate of heat transfer will change. This is called unsteady-state heat transfer, in contrast to steady-state heat transfer when the temperatures do not change. An example of unsteady-state heat transfer is the heating and cooling of cans in a retort to sterilize the contents. Unsteady-state heat transfer is more complex since an additional variable, time, enters into the rate equations.

Heat can be transferred in three ways: by conduction, by radiation and by convection.

In conduction, the molecular energy is directly exchanged, from the hotter to the cooler regions, the molecules with greater energy communicating some of this energy to neighbouring molecules with less energy. An example of conduction is the heat transfer through the solid walls of a refrigerated store.

Radiation is the transfer of heat energy by electromagnetic waves, which transfer heat from one body to another in the same way as electromagnetic light waves transfer light energy. An example of radiant heat transfer is when a foodstuff is passed below a bank of electric resistance heaters which are red hot.

Convection is the transfer of heat by the movement of groups of molecules in a fluid. The groups of molecules may be moved by density changes or by forced motion of the fluid. An example of convection heating is cooking in a jacketed pan: without a stirrer, density changes cause heat transfer by natural convection; with a stirrer the convection is forced.

In general, heat is transferred in solids by conduction, in fluids by conduction and convection. Heat transfer by radiation occurs through open space in the same way as with the transfer of light.

In practice, the three types of heat transfer may occur together. For calculations it is often best to consider the mechanisms separately, and then to combine them where necessary.

HEAT CONDUCTION

In the case of heat conduction, the equation, rate = driving force/resistance, can be applied directly. The driving force is the temperature difference per unit length of heat-transfer path, also known as the temperature gradient. Instead of resistance to heat flow its reciprocal, called the conductance, is used. This changes the form of the general equation to:

$$\text{rate of heat transfer} = \text{driving force} \times \text{conductance},$$

that is:

$$dQ/d\theta = kA\,dt/dx, \qquad (5.1)$$

where $dQ/d\theta$ is the rate of heat transfer, the quantity of heat energy transferred per unit of time, A is the area of cross-section of the heat flow path, dt/dx is the temperature gradient, that is the rate of change of temperature per unit length of path and k is the thermal conductivity of the medium. Notice the distinction between thermal conductance which relates to the actual thickness of a given material (k/x) and thermal conductivity which relates only to unit thickness.

The units of k, the thermal conductivity, can be found from eqn. (5.1) by transposing the terms

$$\begin{aligned} k &= dQ/d\theta \times 1/A \times 1/(dt/dx) \\ &= J\,s^{-1} \times m^{-2} \times 1/(^\circ C\,m^{-1}) \\ &= J\,m^{-1}\,s^{-1}\,{}^\circ C^{-1}. \end{aligned}$$

Equation (5.1) is known as the Fourier equation for heat conduction. *Note:* Heat flows from a hotter to a colder body, that is in the direction of the negative temperature gradient. Thus a minus sign should appear in the Fourier equation. However, in simple problems the direction of heat flow is obvious and the minus sign is considered to be confusing rather than helpful, so it has not been used.

Thermal Conductivity

On the basis of eqn. (5.1) thermal conductivities of materials can be measured. Thermal conductivity

does change slightly with temperature, but in many applications it can be regarded as a constant for a given material. Thermal conductivities are given in Appendices 3, 4, 5, 6, which give physical properties of many materials used in the food industry.

In general, metals have a high conductivity, in the region $50\text{--}400\,J\,m^{-1}\,s^{-1}\,{}^\circ C^{-1}$. Most foodstuffs contain a high proportion of water and as the thermal conductivity of water is about $0.7\,J\,m^{-1}\,s^{-1}\,{}^\circ C^{-1}$ above $0^\circ C$, thermal conductivities of foods are in this range. Ice has a substantially higher thermal conductivity than water, about $2.3\,J\,m^{-1}\,s^{-1}\,{}^\circ C^{-1}$. The thermal conductivity of frozen foods is, therefore, higher than foods at normal temperatures.

Most dense non-metallic materials have thermal conductivities of $0.5\text{--}2\,J\,m^{-1}\,s^{-1}\,{}^\circ C^{-1}$. Insulating materials, such as those used in walls of cold stores, approximate closely to the conductivity of gases as they are made from non-metallic materials enclosing small bubbles of gas or air. The conductivity of air is $0.024\,J\,m^{-1}\,s^{-1}\,{}^\circ C^{-1}$ at $0^\circ C$, and insulating materials such as foamed plastics, cork and expanded rubber, are in the range $0.038\text{--}0.052\,J\,m^{-1}\,s^{-1}\,{}^\circ C^{-1}$. Some of the new insulating materials have thermal conductivities as low as $0.026\,J\,m^{-1}\,s^{-1}\,{}^\circ C^{-1}$.

When using published tables of data the units should be carefully checked. Mixed units, convenient for particular applications, are sometimes used and they may need to be converted.

Conduction through a Slab

If a slab of material, as shown in Fig. 5.1, has two faces at different temperatures t_1 and t_2 heat will flow from the face at the higher temperature t_1 to the other face at the lower temperature t_2.

The rate of heat transfer is given by Fourier's equation:

$$dQ/d\theta = kA\,dt/dx.$$

Under steady temperature conditions $dQ/d\theta = \text{constant}$, which is called q:

$$\therefore \quad q = kA\,dt/dx$$

but dt/dx, the rate of change of temperature per unit

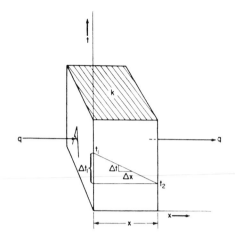

FIG. 5.1. Heat conduction through a slab.

length of path, is given by $(t_1 - t_2)/x$ where x is the thickness of the slab,

$$\therefore \quad q = kA(t_1 - t_2)/x$$

or

$$q = kA\,\Delta t/x = (k/x)A\,\Delta t. \qquad (5.2)$$

This may be regarded as the basic equation for simple heat conduction. It can be used to calculate the rate of heat transfer through a uniform wall if the temperature difference across it and the thermal conductivity of the wall material are known.

EXAMPLE 5.1. A cork slab 10 cm thick has one face at $-12°C$ and the other face at $21°C$. If the mean thermal conductivity of cork in this temperature range is $0.042\,\mathrm{J\,m^{-1}\,s^{-1}\,°C^{-1}}$ what is the rate of heat transfer through $1\,\mathrm{m}^2$ of wall?

$$t_1 = 21°C \qquad t_2 = -12°C, \qquad \therefore \quad \Delta t = 33°C,$$
$$A = 1\,\mathrm{m}^2,\ k = 0.042\,\mathrm{J\,m^{-1}\,s^{-1}\,°C^{-1}}, \qquad x = 0.1\,\mathrm{m},$$
$$\therefore \quad q = \frac{0.042}{0.1} \times 1 \times 33 = \underline{13.9\,\mathrm{J\,s^{-1}}}.$$

Heat Conductances

In tables of properties of insulating materials, heat conductances are sometimes used instead of thermal conductivities. The heat conductance is the quantity of heat that will pass in unit time, through unit area of a specified thickness of material, under

unit temperature difference. For a thickness x of material with a thermal conductivity of k in $\mathrm{J\,m^{-1}\,s^{-1}\,°C^{-1}}$, the conductance is $k/x = C$ and the units of conductance are $\mathrm{J\,m^{-2}\,s^{-1}\,°C^{-1}}$.

$$\therefore \quad \text{heat conductance} = C = k/x.$$

Heat Conductances in Series

Frequently, in heat conduction, heat passes through several consecutive layers of different materials. For example, in a cold store wall, heat might pass through brick, plaster, wood and cork. In this case, eqn. (5.2) can be applied to each layer. This is illustrated in Fig. 5.2(a).

In the steady state, the same quantity of heat per unit time must pass through each layer.

$$\therefore \quad q = A_1\Delta t_1 k_1/x_1 = A_2\Delta t_2 k_2/x_2$$
$$= A_3\Delta t_3 k_3/x_3 = \cdots$$

If the areas are the same,

$$A_1 = A_2 = A_3 = \cdots = A.$$
$$q = A\,\Delta t_1 k_1/x_1 = A\,\Delta t_2 k_2/x_2$$
$$= A\,\Delta t_3 k_3/x_3 = \cdots .$$
$$\therefore \quad A\,\Delta t_1 = q(x_1/k_1) \ \text{ and } \ A\,\Delta t_2 = q(x_2/k_2) \ \text{ and }$$
$$A\,\Delta t_3 = q(x_3/k_3)\ldots$$
$$\therefore \quad A\,\Delta t_1 + A\,\Delta t_2 + A\,\Delta t_3 + \cdots = q(x_1/k_1)$$
$$+ q(x_2/k_2)$$
$$+ q(x_3/k_3) + \cdots$$
$$\therefore \quad A(\Delta t_1 + \Delta t_2 + \Delta t_3 + \cdots) = q(x_1/k_1 + x_2/k_2$$
$$+ x_3/k_3 + \cdots).$$

The sum of the temperature differences over each layer is equal to the difference in temperature of the two outside surfaces of the complete system, i.e.

$$\Delta t_1 + \Delta t_2 + \Delta t_3 + \cdots = \Delta t,$$

and since k_1/x_1 is equal to the conductance of the material in the first layer, C_1, and k_2/x_2 is equal to the conductance of the material in the second layer C_2,

$$\therefore \quad x_1/k_1 + x_2/k_2 + x_3/k_3 + \cdots = 1/C_1 + 1/C_2$$
$$+ 1/C_3\ldots,$$
$$= 1/U,$$

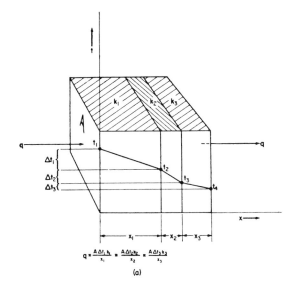

$$q = \frac{A \Delta t_1 k_1}{x_1} = \frac{A \Delta t_2 k_2}{x_2} = \frac{A \Delta t_3 k_3}{x_3}$$

(a)

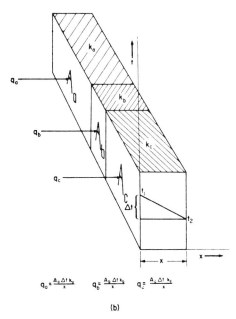

$$q_a = \frac{A_a \Delta t \, k_a}{x} \qquad q_b = \frac{A_b \Delta t \, k_b}{x} \qquad q_c = \frac{A_c \Delta t \, k_c}{x}$$

(b)

Fig. 5.2. Heat conductances (a) Conductances in series. (b) Conductances in parallel.

where U = overall conductance for the combined layers.

$$\therefore \quad A \Delta t = q(1/U).$$
$$\therefore \quad q = UA \Delta t. \tag{5.3}$$

This is of the same form as eqn. (5.2) but extended to cover the composite slab.

U is called the overall heat-transfer coefficient as it can also include combinations involving the other methods of heat transfer – convection and radiation.

Example 5.2. A cold store has a wall comprising 11 cm of brick on the outside, then 7.5 cm of concrete and then 10 cm of cork. The mean temperature within the store is maintained at $-18°C$ and the mean temperature of the outside surface of the wall is $18°C$. Calculate the rate of heat transfer through the wall and the temperature at the interface between cork and concrete. The appropriate thermal conductivities are for brick, concrete and cork, respectively 0.69, 0.76 and $0.043 \, J \, m^{-1} \, s^{-1} \, °C^{-1}$.

Determine also the temperature at the interface between the concrete and the cork layers.

For brick $x_1/k_1 = 0.11/0.69 = 0.16$.

For concrete $x_2/k_2 = 0.075/0.76 = 0.10$.

For cork $x_3/k_3 = 0.10/0.043 = 2.33$.

But
$$1/U = x_1/k_1 + x_2/k_2 + x_3/k_3$$
$$= 0.16 + 0.10 + 2.33$$
$$= 2.6.$$
$$\therefore \quad U = 0.38 \, J \, m^{-2} \, s^{-1} \, °C^{-1},$$
$$t = 18 - (-18) = 36°C,$$
$$A = 1 \, m^2.$$
$$\therefore \quad q = UA \Delta t$$
$$= 0.38 \times 1 \times 36$$
$$= 13.7 \, J \, s^{-1}.$$

Further, $q = A_3 \Delta t_3 k_3/x_3$

and for the cork wall $A_3 = 1 \, m^2 \, x_3/k_3 = 2.33$

and $q = 13.7 \, J \, s^{-1}$.

$$\therefore \quad 13.7 = 1 \times \Delta t_3 \times 1/2.33 \text{ from eqn. (5.2)}.$$
$$\therefore \quad \Delta t_3 = 32°C.$$

But Δt_3 is the difference between the temperature of the cork/concrete surface and the temperature of the cork surface inside the cold store.

$$\therefore \quad t - (-18) = 32$$

where t is the temperature at the cork/concrete surface

$$\therefore \quad t = 14°C.$$

Heat Conductances in Parallel

Heat conductances in series have a sandwich construction at right angles to the direction of the heat transfer, but with heat conductances in parallel, the material surfaces are parallel to the direction of heat transfer and to each other. The heat is therefore passing through each material at the same time, instead of through one material and then the next. This is illustrated in Fig. 5.2(b).

An example is the insulated wall of a refrigerator or an oven, in which the walls are held together by bolts. The bolts are in parallel with the direction of the heat transfer through the wall: they carry most of the heat transferred and thus account for most of the losses.

EXAMPLE 5.3. The wall of a bakery oven is built of insulating brick 10 cm thick and of thermal conductivity $0.22 \, J \, m^{-1} s^{-1} °C$. Steel reinforcing members penetrate the brick, and their total area of cross-section represents 1 % of the inside wall area of the oven. If the thermal conductivity of the steel is $45 \, J \, m^{-1} s^{-1} °C$ calculate (a) the relative proportions of the total heat transferred through the wall by the brick and by the steel and (b) the heat loss for each m^2 of oven wall if the inner side of the wall is at 230°C and the outer side is at 25°C.

Applying eqn. (5.1). $q = A \, \Delta t k / x$, we know that Δt is the same for the bricks and for the steel. Also x, the thickness, is the same.

(a) Consider the loss through an area of 1 m^2,

$\therefore$ for brick $q_b = A_b \Delta t k_b / x$

$$= \frac{0.99(230 - 25)0.22}{0.10}$$

$$= 446 \, J \, x^{-1}$$

and for steel

$$q_s = A_s \Delta t k_s / x$$

$$= \frac{0.01(230 - 25)45}{0.10}$$

$$= 923 \, J \, s^{-1}$$

$\therefore$ $q_b / q_s = 0.48$,

$\therefore$ percentage of heat carried by steel

$$= 1/1.49 \times 100$$

$$= 67 \%.$$

(b) Total heat loss

$$q = q_b + q_s \text{ per } m^2 \text{ of wall}$$

$$= 446 + 923$$

$$= 1369 \, J \, s^{-1}.$$

SURFACE-HEAT TRANSFER

Newton found, experimentally, that the rate of cooling of the surface of a solid, immersed in a colder fluid, was proportional to the difference between the temperature of the surface of the solid and the temperature of the cooling fluid. This is known as Newton's Law of Cooling, and it can be expressed by the equation, analogous to eqn. (5.2),

$$q = h_s A(t_a - t_s), \tag{5.4}$$

where h_s is the surface heat-transfer coefficient, t_a is the temperature of the cooling fluid and t_s is the temperature at the surface of the solid. The surface heat-transfer coefficient can be regarded as the conductance of a hypothetical surface film of the cooling medium of thickness x_f such that $h_s = k_f / x_f$, where k_f is the thermal conductivity of the cooling medium.

Following on this reasoning, it may be seen that h_s can be considered as arising from the presence of another layer, this time at the surface, added to the case of the composite slab considered previously. The heat passes through the surface, then through the various elements of a composite slab and then it may pass through a further surface film. We can at once write the important equation

$$q = A \, \Delta t [(1/h_{s1}) + x_1/k_1 + x_2/k_2 + \cdots$$
$$+ (1/h_{s2})] \tag{5.5}$$
$$= U A \, \Delta t$$

where $1/U = (1/h_{s1} + x_1/k_1 + x_2/k_2 + \cdots 1/h_{s2})$ and h_{s1}, h_{s2} are the surface coefficients on either side of the composite slab, $x_1, x_2 \ldots$ are the thicknesses of the layers making up the slab, and $k_1, k_2 \ldots$ are the conductivities of layers of thickness $x_1, x_2 \ldots$. The coefficient h_s is also known as the convection heat-transfer coefficient and values for it will be discussed in detail under the heading of convection. It is useful at this point, however, to appreciate the magnitude of h_s under various common conditions and these are shown in Table 5.1.

TABLE 5.1
APPROXIMATE RANGE OF SURFACE HEAT-TRANSFER
COEFFICIENTS

	h $\mathrm{J\,m^{-2}\,s^{-1}\,{}^\circ C^{-1}}$
Boiling liquids	2400–24,000
Condensing liquids	1800–18,000
Still air	6
Moving air (3 m s^{-1})	30
Liquids flowing through pipes	1200–6000

EXAMPLE 5.4. Sugar solution is being heated in a jacketed pan made from stainless steel, 1.6 mm thick. Heat is supplied by condensing steam at 200 kPa gauge in the jacket. The surface transfer coefficients are, for condensing steam and for the sugar solution, 12,000 and 3000 J m^{-2} s^{-1} °C^{-1} respectively, and the thermal conductivity of stainless steel is 21 J m^{-1} s^{-1} °C^{-1}. Calculate the quantity of steam being condensed per minute if the transfer surface is 1.4 m^{-2} and the temperature of the sugar solution is 83°C.

From steam tables, Appendix 8, the saturation temperature of steam at 200 kPa gauge = 134°C and the latent heat = 2164 kJ kg^{-1}.

For stainless steel x/k = 0.0016/21
$$= 7.6 \times 10^{-5},$$

Δt = (condensing temperature of steam)
   − (temperature of sugar solution)
$$= 134 - 83 = 51°C.$$

From eqn. (5.5)

$$1/U = 1/12{,}000 + 7.6 \times 10^{-5} + 1/3000,$$
$$\therefore \quad U = 2032 \text{ J m}^{-2}\text{s}^{-1}°C^{-1}$$

and since A = 1.4 m^2,

$$q = UA\,\Delta t$$
$$= 2032 \times 1.4 \times 51$$
$$= 1.45 \times 10^5 \text{ J s}^{-1},$$

$\therefore$ steam required per sec = heat transferred per sec
$$\div \text{ latent heat from steam}$$
$$= 1.45 \times 10^5/(2.164 \times 10^6)\,\text{kg s}^{-1}$$
$$= 0.067\,\text{kg s}^{-1}.$$

UNSTEADY-STATE HEAT TRANSFER

In food-process engineering, heat transfer is very often in the unsteady state, in which temperatures are changing and materials are warming or cooling. Unfortunately, study of heat flow under these conditions is complicated. In fact, it is the subject for study in a substantial branch of applied mathematics, involving finding solutions for the Fourier equation written in terms of partial differentials in three dimensions. There are some cases which can be simplified and handled by elementary methods, and also charts have been prepared which can be used to obtain numerical solutions under some conditions of practical importance.

A simple case of unsteady-state heat transfer arises from the heating or cooling of solid bodies made from good thermal conductors. Take, for example, a long cylinder, say a meat sausage, or a metal bar being cooled in air. The rate at which heat is being transferred to the air from the surface of the cylinder is given by eqn. (5.4)

$$dQ/d\theta = h_s A(t_s - t_a),$$

where t_a is the air temperature and t_s is the surface temperature.

Now, the heat being lost from the surface must be transferred to the surface from the interior of the cylinder by conduction. This heat transfer from the interior to the surface is difficult to determine but as an approximation, we can consider that all the heat is being transferred from the centre of the cylinder. In this instance, we evaluate the temperature drop required to produce the same rate of heat flow from the centre to the surface as passes from the surface to the air. This requires a greater temperature drop than the actual case in which much of the heat has in fact a shorter path.

Assuming that all the heat flows from the centre of the cylinder to the outside, we can write the conduction equation

$$dQ/d\theta = (k/L)A(t_c - t_s)$$

where t_c is the temperature at the centre of the cylinder, k is the thermal conductivity of the material of the cylinder and L is the radius of the cylinder.

Equating these rates:

$$h_s(t_s - t_a) = (k/L)(t_c - t_s)$$

and so

$$h_sL/k = (t_c - t_s)/(t_s - t_a).$$

To take a practical case of a copper cylinder of 15 cm radius cooling in air $k_c = 380\,\mathrm{J\,m^{-1}\,s^{-1}\,°C^{-1}}$, $h_s = 30\,\mathrm{J\,m^{-2}\,s^{-1}\,°C^{-1}}$ (from   Table   5.1), $L = 0.15\,\mathrm{m}$,

$$\therefore \quad (t_c - t_s)/(t_s - t_a) = (30 \times 0.15)/380$$
$$= 0.012$$

In this case 99% of the temperature drop occurs between the air and the cylinder surface. By comparison with the temperature drop between the surface of the cylinder and the air, the temperature drop within the cylinder can be neglected. On the other hand, if the cylinder were made of a poor conductor as in the case of the sausage or if it were very large in diameter, or if the surface heat-transfer coefficient were very much larger, the internal temperature drops could not be neglected.

This simple analysis shows the importance of the ratio

$$\frac{\text{heat transfer coefficient at the surface}}{\text{heat conductance to the centre of the solid}} = \frac{h_sL}{k}.$$

This dimensionless ratio is called the Biot number (Bi) and it is important when considering unsteady state heat flow. When (Bi) is small, and for practical purposes this may be taken as any value less than about 0.2, the interior of the solid and its surface may be considered to be all at one uniform temperature.

In the case in which (Bi) is less than 0.2, a simple analysis can be used, therefore, to predict the rate of cooling of a solid body.

$$\therefore \quad \text{for a cylinder of a good conductor, being cooled in air,}$$

$$dQ = h_sA(t_s - t_a)\,d\theta.$$

But this loss of heat cools the cylinder in accordance with the usual specific heat equation:

$$dQ = c\rho V\,dt$$

where c is the specific heat of the material of the cylinder, ρ is the density of this material and V is the volume of the cylinder.

Since the heat passing through the surface must equal the heat lost from the cylinder, these two expressions for dQ can be equated:

$$c\rho V\,dt = h_sA(t_s - t_a)\,d\theta.$$
$$\therefore \quad d\theta h_sA/c\rho V = dt/(t_s - t_a).$$

Integrating between $t_s = t_1$, and $t_s = t_2$, the initial and final temperatures of the cylinder during the cooling period, θ, we have:

$$-\theta h_sA/c\rho V = \log_e(t_2 - t_a)/(t_1 - t_a)$$

or

$$(t_2 - t_a)/(t_1 - t_a) = \exp(-h_sA\theta/c\rho V). \quad (5.6)$$

For this case, the temperatures for any desired interval can be calculated if the surface transfer coefficient and the other physical factors are known. This gives a reasonable approximation so long as (Bi) is less than about 0.2. Where (Bi) is greater than 0.2 the centre of the solid will cool more slowly than this equation suggests. The equation is not restricted to cylinders, it applies to solids of any shape so long as the restriction in (Bi), calculated for the smallest half-dimension, is obeyed.

Charts have been prepared which give the temperature relationships for solids of simple shapes under more general conditions of unsteady-state conduction. These charts have been calculated from solutions of the conduction equation and they are plotted in terms of dimensionless groups so that their application is more general. The form of the solution is:

$$f(t - t_0)/(t_i - t_0) = F(k\theta/c\rho L^2)(h_sL/k) \quad (5.7)$$

where f and F indicate functions of the terms following, t_i is the initial temperature of the solid, t_0 is the temperature of the cooling or heating medium, t is the temperature of the solid at time θ, $(k\theta/c\rho L^2)$ is called the Fourier number (Fo) (this includes the factor $k/c\rho$ the thermal conductance divided by the volumetric heat capacity, which is called the thermal diffusivity) and (h_sL/k) is the Biot number.

A mathematical result which is very useful in these calculations connects results for two- and three-dimensional situations with results from one-dimensional situations. This states that the two- and three-dimensional values called $F(x, y)$ and $F(x, y, z)$ can be obtained from the individual results if these are $F(x)$, $F(y)$ and $F(z)$, by simple multiplication:

$$F(x, y) = F(x)F(y)$$

and

$$F(x, y, z) = F(x)F(y)F(z).$$

Using the above result, the solution for the cooling or heating of a brick is obtained from the product of three slab solutions, and that for a cylinder of finite length, such as a can, from the product of the solution for an infinite cylinder and the solution for a slab.

Charts giving rates of unsteady-state heat transfer to the centre of a slab, a cylinder, or a sphere, are given in Fig. 5.3. On one axis is plotted the fractional unaccomplished temperature change,

$(t - t_0)/(t_i - t_0)$. On the other axis is the Fourier number, which may be thought of in this connection as a time coordinate. The various curves are for different values of the Biot number.

More detailed charts, giving surface and mean temperatures in addition to centre temperatures, may be found in McAdams (1954), Fishenden and Saunders (1950) and Perry (1973).

EXAMPLE 5.5. A process is under consideration in which large cylindrical meat sausages are to be processed in an autoclave. A sausage may be taken as thermally equivalent to a cylinder 30 cm long and 10 cm in diameter.

If the sausages are initially at a temperature of 21°C and the temperature in the autoclave is maintained at 116°C, estimate the temperature of the sausage at its centre 2 h after it has been placed in the autoclave. Assume that the thermal conductivity of the sausage is $0.48 \, \mathrm{J \, m^{-1} \, s^{-1} \, °C^{-1}}$, that its specific gravity is 1.07, and its specific heat is $3350 \, \mathrm{J \, kg^{-1} \, °C}$. The surface heat-transfer coefficient in the autoclave to the surface of the sausage is $1200 \, \mathrm{J \, m^{-2} \, s^{-1} \, °C^{-1}}$.

This problem can be solved by combining the unsteady-state solutions for a cylinder with those for a slab, working from Fig. 3.3.

(a) For the cylinder, of radius $r = 5$ cm (instead of L in this case)

$$\mathrm{Bi} = h_s r/k = (1200 \times 0.05)/0.48 = 125$$

(often in these systems the length dimension is the half thickness, or the radius, but this has to be checked on the graphs used).

$$\therefore \quad 1/(\mathrm{Bi}) = 8 \times 10^{-3}.$$

After 2 hours $\theta = 7200 \, \mathrm{s}$,

$$\therefore \quad k\theta/c\rho r^2 = (0.48 \times 7200)/[3350 \times 1.07$$
$$\times 1000 \times (0.05)^2]$$
$$= 0.39$$

and so from Fig. 5.3

$$(t - t_0)/(t_1 - t_0) = 0.175 = \text{say, } F(x).$$

(b) For the slab of half-thickness $\dfrac{30}{2}$ cm $= 0.15$ m

$$\mathrm{Bi} = h_s L/k = (1200 \times 0.15)/0.48$$
$$= 375,$$

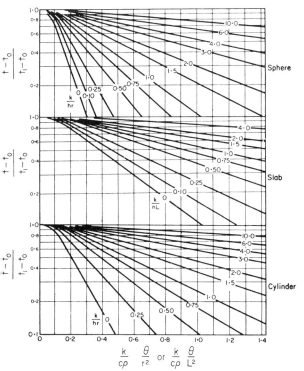

FIG. 5.3. Transient heat conduction: temperatures at the centre of a sphere, a slab and a cylinder (by permission from *Agricultural Process Engineering*, Henderson and Perry, Wiley, New York).

$\therefore 1/(\text{Bi}) = 2.7 \times 10^{-3}$,

$\theta = 7200\,\text{s}$ as before

and

$$k\theta/c\rho r^2 = (0.48 \times 7200)/[3350 \times 1.07$$
$$\times 1000 \times (0.15)]$$
$$= 4.3 \times 10^{-2}$$

and so from Fig. 5.3

$(t - t_0)/(t_1 - t_0) = 0.98 =$ say, $F(y)$,

$\therefore$ overall $(t - t_0)/(t_1 - t_0) = F(x) \cdot F(y)$
$$= 0.175 \times 0.98$$
$$= 0.172,$$

$$\therefore \quad \frac{t_2 - 116}{21 - 116} = 0.172,$$

$\therefore \quad \underline{t_2 = 100°\text{C}.}$

RADIATION-HEAT TRANSFER

Radiation-heat transfer is the transfer of heat energy by electromagnetic radiation. Radiation operates independently of the medium through which it occurs and depends upon the relative temperatures, geometric arrangements and surface structures of the materials that are emitting or absorbing heat.

The calculation of radiant-heat-transfer rates, in detail, is beyond the scope of this book and for most food-processing operations a simplified treatment is sufficient to estimate radiant-heat effects. Radiation can be significant with small temperature differences as, for example, in freeze drying and in cold stores, but it is generally more important where the temperature differences are greater. Under these circumstances, it is often the most significant mode of heat transfer, for example in bakers' ovens and in radiant dryers.

The basic formula for radiant-heat transfer is the Stefan-Boltzmann Law

$$q = A\sigma T^4 \tag{5.8}$$

where T is the absolute temperature (measured from the absolute zero of temperature at $-273°\text{C}$) in degrees Kelvin (K) in the SI system and σ (sigma) is the Stefan–Boltzmann constant $= 5.73 \times 10^{-8}\,\text{J}\,\text{m}^{-2}\,\text{K}^{-4}$. The absolute temperatures are calculated by the formula $K = (°\text{C} + 273)$.

This law gives the radiation emitted by a perfect radiator (a black body as this is called though it could be a red-hot wire in actuality). A black body gives the maximum amount of emitted radiation possible at its particular temperature. Real surfaces at a temperature T do not emit as much energy as predicted by eqn. (5.8), but it has been found that many emit a constant fraction of it. For these real bodies, including foods and equipment surfaces, those which emit a constant fraction of the radiation from a black body, the equation can be rewritten

$$q = \varepsilon A\sigma T^4 \tag{5.9}$$

where ε (epsilon) is called the emissivity of the particular body and is a number between 0 and 1. Bodies obeying this equation are called grey bodies.

Emissivities vary with the temperature T and with the wavelength of the radiation emitted. For many purposes it is sufficient to assume that for dull black surfaces (lamp-black or burnt toast, for example) the emissivity is approximately 1, surfaces such as paper or painted metal or wood and including most foods have emissivities about 0.9, rough un-polished metal surfaces vary from 0.7 to 0.25 and polished metal surfaces have emissivities of about or below 0.05. These values apply at the low and moderate temperatures encountered in food processing.

Just as a black body emits radiation, it also absorbs it and according to the same law, eqn. (5.8). Again grey bodies absorb a fraction of the quantity that a black body would absorb, corresponding to their absorptivity α (alpha). For grey bodies it can be shown that $\alpha = \varepsilon$. The fraction of the incident radiation that is not absorbed is reflected. Thus, there is a further term used, the reflectivity which is equal to $(1 - \alpha)$.

Radiation between Two Bodies

The radiant energy transferred between two surfaces depends upon their temperatures, the geometric arrangement, and their emissivities. For two parallel surfaces, facing each other, each must intercept the total energy emitted by the other, either absorbing or reflecting it. In this case, the net heat transferred from the hotter to the cooler surface is given by

$$q = AC\sigma(T_1^4 - T_2^4) \qquad (5.10)$$

where $1/C = 1/\varepsilon_1 + 1/\varepsilon_2 - 1$, ε_1 is the emissivity of the surface at temperature T_1 and ε_2 is the emissivity of the surface at temperature T_2.

Radiation to a Small Body from its Surroundings

In the case of a relatively small body in surroundings that are at a uniform temperature, the net heat exchange is given by the equation

$$q = \sigma A\varepsilon(T_1^4 - T_2^4) \qquad (5.11)$$

where ε is the emissivity of the body, T_1 is the absolute temperature of the body and T_2 is the absolute temperature of the surroundings.

For many practical purposes in process engineering, eqn. (5.11) covers the situation; for example for a loaf in an oven receiving radiation from the walls around it, or a meat carcase radiating heat to the walls of a freezing chamber.

In order to be able to compare the various forms of heat transfer, it is necessary to see whether an equation can be written for radiant-heat transfer similar to the general heat transfer eqn. (3.5). This means that for radiant-heat transfer

$$q = h_r A(t_1 - t_2) \qquad (5.12)$$

where h_r is the radiation-heat-transfer coefficient, t_1 is the temperature of the body and t_2 is the temperature of the surroundings.

Now

$$(T_1 - T_2) = (t_1 + 273) - (t_2 + 273)$$
$$= (t_1 - t_2)$$

and equating eqn. (5.11) and eqn. (5.12)

$$q = h_r A(T_1 - T_2) = A\varepsilon\sigma(T_1^4 - T_2^4).$$
$$\therefore \quad h_r = \varepsilon\sigma(T_1^4 - T_2^4)/(T_1 - T_2)$$
$$= \varepsilon\sigma(T_1 + T_2)(T_1^2 + T_2^2).$$

If $T_m = (T_1 + T_2)/2$, we can write $T_1 + e = T_m$ and $T_2 - e = T_m$

where

$$2e = T_1 - T_2,$$

also

$$(T_1 + T_2) = 2T_m,$$

and then

$$(T_1^2 + T_2^2) = T_m^2 - 2eT_m + e^2 + T_m^2 + 2eT_m + e^2$$
$$= 2T_m^2 + 2e^2$$
$$= 2T_m^2 + (T_1 - T_2)^2.$$
$$\therefore \quad h_r = \varepsilon\sigma(2T_m)[2T_m^2 + (T_1 - T_2)^2].$$

Now, if $(T_1 - T_2) \ll T_1$ or T_2, that is if the difference between the temperatures is small compared with the numerical values of the absolute temperatures, we can write

$$h_r = \varepsilon\sigma 4T_m^3$$

and so

$$q = h_r A \, \Delta T$$
$$= (4 \times 5.73 \times 10^{-8} \times T_m^3 \times \varepsilon) \times A \, \Delta T$$
$$= 0.23\varepsilon(T_m/100)^3 A \, \Delta T. \qquad (5.13)$$

EXAMPLE 5.6. Calculate the net heat transfer by radiation to a loaf of bread in an oven at a uniform temperature of 177°C, if the emissivity of the surface of the loaf is 0.85, using eqn. (5.11). Compare this result with that obtained by using eqn. (5.13). The total surface area and temperature of the loaf are respectively 0.0645 m² and 100°C.

$$q = A\varepsilon\sigma(T_1^4 - T_2^4)$$
$$= 0.0645 \times 0.85 \times 5.73 \times 10^{-8}$$
$$(450^4 - 373^4)$$
$$= 68.0 \, \text{J s}^{-1}.$$

By eqn. (5.13)

$$q = 0.23\varepsilon(T_m/100)^3 \times A \times (T_1 - T_2)$$
$$= 0.23 \times 0.85 (411/100)^3 \times 0.0645 \times 77$$
$$= \underline{67.4 \, \text{J s}^{-1}}.$$

Notice that even with quite a large temperature difference, eqn. (5.13) gives a close approximation to the result obtained using eqn. (5.11).

CONVECTION-HEAT TRANSFER

Convection-heat transfer is the transfer of energy by the mass movement of groups of molecules. It is restricted to liquids and gases as mass molecular movement cannot occur in solids. It cannot be mathematically predicted as easily as can transfer by conduction or radiation and so its study is based on experimental results rather than on theory. The most satisfactory convection-heat-transfer formulae are relationships between dimensionless groups of physical quantities. Furthermore, since the laws of molecular transport govern both heat flow and viscosity, convection-heat transfer and fluid friction are closely related to each other.

Convection coefficients will be studied under two sections, firstly, natural convection in which movements occur due to density differences on heating or cooling and secondly, forced convection, in which an external source of energy is applied to create movement. In many practical cases, both mechanisms occur together.

Natural Convection

Heat transfer by natural convection occurs when a fluid is in contact with a surface hotter or colder than itself. As the fluid is heated or cooled it changes its density. This difference in density causes movement in the fluid which has been heated or cooled and causes the heat transfer to continue.

There are many examples of natural convection in the food industry. Convection is significant when hot surfaces, such as retorts which may be vertical or horizontal cylinders, are exposed with or without insulation to colder ambient air. It occurs when food is placed inside a chiller or freezer store in which circulation is not assisted by fans. Convection is important when material is placed in ovens without fans and afterwards when the cooked material is removed to cool in air.

It has been found that natural convection rates depend upon the physical constants of the fluid, density ρ, viscosity μ, thermal conductivity k, specific heat at constant pressure c_p, and coefficient of thermal expansion β (beta) which for gases $= 1/T$ by Charles' Law. Other factors that also affect convection-heat transfer are, some linear dimension of the system, diameter D or length L, a temperature difference term, Δt, and the gravitational acceleration g since it is density differences acted upon by gravity that create circulation. Heat-transfer rates are expressed in terms of a convection-heat-transfer coefficient h_c, which is part of the general surface coefficient h_s, in eqn. (5.5).

It has been found, experimentally, that convection-heat transfer can be described in terms of these factors grouped in dimensionless numbers in terms of these factors grouped in dimensionless numbers which are known by the names of eminent workers in this field:

Nusselt number (Nu) $= (h_c D/k)$.

Prandtl number (Pr) $= (c_p \mu/k)$

Grashof number (Gr) $= (D^3 \rho^2 g \beta \, \Delta t/\mu^2)$

and in some cases a length ratio (L/D).

If we assume that these ratios can be related by a simple power function we can then write the most general equation for natural convection:

$$(\text{Nu}) = K(\text{Pr})^k(\text{Gr})^m(L/D)^n. \qquad (5.14)$$

Experimental work has evaluated K, k, m, n, under various conditions. For a discussion, see McAdams (1954). Once K, k, m, n are known for a particular case, together with the appropriate physical characteristics of the fluid, the Nusselt number can be calculated. From the Nusselt number we can find h_c and so determine the rate of convection-heat transfer by applying eqn. (5.5). In natural convection equations, the values of the physical constants of the fluid are taken at the mean temperature between the surface and the bulk fluid. The Nusselt and Biot numbers look similar: they differ in that for Nusselt k and h both refer to the fluid, for Biot k is in the solid and h in the fluid.

Natural Convection Equations

(1) Natural convection about vertical cylinders and planes, such as vertical retorts and oven walls:

$$(\text{Nu}) = 0.53(\text{Pr} \cdot \text{Gr})^{0.25} \text{ for } 10^4 < (\text{Pr} \cdot \text{Gr}) < 10^9,$$
$$(5.15)$$

$$(\text{Nu}) = 0.12(\text{Pr} \cdot \text{Gr})^{0.33} \text{ for } 10^9 < (\text{Pr} \cdot \text{Gr}) < 10^{12}.$$
$$(5.16)$$

For air these equations can be approximated by:

$$h_c = 1.3 \left(\frac{\Delta t}{L}\right)^{0.25}, \qquad (5.17)$$

$$h_c = 1.8(\Delta t)^{0.25}. \qquad (5.18)$$

Equations (5.17) and (5.18) are dimensional equations and are in standard units (Δt in °C and L or D in metres and h_c in $J m^{-2} s^{-1} °C^{-1}$). The characteristic dimension to be used in the calculation of (Nu) and (Gr) in these equations is the height of the plane or cylinder.

(2) Natural convection about horizontal cylinders such as a steam pipe or sausages lying on a rack:

$$(Nu) = 0.54(Pr \cdot Gr)^{0.25} \qquad (5.19)$$

for laminar flow in range $10^3 < (Pr \cdot Gr) < 10^9$.

Simplified equations can be employed in the case of air which is so often encountered in contact with hotter or colder foods giving again:

$$h_c = 1.31 \left(\frac{\Delta t}{D}\right)^{0.25} \qquad (5.20)$$

and for

$$10^9 < (Pr \cdot Gr) < 10^{12}$$

$$h_c = 1.8(\Delta t)^{0.33} \qquad (5.21)$$

(3) Natural convection from horizontal planes, such as slabs of cake cooling: the corresponding cylinder equations may be used, employing the length of the plane instead of the diameter of the cylinder whenever D occurs in (Nu) and (Gr). In the case of horizontal planes, cooled when facing upwards, or heated when facing downwards, which appear to be working against natural convection circulation, it has been found that half of the value of h_c in eqns. (5.19)–(5.21) corresponds reasonably well with the experimental results.

Note carefully that the simplified equations are dimensional. Temperatures must be in °C and lengths in m and then h_c will be in $J m^{-2} s^{-1} °C^{-1}$. Values for σ, k and μ are measured at the film temperature, which is midway between the surface temperature and the temperature of the bulk liquid.

EXAMPLE 5.7. Calculate the rate of convection-heat loss to ambient air from the side walls of a cooking vessel in the form of a vertical cylinder 0.9 m in diameter and 1.2 m high. The outside of the vessel insulation, facing ambient air, is found to be at 49°C and the air temperature is 17°C.

First it is necessary to establish the value of $(Pr \cdot Gr)$. From the properties of air, at the mean film temperature,

$(49 + 17)/2$, that is 33°C, $\mu = 1.9 \times 10^{-5}$ N s m^{-2}, $c_p = 1.0$ kJ kg^{-1} °C^{-1}, $k = 0.025$ J m^{-1} s^{-1} °C^{-1}, $\beta = \dfrac{1}{308}$; $\rho = 1.12$ kg m^{-3}.

From the conditions of the problem, characteristic dimension = height = 1.2 m, $\Delta T = 32°C$.

$$\therefore \quad (Pr \cdot Gr) = (L^3 \rho^2 \beta g \, \Delta t c_p)/(\mu k)$$
$$= [(1.2)^3 \times (1.12)^2 \times 9.81$$
$$\times 32 \times 1.0 \times 10^3]/$$
$$(308 \times 1.9 \times 10^{-5} \times 0.025)$$
$$= 5 \times 10^9.$$

$\therefore$ eqn. (5.18) is applicable.

From eqn. (5.18)

$$h_c = 1.8 \, \Delta t^{0.25} = 1.8(32)^{0.25}$$
$$= 4.3 \, J m^{-2} s^{-1} °C^{-1}.$$

Total area of vessel wall = $\pi DL = \pi \times 0.9$
$$\times 1.2$$
$$= 3.4 \, m^2$$
$$\Delta t = 32°C.$$
$$\therefore \quad \text{heat loss} = h_c A(t_1 - t_2)$$
$$= 4.3 \times 3.4 \times 32$$
$$= 468 \, J s^{-1}.$$

Forced Convection

When a fluid is forced past a solid body and heat is transferred between the fluid and the body, this is called forced-convection heat transfer. Examples in the food industry are in the forced-convection ovens for baking bread, in blast and fluidized freezing, in ice-cream hardening rooms, in agitated retorts, in meat chillers, in all of which foodstuffs of various geometrical shapes are heated or cooled by a surrounding fluid which is moved relative to them by external means. The fluid is constantly being replaced, and the rates of heat transfer are, therefore, higher than for natural convection. Also, as might be expected, the higher the velocity of the fluid the higher the rate of heat transfer. In the case of low velocities, where rates of natural convection heat transfer are comparable to those of forced-convection heat transfer, the Grashof number is still significant. But in general the influence of natural circulation, depending on coefficients of thermal expansion and on the gravitational acceleration, is replaced by dependence on circulation velocities and the Reynolds number.

As with natural convection, the results are substantially based on experiment and are grouped to deal with various commonly met situations such as fluids flowing in pipes, outside pipes, etc.

Forced-convection Equations

(1) Heating and cooling inside tubes, generally fluid foods being pumped through pipes. In cases of moderate temperature differences and where tubes are reasonably long, for laminar flow it is found that

$$(Nu) = 4 \qquad (5.22)$$

and where turbulence is developed for $(Re) > 2100$ and $(Pr) > 0.5$

$$(Nu) = 0.023(Re)^{0.8}(Pr)^{0.4}. \qquad (5.23)$$

For more viscous liquids, such as oils and syrups, the surface heat transfer will be affected depending upon whether the fluid is heating or being cooled. Under these cases, the viscosity effect can be allowed for by using the equation:

$$(Nu) = 0.027(\mu/\mu_s)^{0.14}(Re)^{0.8}(Pr)^{0.33} \qquad (5.24)$$

for $(Re) > 10,000$.

In both cases, the fluid properties are those of the bulk fluid except for μ_s which is the viscosity of the fluid at the temperature of the tube surface.

Since (Pr) varies little for gases, either between gases or with temperature, it can be taken as 0.75 and eqn. (5.23) simplifies for gases to:

$$(Nu) = 0.02(Re)^{0.8}. \qquad (5.25)$$

In this equation the viscosity ratio is assumed to have no effect and all quantities are evaluated at the bulk gas temperature. For other factors constant, this becomes $h_c = k'v^{0.8}$.

(2) Heating or cooling over plane surfaces. Many instances of foods approximate to plane surfaces, such as cartons of meat or ice cream or slabs of cheese. For a plane surface, the problem of characterizing the flow arises as it is no longer obvious what length to choose for the Reynolds number. It has been found, however, that experimental data correlate quite well if the length of the plate measured in the direction of the flow is taken for D in the Reynolds number and the recommended equation is:

$$(Nu) = 0.036 \ (Re)^{0.8}(Pr)^{0.33},$$
$$\text{for } (Re) > 2 \times 10^4. \qquad (5.26)$$

For the flow of air over flat surfaces simplified equations are:

$$h_c = 5.7 + 3.9v \text{ for } v < 5 \, \text{m s}^{-1}, \qquad (5.27)$$
$$h_c = 7.4v^{0.8} \text{ for } 5 < v < 30 \, \text{m s}^{-1}. \qquad (5.28)$$

These again are dimensional equations and they apply only to smooth plates. Values for h_c for rough plates are slightly higher.

(3) Heating and cooling outside tubes such as water chillers, or chilling sausages or spaghetti. Experimental data in this case have been correlated by the usual form of equation

$$(Nu) = K(Re)^n(Pr)^m. \qquad (5.29)$$

The powers n and m vary with the Reynolds number. Values for D in (Re) are again in a difficulty and the diameter of the tube, over which the flow occurs, is used. It should be noted that in this case the same values of (Re) cannot be used to denote streamline or turbulent conditions as for fluids flowing inside pipes.

For gases and for liquids at high or moderate Reynolds numbers:

$$(Nu) = 0.26(Re)^{0.6}(Pr)^{0.3} \qquad (5.30)$$

whereas for liquids at low Reynolds numbers, $1 < (Re) < 200$:

$$(Nu) = 0.86(Re)^{0.43}(Pr)^{0.3}. \qquad (5.31)$$

As in eqn. (5.23), (Pr) for gases is nearly constant so that simplified equations can be written. Fluid properties in these forced-convection equations are evaluated at the mean film temperature which is the arithmetic mean temperature between the temperature of the tube walls and the temperature of the bulk fluid.

EXAMPLE 5.8. Water is flowing at $0.13 \, \text{m s}^{-1}$ across a 7.5-cm diameter sausage at 74°C. If the bulk water temperature is 24°C estimate the heat-transfer coefficient.

$$\text{Mean film temperature} = (74 + 24)/2$$
$$= 49°C.$$

Properties of water at 49°C are $c_p = 4.186 \, \text{kJ kg}^{-1}$,

$$k = 0.64 \, \text{J m}^{-1} \, \text{s}^{-1} \, °\text{C}^{-1},$$
$$\mu = 5.6 \times 10^{-4} \, \text{N s m}^{-2},$$
$$\rho = 1000 \, \text{kg m}^{-3}.$$

$$\therefore \quad (\text{Re}) = (Dv\rho/\mu)$$
$$= (0.075 \times 0.3 \times 1000)/(5.6 \times 10^{-4})$$
$$= 4.02 \times 10^4.$$

$$\therefore \quad (\text{Re})^{0.6} = 580$$
$$(\text{Pr}) = (c_p\mu/k)$$
$$= (4186 \times 5.6 \times 10^{-4})/0.64$$
$$= 3.66.$$

$$\therefore \quad (\text{Pr})^{0.3} = 1.48$$
$$\therefore \quad (\text{Nu}) = (h_c D/k)$$
$$= 0.26(\text{Re})^{0.6}(\text{Pr})^{0.3}.$$
$$\therefore \quad h_c = k/D \times 0.26 \times (\text{Re})^{0.6}(\text{Pr})^{0.3}$$
$$= (0.64 \times 0.26 \times 580 \times 1.48)/0.075$$
$$= \underline{1904 \, \text{J m}^{-2} \, \text{s}^{-1} \, °\text{C}^{-1}.}$$

EXAMPLE 5.9. Calculate the surface heat-transfer coefficient to a vegetable purée which is flowing at an estimated $3 \, \text{m min}^{-1}$ over a flat plate 0.9 m long by 0.6 m wide, if steam is condensing on the other side of the plate and maintaining the surface which is in contact with the purée at 104°C. Assume that the properties of the vegetable purée are, density $1040 \, \text{kg m}^{-3}$, specific heat $3980 \, \text{J kg}^{-1} \, °\text{C}^{-1}$, viscosity $0.002 \, \text{N s m}^{-2}$, thermal conductivity $0.52 \, \text{J m}^{-1} \, \text{s}^{-1} \, °\text{C}^{-1}$.

$$(\text{Re}) = (Lv\rho/\mu)$$
$$= (0.9 \times 3 \times 1040)/(2 \times 10^{-3} \times 60)$$
$$= 2.34 \times 10^4.$$

$\therefore$ eqn. (3.26) is applicable and so
for $(h_c L/k) = 0.036(\text{Re})^{0.8}(\text{Pr})^{0.33}$,

$$\text{Pr} = (c_p\mu/k)$$
$$= (3980 \times 2 \times 10^{-3})/0.52$$
$$= 15.3$$

and so

$$(h_c L/k) = 0.036(2.34 \times 10^4)^{0.8} 15.3^{0.33}$$
$$h_c = (0.52 \times 0.036)$$
$$(3.13 \times 10^3)(2.46)/0.9$$
$$= \underline{160 \, \text{J m}^{-2} \, \text{s}^{-1} \, °\text{C}^{-1}.}$$

EXAMPLE 5.10. What would be the rate of heat loss from the cooking vessel of Example 5.7 on page 57, if a draught caused the air to move past the cooking vessel at a speed of $61 \, \text{m min}^{-1}$?

Assume the vessel is equivalent to a flat plate then from eqn. (5.27)

$$h_c = 5.7 + 3.9v$$
$$= 5.7 + (3.9 \times 61)/60$$
$$= 9.7 \, \text{J m}^{-2} \, \text{s}^{-1} \, °\text{C}^{-1}.$$

So with $A = 3.4 \, \text{m}^2$, $\Delta t = 32°C$,

$$q = 9.7 \times 3.4 \times 32 = \underline{1055 \, \text{J s}^{-1}.}$$

OVERALL HEAT-TRANSFER COEFFICIENTS

It is most convenient to use overall heat-transfer coefficients in heat-transfer calculations as these combine all of the constituent factors into one, and are based on the overall temperature drop. An overall coefficient, U, combining conduction and surface coefficients, has already been introduced in eqn. (5.5). Radiation coefficients, subject to the limitations discussed in the section on radiation, can be incorporated also in the overall coefficient. The radiation coefficients should be combined with the convection coefficient to give a total surface coefficient, as they are in series, and so

$$h_s = (h_r + h_c). \tag{5.32}$$

The overall coefficient U for a composite system, consisting of surface film, composite wall, surface film, in series, can then be calculated as in eqn. (5.5) from

$$1/U = 1/(h_r + h_c)_1 + x_1/k_1 + x_2/k_2 + \cdots$$
$$+ 1/(h_r + h_c)_2. \tag{5.33}$$

EXAMPLE 5.11. In Example 5.2 on page 49, the overall conductance of the materials in a cold-store wall was calculated. If we now assume that on the outside of the wall a wind of $6.7 \, \mathrm{m \, s^{-1}}$ is blowing and that on the inside of the wall a cooling unit moves air over the wall surface at about $0.61 \, \mathrm{m \, s^{-1}}$ and that radiation coefficients can be taken as 6.25 and $1.7 \, \mathrm{J \, m^{-2} \, s^{-1} \, °C^{-1}}$ on the outside and inside of the wall respectively, calculate the overall heat transfer coefficient for the wall.

Outside surface: $v = 6.7 \, \mathrm{m \, s^{-1}}$.

$\therefore$ from eqn. (5.28)

$$h_c = 7.4v^{0.8} = 7.4(6.7)^{0.8}$$
$$= 34 \, \mathrm{J \, m^{-2} \, s^{-1} \, °C^{-1}}$$

and $h_r = 6.25 \, \mathrm{J \, m^{-2} \, s^{-1} \, °C^{-1}}$.

$\therefore \quad h_{s1} = (34 + 6) = 40 \, \mathrm{J \, m^{-2} \, s^{-1} \, °C^{-1}}$.

Inside surface: $v = 0.61 \, \mathrm{m \, s^{-1}}$.

$\therefore$ from eqn. (5.27)

$$h_c = 5.7 + 3.9v = 5.7 + 3.9 \times 0.61$$
$$= 8.1 \, \mathrm{J \, m^{-2} \, s^{-1} \, °C^{-1}}$$

and $\quad h_r = 1.7 \, \mathrm{J \, m^{-2} \, s^{-1} \, °C^{-1}}$.

$\therefore \quad h_{s2} = (8.1 + 1.7)$
$$= 9.8 \, \mathrm{J \, m^{-2} \, s^{-1} \, °C^{-1}}.$$

Now from Example 5.2 the overall conductance of the wall,

$$U_{old} = 0.38 \, \mathrm{J \, m^{-2} \, s^{-1} \, °C^{-1}}$$

and so

$$1/U_{new} = 1/h_{s1} + 1/U_{old} + 1/h_{s2}$$
$$= 1/40 + 1/0.38 + 1/9.8$$
$$= 2.76.$$

$\therefore \quad U_{new} = 0.36 \, \mathrm{J \, m^{-2} \, s^{-1} \, °C^{-1}}.$

In eqn. (5.33) often one or two terms are much more important than other terms because of their numerical values. In such a case the important terms, those signifying the low thermal conductances, are said to be the controlling terms. Thus, in Example 5.11 the introduction of values for the surface coefficients made only a small difference to the overall U value for the insulated wall. The reverse situation might be the case for other walls which were better heat conductors.

EXAMPLE 5.12. Calculate the respective U values for a wall made from either (a) 10 cm of brick of thermal conductivity $0.7 \, \mathrm{J \, m^{-1} \, s^{-1} \, °C^{-1}}$, or (b) 1.3 mm of aluminium sheet, conductivity $208 \, \mathrm{J \, m^{-1} \, s^{-1} \, °C^{-1}}$. Surface heat-transfer coefficients are on the one side 9.9 and on the other $40 \, \mathrm{J \, m^{-2} \, d^{-1} \, °C^{-1}}$.

(a) For brick
$$k = 0.7 \, \mathrm{J \, m^{-1} \, s^{-1} \, °C^{-1}},$$
$$\therefore \quad x/k = 0.1/0.7 = 0.14,$$
$$\therefore \quad 1/U = 1/40 + 0.14 + 1/9.8$$
$$= 0.27,$$
$$\therefore \quad U = 3.7 \, \mathrm{J \, m^{-2} \, s^{-1} \, °C^{-1}}.$$

(b) For aluminium
$$k = 208 \, \mathrm{J \, m^{-2} \, s^{-1} \, °C^{-1}},$$
$$x/k = 0.0013/208$$
$$= 6.3 \times 10^{-6},$$
$$\therefore \quad 1/U = 1/40 + 6.3 \times 10^{-6} + 1/9.8$$
$$= 0.13,$$
$$\therefore \quad U = 7.7 \, \mathrm{J \, m^{-2} \, s^{-1} \, °C^{-1}}.$$

Comparing the calculations in Example 5.11 with those in Example 5.12, it can be seen that the relative importance of the terms varies. In the first example, with the insulated wall the thermal conductivity of the insulation is so low that the neglect of the surface terms makes little difference to the calculated U value. In the case with a wall whose conductance is of the same order as the surface coefficients all terms have to be considered to arrive at a reasonably accurate U value. In the third case with a wall of high conductivity, the wall conductance is insignificant compared with the surface terms and it could be neglected without any appreciable effect on U. The practical significance of this observation is that if the controlling terms are known, then in any overall heat-transfer situation other factors may often be neglected without introducing significant error. On the other hand, if all terms are of the same magnitude there are no controlling terms and all factors have to be taken into account.

HEAT TRANSFER FROM CONDENSING VAPOURS

The rate of heat transfer obtained when a vapour is condensing to a liquid is very often important. In particular, it occurs in the food industry in steam-heated vessels where the steam condenses and gives up its heat and in distillation and evaporation where the vapours produced must be condensed. In condensation, the latent heat of vaporization is given up at constant temperature, the boiling temperature of the liquid.

Two generalized equations have been obtained:

(1) For condensation on vertical tubes or plane surfaces

$$h_v = 0.94 [k^3 \rho^2 g/\mu) \times (\lambda/L \, \Delta t)]^{0.25} \quad (5.34)$$

where λ (lambda) is the latent heat of the condensing liquid in $J \, kg^{-1}$, L is the height of the plate or tube and the other symbols have their usual meanings.

(2) For condensation on a horizontal tube

$$h_h = 0.72 [k^3 \rho^2 g/\mu) \times (\lambda/D \, \Delta t)]^{0.25} \quad (5.35)$$

where D is the diameter of the tube.

These equations apply to condensation in which the condensed liquid forms a film on the condenser surface. This is called film condensation: it is the most usual form and is assumed to occur in the absence of evidence to the contrary. However, in some cases the condensation occurs in drops which remain on the surface and then fall off without spreading a condensate film over the whole surface. Since the condensate film offers heat-transfer resistance, film condensation heat-transfer rates would be expected to be lower than drop condensation heat-transfer rates and this has been found to be true. Surface heat-transfer rates for drop condensation may be as much as ten times as high as the rates for film condensation.

The contamination of the condensing vapour by other vapours which do not condense under the condenser conditions, can have a profound effect on overall coefficients. Examples of a non-condensing vapour are air, in the vapours from an evaporator and in the jacket of a steam pan. The adverse effect of non-condensable vapours on an overall heat-transfer coefficients is due to the difference between the normal range of condensing heat-transfer coefficients, $1200–12{,}000 \, J \, m^{-2} \, s^{-1} \, °C^{-1}$ and the normal range of gas heat-transfer coefficients with natural convection or low velocities, of about $6 \, J \, m^{-2} \, s^{-1} \, °C^{-1}$.

Uncertainties make calculation of condensation coefficients difficult, and for many purposes it is near enough to assume the following coefficients:

for condensing steam, $12{,}000 \, J \, m^{-2} \, s^{-1} \, °C^{-1}$;
for condensing ammonia, $6000 \, m^{-2} \, s^{-1} \, °C^{-1}$;
for condensing organic liquids $1200 \, J \, m^{-2} \, s^{-1} \, °C^{-1}$.

The heat-transfer coefficients for steam with 3% air falls to about $3500 \, J \, m^{-2} \, °C^{-1}$, and with 6% air to about $1200 \, J \, m^{-2} \, s^{-1} \, °C^{-1}$.

EXAMPLE 5.13. A steel tube of 1 mm wall thickness is being used to condense ammonia, using cooling water outside the pipe in a refrigeration plant. If the water side coefficient is estimated at $1750 \, J \, m^{-2} \, s^{-1} \, °C^{-1}$ and the thermal conductivity of steel is $45 \, J \, m^{-1} \, s^{-1} \, °C^{-1}$, calculate the overall heat-transfer coefficient.

Assuming the ammonia condensing coefficient, $6000 \, J \, m^{-2} \, s^{-1} \, °C^{-1}$.

$$1/U = 1/h_1 + x/k + 1/h_2$$
$$= 1/1750 + 0.001/45 + 1/6000$$
$$= 7.6 \times 10^{-4}.$$
$$\therefore \quad U = 1300 \, J \, m^{-2} \, s^{-1} \, °C^{-1}.$$

HEAT TRANSFER TO BOILING LIQUIDS

When the presence of a heated surface causes a liquid near it to boil, the intense agitation gives rise to high local coefficients of heat transfer. A considerable amount of experimental work has been carried out on this, but generalized correlations are still not very adequate. It has been found that the apparent coefficient varies considerably with the temperature difference between the heating surface and the liquid. For temperature differences greater than about 20°C, values of h decrease, apparently because of blanketing of the heating surface by vapours. Over the range of temperature differences from 1°C to 20°C, values of h for boiling water increase from 1200 to about 60,000 J m^{-2} s^{-1} °C^{-1}. For boiling water under atmospheric pressure, the following equation is approximately true:

$$h = 50(\Delta t)^{2.5} \qquad (5.36)$$

where Δt is the difference between the surface temperature and the temperature of the boiling liquid and it lies between 2°C and 20°C.

In many applications the high boiling film coefficients are not of much consequence, as resistance in the heat source controls the overall coefficients.

SUMMARY

1. Heat is transferred by conduction, radiation and convection.

2. Heat-transfer rates are given by the general equation:

$$q = UA\,\Delta t.$$

3. For heat conduction:

$$q = (k/x)A\,\Delta t.$$

4. For radiation:

$$q = \varepsilon A \sigma T^4.$$

5. Overall heat-transfer coefficients are given by:

(a) for heat conductances in series,

$$\frac{1}{U} = \frac{x_1}{k_1} + \frac{x_2}{k_2} + \cdots,$$

(b) for radiation convection and conduction,

$$\frac{1}{U} = 1/(h_{r1} + h_{c1}) + x_1/k_1 + x_2/k_2 + \cdots$$
$$+ 1/(h_{r2} + h_{c2}).$$

6. For convection heat-transfer coefficients are given by equations of the general form:

$$(Nu) = K(Pr)^k(Gr)^m(L/D)^n$$

for natural convection, and

$$Nu = K(Re)^p(Pr)^q$$

for forced convection.

PROBLEMS

1. It is desired to limit the heat loss from a wall of polystyrene foam to 8 J m^{-2} s^{-1} °C^{-1} when the temperature on one side is 20°C and on the other -18°C. How thick should the polystyrene be?

2. Calculate the overall heat-transfer coefficient from air to a product packaged in 3.2 mm of solid cardboard, and 0.1 mm of celluloid, if the surface air coefficient is 11 J m^{-2} s^{-1} °C^{-1}.

3. The walls of an oven are made from steel sheets with asbestos insulation between them of thermal conductivity 0.18 J m^{-1} s^{-1} °C^{-1}. If the maximum internal temperature in the oven is 300°C and the outside surface of the oven wall must not rise above 50°C estimate the minimum necessary thickness of insulation assuming surface heat-transfer coefficients to the air on both sides of the wall are 15 J m^{-2} s^{-1} °c^{-1}. Assume the room air temperature outside the oven to be 25°C and that the insulating effect of the steel sheets can be neglected.

4. Calculate the thermal conductivity of uncooked pastry if measurements show that with a temperature difference of 17°C across a large slab 1.3 cm thick the heat flow is 3×10^{-5} J s^{-1} through an area of 1 cm^2 of slab surface.

5. A thick soup is being boiled in a pan and because of inadequacy of stirring a layer of soup builds up on the bottom of the pan to a thickness of 2 mm. If the hot plate is at 700°C, the heat-transfer coefficient from the plate to the pan is 600 J m^{-2} s^{-1} °C^{-1}, and that from the soup layer to the surface of the bulk soup is 1400 J m^{-2} s^{-1} °C^{-1} and the pan is of aluminium 2 mm thick, find the temperature between the layer of soup and the pan surface.

6. Peas are being blanched by immersing them in hot water at 85°C until the centre of the pea reaches 70°C. The average pea diameter is 0.0048 m and the thermal properties of the peas are, thermal conductivity 0.48 J m^{-1} s^{-1} °C^{-1}, specific heat 3.51×10^3 J kg^{-1} °C^{-1} and density 990 kg m^{-3}. The surface heat-transfer coefficient to the peas has been estimated to be 400 J m^{-2} s^{-1} °C^{-1}. How long should it take the average pea to reach 70°C if its initial temperature was 18°C just prior to immersion? If the diameter of the largest pea is 0.0063 m what temperature will its centre have reached when that of the average pea is 70°C?

7. Some people believe that because of its lower thermal conductivity stainless steel is appreciably thermally inferior to copper or mild steel as constructional material for a steam-jacketed pan to heat food materials. If the condensing coefficient for the steam and the surface boiling coefficient on the two sides of the heating surface are respectively 10,000 J m^{-2} s^{-1} °C^{-1} and 700 J m^{-2} s^{-1} °C^{-1}

and the thickness of all three metal walls is 1.6 mm compare the heating rates from all three constructions.

8. A long cylinder of solid aluminium 7.5 cm in diameter initially at a uniform temperature of 5°C is hung in an air blast at 100°C. If it is found that the temperature at the centre of the cylinder rises to 47.5°C after a time of 850 seconds, estimate the surface heat-transfer coefficient from the cylinder to the air.

9. A can of pumpkin purée 8.73 cm diameter by 11.43 cm in height is being heated in a steam retort in which the steam pressure is 100 kPa above atmospheric pressure. If the pumpkin has a thermal conductivity of $0.83 \, J \, m^{-1} \, s^{-1} \, °C^{-1}$ a specific heat of $3770 \, J \, kg^{-1} \, °C^{-1}$ and a density of $1090 \, kg \, m^{-3}$, plot out the temperature at the centre of the can as a function of time until this temperature reaches 115°C if the temperature in the can prior to retorting was 20°C.

10. If a steam boiler can be represented by a vertical cylindrical vessel 1.1 m diameter and 1.3 m high, and it is maintained internally at a steam pressure of 150 kPa, estimate the energy savings that would result from insulating the vessel with a 5-cm-thick layer of mineral wool assuming heat transfer from the surface is by natural convection. The air temperature of the surroundings is 18°C and the thermal conductivity of the insulation is $0.04 \, J \, m^{-2} \, s^{-1} \, °C^{-1}$.

11. It is desired to chill $3 \, m^3$ of water per hour by means of horizontal coils in which ammonia is evaporated. If the steel coils are 2.13 cm outside diameter and 1.71 cm inside diameter and the water is pumped across the outside of these at a velocity of $0.8 \, m \, s^{-1}$ estimate the length of pipe coil needed if the mean temperature difference between the refrigerant and the water is 8°C, the mean temperature of the water is 4°C and the temperature of the water is decreased by 15°C in the chiller.

CHAPTER 6

HEAT-TRANSFER APPLICATIONS

THE principles of heat transfer are widely used in food processing in many items of equipment. It seems appropriate to discuss these under the various applications which are commonly encountered in nearly every food factory.

HEAT EXCHANGERS

In a heat exchanger, heat energy is transferred from one body or fluid stream to another. In the design of heat-exchange equipment, heat-transfer equations are applied to calculate this transfer of energy so as to carry it out efficiently and under controlled conditions. The equipment goes under many names, such as boilers, pasteurizers, jacketed pans, freezers, air heaters, cookers, ovens and so on. The range is too great to list completely. Heat exchangers are found widely scattered throughout the food-process industry.

Continuous-flow Heat Exchangers

It is very often convenient to use heat exchangers in which one or both of the materials that are exchanging heat are fluids, flowing continuously through the equipment and acquiring or giving up heat in passing. One of the fluids is usually passed through pipes or tubes, and the other fluid stream is passed round or across these. The rate of heat exchange is controlled by the local temperature differences and heat-transfer coefficients at any point in the equipment. The fluids can flow in the same direction through the equipment, this is called

parallel flow; they can flow in opposite directions, called counterflow; they can flow at right angles to each other, called cross flow; or various combinations of these directions of flow can occur in different parts of the exchanger. Most actual heat exchangers of this type have a mixed flow pattern, but it is often possible to treat them from the point of view of the predominant flow pattern. Examples of these exchangers are illustrated in Fig. 6.1.

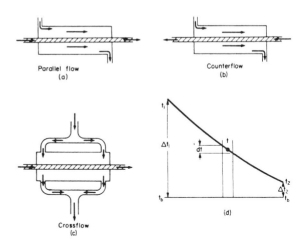

FIG. 6.1. Heat exchanges.

In parallel flow, at the entry to the heat exchanger, there is the maximum temperature difference between the coldest and the hottest stream, but at the exit the two streams can only approach each other's temperature. In a counterflow exchanger, leaving streams can approach the temperatures of the entering stream of the other component and on this account counterflow exchangers are often preferred.

Applying the basic overall heat-transfer equation to the heat exchanger

$$q = U A \Delta t,$$

uncertainty at once arises as to the value to be chosen for Δt, even knowing the temperatures in the entering and leaving streams. Consider a heat exchanger in which fluid is effectively at a constant temperature, t_b as illustrated in Fig. 6.1(d). Constant temperature in one component can result either from a very high flow rate of this component compared with the other component, or from the component being a vapour such as steam or ammonia condensing at a high rate, or from a boiling liquid. The heat-transfer coefficients are assumed to be independent of temperature.

The rate of flow of the fluid which is changing temperature is $G \, \mathrm{kg \, s^{-1}}$, its specific heat is $c_p \, \mathrm{J \, kg^{-1} \, {}^\circ C^{-1}}$. Over a small length of path of area $\mathrm{d}A$, the mean temperature of the fluid is t and the temperature drop is $\mathrm{d}t$. The constant temperature fluid has a temperature t_b.

Therefore the heat balance over the short length is

$$c_p G \, \mathrm{d}t = U(t - t_b) \, \mathrm{d}A$$
$$\therefore \quad (U/c_p G) \, \mathrm{d}A = \mathrm{d}t/(t - t_b).$$

If this is integrated over the length of the tube in which the area changes from $A = 0$ to $A = A$, and t changes from t_1 to t_2, we have

$$A U/c_p G = \log_e(t_1 - t_b)/(t_2 - t_b)$$
$$= \log_e(\Delta t_1/\Delta t_2)$$

in which $\quad \Delta t_1 = (t_1 - t_b)$ and $\Delta t_2 = (t_2 - t_b)$,
$$\therefore \quad c_p G = U A/\log_e(\Delta t_1/\Delta t_2).$$

From the overall equation, the total heat transferred per unit time is given by

$$q = U A \Delta t_m,$$

where Δt_m is the mean temperature difference, but the total heat transferred per unit is also

$$q = c_p G(t_1 - t_2).$$
$$\therefore \quad q = U A \Delta t_m = c_p G(t_1 - t_2),$$
$$= [U A/\log_e(\Delta t_1/\Delta t_2)] \times (t_1 - t_2),$$

but $(t_1 - t_2)$ can be written $(t_1 - t_b) - (t_2 - t_b)$,
$$\therefore \quad (t_1 - t_2) = \Delta t_1 - \Delta t_2.$$

$$\therefore \quad U A \Delta t_m = U A(\Delta t_1 - \Delta t_2)/\log_e(\Delta t_1/\Delta t_2) \tag{6.1}$$

so that

$$\Delta t_m = (\Delta t_1 - \Delta t_2)/\log_e(\Delta t_1/\Delta t_2), \tag{6.2}$$

where Δt_m is called the log mean temperature difference.

In other words, the rate of heat transfer can be calculated using the heat-transfer coefficient, the total area, and the log mean temperature difference. This same result can be shown to hold for parallel and counterflow flow heat exchangers in which both fluids change their temperatures. The analysis of cross-flow heat exchangers is not so simple, but for these also the use of the log mean temperature difference gives a good approximation to the actual conditions if one stream does not change very much in temperature.

EXAMPLE 6.1. Milk is flowing into a pipe cooler and passes through a tube of 2.5 cm internal diameter at a rate of $0.4 \, \mathrm{kg \, s^{-1}}$. Its initial temperature is 49°C and it is wished to cool it to 18°C using a stirred bath of constant 10°C water round the pipe. What length of pipe would be required? Assume an overall coefficient of heat transfer from the bath to the milk of $900 \, \mathrm{J \, m^{-2} \, s^{-1} \, {}^\circ C^{-1}}$, and that the specific heat of milk is $3890 \, \mathrm{J \, kg^{-1} \, {}^\circ C^{-1}}$.

Now
$$\begin{aligned} q &= c_p G(t_1 - t_2) \\ &= 3890 \times 0.4 \times (49 - 18) \\ &= 48{,}240 \, \mathrm{J \, s^{-1}}. \end{aligned}$$

Also
$$q = U A \Delta t_m$$
and
$$\begin{aligned} \Delta t_m &= [(49 - 10) - (18 - 10)]/ \\ &\qquad \log_e[(49 - 10)/(18 - 10)] \\ &= 19.6 \, {}^\circ C. \end{aligned}$$

$$\therefore \quad 48{,}240 = 900 \times A \times 19.6$$
$$\therefore \quad A = 2.73 \, \mathrm{m^2}$$

but
$$A = \pi D L$$

where L is the length of pipe of diameter D.

Now
$$D = 0.025 \, \mathrm{m}.$$
$$\begin{aligned} \therefore \quad L &= 2.73/(\pi \times 0.025) \\ &= 34.8 \, \mathrm{m}. \end{aligned}$$

This can be extended to the situation where there are two fluids flowing, one the cooled fluid and the other the heated fluid. Working from the mass flow rates $(kg\,s^{-1})$ and the specific heats of the two fluids, the terminal temperatures can normally be calculated and these can then be used to determine ΔT_m and so, from the heat-transfer coefficients, the necessary heat-transfer surface.

EXAMPLE 6.2. In a counterflow heat exchanger water is being chilled by a sodium chloride brine. If the rate of flow of the brine is $1.8\,kg\,s^{-1}$ and that of the water is $1.05\,kg\,s^{-1}$, estimate the temperature to which the water is cooled if the brine enters at $-8°C$ and leaves at $10°C$, and if the water enters the exchanger at $32°C$. If the area of the heat-transfer surface of this exchanger is found to be $55\,m^2$, what is the overall heat-transfer coefficient? Take the specific heats to be 3.38 and $4.18\,kJ\,kg^{-1}\,°C^{-1}$ for the brine and the water respectively.

With heat exchangers a small sketch is often helpful.

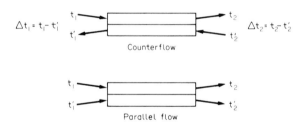

Counterflow

Parallel flow

FIG. 6.2. Diagrammatic heat exchanger.

Figure 6.2 shows three temperatures are known and the fourth t_{w1} can be found from the heat balance

$$1.8 \times 3.38 \times [10-(-8)] = 1.05 \times 4.18$$
$$\times (32-t_{w1})$$

$$\therefore \quad t_{w1} = 7°C.$$

And so $\Delta t_1 = [32-10] = 22°C$
and $\Delta t_2 = [7-(-8)] = 15°C.$

$$\therefore \quad \Delta t_m = (22-15)/\ln(22/15)$$
$$= 7/0.382$$
$$= 18.3°C.$$

For the heat exchanger

$q =$ heat exchanged between fluids
$=$ heat passed across heat transfer surface
$= U A \, \Delta t_m.$

$$\therefore \quad 1.8 \times 3.38 \times 18 = U \times 55 \times 18.3$$
$$\therefore \quad U = 0.11\,kJ\,m^{-2}\,°C^{-1}$$
$$= 110\,J\,m^{-2}\,s^{-1}\,°C^{-1}.$$

In some cases heat-exchanger problems cannot be solved so easily; for example, if the heat-transfer coefficients have to be calculated from the basic equations of heat transfer which depend on flow rates and temperatures of the fluids, and the temperatures themselves depend on the heat-transfer coefficients. The easiest way to proceed then is to make sensible estimates and to go through the calculations. If the final results are coherent then the estimates were reasonable. If not, then make better estimates, on the basis of the results, and go through a new set of calculations; and if necessary repeat until consistent results are obtained.

Jacketed Pans

In a jacketed pan, the liquid to be heated is contained in a vessel which may also be provided with an agitator to keep the liquid on the move across the heat-transfer surface, as shown in Fig. 6.3(a).

The source of heat is commonly steam condensing in the jacket. Practical considerations of importance are: firstly, that there is the minimum of air with the steam in the jacket; secondly, that the steam is not superheated as part of the surface must then be used as a de-superheater over which low gas heat-transfer coefficients apply rather than high condensing coefficients; and thirdly, that steam trapping to remove condensate and air is adequate. The action of the agitator and its ability to keep the fluid moved across the heat-transfer surface are important. Some overall heat-transfer coefficients are shown in Table 6.1.

Save for boiling water which agitates itself, mechanical agitation is assumed. Where there is no agitation coefficients may be halved.

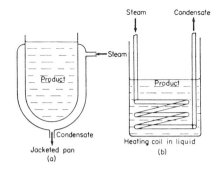

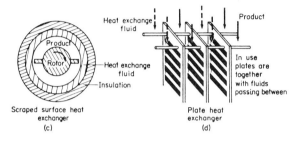

FIG. 6.3. Heat-exchange equipment.

TABLE 6.1
SOME OVERALL HEAT-TRANSFER COEFFICIENTS IN JACKETED PANS

Condensing fluid	Heated fluid	Pan material	$J\ m^{-2}\ s^{-1}\ {}^{\circ}C^{-1}$
Steam	Thin liquid	Cast-iron	1800
Steam	Thick liquid	Cast-iron	900
Steam	Paste	Stainless steel	300
Steam	Water, boiling	Copper	1800

EXAMPLE 6.3. Estimate the steam requirement as you start to heat 50 kg of pea soup in a jacketed pan, if the initial temperature of the soup is 18°C and the steam used is at 100 kPa gauge. The pan has a heating surface of 1 m² and the overall heat-transfer coefficient is assumed to be 300 J m⁻² s⁻¹ °C⁻¹.

From steam tables, saturation temperature of steam at 100 kPa gauge = 120°C and latent heat = λ = 2202 kJ kg⁻¹.

$$q = UA\,\Delta t$$
$$= 300 \times 1 \times (120 - 18)$$
$$= 3.06 \times 10^4\ J\ s^{-1}.$$

$\therefore$ amount of steam
$$= q/\lambda = (3.06 \times 10^4)/2.202 \times 10^6$$
$$= 1.4 \times 10^{-2}\ kg\,s^{-1}$$
$$= 1.4 \times 10^{-2} \times 3.6 \times 10^3$$
$$= \underline{50\ kg\,h^{-1}}.$$

This result applies only to the beginning of heating; as the temperature rises less steam will be consumed as Δt decreases.

The overall heating process can be considered by using the analysis which led up to eqn. (5.6). A stirred vessel to which heat enters from a heating surface with a surface heat-transfer coefficient which controls the heat flow, follows the same heating or cooling path as does a solid body of high internal heat conductivity with a defined surface heating area and surface heat-transfer coefficient.

EXAMPLE 6.4. In the heating of the pan in Example 6.3, estimate the time needed to bring the pea soup up to a temperature of 90°C, assuming the specific heat is 3.95 kJ kg⁻¹ °C⁻¹.

From eqn. (5.6) $\dfrac{t_2 - t_a}{t_1 - t_a} = \exp(-h_s A\theta/c\rho V)$,

$t_a = 120°C$ (temperature of heating medium),

$t_1 = 18°C$ (initial soup temperature),

$t_2 = 90°C$ (soup temperature at end of time θ),

$h_s = 300\ J\ m^{-2}\ s^{-1}\ °C^{-1}$,

$A = 1\ m^2$, $c = 3.95\ kJ\ kg^{-1}\ °C^{-1}$,

$\rho V = 50\ kg$.

$$\therefore \quad \theta = \frac{-3.95 \times 10^3 \times 50}{300 \times 1}\log_e\left(\frac{90-120}{18-120}\right)$$
$$= (-658) \times (-1.22)\,s$$
$$= 803\ s$$
$$= \underline{13.4\ min}.$$

Heating Coils Immersed in Liquids

In some food processes, quick heating is required in the pan, for example, in the boiling of jam. In this case, a helical coil may be fitted inside the pan and steam admitted to the coil as shown in Fig. 6.3(b).

This gives greater heat-transfer rates than jacketed pans, both because it can have a greater heat-transfer surface and because the heat-transfer coefficients are higher for coils than for the pan walls. Examples of the overall heat-transfer coefficient U are quoted as 300–1400 for sugar and molasses solutions heated with steam using a copper coil, 1800 for milk in a coil heated with water outside, and 3600 for a boiling aqueous solution heated with steam in the coil, the units in these coefficients being $J\,m^{-2}\,s^{-1}\,°C^{-1}$.

Scraped Surface Heat Exchangers

One type of heat exchanger, that finds considerable use in the food-processing industry, consists of a jacketed cylinder with an internal cylinder concentric to the first and fitted with scraper blades, as illustrated in Fig. 6.3(c). The blades rotate, causing the fluid to flow through the annular space between the cylinders with the outer heat-transfer surface constantly scraped. Coefficients of heat transfer vary with speeds of rotation but they are of the order of $900–4000\,J\,m^{-2}\,s^{-1}\,°C^{-1}$. These machines are used in the freezing of ice cream and in the cooling of fats during margarine manufacture.

Plate Heat Exchangers

A popular heat exchanger for fluids of low viscosity, such as milk, is the plate heat exchanger, where heating and cooling fluids flow through alternate tortuous passages between vertical plates as illustrated in Fig. 6.3(d). The heating and cooling fluids are arranged so that they flow between alternate plates. Suitable gaskets and channels control the flow and allow parallel or counter-current flow in any desired number of passes. A substantial advantage of this type of heat exchanger is that it offers a large transfer surface which is readily accessible for cleaning. The banks of plates are arranged so that they may be taken apart easily. Overall heat-transfer coefficients are of the order $2400–6000\,J\,m^{-2}\,s^{-1}\,°C^{-1}$.

THERMAL PROCESSING

Thermal processing implies the controlled use of heat to increase, or reduce depending on circumstances, the rates of reactions in foods. A common example is the retorting of canned foods to effect sterilization.

The object of sterilization is to destroy all microorganisms, that is, bacteria, yeasts and moulds, in the food material to prevent decomposition of the food which makes it unattractive or inedible. Also, sterilization prevents any pathogenic (disease-producing) organisms from surviving and being eaten with the food. Pathogenic toxins may be produced during storage of the food if certain organisms are still viable. Microorganisms are destroyed by heat, but the amount of heating required for the killing of different organisms varies. Also, many bacteria can exist in two forms, the vegetative or growing form and the spore or dormant form. The spores are much harder to destroy by heat treatment than are the vegetative forms. Studies of the microorganisms which occur in foodstuffs, have led to the selection of certain types of bacteria as indicator organisms. These are the most difficult to kill, in their spore forms, of the types of bacteria which are likely to be troublesome in foods.

The most commonly used indicator organism is *Clostridium botulinum*. This particular organism is a very important food-poisoning organism as it produces a deadly toxin and also its spores are amongst the most heat resistant. Processes for the heat treatment of foodstuffs are therefore examined with respect to the effect they would have on the spores of *C. botulinum*. If the heat process would not destroy this organism then it is not adequate. As *C. botulinum* is a very dangerous organism, a selected strain of a non-pathogenic organism of similar heat resistance is often used for testing purposes.

Thermal Death Time

It has been found that microorganisms, including *C. botulinum*, are destroyed by heat at rates which depend on the temperature, higher temperatures killing spores more quickly. At any given temperature, the spores are killed at different times, some spores being apparently more resistant to heat than other spores. If a graph is drawn of the number of surviving spores, against time of holding at any chosen temperature, it is found experimentally that the number of surviving spores fall asymptotically to zero. Methods of handling process kinetics are well developed and if the standard methods are applied to such results, it is found that thermal death of microorganisms follows, for practical purposes, a first-order process at a constant temperature. That is the fractional destruction in any fixed time interval, is constant. It is thus not possible, in theory at least, to take the time when all of the organisms are actually destroyed. Instead it is practicable, and very useful, to consider the time needed for a particular fraction of the organisms to be killed.

The rates of destruction can in this way be related to:
(1) The numbers of viable organisms in the initial container or batch of containers.
(2) The number of viable organisms which can safely be allowed to survive.

Of course the surviving number must be small indeed, very much less than one, to ensure adequate safety. However, this concept, which includes the admissibility of survival numbers of much less than one per container, has been found to be very useful. From such considerations, the ratio of the initial to the final number of surviving organisms becomes the criterion which determines adequate treatment. A combination of historical reasons and extensive practical experience has led to this number being set, for *C. botulinum*, at $10^{12}:1$. For other organisms, it may well be different.

The results of experiments to determine the times needed to reduce actual spore counts from 10^{12} to 1 (the lower, open, circles) or to 0 (the upper, closed, circles) are shown in Fig. 6.4. In this graph, these times are plotted against the different temperatures and it shows that when the logarithms of these times are plotted against temperatures, the resulting graph is a straight line. The mean times on this graph are called thermal death times for the corresponding temperatures. Note that these thermal death times do not represent complete sterilization, but a mathematical concept which can be considered as effective sterilization, and which is

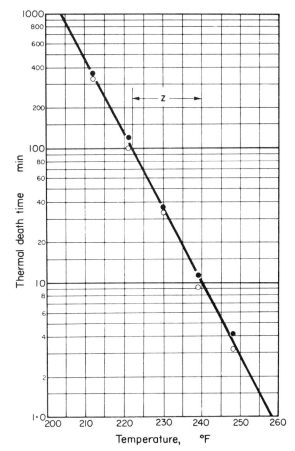

Fig. 6.4. Thermal death time curve for *Clostridium botulinum* (courtesy of Research and Development Department, American Can. Co.).

in fact a survival ratio of $1:10^{12}$.

Any canning process must be considered then from the standpoint of effective sterilization. This is done by combining the thermal death time data with the time–temperature relationships at the point in the can which heats slowest. Generally, this point is on the axis of the can and somewhere close to the geometric centre. Using the unsteady-state heating curves, or experimental measurements with a thermocouple at the slowest heating point in a can, the temperature–time graph for the can under the chosen conditions can be plotted. This curve has then to be evaluated in terms of its effectiveness in destroying *C. botulinum* or any other critical organism, such as thermophilic spore formers, which are important in industry. In this way the engineering data, which provides the temperatures within the container as the process is carried out, are combined with kinetic data to evaluate the effect of processing on the product.

Considering Fig. 6.4 the standard reference temperature is generally selected as 121.1°C and the relative time (in minutes) required to sterilize, effectively, any selected organism at 121°C is spoken of as the F value of that organism. In our example, from Fig. 6.4, the F value is about 2.8 min. For any process which is different from a steady holding at 121°C, our standard process, the F values are worked out by stepwise integration. If the total F value so found is below 2.8 min, then sterilization is not sufficient; if, above 2.8 min, the heat treatment is more drastic than it needs to be.

Equivalent Killing Power at Other Temperatures

The other factor which must be determined, so that the equivalent killing powers at temperatures different from 121°C can be evaluated, is the dependence of thermal death time on temperature. Experimentally, it has been found that if the logarithm of θ, the thermal death time, is plotted against the temperature, a straight-line relationship is obtained. This is shown in Fig. 6.4 and more explicitly in Fig. 6.5.

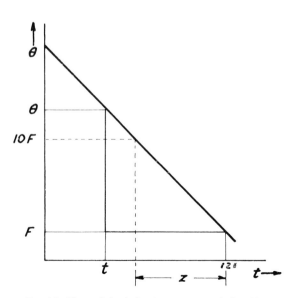

FIG. 6.5. Thermal death time/temperature relationships.

We can then write from the graph

$$\log \theta - \log F = m(121 - t) = \log \theta/F$$

where θ is the thermal death time at temperature t, F is the thermal death time at temperature 121°C and m is the slope of the graph.

Also, if we define z as the number of degrees below 121°C at which θ increases by a factor of 10, that is by one cycle on a logarithmic graph,

$$\theta = 10F \text{ when } t = (121 - z)$$

so that, $\log 10F/F = m[121 - (121 - z)]$.

$$\therefore \quad z = 1/m.$$

$$\therefore \quad \log \theta/F = 1/z(121 - t)$$

or

$$\theta = F \times 10^{(121 - t)/z}. \tag{6.3}$$

Now, the fraction of the process to reach thermal death, dS, accomplished in time $d\theta$ is given by $(1/\theta_1)d\theta$ where θ_1 is the thermal death time at temperature t_1, assuming that the destruction is additive.

$$\therefore \quad dS = (1/\theta_1)d\theta$$
$$= (1/F)10^{-(121 - t_1)/z}d\theta.$$

When the thermal death time has been reached, that is when effective sterilization has been achieved,

$$\int dS = 1,$$

that is

$$\int (1/F)10^{-(121 - t)/z}d\theta = 1$$

or

$$\int 10^{-(121 - t)/z}d\theta = F. \tag{6.4}$$

This implies that the sterilization process is complete, that the necessary fraction of the bacteria have been destroyed, when the integral is equal to F. In this way, the factors F and z can be combined with the time–temperature curve to evaluate any sterilizing process.

The integral can be evaluated graphically or by stepwise numerical integration. In this latter case the contribution towards F of a period of θ min at a temperature t is given by $\theta \times 10^{-(121 - t)/z}$. Breaking up the temperature-time curve into θ_1 min at t_1, θ_2 min at t_2, etc., the total F is given by

$$F = \theta_1 \times 10^{-(121-t_1)/z} + \theta_2$$
$$\times 10^{-(121-t_2)/z} + \cdots$$

This value of F is then compared with the standard value of F for the organism, for example 2.8 min for *C. botulinum* in our example, to decide whether the sterilizing procedure is adequate.

EXAMPLE 6.5. In a retort, the temperatures in the slowest heating region of a can were measured and were found to be shown as in Fig. 6.6. Is the retorting

adequate, if F for the process is 2.8 min and z is 10°C?

Approximate stepped temperature increments are drawn on the curve giving the equivalent holding times and temperatures as shown in Table 6.2. The corresponding F values are calculated for each temperature step.

The above results show that the F value for the process = 2.64 so that the retorting time is not quite adequate. This could be corrected by a further 2 min at 110°C (and proceeding as above, this would add $2 \times 10^{-(121-110)/10} = 0.16$, to 2.64, making 2.8).

TABLE 6.2

Temperature t(°C)	Time θ(min)	$(121 - t)$	$10^{-(121-t)/10}$	$\theta \times 10^{-(121-t)/10}$
80	11	41	7.9×10^{-5}	0.00087
90	8	31	7.9×10^{-4}	0.0063
95	6	26	2.5×10^{-3}	0.015
100	10	21	7.9×10^{-3}	0.079
105	12	16	2.5×10^{-2}	0.30
108	6	13	5.0×10^{-2}	0.30
109	8	12	6.3×10^{-2}	0.50
110	17	11	7.9×10^{-2}	1.34
107	2	14	4.0×10^{-2}	0.08
100	2	21	7.9×10^{-3}	0.016
90	2	31	7.9×10^{-4}	0.0016
80	8	41	7.9×10^{-5}	0.0006
70	6	51	7.9×10^{-6}	0.00005
			Total	2.64

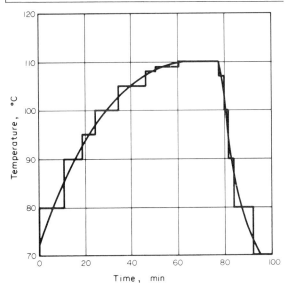

FIG. 6.6. Time/Temperature curve for can processing.

From the example, it may be seen that the very sharp decrease of thermal death times with higher temperatures means that holding times at low temperatures contribute little to the sterilization. Very long times at temperatures below 90°C would be needed to make any appreciable difference to F, and in fact it is the holding time at the highest temperature which virtually determines the F value of the whole process. Calculations can be shortened by neglecting those temperatures which make no significant contribution, although, in each case, both the number of steps taken and their relative contributions should be checked to ensure accuracy in the overall integration.

It is possible to choose values of F and of z to suit specific requirements and organisms which may be suspected of giving trouble. The choice and specification of these is a whole subject in itself and will not be further discussed. From an engineering viewpoint a specification is set, as indicated above, with an F value and a z value, and then the process conditions are designed to accomplish this.

The discussion on sterilization is designed to show, in an elementary way, how heat-transfer calculations can be applied and not as a detailed treatment of the topic. This can be found in appropriate books such as Stumbo (1973).

Pasteurization

Pasteurization is a heat treatment applied to foods, which is less drastic than sterilization, but which is sufficient to inactivate particular disease-producing organisms of importance in a specific foodstuff. Pasteurization inactivates most viable vegetative forms of microorganisms but not heat-resistant spores. Originally, pasteurization was evolved to inactivate bovine tuberculosis in milk. Numbers of viable organisms are reduced by ratios of the order of $10^{15}:1$. As well as in the application to inactivate bacteria, pasteurization may be considered in relation to enzymes present in the food which can be inactivated by heat. The same general relationships as were discussed under sterilization apply to pasteurization. A combination of temperature and time must be used that is sufficient to inactivate the particular species of bacteria or enzyme under consideration. Fortunately, most of the pathogenic organisms which can be transmitted from food to the person who eats it are not very resistant to heat.

The most common application of pasteurization is to liquid milk. In the case of milk, the pathogenic organism which is of importance is the tubercle bacillus, and the time/temperature curve for the inactivation of this bacillus is shown in Fig. 6.7.

This curve can be applied to determine the necessary holding time and temperature in the same way as with the sterilization thermal death curves. However, the times involved are very much shorter, and controlled rapid heating in continuous heat exchangers simplifies the calculations so that only the holding period is really important. For example, 30 min at 62.8°C in the older pasteurizing plants and

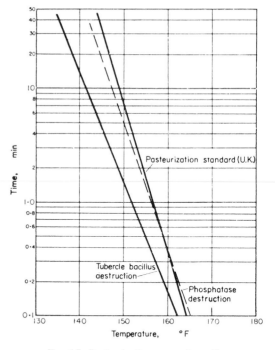

Fig. 6.7. Pasteurization curves for milk.

15 sec at 71.7°C in the so-called high temperature–short time (H.T.S.T.) process are sufficient. An even faster process using a temperature of 126.7°C for 4 sec is claimed to be sufficient. The most generally used equipment is the plate heat exchanger and rates of heat transfer to accomplish this pasteurization can be calculated by the methods explained previously.

An enzyme present in milk, phosphatase, is destroyed under somewhat the same time–temperature conditions as the tubercle bacillus and, since chemical tests for the enzyme can be carried out simply, its presence is used as an indicator of inadequate heat treatment. In this case, the presence or absence of phosphatase is of no importance so far as the storage properties or suitability for human consumption are concerned.

Enzymes are of importance in deterioration processes of fruit juices, fruits and vegetables. If time–temperature relationships, such as those that are shown in Fig. 6.7 for phosphatase, can be determined for these enzymes, heat processes to destroy them can be designed. Most often this is done by steam heating, indirectly for fruit juices and directly for vegetables when the process is known as blanching.

The processes for sterilization and pasteurization illustrate very well the application of heat transfer as a unit operation in food processing. The temperatures and times required are determined and then the heat transfer equipment is designed using the equations developed for heat-transfer operations.

EXAMPLE 6.6. A pasteurization heating process for milk was found, taking measurements and times, to consist essentially of three heating stages being 2 min at 64°C, 3 min at 65°C and 2 min at 66°C. Does this process, in all, meet the standard pasteurization requirements for the milk, and if not what adjustment needs to be made to the period of holding at 66°C?

From Fig. 6.7 pasteurization times θ_t can be read off making conversions to °F:

$$\text{At } 64°C, \theta_{64} = 15.7 \text{ min,}$$

$$\therefore \quad 2 \text{ min is } \frac{2}{15.7} = 0.13,$$

$$65°C, \theta_{65} = 9.2 \text{ min,}$$

$$\therefore \quad 3 \text{ min is } \frac{3}{9.2} = 0.33,$$

$$66°C, \theta_{66} = 5.4 \text{ min,}$$

$$\therefore \quad 2 \text{ min is } \frac{2}{5.4} = 0.37.$$

$$\therefore \quad \text{Total pasteurization effect} = 0.83.$$

Pasteurization remaining to be accomplished $= (1 - 0.83) = 0.17$. At 66°C this would be obtained from (0.17×5.4) min holding $= 0.92$ min.

So an additional 0.92 min (or approximately 1 min) at 66°C would be needed to meet the specification.

REFRIGERATION, CHILLING AND FREEZING

Rates of decay and of deterioration in foodstuffs depend on temperature. At suitable low temperatures, changes in the food can be almost completely prevented. The growth and metabolism of microorganisms is slowed down and if the temperature is low enough, growth of all microorganisms virtually ceases. Enzyme activity and chemical reaction rates (of fat oxidation, for example) are also very much reduced at these temperatures. To reach temperatures low enough for deterioration virtually to cease, most of the water in the food must be frozen. The effect of chilling is only to slow down deterioration changes.

In studying chilling and freezing, it is necessary to look first at the methods for obtaining low temperatures, i.e. refrigeration systems, and then at the coupling of these to the food products in chilling and freezing.

Refrigeration Cycle

The basis of mechanical refrigeration is the fact that at different pressures the saturation (or the condensing) temperatures of vapours are different as clearly shown on the appropriate vapour-pressure/temperature curve. As the pressure increases condensing temperatures also increase. This fact is applied in a cyclic process which is illustrated in Fig. 6.8 and can be followed on the temperature–enthalpy chart shown on Fig. 6.9.

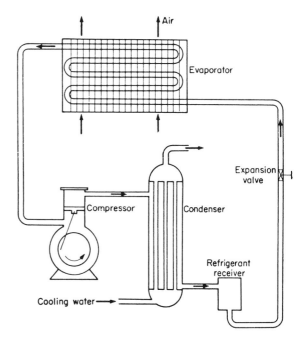

FIG. 6.8. Mechanical refrigeration circuit.

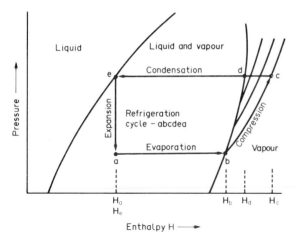

FIG. 6.9. Temperature/enthalpy chart.

This is a thermodynamic diagram which looks very complicated at first sight but which in fact can make calculations straightforward and simple. For the present purposes the most convenient such chart is the one shown with pressure as the vertical axis (for convenience on a logarithmic scale) and enthalpy on the horizontal axis. On such a diagram the properties of the particular refrigerant can be plotted, including the interphase equilibrium lines such as the saturated vapour line, which are important in refrigeration as it depends on evaporation and condensation. Figure 6.9 is a skeleton diagram and Appendix 11 gives charts for the two most common refrigerants ammonia and refrigerant 12; others for common refrigerants can be found in the ASHRAE Guide and Data Books.

To start with the evaporator; in this the pressure above the refrigerant is low enough so that evaporation of the refrigerant liquid to a gas occurs at some suitable low temperature determined by the requirements of the product. This temperature might be, for example, $-18°C$ in which case the corresponding pressures would be for ammonia, 229 k Pa absolute and for dichlorodifluoromethane (also known as refrigerant 12) 168 k Pa. Evaporation then occurs and this extracts the latent heat of vaporization for the refrigerant from the surroundings of the evaporator and it does this at the appropriate low temperature. This process of heat extraction at low temperature represents the useful part of the refrigerator. On the temperature/enthalpy chart this is represented by ab at constant

pressure (the evaporation pressure) in which 1 kg of refrigerant takes in $(H_b - H_a)\,kJ\,kg^{-1}$.

The remainder of the process cycle is included merely so that the refrigerant may be returned to the evaporator to continue the cycle. First, the vapour is sucked into a compressor which is essentially a gas pump and which increases its pressure to exhaust it at the higher pressure to the condensers. This is represented by the line bc which follows an adiabatic compression line, a line of constant entropy (the reasons for this must be sought in a book on refrigeration) and work equivalent to $(H_c - H_b)\,kJ\,kg^{-1}$ has to be performed on the refrigerant to effect the compression. The higher pressure might be, for example, 1150 kPa for ammonia, or 740 kPa for refrigerant 12, and it is determined by the temperature at which cooling water or air is available to cool the condensers.

To complete the cycle the refrigerant must be condensed, giving up its latent heat of vaporization to some cooling medium. This is carried out in a condenser which is a heat exchanger cooled generally by water or air. This appears on Fig. 6.9 as the horizontal line (at the constant condenser pressure), at first cd cooling the gas and then continuing along de until the refrigerant is completely condensed at point e. The total heat given out in this from refrigerant to condenser water is $(H_c - H_e) = (H_c - H_a)\,kJ\,kg^{-1}$. The condensing temperature, corresponding to the above high pressures, is about $30°C$ and so in this example cooling water at about $20°C$, could be used, leaving sufficient temperature difference to accomplish the heat exchange in equipment of reasonable size.

This process of evaporation at a low pressure and corresponding low temperature, followed by compression, followed by condensation at atmospheric temperature and corresponding high pressure, is the refrigeration cycle. The high-pressure liquid passes through a nozzle from the condenser or high-pressure receiver vessel, to the evaporator, and so the cycle continues. Expansion through the expansion valve is at constant enthalpy and so it follows the vertical line ea and there is no enthalpy added to or subtracted from the refrigerant. This line at constant enthalpy from point e explains why the point a is where it is on the pressure line, corresponding to the evaporation (suction) pressure.

By adjusting the high and low pressures, the condensing and evaporating temperatures can be selected as required. The high pressure is determined by the available cooling-water temperature, by the cost of this cooling water and by the cost of condensing equipment. The evaporating pressure is determined by the low temperature that is required for the product, or by the rate of cooling or freezing that has to be provided. Low evaporating temperatures mean higher power requirements for compression and greater volumes of low-pressure vapours to be handled therefore larger compressors, so that the compression is more expensive. It must also be remembered that, in actual operation, temperature differences must be provided to operate

both the evaporator and the condenser. There must be lower pressures than those that correspond to the evaporating coil temperature in the compressor suction line, and higher pressures in the compressor discharge than those that correspond to the condenser temperature.

Overall the energy side of the refrigeration cycle can therefore be summed up: the heat taken in from surroundings at the (low) evaporator temperature and pressure $(H_b - H_a)$, the heat equivalent to the work done by the compressor $(H_c - H_b)$ and the heat rejected at the (high) compressor pressure and temperature $(H_c - H_e)$. A useful measure is the ratio of the heat taken in at the evaporator (the useful refrigeration), $(H_b - H_a)$, to the energy put in by the compressor which must be paid for $(H_c - H_b)$. This ratio is called the coefficient of performance (COP). The unit commonly used to measure refrigerating effect is the ton of refrigeration = 3.52 kW. It arises from the quantity of energy to freeze 2000 lb of water (1 short ton) in one day.

EXAMPLE 6.7. It is wished to freeze 15 tonnes of fish per day from an initial temperature of 10°C to a final temperature of −8°C using a stream of cold air.

Estimate the maximum capacity of the refrigeration plant required, if it is assumed that the maximum rate of heat extraction from the product is twice the average rate. If the heat-transfer coefficient from the air to the evaporator coils, which form the heat exchanger between the air and the boiling refrigerant, is $22 \, \mathrm{J \, m^{-2} \, s^{-1} \, °C^{-1}}$, calculate the surface area of evaporator coil required if the logarithmic mean temperature drop across the coil is 12°C.

From the tabulated data (Appendix 7) the specific heat of fish is $3.18 \, \mathrm{J \, kg^{-1} \, °C^{-1}}$ above freezing and $1.67 \, \mathrm{J \, kg^{-1} \, °C^{-1}}$ below freezing, and the latent heat is $276 \, \mathrm{kJ/kg^{-1}}$.

Enthalpy change in fish:

$$(10 \times 3.2) + (8 \times 1.67) + 276 = 31.8 + 13.4 + 276$$
$$= 321.2 \, \mathrm{kJ \, kg^{-1}}.$$
$$\text{Total heat removed in freezing} = 15 \times 1000 \times 321.2$$
$$= 4.82 \times 10^6 \, \mathrm{kJ \, day^{-1}}.$$
$$\text{Average rate of heat removal} \, (4.82 \times 10^6)/(24 \times 60 \times 60)$$
$$= 55.8 \, \mathrm{kJ \, s^{-1}}.$$

If maximum is twice average
$$\text{then maximum} = q = 111.6 \, \mathrm{kJ \, s^{-1}}.$$
$$\text{Coil rate of heat transfer } q = U A \, \Delta t_m$$
$$\text{and so } A = q/U \, \Delta t_m$$
$$= (111.6)/(22 \times 12)$$
$$= 0.42 \times 10^3 \, \mathrm{m^2}$$
$$= 420 \, \mathrm{m^2}.$$

The great advantage of tracing the cycle on the pressure/enthalpy diagram is that from the numerical co-ordinates of the various cycle points performance parameters can be read off or calculated readily.

EXAMPLE 6.8. Ammonia liquid is boiling in an evaporator under an absolute pressure of 120 kPa. Find the temperature and the volumetric rate of evolution of ammonia gas if the heat extraction rate from the surroundings is 300 watts.

From the chart in Appendix 11(a) the boiling temperature of ammonia at a pressure of 120 kPa is − 30°C, so this is the evaporator temperature.

Also from the chart, the latent heat of evaporation

is (enthalpy of saturated vapour − enthalpy of saturated liquid) = 1.72 − 0.36 = 1.36 MJ kg^{-1}.

For a heat-removal rate of 300 watts = 0.3 kJ s^{-1} the ammonia evaporation rate is therefore (0.3/1360) = 2.2 × 10^{-4} kg s^{-1}. The chart shows at the saturated vapour point for the cycle (b on Fig. 6.8) that the specific volume of ammonia vapour is 0.98 m^3 kg^{-1} and so the volumetric rate of ammonia evolution is:

$$2.2 \times 10^{-4} \times 0.98 = 2.16 \times 10^{-4} \, m^3 \, s^{-1}.$$

So far we have been talking of the theoretical cycle. Real cycles differ by, for example, pressure drops in piping, superheating of vapour to the compressor and non-adiabatic compression, but these are relatively minor. Approximations quite good enough for our purposes can be based on the theoretical cycle. If necessary, allowances can be included for particular inefficiencies.

The refrigerant vapour has to be compressed so it can continue round the cycle and be condensed. From the refrigeration demand, the weight of refrigerant required to be circulated can be calculated (each kg s^{-1} extracts so many J s^{-1}

amount taken in, to the theoretical compressor displacement, is called the volumetric efficiency of the compressor. Both mechanical and volumetric efficiencies can be measured, or taken from manufacturer's data, and they depend on the actual detail of the equipment used.

Consideration of the data from the thermo-dynamic chart and of the refrigeration cycle enables quite extensive calculations to be made about the operation.

EXAMPLE 6.9. To meet the requirements of Example 6.7 calculate the speed at which it would be necessary to run a six-cylinder reciprocating ammonia compressor with each cylinder having a 10-cm bore (diameter) and a 12-cm stroke (length of piston travel), assuming a volumetric efficiency of 80%. The condensing temperature is 30°C (determined from the available cooling water temperature) and the evaporating temperature needed is −15°C. Calculate also the theoretical coefficient of performance of this refrigeration system.

From the chart Appendix 11(a) the heat extracted by ammonia at the evaporating temperature of −15°C is (1.74 − 0.63) = 1.11 MJ kg^{-1}.

Maximum rate of refrigeration = 111.6 kJ kg^{-1}.

Rate of refrigerant circulation = 111.6/1110
= 0.100 kg s^{-1}.

Specific volume of refrigerant (from chart) 0.49 m^3 kg^{-1}.

Theoretical displacement volume = 0.49 × 0.100
= 0.049 m^3 s^{-1}.

Actual displacement needed = (0.049 × 100)/80 m^3 s^{-1}.

Volume of cylinders = (π/4) × (0.10)^2 × 0.12 × 6
= 5.7 × 10^{-3} m^3 swept out per rev.

Speed of compressor = (0.049 × 60 × 100)/(5.7 × 10^{-3} × 80)
= 645 rev. min^{-1}.

according to the value of $(H_b − H_a)$ and from the volume of this the compressor displacement can be calculated, as the compressor has to handle this volume. Because the compressor piston cannot entirely displace all of the working volume of the cylinder there must be a clearance volume and because of inefficiencies in valves and ports the actual amount of refrigerant vapour taken in is less than the theoretical. The ratio of these, actual

Coefficient of performance = (heat extracted in evaporator)/(heat equivalent of theoretical shaft work in the compressor)

$$= (H_b − H_a)/(H_c − H_b).$$

Under cycle conditions, from chart, the coefficient of performance

$$= (1.74 − 0.63)/(1.97 − 1.74) = 1.11/0.23$$
$$= 4.8.$$

Performance Characteristics

Variations in load and in the evaporating or condensing temperatures are often encountered when considering refrigeration systems. Their effects can be predicted by relating them to the basic cycle.

If the heat load increases in the cold store then the temperature tends to rise and this increases the amount of refrigerant boiling off. If the compressor cannot move this, then the pressure on the suction side of the compressor increases and so the evaporating temperature increases tending to reduce the evaporation rate and correct the situation. However, the effect is to lift the temperature in the cold space and if this is to be prevented additional compressor capacity is required.

As the evaporating pressure, and resultant temperature, change, so the volume of vapour per kilogram of refrigerant changes. If the pressure decreases, this volume increases, and therefore the refrigerating effect, which is substantially determined by the rate of circulation of refrigerant, must also decrease. Therefore if a compressor is required to work from a lower suction pressure its capacity is reduced, and conversely.

So at high suction pressures giving high circulation rates, the driving motors may become overloaded because of the substantial increase in quantity of refrigerant circulated in unit time.

Changes in the condenser pressure have relatively little effect on the quantity of refrigerant circulated. However, they, and also decreases in suction pressure, have quite a substantial effect on the power consumed per ton of refrigeration. Therefore for an economical plant, it is important to keep the suction pressure as high as possible compatible with the product requirement for low temperature or rapid freezing, and the condenser pressure as low as possible compatible with the available cooling water or air temperature.

Refrigerants

Although in theory a considerable number of fluids might be used in mechanical refrigeration, and historically quite a number including cold air and carbon dioxide have been, those actually in use today are only a very small number. Substantially they include only ammonia which is used in many large industrial systems, and a family of halogenated hydrocarbons containing differing proportions of chlorine and fluorine and chosen according to the particular refrigeration duty required. The reasons for this very small group of practical refrigerants are many; important amongst them are the actual vapour pressure/temperature curve for the refrigerant which determines the pressures between which the system must operate for any particular pair of evaporator and condenser temperatures, the refrigerating effect per cubic metre of refrigerant pumped around the system which in turn governs the size of compressors and piping, and the stability and cost of the refrigerant itself. Ammonia is in most ways the best refrigerant from the mechanical point of view, but its great problem is its toxicity. The thermodynamic chart for ammonia, refrigerant 717 is given in Appendix 11(a). In working spaces, such as encountered in air conditioning, the halogenated hydrocarbons (often known, after the commercial name, as Freons) are very often used because of safety considerations. They are also used in domestic refrigerators. A thermodynamic chart for refrigerant 12 (the reasons for the numbering system are obscure, ammonia being refrigerant 717), the commonest of the halogenated hydrocarbon refrigerants, is given in Appendix 11(b), and other charts are available in references such as the ASHRAE Guide and Data Books.

Mechanical Equipment

Compressors are just basically vapour pumps and much the same types as shown in Fig. 4.3 for liquid pumps are encountered. Their design is highly specialized, particular problems arising from the lower density and viscosity of vapours when compared with liquids. The earliest designs were reciprocating machines with pistons moving horizontally or vertically, at first in large cylinders and at modest speeds, and then increasingly at higher speeds in smaller cylinders. An important aspect to compressor choice is the compression ratio, being the ratio of the absolute pressure discharge from the compressor, to the inlet suction pressure. Reciprocating compressors can work effectively at quite high compression ratios (up to 6 or 7 to 1). Higher overall compression ratios are handled by putting two or more compressors in series and so sharing the overall compression ratio between them.

For smaller compression ratios and for handling the large volumes of vapours encountered at low temperatures and pressures, rotary vane compressors are often used, and for even larger volumes, centrifugal compressors, often with many stages, can be used. A recent popular development is the screw compressor, analogous to a gear pump, which has considerable flexibility. Small systems are often termed "hermetic", implying that the motor and compressor are sealed into one casing with the refrigerant circulating through both. This avoids rotating seals through which refrigerant can leak. The familiar and very dependable units in household refrigerators are almost universally of this type.

The Evaporator

The evaporator is the only part of the refrigeration equipment that enters directly into food-processing operations. Heat passes from the food to the heat-transfer medium, which may be air or liquid, thence to the evaporator and so to the refrigerant. Thermal coupling is in some cases direct, as in a plate freezer. In this, the food to be frozen is placed directly on or between plates, within which the refrigerant circulates. Another familiar example of direct thermal coupling is the chilled slab in a shop display.

Generally, however, the heat-transfer medium is air which moves either by forced or natural circulation between the heat source, the food and the walls warmed by outside air, and the heat sink which is the evaporator. Sometimes the medium is liquid such as in the case of immersion freezing in, say, propylene glycol or in alcohol–water mixtures. Then there are some cases in which the refrigerant is, in effect, the medium such as immersion or spray with liquid nitrogen and immersion in liquid halogenated hydrocarbons: in the former case the evaporated nitrogen is wasted but in the latter the medium must be recondensed because of its cost.

Sometimes there is also a further intermediate heat-transfer medium, so as to provide better control, or convenience, or safety. An example is in some milk chillers where the basic refrigerant is ammonia, this cools glycol which is pumped through a heat exchanger where it cools the milk. A sketch of some types of evaporator system is given in Fig. 6.10.

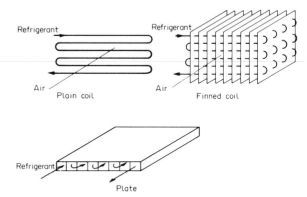

FIG. 6.10. Refrigeration evaporators.

In the freezer or chiller the heat-transfer rates, both from the food and to the evaporator, depend upon fluid or gas velocities and upon temperature differences. The values for the respective heat-transfer coefficients can be estimated by use of the standard heat-transfer relationships. Typical values which occur in freezing equipment are given in Table 6.3.

TABLE 6.3
EXPECTED SURFACE HEAT-TRANSFER COEFFICIENTS (h_s)

	$\mathrm{J\ m^{-2}\ s^{-1}\ {}^{\circ}C^{-1}}$
Still-air freezing (including radiation to coils)	9
Still-air freezing (no radiation)	6
Air-blast freezing 3 m s^{-1}	18
Air-blast freezing 5 m s^{-1}	30
Liquid-immersion freezing	600
Plate freezing	120

Temperature differences across evaporators are generally of the order 3–10°C. The calculations for heat transfer can be carried out using the methods which have been discussed in other sections, including their relationship to freezing and freezing times, as the evaporators are just refrigerant-to-air heat exchangers.

The evaporator surfaces are often extended by the use of metal fins which are bonded to the evaporator pipe surface. The reason for this construction is that the relatively high metal conductance, compared with the much lower surface conductance from the metal surface to the air, maintains the fin surface substantially at the coil temperature. A slight rise in temperature along the fin can be accounted for by including in calculations a fin efficiency factor. The effective evaporator area is then calculated by the relationship

$$A = A_p + \phi A_s \qquad (6.5)$$

where A is the equivalent total evaporator surface area, A_p is the coil surface area, called the primary surface, A_s is the fin surface area, called the secondary surface and ϕ (phi) is the fin efficiency.

Values of ϕ lie between 65% and 95% in the usual designs, as shown in DKV Arbeitsblatt 2-02, 1950.

Chilling

Chilling of foods is a process by which their temperature is reduced to the desired holding temperature just above the freezing point of food, usually in the region of -2 to $2°C$.

Many commercial chillers operate at higher temperatures, up to 10–12°C. The effect of chilling is only to slow down deterioration changes and the reactions are temperature dependent. So the time and temperature of holding the chilled food determine the storage life of the food.

Rates of chilling are governed by the laws of heat transfer which have been described in previous sections. It is an example of unsteady-state heat transfer by convection to the surface of the food and by conduction within the food itself. The medium of heat exchange is generally air, which extracts heat from the food and then gives it up to refrigerant in the evaporator. As explained in the heat-transfer section, rates of convection heat transfer from the surface of food and to the evaporator are much greater if the air is in movement, being roughly proportional to $v^{0.8}$.

To calculate chilling rates it is therefore necessary to evaluate:

(a) the surface heat transfer coefficient,

(b) the resistance offered to heat flow by any packing material that may be placed round the food,

(c) the appropriate unsteady-state heat-conduction equation.

Although the shapes of most foodstuffs are not regular they often approximate the shapes of slabs, bricks, spheres and cylinders.

EXAMPLE 6.10. Before apples are loaded into a cool store it is wished to chill them to a central temperature of 5°C so as to avoid problems of putting warm apples with the colder ones in storage. The apples, initially at 25°C, are considered to be spheres of 7 cm diameter and the chilling is to be carried out using air at $-1°C$ and at a velocity which provides a surface heat-transfer coefficient of $30\,J\,m^{-2}\,s^{-1}\,°C^{-1}$. The physical properties of the apples are $k = 0.5\,J\,m^{-1}\,s^{-1}\,°C^{-1}$, $\rho = 930\,kg\,m^{-3}$, $c = 3.6\,kJ\,kg^{-1}\,°C^{-1}$. Calculate the time necessary to chill the apples so that their centres reach 3°C.

This is an example of unsteady-state cooling and can be solved by application of Fig. 5.3,

$$\mathrm{Bi} = \frac{hr}{k} = \frac{30 \times 0.035}{0.5} = 2.1,$$

$$\therefore \quad 1/\mathrm{Bi} = 0.48$$

$$(t - t_0)/(t_1 - t_0) = [5 - (-1)]/$$
$$[25 - (-1)] - 0.23,$$

$$\therefore \quad F_0 = 0.46 = \frac{k}{pc}\frac{\theta}{r^2},$$

$$\therefore \quad \theta = [0.46 \times 930 \times 3600 \times (0.035)^2]/0.5$$
$$= 3773\,s$$
$$= 1.05\,h.$$

A full analysis of chilling must, in addition to heat transfer, take mass transfer into account if the food surfaces are moist and the air is unsaturated. This is a common situation and complicates chilling analysis.

Freezing

Water makes up a substantial proportion of almost all foodstuffs and so freezing has a marked physical effect on the food. Because of the presence of substances dissolved in the water, food does not freeze at one temperature but rather over a range of temperatures. At temperatures just below the freezing point of water, crystals that are almost pure ice form in the food and so the remaining solutions become more concentrated. Even at low temperatures some water remains unfrozen, in very concentrated solutions.

In the freezing process, added to chilling is the removal of the latent heat of freezing. This latent heat has to be removed from any water that is present. Since the latent heat of freezing of water is $335 \, \text{kJ kg}^{-1}$, this represents the most substantial thermal quantity entering into the process. There may be other latent heats, for example the heats of solidification of fats which may be present, and heats of solution of salts, but these are of smaller magnitude than the latent heat of freezing of water, and also the fats themselves are seldom present in foods in as great a proportion as water.

Because of the latent-heat-removal requirement, the normal unsteady-state equations cannot be applied to the freezing of foodstuffs. The coefficients of heat transfer can be estimated by the following equation:

$$1/h_s = 1/h_c + (x/k) + 1/h_r$$

where h_s is the total surface heat-transfer coefficient, h_c is the convection heat transfer coefficient, x is the thickness of packing material, k is the thermal conductivity of the packing material and h_r is the radiation heat-transfer coefficient.

A full analytical solution of the rate of freezing of food cannot be obtained. However, an approximate solution, due to Plank, is sufficient for most practical purposes. Plank assumed that the freezing process:

(a)   commences with all of the food unfrozen but at its freezing temperature,
(b)   occurs sufficiently slowly for heat transfer in the frozen layer to take place under steady-state conditions.

Making these assumptions, freezing rates for bodies of simple shapes can be calculated. As an example of the method, the time taken to freeze to the centre of a slab whose length and breadth are large compared with the thickness, will be calculated.

Rates of heat transfer are equal from either side of the slab. Assume that at time θ a thickness x of the slab of area A has been frozen as shown in Fig. 6.11. The temperature of the freezing medium is t_a. The freezing temperature of the foodstuff is t, and the surface temperature of the food is t_s. The thermal conductivity of the frozen food is k, λ is the latent heat of the foodstuff and ρ is its density.

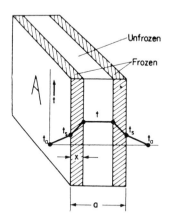

FIG. 6.11. Freezing of a slab.

The rate of movement of the freezing boundary multiplied by the latent heat equals the rate of heat transfer of heat to the boundary:

$$q = A\lambda\rho \, dx/d\theta.$$

Now, all of the heat removed at the freezing boundary must be transmitted to the surface through the frozen layer; if the frozen layer is in the steady-state condition we have:

$$q = (t - t_s)k/x.$$

Similarly, this quantity of heat must be transferred to the cooling medium from the food surface, so:

$$q = Ah_s(t_s - t_a),$$

where h_s is the surface heat-transfer coefficient.

Eliminating t_s between the two equations gives:

$$q = (t - t_a)A \times 1/(1/h_s + x/k).$$

Since the same heat flow passing through the surface also passes through the frozen layer and is removed from the water as it freezes in the centre of the block:

$$A(t - t_a)/(1/h_s + x/k) = A\lambda\rho \, dx/d\theta.$$

$\therefore \quad (t - t_a)/(1/h_s + x/k) = \lambda\rho \, dx/d\theta.$

$\therefore \quad d\theta(t - t_a) = \lambda\rho(1/h_s + x/k) \, dx.$

Now, if the thickness of the slab is a, the time taken for the centre of the slab at $x = a/2$ to freeze can be obtained by integrating from $x = 0$, to $x = a/2$ during which time θ goes from 0 to θ_f.

$\therefore \quad \theta_f(t - t_a) = \lambda\rho(a/2h_s + a^2/8k).$

$$\therefore \quad \theta_f = \frac{\lambda\rho}{t - t_a}\left[\frac{a}{2h_s} + \frac{a^2}{8k}\right]. \qquad (6.6)$$

In his papers Plank (1913, 1941) derives his equation in more general terms and finds that for brick-shaped solids the change is in numerical factors only. The general equation can thus be written

$$\theta = \frac{\lambda\rho}{t - t_a} \times (Pa/h_s + Ra^2/k) \qquad (6.7)$$

where $P = 1/2$, $R = 1/8$ for a slab, $P = 1/4$, $R = 1/16$ for an infinitely long cylinder, and $P = 1/6$ and $R = 1/24$ for a cube or a sphere. Brick-shaped solids have values of P and R lying between those for slabs and those for cubes. Appropriate values of P and R for a brick-shaped solid can be obtained from the graph in Fig. 6.12. In this figure, β_1 and β_2 are the ratios of the two longest sides to the shortest. It does not matter in what order they are taken.

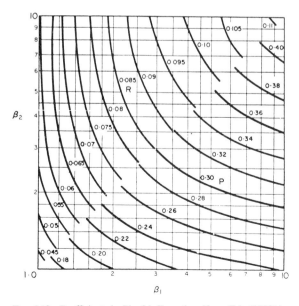

β_1

FIG. 6.12. Coefficients in Plank's Equation [from Ede (1949) by permission].

Because the assumptions made in the derivation of Plank's equation lead to errors which tend towards under-estimation of freezing times, more accurate predictions can be made if some allowances are made for this. One step is to use the total enthalpy changes from the initial to the final state of the product being frozen, that is to include the sensible heat changes both above and below the freezing temperature in addition to the latent heat. Even with this addition the prediction will still be about 20% or so lower than equivalent experimental measurements for brick shapes indicate. Adaptations of Plank's equation have been proposed which correspond better with experimental results, such as those in Cleland and Earle (1982), but they are more complicated.

EXAMPLE 6.11. If a slab of meat is to be frozen between refrigerated plates with the plate temperature at $-34°C$, how long will it take to freeze if the slab is 10 cm thick and the meat is wrapped in cardboard 1 mm thick on either side of the slab? What would be the freezing time if the cardboard were not present? Assume that for the plate freezer the surface heat-transfer coefficient is $600 \, J \, m^{-2} \, s^{-1} \, °C^{-1}$, the thermal conductivity of cardboard is $0.06 \, J \, m^{-1} \, s^{-1} \, °C^{-1}$, the thermal conductivity of frozen meat is $1.6 \, J \, m^{-1} \, s^{-1} \, °C^{-1}$, its latent heat is $2.56 \times 10^5 \, J \, kg^{-1}$ and density $1090 \, kg \, m^{-3}$. Assume also that meat freezes at $-2°C$.

Conductance of cardboard packing $= x/k$
$= 0.017.$

$\therefore \quad 1/h_s = x/k + 1/h = 0.017 + 1/600$
$\qquad\qquad = 0.019.$

In a plate freezer, the thickness of the slab is the only dimension that is important. The case can be treated as equivalent to an infinite slab, and therefore the constants in Plank's equation are $1/2$ and $1/8$.

$\therefore \quad \theta_f = \lambda\rho/(t - t_a) \times (Pa/h_s + Ra^2/k)$
$= (2.56 \times 10^5 \times 1090)/[-2 - (-34)]$
$\times [(1/2 \times 0.1 \times 0.019)$
$+ (1/8 \times (0.1)^2 \times 1/1.6)]$
$= 1.51 \times 10^4 \, sec$
$= 4.2 \, h$

and with no packing $h_s = 600$ so that

$1/h_s = 1.7 \times 10^{-3}$ and

$$\theta_f = (2.56 \times 10^5 \times 1090)/[-2-(-34)]$$
$$\times [(1/2 \times 0.1 \times 1.7 \times 10^{-3})$$
$$+ (1/8 \times (0.1)^2 \times 1/1.6)]$$
$$= 7.54 \times 10^3 \, \text{sec}$$
$$= 2.1 \, \text{h}.$$

This estimate can be improved by adding to the latent heat of freezing the enthalpy change above the freezing temperature (assuming the meat with a specific heat of $3.22 \times 10^3 \, \text{J kg}^{-1}$ starts at $+10°\text{C}$ and goes to $-2°\text{C}$, giving $3.9 \times 10^4 \, \text{J kg}^{-1}$) and below the freezing temperature (assuming the meat goes from $-2°\text{C}$) to the mean of $-2°\text{C}$ and $-34°\text{C}$, that is $-18°\text{C}$, with a specific heat of $1.67 \times 10^3 \, \text{J kg}^{-1}$, giving $2.8 \times 10^4 \, \text{J kg}^{-1}$. This gives a total of $3.23 \times 10^5 \, \text{J kg}^{-1}$ and amended freezing times of

$4.1 \times (3.23/2.56) = 5.2 \, \text{h}$ and $2.0 \times (3.23/2.56) = 2.5 \, \text{h}$.

If instead of a slab, cylinder, or cube, it were closer to a brick shape then an additional 20% should be added.

Thus, with a knowledge of the thermal constants of a foodstuff, required freezing times can be estimated by the use of Plank's equation. Appendix 7 gives values for the thermal conductivities, and the latent heats and densities, of some common foodstuffs.

Because the analysis using Plank's equation can separate the total freezing time into two terms, one intrinsic to the food material to be frozen, and the other containing the surface heat-transfer coefficient which can be influenced by the process equipment, it is useful to write Plank's equation in dimensionless form, substituting ΔH for $\rho\lambda$:

$$\frac{\theta_f h \Delta t}{a \, \Delta H P} = \left(1 + \frac{R}{P} \text{Bi}\right) \text{ where } \text{Bi} = \frac{ha}{k}$$

This leads to putting

$$\eta = \frac{R \, \text{Bi}}{P} \bigg/ \left(1 + \frac{R \, \text{Bi}}{P}\right) = \frac{\text{Bi}}{\dfrac{P}{R} + \text{Bi}} \qquad (6.8)$$

in which η can be regarded as an efficiency of coupling of the freezing medium to the food varying from 1 for $\text{Bi} \to \infty$ to 0 for $\text{Bi} \to 0$. Taking an intrinsic freezing time θ_f' for the case of $\Delta t = 1$ then

$$\theta_f = \theta_f' \frac{1}{\Delta t} \cdot \frac{1}{\eta} \qquad (6.9)$$

and this can be used very quickly to examine the influence of freezing medium temperature and of surface heat-transfer coefficient on the actual freezing time, so as to take process variations in these into account.

EXAMPLE 6.12. Determine the intrinsic freezing time for the carton of Example 6.11 and by putting the equation for the freezing time in the form of eqn. (6.9) evaluate the effect of (a) changes in the temperature of the plates to $-20°\text{C}$ and (b) the effect of doubling the thickness of the cardboard and (c) the effect of decreased surface coefficients due to

poor contact which drops the surface transfer coefficient to $100 \, \text{J m}^{-2} \text{s}^{-1} °\text{C}^{-1}$.

Calculating $\text{Bi} = \dfrac{ha}{k} = \dfrac{52.6 \times 0.1}{1.6} = 3.3$

$P/R = 4$, $\therefore \quad \eta = 3.3/(4 + 3.3) = 0.45$,

$\therefore \quad \theta_f' = 4.2 \times 0.45 \times 32 = 60.5 \, \text{h}$,

for (a) $\theta_f = 60.5 \times \dfrac{1}{0.45} \times \dfrac{1}{18} = 7.5 \, \text{hours}$,

for (b) $\dfrac{x}{k}$ becomes 0.034, $\therefore \quad \dfrac{1}{h_s} = 0.034 + 0.0017$,

$\therefore \quad h_s$ becomes 28,

$\therefore \quad \text{Bi}$ becomes $\dfrac{28 \times 0.1}{1.6} = 1.75$,

$\therefore \quad \eta$ becomes 0.30,

$\therefore \quad \theta_f = 60.5 \times \dfrac{1}{0.30} \times \dfrac{1}{32}$

$\quad = 6.3 \, \text{hours}$,

for (c) $1/h_s$ becomes $0.017 + 0.01 = 0.027$,

$\therefore$ Bi becomes $\dfrac{37 \times 0.1}{1.6} = 2.3$

$\therefore$ η becomes 0.36,

$\therefore$ $\theta_f = 60.5 \times \dfrac{1}{32} \times \dfrac{1}{0.36}$

$\qquad = \underline{5.2 \text{ hours.}}$

Cold Storage

For cold storage, the requirement for refrigeration comes from the need to remove the heat coming into the store from the external surroundings through insulation and from other heat sources within the store such as motors, lights and workers (each man contributing something of the order of 0.5 kW) as well as from the foodstuffs. Heat penetrating the walls can be estimated, knowing the overall heat-transfer coefficients including the surface terms and the conductances of the insulation which may include several different materials. The other heat sources require to be considered and summed. Detailed calculations can be quite complicated but for many purposes simple methods give a reasonable estimate.

SUMMARY

1. For heat exchangers:

$$q = UA\,\Delta t_m$$

where $\Delta t_m = \dfrac{\Delta t_1 - \Delta t_2}{\log_e \Delta t_1 / \Delta t_2}$

2. For jacketed pans:

$$q = UA\,\Delta t$$

and $\qquad \dfrac{t_1 - t_0}{t_2 - t_0} = \exp(-h_s A\theta / c\rho v).$

3. For sterilization of cans
   (a) thermal death time is the time taken to reduce bacterial spore counts by a factor of 10^{12},
   (b) F value is the thermal death time at 121°C. For *Clostridium botulinum* it is about 2.8 m,

(c) z is the temperature difference corresponding to a ten-fold change in the thermal death time,
(d) $\theta_{121} = \theta_t \times 10^{-(121-t)/z}$ or $\theta_t = \theta_{121} \times 10^{(121-t)/z}$.

4. The coefficient of performance of refrigeration plant is: (energy extracted in evaporator)/(energy input to compressor).

5. Freezing times can be calculated from:

$$\theta = \dfrac{\lambda\rho}{(t - t_a)}\left[P\dfrac{a}{h_s} + R\dfrac{a^2}{k} \right]$$

where for a slab $P = 1/2$ and $R = 1/8$ and for a sphere $P = 1/6$ and $R = 1/24$. A better approximation is to substitute ΔH over the whole range, for $\rho\lambda$. In addition for brick shapes a multiplier of around 1.20 is needed.

PROBLEMS

1. A stream of milk is being cooled by water in a counterflow heat exchanger. If the milk flowing at a rate of 2 kg s^{-1} is to be cooled from 50°C to 10°C estimate the rate of flow of the water if it is found to rise 22°C in temperature and calculate the log mean temperature difference across the heat exchanger, if the water enters the exchanger at 11°C.

2. A flow of 9.2 kg s^{-1} of milk is to be heated to 65°C from 150°C in a heat exchanger, using 16.7 kg s^{-1} of water at 95°C. If the overall heat-transfer coefficient is 1300 J m^{-2} s^{-1} °C^{-1} calculate the area of heat exchanger required if the flows are (a) parallel and (b) counterflow.

3. If in the heat exchanger of worked Example 6.2 it is desired to cool the water by a further 3°C, estimate the increase in the flow rate of the brine that would be necessary to achieve this, assuming that the surface heat transfer on the brine side is proportional to $v^{0.8}$, that the surface coefficient under the conditions of Example 2.6 are equal on both sides of the heat-transfer surface and they control the overall heat-transfer coefficient.

4. A counterflow regenerative heat exchanger is to be incorporated into a pasteurization plant for milk, with a heat-exchange area of 23 m^2 and an estimated overall heat-transfer coefficient of 950 J m^{-2} s^{-1} °C^{-1}. (Regenerative flow implies that the milk passes from the heat exchanger through further heating and processing and then proceeds back through the same heat exchanger so that the outgoing hot stream transfers heat to the incoming cold stream.) Calculate the temperature at which the incoming colder milk leaves the exchanger if it enters at 10°C and if the hot milk enters the exchanger at 72°C.

5. Olive oil is to be heated in a hemispherical steam-jacketed pan which is 0.85 m in diameter. If the pan is filled with oil at room temperature (21°C) and steam at a pressure of 200 kPa above atmospheric is admitted to the jacket, which covers the whole of the surface of the hemisphere, estimate the time

required for the oil to heat to 115°C. Assume an overall heat-transfer coefficient of 550 J m^{-2} s^{-1} °C^{-1} and no heat losses to the surroundings.

6. The milk pasteurizing plant using the programme calculated in worked Example 6.6 was found in practice to have a 1°C error in its thermometers so that temperatures thought to be 65°C were in fact 64°C and so on. Under these circumstances what would the holding time at the highest temperature (a true 65°C) need to be?

7. If the contents of the can of pumpkins, whose heating curve was to be calculated in unworked Example 9 of Chapter 5, has to be processed to give the equivalent at the centre of the can of a 10^{12} reduction in the spore count of *C. botulinum* (assume a *z* value of 10°C and a 10^{12} reduction is effected after 2.5 m at 121°C) calculate the holding time that would be needed at 115°C. Take the effect of the heating curve previously calculated into consideration but ignore any cooling effects.

8. A cold store is to be erected to maintain an internal temperature of −18°C with a surrounding air temperature of 25°C. It is to be constructed of concrete blocks 20 cm thick and then 15 cm of polystyrene foam. If the external surface coefficient of heat transfer is 10 J m^{-2} s^{-1} °C^{-1} and the internal one is 6 J m^{-2} s^{-1} °C^{-1} and the store is 40 × 20 × 7 m high determine the refrigeration load due to building heat gains from its surrounding air. Assume that ceiling and floor loss rates per m^2 are one-half of those for the walls. Determine also the distance from the inside face of the walls of the 0°C plane, assuming that the concrete blocks are on the outside.

9. For a refrigeration system with a coefficient of performance of 2.8, if you measure the power of the driving motor and find it to be producing 8.3 horsepower estimate the refrigeration capacity available at the evaporator, the tons of refrigeration extracted per kW of electricity consumed, and the rate of heat extraction in the condenser. Assume the mechanical and electrical efficiency of the drive to be 74%.

10. A particular refrigeration plant using ammonia as refrigerant is evaporating at −30°C and condensing at 38°C, and extracting 25 tons of refrigeration at the evaporator. For this plant calculate, assuming a theoretical cycle:
    (a) the rate of circulation of ammonia, kg s^{-1},
    (b) the theoretical power required for compression, kW,
    (c) the rate of heat rejection to the cooling water, kW,
    (d) the COP,
    (e) the volume of ammonia entering the compressor per unit time, m^3 s^{-1}.

11. It is wished to consider the possibility of chilling the apples of worked Example 6.11 in chilled water instead of in air. If water is available at 1°C and is to be pumped past the apples at 0.5 m s^{-1} estimate the time needed for the chilling process.

12. Estimate the time needed to freeze a meat sausage, initially at 15°C which may be taken to be a finite cylinder 2 cm in diameter and 15 cm long, in an air blast whose velocity across the sausage is 3 m s^{-1} and temperature is −18°C.

13. If the velocity of the air blast in the previous example were doubled, what would be the new freezing time? Management then decide to pack the sausages in individual tight-fitting cardboard wraps. What would be the maximum thickness of the cardboard permissible if the freezing time using the higher velocity of 6 m s^{-1} were to be no more than it had been originally in the 3 m s^{-1} air blast.

14. If you found by measurements that a roughly spherical thin plastic bag, measuring 30 cm in diameter, full of wet fish fillets, froze in a −30°C air blast in 16 h, what would you estimate to be the surface heat-transfer coefficient from the air to the surface of the bag?

CHAPTER 7

DRYING

DRYING is one of the oldest methods of preserving food. Primitive societies practised the drying of meat and fish in the sun long before recorded history. Today the drying of foods is still important as a method of preservation. Dried foods can be stored for long periods without deterioration occurring. The principal reasons for this are that the microorganisms which cause food spoilage and decay are unable to grow and multiply in the absence of sufficient water and many of the enzymes which promote undesired changes in the chemical composition of the food cannot function without water.

Preservation is the principal reason for drying, but drying can also occur in conjunction with other processing, for example in the baking of bread in which application of heat expands gases, changes the structure of the protein and starch and dries the loaf. Losses of moisture may also occur when they are not desired, for example during curing of cheese and in the fresh or frozen storage of meat, and in innumerable other moist food products during holding in air.

Drying of foods implies the removal of water from the foodstuff. In most cases, drying is accomplished by vaporizing the water that is contained in the food, and to do this the latent heat of vaporization must be supplied. There are, thus, two important process-controlling factors which enter into the unit operation of drying:

(a) the transfer of heat to provide the necessary latent heat of vaporization,

(b) the movement of water or water vapour through the food material and then away from it to effect the separation of water from foodstuff.

Drying processes fall into three categories:

(1) Air and contact drying under atmospheric pressure. In air and contact drying, heat is transferred through the foodstuff either from heated air or from heated surfaces. The water vapour is removed with the air.

(2) Vacuum drying. In vacuum drying, advantage is taken of the fact that evaporation of water occurs more readily at lower pressures than at higher ones. Heat transfer in vacuum drying is generally by conduction, sometimes by radiation.

(3) Freeze drying. In freeze drying, the water vapour is sublimed off from frozen food. The food structure is better maintained under these conditions. Suitable temperatures and pressures must be established in the dryer to ensure that sublimation occurs.

BASIC DRYING THEORY

Three States of Water

Pure water can exist in three states, solid, liquid and vapour. The state in which it is at any time depends on the temperature and pressure conditions and it is possible to illustrate this on a phase diagram, as in Fig. 7.1.

If we choose any condition of temperature and pressure and find the corresponding point on the diagram this point will lie, in general, in one of the three labelled regions, solid, liquid, or gas. This will give the state of the water under the chosen conditions.

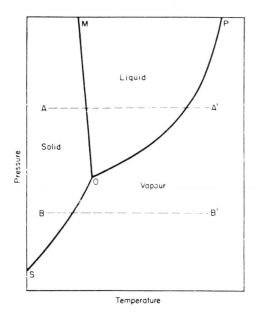

Fig. 7.1. Phase diagram for water.

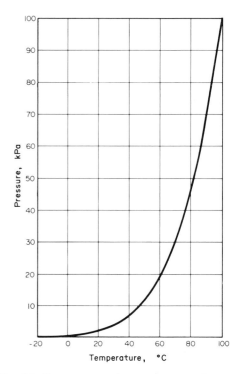

Fig. 7.2. Vapour pressure/temperature curve for water.

Under certain conditions, two states may exist side by side, and such conditions are found only along the lines of the diagram. Under one condition, all three states may exist together; this condition arises at what is called the triple point, indicated by point 0 on the diagram. For water it occurs at 0.0098°C and 0.64 kPa (4.8 mm of mercury) pressure.

If heat is applied to water in any state at constant pressure, the temperature rises and the condition moves horizontally across the diagram, and as it crosses the boundaries a change of state will occur. For example, starting from condition A on the diagram adding heat warms the ice, then melts it, then warms the water and finally evaporates the water to condition A'. Starting from condition B, situated below the triple point, when heat is added, the ice warms and then sublimes without passing through any liquid state.

Liquid and vapour coexist in equilibrium only under the conditions along the line OP. This line is called the vapour-pressure line. The vapour pressure is the measure of the tendency of molecules to escape as a gas from the liquid. The vapour pressure/temperature curve for water is shown in Fig. 7.2 which is just an enlargement for water of the curve OP of Fig. 7.1. Boiling occurs when the vapour

pressure of the water is equal to the total pressure on the water surface. The boiling point at atmospheric pressure is of course 100°C. At pressures above or below atmospheric, water boils at the corresponding temperatures above or below 100°C as shown in Fig. 7.2 for temperatures below 100°C.

Heat Requirements for Vaporization

The energy which must be supplied to vaporize the water at any temperature depends upon this temperature. The quantity of energy required per kg of water is called the latent heat of vaporization, if it is from a liquid, or latent heat of sublimation if it is from a solid. The heat energy required to vaporize water under any given set of conditions can be calculated from the latent heats given in the steam table in Appendix 6, as steam and water vapour are the same thing.

EXAMPLE 7.1. A food containing 80 % water is to be dried at 100°C down to a moisture content of 10 %.

If the initial temperature of the food is 21°C calculate the quantity of heat energy required, per unit weight of the original material, for drying under atmospheric pressure. The latent heat of vaporization of water at 100°C and at standard atmospheric pressure is 2257 kJ kg^{-1}. The specific heat capacity of the food is 3.8 kJ kg^{-1} °C^{-1} and of water is 4.186 kJ kg^{-1} °C^{-1}. Find also the energy requirement/kg water removed.

Calculating for 1 kg food

Initial moisture = 80%,

∴ 800 g moisture are associated with 200 g dry matter.

Final moisture = 10%,

∴ 100 g moisture are associated with 900 g dry matter,

∴ $(100 \times 200)/900$ g = 22.2 g moisture are associated with 200 g dry matter.

∴ 1 kg of original matter must lose $(800 - 22)$ g moisture = 778 g moisture.

Heat energy required for 1 kg original material = heat energy to raise temperature to 100°C + latent heat to remove water

$$= (100 - 21) \times 3.8 + 0.778 \times 2257$$
$$= 300.2 + 1755.9 = 2056 \text{ kJ}.$$

Energy/kg water removed, as 2056 kJ are required to remove 0.778 kg of water:

$$= 2056/0.778$$
$$= 2643 \text{ kJ}.$$

Steam is often used to supply heat to air or to surfaces used for drying. In condensing, steam gives up its latent heat of vaporization and, in drying, the substance being dried must take up latent heat of vaporization to convert its liquid into vapour, so it might be reasoned that 1 kg of steam condensing will produce 1 kg vapour. This is not exactly true, as the steam and the food will in general be under different pressures with the food at the lower pressure. Latent heats of vaporization are slightly higher at lower pressures, as shown in Table 7.1. In practice, there are also heat losses to be considered.

EXAMPLE 7.2. Using the same material as in Example 7.1, if vacuum drying is to be carried out at 60°C under the corresponding saturation pressure of

TABLE 7.1
LATENT HEAT AND SATURATION TEMPERATURE OF WATER

Absolute pressure (kPa)	Latent heat of vaporization (kJ kg^{-1})	Saturation temperature (°C)
1	2485	7
2	2460	18
5	2424	33
10	2393	46
20	2358	60
50	2305	81
100	2258	99.6
101.35 (1 atm)	2257	100
110	2244	102
120	2238	105
200	2202	120
500	2109	152

20 kPa abs. (or a vacuum of 81.4 kPa), calculate the heat energy required to remove the moisture per unit weight of raw material.

Heat energy required per kg raw material = heat energy to raise temperature to 60°C + latent heat of vaporization at 20 kPa abs.

$$= (60 - 21) \times 3.8 + 0.778 \times 2358$$
$$= 148.2 + 1834.5$$
$$= 1983 \text{ kJ}.$$

In freeze drying the latent heat of sublimation must be supplied. Pressure has little effect on the latent heat of sublimation, which can be taken as 2838 kJ kg^{-1}.

EXAMPLE 7.3. If the foodstuff in the two previous examples were to be freeze dried at 0°C, how much energy would be required per kg of raw material, starting from frozen food at 0°C?

Heat energy required = 0.778×2838
$$= 2208 \text{ kJ kg}^{-1}.$$

Heat Transfer in Drying

We have been discussing the heat-energy requirements for the drying process. The rates of drying are generally determined by the rates at which heat energy can be transferred to the water or to the ice in order to provide the latent heats, though under some circumstances the rate of mass transfer (removal of the water) can be limiting. All three of the mechanisms by which heat is transferred – conduction, radiation and convection – may enter into drying. The relative importance of the mechanisms varies from one drying process to another and very often one mode of heat transfer predominates to such an extent that it governs the overall process.

As an example, in air drying the rate of heat transfer is given by

$$q = h_s A(t_a - t_s)$$

where q is the heat transfer rate in $kJ\,kg^{-1}\,s^{-1}$, h_s is the surface heat-transfer coefficient $J\,m^{-2}\,s^{-1}\,°C^{-1}$, A is the area through which heat flow is taking place, m^2, t_a is the air temperature and t_s is the temperature of the surface which is drying, °C.

To take another example, in a roller dryer where moist material is spread over the surface of a heated drum, heat transfer occurs by conduction from the drum to the foodstuff, so that the equation is

$$q = U A(t_i - t_s)$$

where U is the overall heat-transfer coefficient, t_i is the drum temperature (usually very close to that of the steam), t_s is the surface temperature of the food (boiling point of water or slightly above) and A is the area of drying surface on the drum.

The value of U can be estimated from the conductivity of the drum material and of the layer of foodstuff. Values of U have been quoted as high as $1800\,J\,m^{-2}\,s^{-1}\,°C^{-1}$, under very good conditions and down to about $60\,J\,m^{-2}\,s^{-1}\,°C^{-1}$ under poor conditions.

In cases where substantial quantities of heat are transferred by radiation, it should be remembered that the surface temperature of the food may be higher than the air temperature. Estimates of surface temperature can be made using the relationships developed for radiant heat transfer although the actual effect of combined radiation and evaporative cooling is complex. Convection coefficients also can be estimated using the standard equations.

For freeze drying, energy must be transferred to the surface at which sublimation occurs. However, it must be supplied at such a rate as not to increase the temperature at the drying surface above the freezing point. In many applications of freeze drying, the heat transfer occurs mainly by conduction.

As drying proceeds, the character of the heat-transfer situation changes. Dry material begins to occupy the surface layers and conduction must take place through these dry surface layers which are poor heat conductors so that heat is transferred to the drying region progressively more slowly.

Dryer Efficiencies

The efficiency of operation of a dryer can be considered as the ratio of the heat that would be theoretically required to supply the latent heat of vaporization of the water that has been dried off, to the actual heat used in the dryer. This efficiency is useful when assessing the performance of a dryer and in making comparisons between the various classes of dryers which may be alternatives for a particular drying operation.

The overall efficiency will also take into account losses on the heating side and therefore it is based on the total heat available from fuel which is burned to provide heat for the dryer.

EXAMPLE 7.4. A dryer reduces the moisture content of 100 kg of a potato product from 80% to 10% moisture. If 250 kg of steam at 70 kPa gauge is used to heat 49,800 m^3 of air to 80°C, and if the air is cooled to 71°C in passing through the dryer, calculate the efficiency of the dryer in terms of the heat supplied (a) from the air and (b) from the steam. The specific heat of potato is $3.43\,kJ\,kg^{-1}\,°C$. Assume potato enters at 24°C and leaves at the same temperature as the exit air.

In 100 kg of raw material there is 80% moisture, that is 80 kg water and 20 kg dry material,

∴   total weight of dry product = 20 × (10/9)
     = 22.2 kg, and weight of water
     = (22.2 − 20) = 2.2 kg.
∴   water removed = (80 − 2.2) = 77.8 kg.

Heat supplied to potato product = sensible heat to raise raw material temperature from 24°C to 71°C + latent heat of vaporization.

Now, the latent heat of vaporization corresponding to a saturation temperature of 71°C is $2331\,kJ\,kg^{-1}$,

∴ heat supplied/100 kg potato

> $= 100(71 - 24)3.43 + 77.8 \times 2331$
>
> $= 16 \times 10^3 + 181 \times 10^3$
>
> $= 1.97 \times 10^5$ kJ.

The specific heat of air can be assumed to be $1.0 \, \text{kJ kg}^{-1} {}^{\circ}\text{C}^{-1}$ and the density of the air to be $1.06 \, \text{kg m}^{-3}$.

∴ heat given up by air/100 kg potato

> $= 1.0 \times (80 - 71) \times 49{,}800 \times 1.06$
>
> $= 4.75 \times 10^5$ kJ.

∴ thermal efficiency of air drying

> $= (1.97/4.75) \times 100$
>
> $= 41\%$.

The latent heat of stem at 70 kPa gauge is $2216 \, \text{kJ kg}^{-1}$

∴ heat in steam $= 250 \times 2216$

> $= 5.54 \times 10^5$ kJ.

∴ overall thermal efficiency

> $= (1.97/5.54) \times 100$
>
> $= 35.5\%$.

Notice that the overall efficiency is the lower as there are additional heat losses in the air heating operation.

Examples of overall thermal efficiencies are:

drum dryers	35–80%
spray dryers	20–50%
radiant dryers	30–40%

After sufficient energy has been provided to vaporize or to sublime moisture from the food, some way must be found to remove this moisture. In freeze-drying and vacuum systems it is normally convenient to condense the water to a liquid or a solid and then the vacuum pumps have to handle only the non-condensible gases. In atmospheric drying a current of air is normally used.

MASS TRANSFER IN DRYING

In heat transfer, heat energy is transferred under the driving force provided by a temperature difference, and the rate of transfer is proportional to the potential (temperature) difference and to the properties of the transfer system characterized by the heat-transfer coefficient. In the same way, mass is transferred under the driving force provided by a partial pressure or concentration difference and the rate is proportional to the potential (pressure or concentration) difference and to the properties of the transfer system characterized by the mass-transfer coefficient.

Writing these symbolically, analogous to $q = U A \Delta t$, we have

$$\frac{\mathrm{d}w}{\mathrm{d}\theta} = k'_g \, A \, \Delta Y \qquad (7.1)$$

where w is the mass being transferred kg s^{-1}, A is the area through which the transfer is taking place, k'_g is the mass-transfer coefficient in this case in units $\text{kg m}^{-2} \text{s}^{-1}$, and Y is the humidity difference in kg kg^{-1}. Unfortunately the application of mass-transfer equation is not as straightforward as heat transfer, because the movement of moisture changes as drying proceeds. Initially, the mass (moisture) is transferred from the surface of the material and later, to an increasing extent, from deeper within the food to the surface and thence to the air. So the first stage is to determine the relationships between the moist surface and the ambient air and then to consider the diffusion through the food. In studying the surface/air relationships, it is necessary to consider mass and heat transfer simultaneously.

The air for drying is usually heated and it is also the heat-transfer medium. Therefore it is necessary to consider the relationships between air and the moisture it contains.

PSYCHROMETRY

The capacity of air for moisture removal depends on its humidity and its temperature. The study of relationships between air and its associated water is called psychrometry.

Humidity (Y) is the measure of the water content of the air. The absolute humidity is the mass of water vapour per unit mass of dry air and the units are therefore kg kg^{-1}.

Air is said to be saturated with water vapour at a given temperature and pressure if its humidity is a maximum under these conditions. If further water is added to saturated air, it must appear as liquid water in the form of a mist or droplets. Under conditions of saturation, the partial pressure of the water vapour in the air is equal to the saturation vapour pressure of water at that temperature.

The total pressure of a gaseous mixture, such as air and water vapour, is made up from the sum of the pressures of its constituents, which are called the partial pressures. Each partial pressure arises from the molecular concentration of the constituent and the pressure exerted is that which corresponds to the number of moles present and the total volume of the system. The partial pressures are added to obtain the total pressure.

EXAMPLE 7.5. If the total pressure of moist air is 100 kPa (approximately atmospheric) and the humidity is measured as $0.03 \, kg \, kg^{-1}$, calculate the partial pressure of the water vapour.

The molecular weight of air is 29, and of water 18 so that the mole fraction of water is

$$\frac{0.03}{18} \bigg/ \left(\frac{1.00}{29} + \frac{0.03}{18} \right) = 0.0017/(0.034 + 0.0017)$$

$$= 0.048.$$

Therefore the water vapour pressure

$$= 0.048 \times 100 \, kPa$$

$$= 4.8 \, kPa.$$

The relative humidity (RH) is defined as the ratio of the partial pressure of the water vapour to the partial pressure of saturated water vapour at the same temperature. Therefore

$$RH = p/p_s$$

and is often expressed as a percentage.

EXAMPLE 7.6. If the air in Example 7.5 is at 60°C, calculate the relative humidity.

From steam tables, the saturation pressure of water vapour at 60°C is 19.9 kPa.

Therefore the relative humidity $= p/p_s$

$$= 4.8/19.9$$

$$= 0.24$$

$$\text{or } 24\%.$$

If such air were cooled, then when the percentage relative humidity reached 100% the air would be saturated and this would occur at that temperature at which $p = p_s = 4.8 \, kPa$.

Interpolating from the steam tables, or reading

from the water vapour pressure/temperature graph, this occurs at a temperature of 32°C and this temperature is called the dew point of the air at this particular moisture content. If cooled below the dew point, the air can no longer retain this quantity of water as vapour and so water must condense out as droplets or a fog, and the water remaining as vapour in the air will be that corresponding to saturation at the temperature reached.

The humidity Y can therefore be related to the partial pressure p_w of the water in air vapour by the equation

$$Y = 18p_w/[29(P - p_w)] \qquad (7.2)$$

where P is the total pressure. In circumstances where p_w is small compared with P, and this is approximately the case in air/water systems at room temperatures $Y \doteqdot 18p_w/29P$.

Corresponding to the specific heat capacity of gases, c_p, is the humid heat, c_s of moist air. It is used in the same way as a specific heat, the enthalpy change being the mass of dry air multiplied by the temperature difference and by the humid heat. The units are $J \, kg^{-1} \, {}^{\circ}C^{-1}$ and the numerical values can be read off the psychrometric chart. Where it differs from specific-heat capacity at constant pressure is that it is based only on the mass of the dry air, and the specific heat of the water it contains is effectively incorporated into the humid heat which therefore is numerically a little larger than the specific-heat capacity to allow for this.

Wet-bulb Temperatures

A useful concept in psychrometry is the wet-bulb temperature, as compared with the ordinary temperature which is called the dry-bulb temperature. The wet-bulb temperature is the temperature reached by a water surface, such as that registered by a thermometer bulb surrounded by a wet wick, when exposed to air passing over it. The wick and therefore the thermometer bulb decreases in temperature below the dry-bulb temperature until the rate of heat transfer from the warmer air to the wick is just equal to the rate of heat transfer needed to provide for the evaporation of water from the wick into the air stream.

Equating these two rates of heat transfer gives

$$h_c A(t_a - t_s) = \lambda k_g' A(Y_s - Y_a)$$

where a and s denote actual and saturation temperatures and humidities; h_c is the heat-transfer coefficient and k'_g the mass transfer coefficient from the air to the wick surface; λ is the latent heat of evaporation of water.

As the relative humidity of the air decreases, so the difference between the wet-bulb and dry-bulb temperatures, called the wet-bulb depression, increases and a line connecting wet-bulb temperature and relative humidity can be plotted on a suitable chart. When the air is saturated, the wet-bulb temperature and the dry-bulb temperature are identical.

Therefore if $(t_a - t_s)$ is plotted against $Y_s - Y_a$ remembering that the point (t_s, Y_s) must correspond to a dew-point condition, we then have a wet-bulb straight line on a temperature/humidity chart sloping down from the point (t_s, Y_s) with a slope of $-(\lambda k'_g / h_c)$.

A further important concept is that of the adiabatic saturation condition. This is the situation reached by a stream of water, in contact with the humid air, both of which ultimately reach a temperature at which the heat lost by the humid air on cooling is equal to the heat of evaporation of the water leaving the stream of water by evaporation.

Under this condition with no heat exchange to the surroundings, the total enthalpy change

$$\Delta H = c_s(t_a - t_s) + \lambda(Y_s - Y_a) = 0$$

where c_s is the humid heat of the air.

Now it just so happens, for water, that the numerical magnitude of

$$\frac{h_c}{c_s k_g} = 1 \text{ (known as the Lewis number)}.$$

Therefore the wet bulb line and the adiabatic saturation line coincide when the Lewis number $= 1$. It is now time to examine the chart we have spoken about. It is called a psychrometric chart.

Psychrometric Charts

In the preceding discussion, we have been considering a chart of humidity against temperature, and such a chart is given in skeleton form on Fig. 7.3 and more fully in Appendix 9. The two main axes are temperature (dry bulb) and humidity. The saturation curve is plotted on this dividing the whole area into an unsaturated and a two-phase region. Taking a point on the saturation curve (t_s, Y_s) a line can be drawn from this with a slope

$$-\frac{\lambda k'_g}{h_c} \left(= -\frac{\lambda}{C_s} \right)$$

running down into the unsaturated region of the chart – this is the wet bulb or adiabatic cooling line and a net of such lines is shown. Any constant temperature line between the saturation curve and the zero humidity axis can be divided evenly into

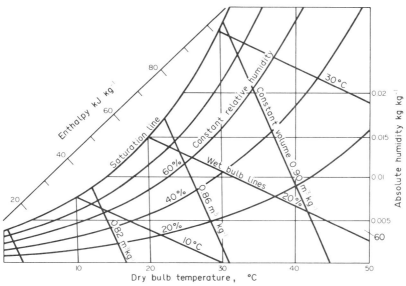

FIG. 7.3. Psychrometric chart — simplified.

fractional humidities which will correspond to fractional relative humidities [for example, a 0.50 humidity ratio will correspond to a 50% RH because of eqn. (7.2) if $P \gg p_w$].

This discussion is somewhat over-simplified and close inspection of the chart shows that the axes are not exactly rectangular and that the lines of constant dry-bulb temperature are not exactly parallel. The reasons are beyond the scope of the present discussion but can be found in appropriate texts such as Keey (1978).

This chart can be used as the basis of many calculations. It can be used to calculate relative humidities and other properties.

EXAMPLE 7.7. If the wet-bulb temperature in a particular room is measured and found to be 20°C in air whose dry-bulb temperature is 25°C (that is the wet-bulb depression is 5°C) estimate the relative humidity, the enthalpy and the specific volume of the air in the room.

On the humidity chart follow down the wet-bulb line for a temperature of 20°C until it meets the dry-bulb temperature line for 25°C. Examining the location of this point of intersection with reference to the lines of constant relative humidity, it lies between 60% and 70% RH and about 4/10 of the way between them but nearer to the 60% line. Therefore the RH is estimated to be 64%. Similar examination of the enthalpy lines gives an estimated enthalpy of 57 kJ kg^{-1}, and from the volume lines a specific volume of 0.862 m^3 kg^{-1}.

Once the properties of the air have been determined other calculations can easily be made.

EXAMPLE 7.8. If the air in Example 7.7 is then to be heated to a dry-bulb temperature of 40°C, calculate the heat needed for a flow of 1000 m^3 h^{-1} of the hot air to be supplied to a dryer, and the relative humidity of the heated air.

On heating, the air condition moves, at constant absolute humidity as no water vapour is added or subtracted, to the condition at the higher (dry bulb) temperature of 40°C. At this condition, reading from the chart, the enthalpy is 73 kJ kg^{-1}, specific volume is 0.906 m^3 kg^{-1} and RH 27%.

$\therefore$ Mass of 1000 m^3 is 1000/0.906 = 1104 kg,

$$\Delta H = (73 - 57) = 16 \text{ kJ kg}^{-1}.$$

So rate of heating required

$$= 1104 \times 16 \text{ kJ h}^{-1}$$
$$= (1104 \times 16)/3600 \text{ kJ s}^{-1}$$
$$= 5 \text{ kW}.$$

If the air is used for drying, with the heat for evaporation being supplied by the hot air passing over a wet solid surface, the system behaves like the adiabatic saturation system. It is adiabatic because no heat is obtained from any source external to the air and the wet solid, and the latent heat of evaporation must be obtained by cooling the hot air. Looked at from the viewpoint of the solid, this is a drying process; from the viewpoint of the air it is humidification.

EXAMPLE 7.9. Air at 60°C and 8% RH is blown through a continuous dryer from which it emerges at a temperature of 35°C. Estimate the quantity of water removed per kg of air passing, and the volume of drying air required to remove 20 kg water h^{-1}.

Using the psychrometric chart (high-temperature version, to take in the conditions) the inlet air condition shows the humidity of the drying air to be 0.01 kg kg^{-1} and its specific volume to be 0.96 m^3 kg^{-1}. Through the dryer, the condition of the air follows a constant wet-bulb line, so at 35°C its condition is a humidity of 0.0207.

$\therefore$ water removed = (0.0207 − 0.010)
$$= 0.0107 \text{ kg kg}^{-1} \text{ of air.}$$

So each kg, i.e. 0.96 m^3, of air passing will remove 0.0107 kg water,

$\therefore$ volume of air to remove 20 kg h^{-1}
$$= (20/0.0107) \times 0.96$$
$$= 1794 \text{ m}^3 \text{ h}^{-1}.$$

If air is cooled, then initially its condition moves along a line of constant humidity, horizontally on a psychrometric chart, until it reaches the saturation curve at its dew point. Further cooling then proceeds down the saturation line to the final temperature, with water condensing to adjust the humidity as the saturation humidity cannot be exceeded.

EXAMPLE 7.10. The air emerging from a dryer with an exit temperature of 45°C, passes over a surface which is gradually cooled. It is found that the first traces of moisture appear on this surface when it is at 40°C. Estimate the humidity of the air leaving the dryer.

On the psychrometric chart, the saturation temperature is 40°C and proceeding at constant humidity from this, the 45°C line is intersected at a point indicating a relative humidity of 76%.

In dryers, it is sometimes useful to reheat the air so as to reduce its relative humidity and thus to give it an additional capacity to evaporate more water from the material being dried. This process can easily be followed on a psychrometric chart.

EXAMPLE 7.11. A flow of 1800 m³ h⁻¹ of air initially at a temperature of 18°C and 50% RH is to be used in an air dryer. It is heated to 140°C and passed over a set of trays in a shelf dryer, which it leaves at 60% RH. It is then reheated to 140°C and passed over another set of trays which it leaves at 60% RH again. Estimate the energy necessary to heat the air and the quantity of water removed per hour.

From the psychrometric chart (normal temperatures) the humidity of the initial air is 0.0062 kg kg⁻¹, specific volume is 0.834 m³ kg⁻¹, and enthalpy 35 kJ kg⁻¹. Proceeding at constant humidity to a temperature of 140°C, the enthalpy is found (high temperature chart) to be 160 kJ kg⁻¹. Proceeding along a wet-bulb line to an RH of 60% gives the corresponding temperature as 48°C and humidity as 0.045 kg kg⁻¹.

Reheating to 140°C keeps humidity constant and enthalpy goes to 268 kJ kg⁻¹.

Thence along a wet-bulb line to 60% RH gives humidity of 0.082 kg kg⁻¹.

$$\text{Thus total energy supplied} = \Delta H = 268 - 35$$
$$= 233 \text{ kJ kg}^{-1}$$
$$\text{and total water removed} = \Delta Y = 0.082 - 0.0064$$
$$= 0.0756 \text{ kg kg}^{-1}.$$

$$\text{Now } 1800 \text{ m}^3 \text{ of air h}^{-1} = 1800/0.834$$
$$= 2158 \text{ kg h}^{-1}$$
$$= 0.6 \text{ kg s}^{-1}.$$
$$\therefore \text{ energy taken in by air} = 233 \times 0.6 \text{ kJ s}^-$$
$$= 140 \text{ kW}.$$
$$\text{Water removed in dryer} = 0.6 \times 0.0756$$
$$= 0.045 \text{ kg s}^{-1}$$
$$= 163 \text{ kg h}^{-1}.$$

Exit temperature of air (from chart) = 60°C.

Consideration of psychrometric charts and what has been said about them will show that they can be used for calculations focused on the air, for the purposes of air conditioning as well as for drying.

EXAMPLE 7.12. In a tropical country, it is desired to provide processing air conditions of 15°C and 80% RH. The ambient air is at 31.5°C and 90% RH. If the chosen method is to cool the air to condense out enough water to reduce the water content of the air sufficiently, then to reheat if necessary, determine the temperature to which the air should be cooled, the quantity of water removed and the amount of reheating necessary. The processing room has a volume of 1650 m³ and it is estimated to require six air changes per hour.

Using the psychrometric chart (normal temperatures) the initial humidity can be found to be 0.0266 kg kg⁻¹.

At the final condition the humidity is 0.0085 kg kg⁻¹.

The saturation temperature for this humidity is 13°C.

At the saturation temperature of 13°C the enthalpy is 33.5 kJ kg⁻¹.

At the final conditions, 15°C and 80% RH, the enthalpy is 37 kJ kg⁻¹ and the specific volume of air is 0.827 m³ kg⁻¹.

Assuming that the air changes are calculated at the conditions in the working space.

$$\therefore \text{ mass of air to be conditioned} = (1650 \times 6)/0.827$$
$$= 11{,}970 \text{ kg h}^{-1},$$
$$\text{mass of water removed per kg of dry air} = \Delta Y = 0.0266 - 0.0085$$
$$= 0.018 \text{ kg kg}^{-1}.$$

$$\therefore \text{ mass of water removed per hour} = 11{,}970 \times 0.018$$
$$= 215 \, \text{kg h}^{-1}.$$
$$\text{Reheat required } \Delta H = (37 - 33.5)$$
$$= 3.5 \, \text{kJ kg}^{-1}.$$
$$\text{Total reheat required} = 11{,}970 \times 3.5$$
$$= 41{,}895 \, \text{kJ h}^{-1}$$
$$= 11.6 \, \text{kJ s}^{-1}$$
$$= \underline{11.6 \, \text{kW}.}$$

Measurement of Humidity

Methods depend largely upon the concepts that have been presented in the preceding sections, but because they are often needed it seems useful to set them out specifically.

(1) Wet- and dry-bulb thermometers. The dry-bulb temperature is the normal air temperature and about the only caution that is needed is that if the thermometer bulb, or element, is exposed to a surface at a substantially higher or lower temperature the possibility of radiation errors should be considered. A simple method to greatly reduce any such error is to interpose a radiation shield, e.g. a metal tube, which stands off from the thermometer bulb 1 cm or so and prevents exposure to the radiation source or sink. A piece of wicking such as a hollow shoelace of the correct size, dipping into water to moisten the wet bulb, is adequate and the necessary aspiration of air past this bulb can be effected by a small fan or by swinging bulb, wick, water bottle and all as in a sling psychrometer. The maximum difference between the two bulbs gives the wet-bulb depression and a psychrometric chart or appropriate tables will then give the relative humidity.

(2) Dew-point meters. These measure the saturation or dew-point temperature by cooling a sample of air until condensation occurs. The psychrometric chart or a scale on the instrument is then used to give the humidity. For example, a sample of air at 20°C is found to produce the first signs of condensation on a mirror when the mirror is cooled to 14°C. The chart shows by moving horizontally across, from the saturation temperature of 14°C to the constant temperature line at 20°C, that the air must have a relative humidity of 69%.

(3) The hair hygrometer. Hairs expand and contract in length according to the relative humidity. Instruments are made which give accurately the length of the hair and so they can be calibrated in humidities.

(4) Electrical resistance hygrometers. Some materials vary in their surface electrical resistance according to the relative humidity of the surrounding air. Examples are aluminium oxide, phenol-formaldehyde polymers, and styrene polymers. Calibration allows resistance measurements to be interpreted as humidity.

(5) Lithium chloride hygrometers. In these the solution of lithium chloride is maintained at a temperature such that its partial pressure equals the partial pressure of water vapour in the air. The vapour pressure–temperature relationships for lithium chloride can be used to determine the humidity of the air.

EQUILIBRIUM MOISTURE CONTENT

The equilibrium vapour pressure above a food is determined not only by the temperature but also by the water content of the food, by the way in which the water is bound in the food, and by the presence of constituents soluble in water. Under a given vapour pressure of water in the surrounding air, a food attains a moisture content in equilibrium with its surroundings, and this is called its equilibrium moisture content. It is possible, therefore, to plot the equilibrium vapour pressure against moisture content or to plot the relative humidity of the air in equilibrium with the food against moisture content of the food. Often, instead of the relative humidity, the water activity of the food surface is used. This is the ratio of the partial pressure of water in the food to the vapour pressure of water at the same temperature. The equilibrium curves obtained vary with different types of foodstuffs and examples are shown in Fig. 7.4.

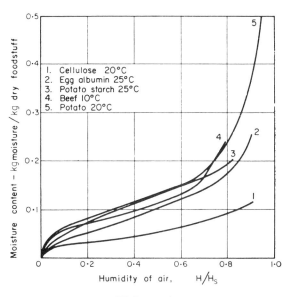

Fig. 7.4. Equilibrium moisture contents.

Thus, for the potato as shown in Fig. 7.4, at a temperature of 20°C in an atmosphere of relative humidity 30% (giving a water activity of 0.3), the equilibrium moisture content is 0.1 kg water/kg dry potato. It would not be possible to dry potatoes below 10% using an air dryer with air at 20°C and relative humidity 30%. It will be noted from the shape of the curve that above a certain relative humidity, about 80% in the case of potatoes, the equilibrium content increases very rapidly with increase in relative humidity. There are marked differences between foods, both in shape of the curves and in the amount of water present at any relative humidity and temperature, in the range of relative humidity between 0 and 65%. The sigmoid (S-shaped) character of the curve is most pronounced, and the moisture content at low humidities is greatest, for food whose dry solids are high in protein,

starch, or other high molecular weight polymers. They are low for foods high in soluble solids. Fats and crystalline salts and sugars in general absorb negligible amounts of water when the RH is low or moderate, Sugars in the amorphous form absorb more than in the crystalline form.

AIR DRYING

In air drying, the rate of removal of water depends on the conditions of the air, the properties of the food and the design of the dryer.

Moisture can be held in varying degrees of bonding.

Formerly, it was considered that water in a food came into one or other of two categories, free water or bound water. This now appears to be an over-simplification and such clear demarcations are no longer considered useful. Water is held by forces whose intensity ranges from the very weak forces retaining surface moisture to very strong chemical bonds. In drying, it is obvious that the water which is loosely held will be removed most easily. Thus it would be expected that drying rates would decrease as moisture content decreases, with the remaining water being bound more and more strongly as its quantity decreases.

In many cases, a substantial part of the water is found to be loosely bound and this part can, for drying purposes, be considered as free water at the surface. We may then compare drying rates for a material such as sand with those of a food such as meat. These are shown in Fig. 7.5.

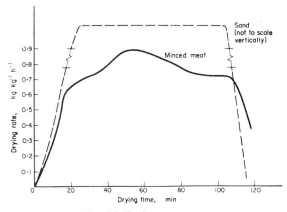

Fig. 7.5. Drying-rate curves.

This behaviour, in which the drying behaves as though the water were at a free surface, is called constant-rate drying. If w is the mass of the material being dried then for constant rate drying

$$\frac{dw}{d\theta} = \text{constant}.$$

However, in food, unlike sand, after a period of drying at a constant rate, it is found that the water then comes off more slowly. A complete drying curve for fish, adapted from Jason (1958), is shown in Fig. 7.6. The drying temperature was low and this accounts for the long drying time. A more generalized drying curve plotting the rate of drying as a percentage of the constant rate against moisture content is shown in Fig. 7.7.

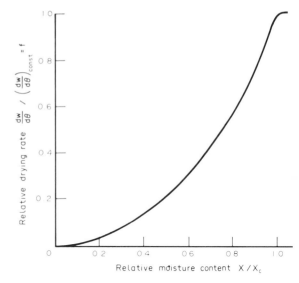

FIG. 7.7. Generalized drying curve.

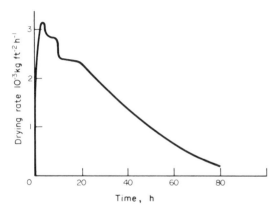

FIG. 7.6. Drying curve for fish.

The change from constant drying rate to a slower rate occurs at different moisture contents for different foods. However, for many foods the change from constant drying rate occurs at a moisture content in equilibrium with air of 58–65% relative humidity, that is at $a_w = 0.58$–0.65. The moisture content at which this change of rate occurs is known as the critical moisture content, X_c.

Another point of importance is that many foods such as potato do not show a true constant-rate drying period. They do, however, often show quite a sharp break after a slowly and steadily declining drying-rate period and the concept of constant rate is still a useful approximation.

The end of the constant-rate period, when $X = X_c$ at the break point of drying-rate curves, signifies that the water has ceased to behave as if it

were at a free surface and that factors other than vapour-pressure differences are influencing the rate of drying. Thereafter the drying rate decreases and this is called the falling-rate period of drying. The rate-controlling factors in the falling-rate period are complex, depending upon diffusion through the food, and upon the changing energy-binding pattern of the water molecules. Very little theoretical information is available for drying of foods in this region and experimental drying curves are the only adequate guide to design.

Calculation of Constant Drying Rates

In the constant-rate period, the water is being evaporated from what is effectively a free water surface. The rate of removal of water can then be related to the rate of heat transfer, if there is no change in the temperature of the material and therefore all heat energy transferred to it must result in evaporation of water. The rate of removal of the water is also the rate of mass transfer, from the solid to the ambient air. These two – mass and heat transfer – must predict the same rate of drying for a given set of circumstances.

Considering mass transfer which is fundamental to drying, the driving force is the partial difference of the water vapour between the food and the air. The extent of this difference can be obtained, knowing the temperatures and the conditions, by reference to tables or the psychrometric chart. Alternatively, the driving force may be expressed in terms of humidity driving forces and the numerical values of the mass-transfer coefficients in this case are linked to the others through the partial pressure/humidity relationships such as eqns. (7.1) and (7.2).

EXAMPLE 7.13. If the mass-transfer coefficient from a free water surface to an adjacent moving air stream is $0.015 \text{ kg m}^{-2} \text{ s}^{-1}$, estimate the rate of evaporation from a surface of 1 m^2 at a temperature of 28°C into an air stream with a dry-bulb temperature of 40°C and RH of 40% and the necessary rate of supply of heat energy to effect this evaporation.

From charts, the humidity of saturated air at 40°C is $0.0495 \text{ kg kg}^{-1}$.

∴ humidity of air at 40°C and 40% RH = 0.0495×0.4

$= 0.0198 \text{ kg kg}^{-1} = Y_a$.

From charts the saturated humidity at 28°C $= 0.0244 \text{ kg kg}^{-1} = Y_s$.

∴ Driving force $= (Y_s - Y_a)$

$$= (0.0244 - 0.0198) \text{ kg kg}^{-1}$$

$$= 0.0048 \text{ kg kg}^{-1}.$$

∴ Rate of evaporation $= k_g A (Y_s - Y_a)$

$$= 0.015 \times 1 \times 0.0048$$

$$= 7.2 \times 10^{-5} \text{ kg s}^{-1}.$$

Latent heat of evaporation of water at 28°C $= 2.44 \times 10^3 \text{ kJ kg}^{-1}$.

∴ Rate of heat energy supply $= 7.2 \times 10^{-5} \times 2.44 \times 10^3 \text{ kJ s}^{-1}$

$$= 0.176 \text{ kJ s}^{-1}$$

$$= 0.176 \text{ kW}.$$

The problem in applying such apparently simple relationships to provide the essential rate information for drying, is in the prediction of the mass-transfer coefficients. In the section on heat transfer, methods and correlations were given for the prediction of heat-transfer coefficients. Such can be applied to the drying situation and the heat-transfer rates used to estimate rates of moisture removal. The reverse can also be applied.

EXAMPLE 7.14. Using the data from Example 7.13, estimate the heat-transfer coefficients from the air stream to the water surface.

Heat-flow rate $= q = 176 \text{ J s}^{-1}$ from Example 7.13.

Temperature difference = dry-bulb temperature of air − wet-bulb temperature (at food surface)

$$= (40 - 28)$$

$$= 12°C = (t_a - t_s).$$

Since $q = h_c A (t_a - t_s)$,

∴ $176 = h_c \times 1 \times 12$,

∴ $h_c = 15 \text{ J m}^{-2} \text{ s}^{-1} °\text{C}^{-1}$.

Mass balances are also applicable and can be used in drying and related calculations.

EXAMPLE 7.15. In a low-temperature drying situation, air at 60°C and 10% RH is being passed over a bed of diced carrots at the rate of 20 kg dry air per second. If the rate of evaporation of the carrots, measured by the rate of change of weight of the carrots, is 0.16 kg s^{-1}, estimate the temperature and RH of the air leaving the dryer.

From the psychrometric chart:

Humidity of air at

60°C and 10% RH $= 0.013 \text{ kg kg}^{-1}$.

Humidity added in drying = 0.16 kg/20 kg air

$$= 0.008 \text{ kg kg}^{-1},$$

∴ humidity of air leaving dryer $= 0.013 + 0.008$

$$= 0.021 \text{ kg kg}^{-1}.$$

Following on the psychrometric chart the wet-bulb line from the entry point at 60°C and 10% RH up to the intersection of that line with a constant humidity line of 0.021 kg kg^{-1}, the resulting temperature is 41°C and the RH 42%.

Because the equation for predicting heat-transfer coefficients, for situations commonly encountered, are extensive and much more widely available than mass-transfer coefficients, the heat-transfer rates can be used to estimate drying rates, through the Lewis ratio. Remembering that $Le = (h_c/k'_g C_s) = 1$ for the air/water system (strictly speaking the Lewis number, which arises in gaseous diffusion theory, is $h_c/k'_g C_p$ but for air of the humidity encountered in ordinary practice $C_s \doteqdot C_p \doteqdot 1.02\,kJ\ kg^{-1}\,°C^{-1}$). Therefore numerically, if h_c is in $J\,m^{-2}\,s^{-1}\,°C^{-1}$, and k'_g in $kg\,m^{-2}\,s^{-1}$, $k'_g = h_c/1000$. The values of h_c can be predicted using the standard relationships for heat-transfer coefficients which have been discussed in Chapter 4.

EXAMPLE 7.16. In Examples 7.12 and 7.13 a value for k'_g of $0.0150\,kg\,m^{-2}\,s^{-1}$ was used. It was also found that the corresponding heat-transfer coefficient for this situation was $15\,J\,m^{-2}\,s^{-1}\,°C^{-1}$. Does this agree with the expected value from the Lewis relationship for the air/water system?

$h_c = 15\,J\,m^{-2}\,s^{-1}\,°C^{-1}$

$\quad = 1000 \times 0.0150$

$\quad = 1000 \times k'_g$ as the Lewis relationship predicts.

A convenient way to remember the inter-relationship is that the mass-transfer coefficient from a free water surface into air expressed in $g\,m^{-2}\,s^{-1}$ is numerically equal to the heat-transfer coefficient from the air to the surface expressed in $J\,m^{-2}\,s^{-1}\,°C^{-1}$.

Falling-rate Drying

The highest rate of drying is normally the constant-rate situation, then as drying proceeds the moisture content falls and the access of water from the interior of the food to the surface affects the rate and decreases it. The situation then is complex with moisture gradients controlling the observed drying rates. Actual rates can be measured, showing in the idealized case a constant rate continuing up to the critical moisture content and thereafter a declining rate as the food, on continued drying, approaches the equilibrium moisture content for the food. This is clearly shown by the drying curve of Fig. 7.7 and at low moisture contents the rates of drying become very low. The actual detail of such curves depends,

of course, on the specific material and conditions of the drying process.

Calculation of Drying Times

Drying rates, once determined experimentally or predicted from theory, can then be used to calculate drying times so that drying equipment and operations can be designed. In the most general cases, the drying rates vary throughout the dryer with time as drying proceeds, and with the changing moisture content of the material. So the situation is complicated. However, in many cases a simplified approach can provide useful results. One simplification is to assume that the temperature and RH of the drying air are constant.

In this case, for the constant-rate period, the time needed to remove the quantity of water which will reduce the food material to the critical moisture content X_c (that corresponding to the end of the constant-rate period and below which the drying rate falls) can be calculated by dividing this quantity by the rate.

$$\text{So } \theta = w(X_0 - X_f)/\left(\frac{dw}{d\theta}\right)_{const.} \quad (7.3)$$

where $\left(\frac{dw}{d\theta}\right)_{const.} = k'_g A(Y_s - Y_a)$

and X_0 is the initial moisture content and X_f the final moisture content $(= X_c$ in this case) both on a dry basis, w is the amount of dry material in the food and $(dw/d\theta)_{const.}$ is the constant-drying rate. Where the drying rate is reduced by a factor f then this is incorporated to give

$$\theta = W(X_0 - X_f)/f\left(\frac{dw}{d\theta}\right)_{const.} \quad (7.4)$$

and f therefore expresses the ratio of the actual drying rate to the maximum drying rate corresponding to the free surface-moisture situation.

EXAMPLE 7.17. For $100\,kg$ of food material with an initial water content of 80% on a wet basis and with a surface area of $12\,m^2$, estimate the time needed to dry to 50% moisture content on a wet basis assuming constant-rate drying in air at a temperature of $120°C$ dry bulb and $50°C$ wet bulb. Under the conditions in the dryer, measurements indicate the heat-transfer coefficient to the food surface from the air to be $18\,\mathrm{J\,m^{-2}\,s^{-1}\,{}^{\circ}C^{-1}}$.

From the data

$$X_0 = 0.8/(1 - 0.8) = 4\,\mathrm{kg\,kg^{-1}},$$
$$X_f = 0.5/(1 - 0.5) = 1\,\mathrm{kg\,kg^{-1}}$$

and from the psychrometric chart, $Y_s = 0.087$ and $Y_a = 0.054\,\mathrm{kg\,kg^{-1}}$.

Moisture content X	0.5		0.4		0.3		0.2		0.18		0.17
$w(X_1 - X_2)$			2		2		2		0.4		0.2
f			0.86		0.57		0.29		0.11		0.005
$\dfrac{1}{f\left(\dfrac{dw}{d\theta}\right)_{const.}}\left[= \dfrac{1}{f(7.128 \times 10^{-3})}\right]$			1.63×10^2		2.46×10^2		4.84×10^2		1.28×10^3		2.81×10^4
θ			326		492		968		512		5620

$\sum \theta$ $7918\,\mathrm{s} = 2.2\,\mathrm{h}$ (to remove 6.6 kg of water)
$\therefore$ total drying time $(2.3 + 2.2)\mathrm{h} = 4.5\,\mathrm{h}$.

From the Lewis relationship

$$k'_g = 18\,\mathrm{g\,m^{-2}\,s^{-1}} = 0.018\,\mathrm{kg\,m^{-2}\,s^{-1}}$$
$$w = 100(1 - 0.8) = 20\,\mathrm{kg}$$

$\therefore$ using eqn. (7.3)

$$\theta = 20(4 - 1)/[0.018 \times 12 \times (0.087 - 0.054)]$$
$$= 60/7.128 \times 10$$
$$= 8417\,\mathrm{s}$$
$$= 2.3\,\mathrm{h} \text{ (to remove 60 kg of water)}.$$

During the falling-rate period, the procedure outlined above can be extended, using the drying curve for the particular material and the conditions of the dryer. Sufficiently small differential quantities of moisture content to be removed have to be chosen, over which the drying rate is effectively constant, so as to give an accurate value of the total time. As the moisture content above the equilibrium level decreases so the drying rates decrease, and drying times become long.

EXAMPLE 7.18. Continuing Example 7.17, if for the particular food material, the critical moisture content, X_c, is 100% and the equilibrium moisture content under the conditions in the dryer is 15%, and if the drying curve is that illustrated in Fig. 7.7, estimate the total time to dry down to 17%, all moisture contents being on a dry basis.

Equation (7.4) can be applied, over small intervals of moisture content and multiplying the constant rate by the appropriate reduction factor (f) read off from Fig. 7.7. This can be set out in a table. Note the temperature and humidity of the air were assumed to be constant throughout the drying.

The example shows how as the moisture level descends toward the equilibrium value so the drying rate becomes slower and slower. In terms of the mass-transfer equations, the humidity or partial pressure driving force is tending to zero as the equilibrium moisture content is approached. In terms of the heat-transfer equations, the surface temperature has risen above the wet-bulb temperature once the surface ceases to behave as a wet surface and it climbs towards the dry-bulb temperature of the air as the moisture level continues to fall.

This calculation procedure can be applied to more complicated dryers, considering them as divided into sections, and applying the drying-rate equations and the input and output conditions to these sections sequentially to build up the whole situation in the dryer.

CONDUCTION DRYING

So far the drying considered has been by hot air. Other methods of drying which are quite commonly encountered are drying by contact with a hot surface, and a continuous version of this is the drum or roller dryer where the food is coated as a thin paste over the surface of a slowly revolving heated horizontal cylinder. In such a case, the food dries for as much of one revolution of the cylinder as is mechanically feasible, after which it is scraped off. The amount of drying is substantially controlled by the rate of heat transfer and estimates of the heat-transfer rate can be used for calculations of the extent of drying.

EXAMPLE 7.19. A drum dryer is being used to dry a starch-based breakfast food. The initial moisture content of the food is 75% on a wet basis, the drum surface temperature is 138°C and the estimated heat-transfer coefficient from the drum surface to the drying food is $800 \, J \, m^{-2} \, s^{-1} \, °C^{-1}$. Assume that the thickness of the food on the drum is 0.3 mm and the thermal conductivity of the food is $0.55 \, J \, m^{-1} \, s^{-1} \, °C^{-1}$. If the drum, 1 m diameter and 1 m in length, is rotating at 2 rev min^{-1} and the food occupies three-quarters of the circumference, estimate the moisture content of the film being scraped off. Assume the critical moisture content for the food material is 14% on a dry basis.

Initial moisture content = 75% wet basis

$$= 0.75/(1 - 0.75)$$
$$= 3 \, kg \, kg^{-1} \text{ dry basis.}$$

Total quantity of material on drum

$$= (\pi \times D \times 3/4) \times 1 \times 0.0003 \, m^3$$
$$= \pi \times 1 \times 3/4 \times 1 \times 0.0003$$
$$= 7.1 \times 10^{-4} \, m^3.$$

Assuming a density of the food paste of $1000 \, kg \, m^3$,

$$\therefore \quad \text{weight on drum} = 7.1 \times 10^{-4} \times 10^3$$
$$= 0.71 \, kg.$$

Overall resistance to heat transfer

$$1/U = 1/800 + 0.0003/0.55$$
$$= 1.25 \times 10^{-3} + 0.55 \times 10^{-3}$$
$$= 1.8 \times 10^{-3}.$$
$$\therefore \quad U = 556,$$
$$q = U A \, \Delta t$$
$$= 556 \times \pi \times D \times 1 \times 0.75 \times (138 - 100)$$
$$= 4.98 \times 10^4 \, J \, s^{-1}.$$

Latent heat of evaporation of water
$$= 2257 \, kJ \, kg^{-1},$$

$$\therefore \quad \text{rate of evaporation} = \frac{q}{\lambda}$$
$$= 0.022 \, kg \, s^{-1}.$$

Residence time of food on drum: at 2 rev min^{-1}, 1 revolution takes 30 s, but the material is on for 3/4 rev.

$$\therefore \quad \text{residence time} = (3/4) \times 30$$
$$= 22.5 \, sec.$$
$$\therefore \quad \text{water removed} = 22.5 \times 0.022$$
$$= 0.495 \, kg.$$

Initial quantity of water = $0.71 \times 3/4$
$$= 0.53 \, kg$$

and dry solids $= 0.71 \times 1/4 = 0.18 \, kg.$

$$\therefore \quad \text{Residual water} = (0.53 - 0.495)$$
$$= 0.035 \, kg.$$

$\therefore$ Water content (wet basis) remaining

$$= 0.035/(0.18 + 0.035) = 16\%.$$

DRYING EQUIPMENT

In an industry so diversified and extensive as the food industry, it would be expected that a great number of different types of dryer would be in use. This is the case and the total range of equipment is much too wide to be described in any introductory book such as this. The principles of drying may be applied to any type of dryer, but it should help the understanding of these principles if a few common types of dryers are described.

The major problem in calculations of real dryers is that conditions change as the drying air and the drying solids move along the dryer in a continuous dryer, or change with time in the batch dryer. Such implications take them beyond the scope of the present book, but the principles of mass and heat balances are the basis and the analysis is not difficult once the fundamental principles of drying are understood.

Tray Dryers

In tray dryers, the food is spread out, generally quite thinly, on trays in which the drying takes place. Heating may be by an air current sweeping across the trays, by conduction from heated trays or heated shelves on which the trays lie, or by radiation from heated surfaces. Most tray dryers are heated by air which also removes the vapours.

Tunnel Dryers

These may be regarded as developments of the tray dryer, in which the trays on trolleys move through a tunnel where the heat is applied and the vapours removed. In most cases, air is used in tunnel drying and the material can move through the dryer either parallel or countercurrent to the air flow.

Roller or Drum Dryers

In these the food is spread over the surface of a heated drum. The drum rotates, with the food being applied to the drum at one part of the cycle. The food remains on the drum surface for the greater part of the rotation, during which time the drying takes place, and is then scraped off. Drum drying may be regarded as conduction drying.

Fluidized Bed Dryers

In a fluidized bed dryer, the food material is maintained suspended against gravity in an upward-flowing air stream. There may also be a horizontal air flow to convey the food through the dryer. Heat is transferred from the air to the food material, mostly by convection.

Spray Dryers

In a spray dryer, liquid or fine solid material in a slurry is sprayed in the form of a fine dispersion into a current of heated air. Drying occurs very rapidly, so that this process is very useful for materials which are damaged by exposure to heat for any appreciable length of time. The dryer body is large so that the particles can settle, as they dry, without touching the walls on which they might otherwise stick.

Pneumatic Dryers

In a pneumatic dryer, the solid food particles are conveyed rapidly in an air stream, the velocity and turbulence of the stream maintaining the particles in suspension. Heated air accomplishes the drying and often some form of classifying device is included in the equipment. In the classifier, the dried material is separated, the dry material passes out as product and the moist remainder is recirculated for further drying.

Rotary Dryers

The foodstuff is contained in a horizontal inclined cylinder through which it travels, being heated either by air flow through the cylinder, or by conduction of heat from the cylinder walls. In some cases, the cylinder rotates and in others the cylinder is stationary and a paddle or screw rotates within the cylinder conveying the material through.

Trough Dryers

The materials to be dried are contained in a trough-shaped conveyor belt, made from mesh, and air is blown through the bed of material. The movement of the conveyor continually turns over the material, exposing fresh surfaces to the hot air.

Bin Dryers

In bin dryers, the foodstuff is contained in a bin with a perforated bottom through which warm air is blown vertically upwards, passing through the material and so drying it.

Belt Dryers

The food is spread as a thin layer on a horizontal mesh or solid belt and air passes through or over the material. In most cases the belt is moving, though in some designs the belt is stationary and the material is transported by scrapers.

Vacuum Dryers

Batch vacuum dryers are substantially the same as tray dryers, except that they operate under a vacuum, and heat transfer is by conduction or by radiation. The trays are enclosed in a large cabinet which is evacuated. The water vapour produced is generally condensed, so that the vacuum pumps have only to deal with non-condensible gases. Another type consists of an evacuated chamber containing a roller dryer.

Freeze Dryers

The material is held on shelves or belts in a chamber which is under high vacuum. In most cases, the food is frozen before being loaded into the dryer. Heat is transferred to the food by conduction or radiation and the vapour is removed by vacuum pump and then condensed. In one process, known as accelerated freeze drying, heat transfer is by conduction; sheets of expanded metal are inserted between the foodstuffs and heated plates to improve heat transfer and moisture removal. The pieces of food must be shaped so as to present the largest possible flat surface to the expanded metal and the plates to obtain good heat transfer. A refrigerated condenser may be used to condense the water vapour.

Various types of dryers are illustrated in Fig. 7.8.

MOISTURE LOSS IN FREEZERS AND CHILLERS

When a moist surface is cooled by an air flow, and if the air is unsaturated, water will evaporate from the surface to the air. This contributes to the heat

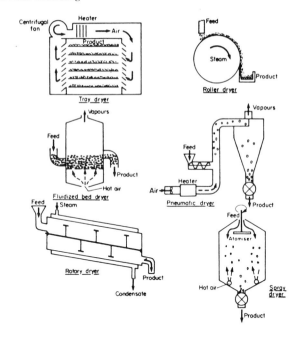

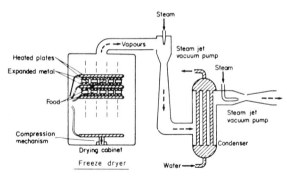

FIG. 7.8. Dryers.

transfer, but a more important effect is to decrease the weight of the foodstuff by the amount of water removed. The loss in weight has serious economic consequences, since food is most often sold by weight, and also in many foodstuffs the moisture loss may result in a less attractive surface appearance. To give some idea of the quantities involved, meat on cooling from animal body temperature to air temperature loses about 2 % of its weight, on freezing it may lose a further 1 % and thereafter if held in a freezer store it loses weight at a rate of about 0.25 % per month. After a time, this steady rate of loss in store falls off, but over the course of a year the total store loss may easily be of the order of 2–2.5 %.

To minimize these weight losses, the humidity of the air in freezers, chillers and stores and the rate of chilling and freezing, should be high. The design of the evaporator equipment can help if a relatively large coil area has been provided for the freezing or cooling duty. The large area means that the cooling demand can be accomplished with a small air-temperature drop. This may be seen from the standard equation

$$q = U A \, \Delta t \qquad (7.5)$$

For fixed q (determined by the cooling demand) and for fixed U (determined by the design of the freezer) a large A will mean a small Δt, and vice versa. Since the air leaving the coils will be nearly saturated with water vapour as it leaves, the larger the Δt the colder the air at this point, and the dryer it becomes. The dryer it becomes (the lower the RH) the greater its capacity for absorbing water from the meat. So a low Δt decreases the drying effect. The water then condenses from the air, freezes to ice on the coils and must be removed, from time to time, by defrosting. Similarly for fixed U and A, a large q means a large Δt, and therefore better insulation leading to a lower q will decrease weight losses.

SUMMARY

1. In drying:
   (a) the latent heat of vaporization must be supplied,
   (b) the moisture must be transported out from the food.

2. Rates of drying depend on:
   (a) vapour pressure of water at the drying temperature,
   (b) vapour pressure of water in the external environment,
   (c) the equilibrium vapour pressure of water in the food,
   (d) the moisture content of the food.

3. For most foods, drying proceeds initially at a constant rate given by:

$$\mathrm{d}w/\mathrm{d}\theta = k_g' A (Y_s - Y_a) = h_c A (t_a - t_s)/\lambda$$
$$= q/\lambda$$

for air drying. After a time the rate of drying decreases as the moisture content of the food reaches low values.

4. Air is saturated with water vapour when the partial pressure of water vapour in the air equals the saturation pressure of water vapour at the same temperature.

5. Humidity of air is the ratio of the weight of water vapour to the weight of the dry air in the same volume.

6. Relative humidity is the ratio of the actual to the saturation partial pressure of the water vapour at the air temperature.

7. Water vapour/air humidity relationships are shown on the psychrometric chart.

PROBLEMS

1. Cabbage containing 89 % of moisture is to be dried in air at 65°C down to a moisture content on a dry basis of 5 %. Calculate the heat energy required per tonne of raw cabbage and per tonne of dried cabbage, for the drying. Ignore the sensible heat.

2. The efficiency of a spray dryer is given by the ratio of the heat energy in the hot air supplied to the dryer and actually used for drying, divided by the heat energy supplied to heat the air from its original ambient temperature. Calculate the efficiency of a spray dryer with an inlet air temperature of 150°C, an outlet temperature of 95°C, operating under an ambient air temperature of 15°C. Suggest how the efficiency of this dryer might be raised.

3. Calculate the humidity of air at a temperature of 65°C and in which the RH is 42 % and check from a psychrometric chart.

4. Water at 36°C is to be cooled in an evaporative cooler by air which is at a temperature of 18°C and in which the RH is measured to be 43 %. Calculate the minimum temperature to which the air could be cooled, and if the air is cooled to 5°C above this temperature, what is the actual cooling effected. Check your results on a psychrometric chart.

5. In a chiller store for fruit, which is to be maintained at 5°C, it is important to maintain a daily record of the relative humidity. A wet- and dry-bulb thermometer is available so prepare a chart giving the relative humidity for the store in terms of the wet-bulb depression.

6. A steady stream of 1300 m³ h⁻¹ of room air at 16°C and 65 % RH is to be heated to 150°C to be used for drying. Calculate the heat input required to accomplish this. If the air leaves the dryer at 92°C and at 98 % RH calculate the quantity of water removed per hour by the dryer.

7. In a particular situation, the heat-transfer coefficient from a food material to air has been measured and found to be 25 J m⁻² s⁻¹ °C⁻¹. If this material is to be dried in air at 90°C and 15 % RH, estimate the maximum rate of water removal.

8. Considering apples to be spheres of diameter 0.07 m and of density 960 kg m⁻³, estimate the rate of drying of apples, per cent per week, if they are in air at 12°C and 65 % RH flowing over the apples at 0.5 m s⁻¹.

9. Assume that the food material from worked Example 7.17 is
   to be dried in air at 130°C with a relative humidity of 8 % and
   that under these conditions the equilibrium moisture content
   in the food is 11 %. Estimate the time required to dry from
   400 % down to 12 %, taking it that constant-rate drying
   obtains down to a 50 % moisture content, all moistures being
   measured on a dry basis.

CHAPTER 8

EVAPORATION

FREQUENTLY in the food industry a raw material or a potential foodstuff contains more water than is required in the final product. When the foodstuff is a liquid, the easiest method of removing the water, in general, is to apply heat to evaporate it. Evaporation is thus a process which is often used by the food technologist.

The basic factors which affect the rate of evaporation are:

(a) the rate at which heat can be transferred to the liquid,

(b) the quantity of heat required to evaporate each kg of water,

(c) the maximum allowable temperature of the liquid,

(d) the pressure at which the evaporation takes place,

(e) any changes which may occur in the foodstuff during the course of the evaporation process.

Considered as a piece of process plant, the evaporator has two principal functions, to exchange heat and to separate the vapour that is formed from the liquid. Important practical considerations in evaporators are:

(a) the maximum allowable temperature, which may be substantially below 100°C.

(b) the promotion of circulation of the liquid across the heat-transfer surfaces, to attain reasonably high heat-transfer coefficients and to prevent any local overheating,

(c) the viscosity of the fluid which will often increase substantially as the concentration of the dissolved materials increases,

(d) any tendency to foam which makes separation of liquid and vapour difficult.

THE SINGLE-EFFECT EVAPORATOR

The typical evaporator is made up of three functional sections: the heat exchanger, the evaporating section, where the liquid boils and evaporates, and the separator in which the vapour leaves the liquid and passes off to the condenser or to other equipment. In many evaporators, all three sections are contained in a single vertical cylinder. In the centre of the cylinder there is a steam-heating section, with pipes passing through it in which the evaporating liquors rise. At the top of the cylinder, there are baffles which allow the vapours to escape but check liquid droplets which may accompany the vapours from the liquid surface. A diagram of this type of evaporator, which may be called the conventional evaporator, is given in Fig. 8.1.

In the heat-exchanger section, called a calandria in this type of evaporator, steam condenses in the jacket and the liquid being evaporated boils on the inside of the tubes and in the space above the upper tube plate. The resistance to heat flow is imposed by the steam and liquid film coefficients and by the material of the tube walls. The circulation of the liquid greatly affects evaporation rates, but circulation rates and patterns are very difficult to predict in any detail. Values of overall heat-transfer coefficients that have been reported for evaporators are of the order of $1800-5000 \, \text{J m}^{-2} \text{s}^{-1} {}^{\circ}\text{C}^{-1}$ for the evaporation of distilled water in a vertical-tube evaporator with heat supplied by condensing steam. However, with dissolved solids, in increasing quantities as evaporation proceeds leading to increased viscosity and poorer circulation, heat-transfer coefficients in practice may be much lower than this.

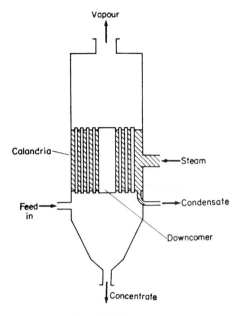

Vapour

Calandria

Steam

Feed in

Condensate

Downcomer

Concentrate

FIG. 8.1. Evaporator.

As evaporation proceeds, the remaining liquors become more concentrated and because of this the boiling temperatures rise. The rise in the temperature of boiling reduces the available temperature drop, assuming no change in the heat source. And so the total rate of heat transfer will drop accordingly. Also, the viscosity of the liquid will increase, often quite substantially, and this affects circulation and the heat-transfer coefficients leading again to lower rates of boiling. Yet another complication is that measured, overall, heat-transfer coefficients have been found to vary with the actual temperature drop, so that the design of an evaporator on theoretical grounds is inevitably subject to wide margins of uncertainty.

Perhaps because of this uncertainty, evaporator designs have tended to follow traditional patterns of which the calandria type of Fig. 8.1 is a typical example.

Vacuum Evaporation

For the evaporation of liquids which are affected by high temperatures, it may be necessary to reduce the temperature of boiling by operating under reduced pressure. The relationship between vapour pressure and boiling temperature, for water, is shown in Fig. 7.1. When the vapour pressure of the liquid reaches the pressure of its surroundings, the liquid boils. The reduced pressures required to boil the liquor at lower temperatures are obtained by mechanical, or steam jet ejector, vacuum pumps, combined generally with condensers for the vapours from the evaporator. Mechanical vacuum pumps are generally cheaper in running costs but more expensive in terms of capital than are steam jet ejectors. The condensed liquid can either be pumped from the system or discharged through a barometric column in which a static column of liquid balances the atmospheric pressure. Vacuum pumps are then left to deal with the non-condensibles, which of course are much less in volume but still have to be discharged to the atmosphere.

Heat Transfer in Evaporators

Heat transfer in evaporators is governed by the equations for heat transfer to boiling liquids and by the convection and conduction equations. The heat must be provided from a source at a suitable temperature and this is condensing steam in most cases. The steam comes either directly from a boiler or from a previous stage of evaporation in another evaporator. Major objections to other forms of heating, such as direct firing or electric resistance heaters, arise because of the need to avoid local high temperatures and because of the high costs in the case of electricity. In some cases the temperatures of condensing steam may be too high for the product and warm water may be used. Low-pressure steam can also be used but the large volumes create design problems.

Calculations on evaporators can be carried out combining mass and energy balances with the principles of heat transfer.

EXAMPLE 8.1. A single-effect evaporator is required to concentrate a solution from 10% solids to 30% solids at the rate of 250 kg of feed per hour. If the pressure in the evaporator is 77 kPa absolute, and if steam is available at 200 kPa gauge, calculate the quantity of steam required per hour and the area of heat-transfer surface if the overall heat-transfer coefficient is $1700\,\mathrm{J\,m^{-2}\,s^{-1}\,{}^\circ C^{-1}}$. Assume that the temperature of the feed is 18°C and that the boiling point of the solution under the pressure of 77 kPa absolute is 91°C. Assume, also, that the specific heat of the solution is the same as for water, that is $4.186 \times 10^3\,\mathrm{J\,kg^{-1}}$, and the latent heat of vaporization of the solution is the same as that for water under the same conditions.

From steam tables, the condensing temperature of steam at 200 kPa (g) is 134°C and latent heat $2164\,\mathrm{kJ\,kg^{-1}}$, and latent heat at 77 kPa (abs.) is $2281\,\mathrm{kJ\,kg^{-1}}$ and condensing temperature 91°C.

Mass balance (kg h^{-1})

	Solids	Liquids	Total
Feed	25	225	250
Product	25	58	83
Evaporation			167

Heat balance

Heat available per kg of steam

= latent heat + sensible heat

in cooling to 91°C

$= 2.164 \times 10^6 + 4.186 \times 10^3 (134 - 91)$

$= 2.164 \times 10^6 + 1.8 \times 10^5$

$= 2.34 \times 10^6$ J.

Heat required by the solution

= latent heat + sensible heat in
heating from 18°C to 91°C

$= 2281 \times 10^3 \times 167 + 250 \times 4.186 \times 10^3$

$\times (91 - 18)$

$= 3.81 \times 10^8 + 7.6 \times 10^7$

$= 4.57 \times 10^8$ J.

Now, heat from steam = heat required by the solution,

∴ quantity of steam required per hour

$= (4.57 \times 10^8)/(2.34 \times 10^6)$

$= 195\,\mathrm{kg\,h^{-1}}$ of steam,

∴ quantity of steam/kg of water evaporated

$= 195/167$

$= 1.17$ kg steam/kg water.

Heat-transfer area

Temperature of condensing steam = 134°C.

Temperature difference across the evaporator $= (134 - 91) = 43°C$.

Writing the heat-transfer equation for q in joules/sec,

$$q = UA\,\Delta t,$$

$$(4.57 \times 10^8)/3600 = 1700 \times A \times 43,$$

$$\therefore \quad A = 1.74\,\mathrm{m^2}.$$

Condensers

In evaporators, which are working under reduced pressure, the vacuum pump is often preceded by a condenser to remove the bulk of the volume of the vapours by condensing them to a liquid. Condensers for the vapour may be either surface or jet condensers. Surface condensers provide sufficient heat-transfer surface, pipes for example, through which the condensing vapour transfers latent heat of vaporization to cooling water circulating through the pipes. In a jet condenser, the vapours are mixed with a stream of condenser water sufficient in quantity to transfer latent heat from the vapours.

EXAMPLE 8.2. How much water would be required in a jet condenser to condense the vapours from an evaporator evaporating $5000\,\mathrm{kg\,h^{-1}}$ of water under a vacuum of 6 cm of mercury? The condensing water is available at 18°C and the highest allowable temperature for water discharged from the condenser is 35°C.

Heat balance

The pressure in the evaporator is 15 cm mercury $= Z\rho g = 0.15 \times 13.6 \times 1000 \times 9.81 = 20\,\mathrm{kPa}$. From Steam Tables, the condensing temperature of water under pressure of 20 kPa is 60°C and the corresponding latent heat of vaporization is $2358\,\mathrm{kJ\,kg^{-1}}$.

Heat removed from condensate

$= 2358 \times 10^3 + (60 - 35) \times 4.186 \times 10^3$

$= 2.46 \times 10^6\,\mathrm{J\,kg^{-1}}$.

Heat taken by cooling water

$$= (35 - 18) \times 4.186 \times 10^3$$
$$= 7.1 \times 10^4 \, \text{J kg}^{-1}.$$

Quantity of heat required by condensate per hour

$$= 5000 \times 2.46 \times 10^6 \, \text{J},$$

∴   quantity of cooling water per hour

$$= (5000 \times 2.46 \times 10^6)/7.1 \times 10^4$$
$$= 1.7 \times 10^5 \, \text{kg}.$$

EXAMPLE 8.3. What heat-exchange area would be required for a surface condenser working under the same conditions as the jet condenser in Example 8.3, assuming a U value of $2270 \, \text{J m}^{-2} \text{s}^{-1} \, ^\circ\text{C}^{-1}$, and disregarding any sub-cooling of the liquid. The temperature differences are small so that the arithmetic mean temperature can be used for the heat exchanger (condenser). The mean temperature difference equals

$$(60 - 18)/2 + (60 - 35)/2 = 33.5^\circ\text{C}.$$

Since, from the previous problem, and remembering to put time in hours,

$$2.46 \times 10^6 \times 5000 = 2270 \times A \times 33.5 \times 3600,$$
$$\therefore \quad A = 45 \, \text{m}^2$$

and this would be a large condenser so that the jet condenser is often preferred.

MULTIPLE-EFFECT EVAPORATION

An evaporator is essentially a heat exchanger in which a liquid is boiled to give a vapour, so that it is also a low-pressure steam generator. It may be possible to make use of this, to treat an evaporator as a low-pressure boiler, and to make use of the steam produced for further heating in another evaporator, called another effect.

Consider two evaporators connected so that the vapour line from one is connected to the steam chest of the other as shown in Fig. 8.2, making up a two-effect evaporator.

If liquid is to be evaporated in each effect, and if the boiling point of this liquid is unaffected by the

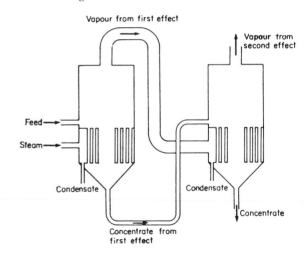

FIG. 8.2. Double effect evaporator — forward feed.

solute concentration, then writing a heat balance for the first evaporator,

$$q_1 = U_1 A_1 (t_s - t_1) = U_1 A_1 \Delta t_1 \qquad (8.1)$$

where q_1 is the rate of heat transfer, U_1 is the overall heat transfer coefficient in evaporator 1, A_1 is the heat-transfer area in evaporator 1, t_s is the temperature of condensing steam from the boiler, t_1 is the boiling temperature of the liquid in evaporator 1 and Δt_1 is the temperature difference in evaporator 1, $= (t_s - t_1)$.

Similarly, in the second evaporator, remembering that the "steam" in the second is the vapour from the first evaporator and that this will condense at approximately the same temperature as it boiled, since pressure changes are small,

$$q_2 = U_2 A_2 (t_1 - t_2) = U_2 A_2 \Delta t_2,$$

in which the subscripts 2 indicate the conditions in the second evaporator.

If the evaporators are working in balance, then all of the vapours from the first effect are condensing and in their turn evaporating vapours in the second effect. Also, if heat losses can be neglected, if there is no appreciable boiling-point elevation of the more concentrated solution and if the feed is supplied at its boiling point,

$$q_1 = q_2.$$

Further, if the evaporators are so constructed that $A_1 = A_2$, the foregoing equations can be combined.

$$\therefore \quad U_2/U_1 = \Delta t_1/\Delta t_2. \tag{8.2}$$

Equation (8.2) states that the temperature differences are inversely proportional to the overall heat-transfer coefficients in the two effects. This analysis may be extended to any number of effects operated in series in this way.

Feeding of Multiple-effect Evaporators

In a two-effect evaporator, the temperature in the steam chest is higher in the first than in the second effect. In order that the steam provided by the evaporation in the first effect will boil off liquid in the second effect, the boiling temperature in the second effect must be lower and so that effect must be under lower pressure.

Consequently, the pressure in the second effect must be reduced below that in the first. In some cases, the first effect may be at a pressure above atmospheric, or the first effect may be at atmospheric pressure; the second and subsequent effects have therefore to be under increasingly lower pressures. Often many of the later effects are under vacuum. Under these conditions, the liquid-feed progress is simplest if it passes from effect one to effect two, to effect three, and so on, as in these circumstances the feed will flow without pumping. This is called forward feed. It means that the most concentrated liquids will occur in the last effect. Alternatively, feed may pass in the reverse direction, starting in the last effect and proceeding to the first, but in this case the liquid has to be pumped from one effect to the next against the pressure drops. This is called backward feed and because the concentrated viscous liquids can be handled at the highest temperatures in the first effects it usually offers larger evaporation capacity than forward-feed systems, but it may be disadvantageous from the viewpoint of product quality.

Advantages of Multiple-effect Evaporators

At first sight, it may seem that the multiple-effect evaporator has all the advantages, the heat is used over and over again and we appear to be getting the evaporation in the second and subsequent effects for nothing. Closer examination shows, however, that there is a price to be paid for the heat economy.

In the first effect, $q_1 = U_1 A_1 \Delta t_1$ and in the second effect, $q_2 = U_2 A_2 \Delta t_2$. We shall now consider a single-effect evaporator, working under the same pressure as the first effect $q_s = U_s A_s \Delta t_s$, where subscript s indicates the single-effect evaporator. Also, since the overall conditions are the same $\Delta t_s = \Delta t_1 + \Delta t_2$, as the overall temperature drop is between the steam-condensing temperature in the first effect and the evaporating temperature in the second effect. Each successive steam chest in the multiple-effect evaporator condenses at the same temperature as that at which the previous effect is evaporating. Now, consider the case in which $U_1 = U_2 = U_s$, and $A_1 = A_2$. The problem then becomes to find A_s for the single-effect evaporator which will evaporate the same quantity as the two effects.

From the given conditions and from eqn. (8.2),

$$\Delta t_1 = \Delta t_2$$

and $$\Delta t_s = \Delta t_1 + \Delta t_2 = 2\Delta t_1,$$

$$\therefore \quad \Delta t_1 = 0.5\Delta t_s$$

Now, $$q_1 + q_2 = U_1 A_1 \Delta t_1 + U_2 A_2 \Delta t_2$$
$$= U(A_1 + A_2)\Delta t_s/2$$

but $$q_1 + q_2 = q_s$$

and $$q_s = U A_s \Delta t_s$$

so that, $(A_1 + A_2)/2 = 2A_1/2 = A_s.$

That is, $A_1 = A_2 = A_s.$

The analysis shows that if the same total quantity is to be evaporated, then the heat-transfer surface of each of the two effects must be the same as that for a single-effect evaporator working between the same overall conditions. The analysis can be extended to cover any number of effects and leads to the same conclusions. In multiple-effect evaporators, steam economy has to be paid for by increased capital costs of the evaporators. Since the heat-transfer areas are generally equal in the various effects and since in a sense what you are buying in an evaporator is suitable heat-transfer surface, the n effects will cost approximately n times as much as a single effect.

Comparative costs of the auxiliary equipment do not altogether follow the same pattern. Condenser requirements are less for multiple-effect evaporators. The condensation duty is distributed between the steam chests of the effects, except for the first one, and so condenser and cooling-water requirements will be less. The optimum design of evaporation plant must then be based on a balance between operating costs which are lower for multiple effects, because of their reduced steam consumption, and capital charges which will be lower for fewer evaporators. The comparative operating costs are illustrated by the figures in Table 8.1 based on data from Grosse and Duffield (1954).

TABLE 8.1
STEAM CONSUMPTION AND RUNNING COSTS OF EVAPORATORS

Number of effects	Steam consumption (kg steam/kg water evaporated)	Total running cost (relative to a single-effect evaporator)
One	1.1	1
Two	0.57	0.52
Three	0.40	0.37

EXAMPLE 8.4. Estimate the requirements of steam and heat-transfer surface, and the evaporating temperatures in each effect, for a triple effect evaporator evaporating $500 \, \text{kg h}^{-1}$ of a 10% solution up to a 30% solution. Steam is available at $200 \, \text{kPa}$ gauge and the pressure in the evaporation space in the final effect is $60 \, \text{kPa}$ absolute. Assume that the overall heat-transfer coefficients are 2270, 2000 and $1420 \, \text{J m}^{-2} \text{s}^{-1} {}^{\circ}\text{C}^{-1}$ in the first, second and third effects respectively. Neglect sensible-heat effects and assume no boiling-point elevation, and equal heat transfer in each effect.

Mass balance (kg h^{-1})

	Solids	Liquids	Total
Food	50	450	500
Product	50	117	167
Evaporation			333

Heat balance

From steam tables, the condensing temperature of steam at $200 \, \text{kPa}$ (g) is 134°C and the latent heat is $2164 \, \text{kJ/kg}^{-1}$. Evaporating temperature in final

effect under pressure of $60 \, \text{kPa}$ (abs.) is 86°C, as there is no boiling-point rise and latent heat is $2294 \, \text{kJ/kg}$.

Equating the heat transfer in each effect:

$$q_1 = q_2 = q_3,$$
$$\therefore \quad U_1 A_1 \, \Delta t_1 = U_2 A_2 \, \Delta t_2 = U_3 A_3 \, \Delta t_3$$

and $\Delta t_1 + \Delta t_2 + \Delta t_3 = (134 - 86) = 48^{\circ}\text{C}$.

Now, if $A_1 = A_2 = A_3$

then $\Delta t_2 = \Delta t_1 U_1 / U_2$ and $\Delta t_3 = \Delta t_1 U_1 / U_3$

so that $\Delta t_1 (1 + U_1 / U_2 + U_1 / U_3) = 48$,

$$\therefore \quad \Delta t_1 \times [1 + (2270/2000) +$$
$$(2270/1420)] = 3.73 \, \Delta t_1$$
$$= 48,$$
$$\therefore \quad \Delta t_1 = 12.9^{\circ}\text{C},$$
$$\therefore \quad \Delta t_2 = \Delta t_1 \times (2270/2000) = 14.6$$

and $\Delta t_3 = \Delta t_1 \times (2270/1420) = 20.6$

and so the evaporating temperature in the first effect is $(134 - 12.9) = 121^{\circ}\text{C}$, and the latent heat (from Steam Tables) $2200 \, \text{kJ kg}^{-1}$. That in the second effect is $(121 - 14.5) = 106.5^{\circ}\text{C}$, latent heat $2240 \, \text{kJ kg}^{-1}$, and in the third effect $(106.5 - 20.6) = 86^{\circ}\text{C}$, latent heat $2294 \, \text{kJ kg}^{-1}$.

Equating the quantities evaporated in each effect and neglecting the sensible heat changes, if w_1, w_2, w_3 are the respective quantities evaporated in effects 1, 2 and 3, and w_s, is the quantity of steam condensed per hour in effect 1, then

$$w_1 \times 2200 \times 10^3 = w_2 \times 2240 \times 10^3$$
$$= w_3 \times 2294 \times 10^3$$
$$= w_s \times 2164 \times 10^3.$$

The sum of the quantities evaporated in each effect must equal the total evaporated in all three effects so that

$w_1 + w_2 + w_3 = 333$ and solving as above,

$$\therefore \quad w_1 = 113 \quad w_2 = 111 \quad w_3 = 108$$
$$w_s = 115.$$

Steam consumption

It required $115 \, \text{kg}$ steam (w_s) to evaporate a total of $333 \, \text{kg}$ water, that is $0.35 \, \text{kg}$ steam/kg water evaporated.

Heat exchanger surface.

Writing a heat balance on the first effect:

$(113 \times 2200 \times 1000)/3600 = 2270 \times A \times 12.9,$

$\therefore \quad A_1 = 2.4\,\mathrm{m}^2 = A_2 = A_3,$

$\therefore \quad \text{total area} = A_1 + A_2 + A_3 = 7.2\,\mathrm{m}^2.$

Note that the conditions of this example are considerably simplified, in that sensible heat and feed heating effects are neglected, and no boiling-point rise occurs. The general method remains the same in the more complicated cases, but it is often easier to solve the heat-balance equations by trial and error rather than by analytical methods, refining the approximations as far as necessary.

VAPOUR RECOMPRESSION

In addition to the possibility of taking the steam from one effect and using it in the steam chest of another, a further possibility for economy of steam is to take the vapour and, after compressing it, return it to the steam chest of the evaporator from which it was evaporated. The compression can be effected either by using some fresh steam, at a suitably high pressure, in a jet pump, or by mechanical compressors. The use of jet ejectors is the more common. By this means a proportion of the vapours are re-used, together with fresh steam, and so considerable overall steam economy achieved by reusing the latent heat of the vapours over again. The price to be paid for the recompression is in the pressure drop of the fresh steam which may be wasted through a reducing valve in any case, or in the mechanical energy expended in mechanical compressors. Vapour recompression is similar in many ways to the use of multiple effects. The available temperature in the fresh steam is reduced before use for evaporation and so additional heat-exchange surface has to be provided: roughly one stage equals one extra effect.

The steam economy of an evaporator is also affected by the temperature of the feed. If the feed is not at its boiling point, heat has to be used in raising it to this temperature. A convenient source of this feed pre-heat may be in the vapours from a single effect evaporator and a separate feed pre-heater can be used for this purpose.

BOILING-POINT ELEVATION

As evaporation proceeds, the liquor remaining in the evaporator becomes more concentrated and its boiling point will rise. The extent of the boiling-point elevation depends upon the nature of the material being evaporated and upon the concentration changes that are produced. The extent of the rise can be predicted by Raoult's Law which leads to

$$\Delta t = kx \qquad (8.3)$$

where Δt is the boiling point elevation, x is the mole fraction of the solute and k is a constant of proportionality. In multiple-effect evaporators, where the effects are fed in series, the boiling points will rise from one effect to the next as the concentrations rise. Relatively less of the apparent temperature drops are available for heat transfer, although boiling points are higher, as the condensing temperature of the vapour in the steam chest of the next effect is still that of the pure vapour. Boiling-point elevation complicates evaporator analysis but heat balances can still be drawn up along the lines indicated previously. Often food-stuffs are made up from large molecules in solution, in which boiling-point elevation can be ignored.

As the concentrations rise, the viscosity of the liquor also rises. The increase in the viscosity of the liquor affects the heat transfer and it often imposes a limit on the extent of evaporation that is practicable.

There is no straightforward method of predicting the extent of the boiling-point elevation in the concentrated solutions that are met in some evaporators in practical situations. Many liquors have their boiling points at some concentrations tabulated in the literature, and these can be extended by the use of a relationship known as Duhring's rule. Duhring's rule states that the ratio of the temperatures at which two solutions exert the same vapour pressure is constant. Thus, if we take the vapour pressure–temperature relation of a reference liquid, usually water, and if we know two points on the vapour pressure–temperature curve of the solution that is being evaporated, the boiling points of the solution to be evaporated at various pressures can be read off from the diagram called a Duhring plot. The Duhring plot will give the boiling point of solutions of various concentrations by interpolation, and at various pressures by proceeding along a line of constant composition. A Duhring plot of the boiling points of sodium chloride solutions is given in Fig. 8.3.

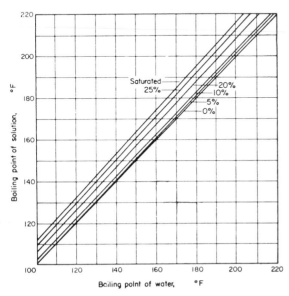

FIG. 8.3. Dühring plot for boiling point of sodium chloride solutions.

EXAMPLE 8.5. It is found that a saturated solution of sodium chloride in water boils under atmospheric pressure at 109°C. Under a total pressure of 25.4 kPa, water boils at 65.6°C and saturated sodium chloride at 73.3°C. From these, draw a Duhring plot for saturated salt solution and, knowing the vapour pressure–temperature relationship for water from Fig. 7.2, find the boiling temperature of saturated salt solution under a total pressure of 33.3 kPa.

The Duhring plot for salt solution has been given in Fig. 8.3, and since the line is straight it may be seen that knowledge of two points on it, and the corresponding boiling points for the reference substance, water, would enable the line to be drawn. From the line, and using Fig. 7.2 again to find that the boiling point of water under a pressure of

33.3 kPa is 71.7°C, we can read off the corresponding boiling temperature for saturated salt solution as 79.4°C.

By finding the boiling points of salt solutions of various concentrations under two pressures, the Duhring lines can then, also, be filled in for solutions of these concentrations. Such lines are also on Fig. 8.3. Intermediate concentrations can be estimated by interpolation and so the complete range of boiling points at any desired concentration, and under any given pressure, can be determined.

Latent heats of vaporization also increase as pressures are reduced, as shown for water in Table 7.1. Methods for determining these changes can be found in the literature, for example in Perry (1973).

EVAPORATION OF HEAT-SENSITIVE MATERIALS

In evaporators which have large volumes into which incoming feed is mixed, the retention time of a given food particle may be considerable. The average retention time can be obtained simply, by dividing the volume of the evaporator by the feed rate, but a substantial proportion of the liquor remains for much longer than this. Thus with heat-sensitive materials a proportion may deteriorate and lead to general lowering of product quality.

This difficulty is overcome in modern high flow-rate evaporators in which there is a low hold-up volume and in which little or no mixing occurs. Examples are long-tube evaporators, plate evaporators, and the various scraped-plate thin-film evaporators.

EXAMPLE 8.6. Tomato juice is to be concentrated from 12% solids to 28% solids in a climbing film evaporator, 3 m high and 4 cm diameter. The maximum allowable temperature for tomato juice is 57°C. The juice is fed to the evaporator at 57°C and at this temperature the latent heat of vaporization is 2366 kJ kg^{-1}. Steam is used in the jacket of the evaporator at a pressure of 170 kPa (gauge). If the overall heat-transfer coefficient is 6000 J m^{-2} s^{-1} °C^{-1}, estimate the quantity of tomato juice feed per hour. Take heating surface as 3 m × 0.04 m diameter.

Mass balance: basis 100-kg feed

	Solids	Liquids	Total
Food	12	88	100
Product	12	31	43
Evaporation			57

Heat balance

Area of evaporator tube πDH

$$= \pi \times 0.04 \times 3$$
$$= 0.38 \, \text{m}^2.$$

Condensing steam temperature at $170 \, \text{kPa} = 115°\text{C}$ from Steam Tables. Making a heat balance across the evaporator

$$q = UA \, \Delta t$$
$$= 6000 \times 0.38 \times (115 - 57)$$
$$= 1.32 \times 10^5 \, \text{J s}^{-1}.$$

Heat required per kg of feed for evaporation

$$= 0.57 \times 2366 \times 103$$
$$= 1.34 \times 10^6 \, \text{J},$$

$\therefore$ quantity evaporated $= (1.32 \times 10^5)/$
$$1.34 \times 10^6$$
$$= 0.1 \, \text{kg s}^{-1},$$

$\therefore$ rate of evaporation $= 360 \, \text{kg h}^{-1}.$

EVAPORATION EQUIPMENT

Open Pans

The most elementary form of evaporator consists of an open pan in which the liquid is boiled. Heat can be supplied through a steam jacket, or through coils, and scrapers or paddles may be fitted to provide agitation. Such evaporators are simple and low in capital cost, but they are expensive in their running costs as heat economy is poor.

Horizontal-tube Evaporators

The horizontal-tube evaporator is a development of the open pan in which the pan is closed in, generally in a vertical cylinder. The heating tubes are arranged in a horizontal bundle immersed in the liquid at the bottom of the cylinder. Liquid circulation is rather poor in this type of evaporator.

Vertical-tube Evaporators

By using vertical, rather than horizontal tubes, the natural circulation of the heated liquid can be made to give good heat transfer. The standard evaporator, shown in Fig. 8.1, is an example of this type. Recirculation of the liquid is through a large "downcomer" so that the liquors rise through the vertical tubes about 5–8 cm diameter, boil in the space just above the upper tube plate and recirculate through the downcomers. The hydrostatic head reduces boiling on the lower tubes which are covered by the circulating liquid. The length to diameter ratio of the tubes is of the order of 15:1. The basket evaporator shown in Fig. 8.4(a) is a variant of the calandria evaporator in which the

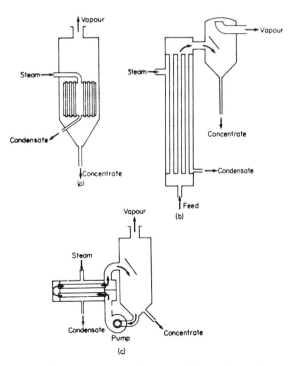

FIG. 8.4. Evaporators: (a) basket type, (b) long tube, (c) forced circulation.

steam chest is contained in a basket suspended in the lower part of the evaporator, and recirculation occurs through the annular space round the basket.

Plate Evaporators

The plate heat exchanger can be adapted for use as an evaporator. The spacings can be increased between the plates and appropriate passages provided so that the much larger volume of the vapours, when compared with the liquid, can be accommodated. Plate evaporators can provide good heat transfer and also ease of cleaning.

Long-tube Evaporators

Tall slender vertical tubes may be used for evaporators as shown in Fig. 8.4(b). The tubes, which have a length to diameter ratio of the order of 100:1, pass vertically upward inside the steam chest. The liquid may either pass down through the tubes, called a falling-film evaporator, or be carried up by the evaporating liquor in which case it is called a climbing-film evaporator. Evaporation occurs on the walls of the tubes. Because circulation rates are high and the surface films are thin, good conditions are obtained for the concentration of heat-sensitive liquids due to high heat-transfer rates and short heating times.

Generally, the liquid is not recirculated, and if sufficient evaporation does not occur in one pass, the liquid is fed to another pass. In the climbing-film evaporator, slugs of vapour form as the liquid boils on the inside of the tube and this vapour carries up the remaining liquid which continues to boil. Tube diameters are of the order of 2.5 to 5 cm, contact times may be as low as 5–10 sec. Overall heat-transfer coefficients may be up to five times as great as from a heated surface immersed in a boiling liquid. In the falling-film type, the tube diameters are rather greater, about 8 cm, and these are specifically suitable for viscous liquids.

Forced-circulation Evaporators

The heat-transfer coefficients from condensing steam are high, so that the major resistance to heat flow in an evaporator is usually in the liquid film. Tubes are generally made of metals with a high thermal conductivity, though scale formation may occur on the tubes to reduce the tube conductance. The liquid-film coefficients can be increased by improving the circulation of the liquid and by increasing its velocity of flow across the heating surfaces. Pumps, or impellers, can be fitted in the liquid circuit to help with this. Using pump circulation, the heat-exchange surface can be divorced from the boiling and separating sections of the evaporator, as shown in Fig. 8.4(c). Alternatively, impeller blades may be inserted into flow passages such as the downcomer of a calandria-type evaporator. Forced circulation is used particularly with viscous liquids. It may also be worth consideration for expensive heat-exchange surfaces when these are required because of corrosion or hygiene requirements. In this case it pays to obtain the greatest possible heat flow through each square metre of heat-exchange surface.

Coming also under the heading of forced-circulation evaporators are various scraped surface and agitated film evaporators. In one type the material to be evaporated passes down over the interior walls of a heated cylinder and it is scraped by rotating scraper blades to maintain a thin film, high heat transfer and a short and controlled residence time exposed to heat.

Evaporation for Heat-sensitive Liquids

Many food products with volatile flavour constituents retain more of these if they are evaporated under conditions favouring short contract times with the hot surfaces. This can be achieved for solutions of low viscosity by climbing- and falling-film evaporators either tubular or plate types. As the viscosities increase, for example at higher concentrations, mechanical transport across heated surfaces is used to advantage and methods include mechanically scraped surfaces, and the flow of the solutions over heated spinning surfaces. Under such conditions residence times can be fractions of a minute and when combined with a pressure vacuum as low as can reasonably be maintained, volatile retention can be maximized.

SUMMARY

1. Heat and material balances are the basis for evaporator calculations.

2. The rate of boiling is governed by the heat-transfer equations.

3. For multiple effect evaporators, i.e. two or more evaporators used in series, $q_1 = q_2$,

$$U_1 A_1 \Delta t_1 = U_2 A_2 \Delta t_2$$

and if A_1 and A_2 are equal $\dfrac{U_2}{U_1} = \dfrac{\Delta t_1}{\Delta t_2}$.

4. Multiple-effect evaporators use less heat than single-effect evaporators; for an n-effect evaporator, the steam requirement is approximately $1/n$, but require more heat-exchange surface, the heat-exchange surface is approximately n times. From the energy viewpoint evaporators can be very much more efficient than dryers.

5. Condensers on an evaporator must provide sufficient cooling to condense all water vapour from the evaporator. Condenser calculations are based on the heat-transfer equation.

6. Boiling-point elevation in evaporators can be determined using Duhring's rule that the ratio of the temperatures at which two solutions exert the same pressure is constant.

7. Special provisions including short residence times and low pressures to give low boiling points are necessary if the maximum retention of volatile constituents is important, and to handle heat-sensitive materials.

PROBLEMS

1. A single-effect evaporator is to produce a 35% solids tomato concentrate from a 6% solids raw juice. The pressure in the evaporator is 20 kPa absolute and steam is available at 100 kPa gauge. If the overall heat-transfer coefficient is 440 J m^{-2} s^{-1} °C^{-1}, the boiling temperature of the tomato juice under the conditions in the evaporator is 61°C, and the area of the heat-transfer surface of the evaporator is 12 m^2, estimate the rate of raw juice feed that is required to supply the evaporator.

2. Estimate the requirements of steam, the area of the heat-transfer surface and the evaporating temperature in each effect, for a two-effect evaporator. Steam is available at 100 kPa gauge pressure and the pressure in the second effect is 20 kPa absolute. Assume an overall heat-transfer coefficient of 600 and 450 J m^{-2} s^{-1} °C^{-1} in the first and second effects respectively. The evaporator is to concentrate 15,000 kg h^{-1} of raw milk from 9.5% solids to 35% solids.

3. A plate evaporator is concentrating milk from 10% solids to 30% solids at a feed rate of 1500 kg h^{-1}. Heating is by steam at 200 kPa absolute and the evaporating temperature is 75°C. Calculate the number of plates needed if the area of heating surface on each plate is 0.44 m^2 and the overall heat-transfer coefficient 650 J m^{-2} s^{-1} °C^{-1}. If the plates after several hours running become fouled by a film of thickness 0.1 mm of thermal conductivity 0.1 J m^{-1} s^{-1} °C^{-1} by how much would the capacity of the evaporator be reduced?

4. Calculate the evaporation in each effect of a triple-effect evaporator concentrating a solution from 5% to 25% total solids at a total input rate of 10,000 kg h^{-1}. Steam is available at 200 kPa absolute pressure and the pressure in the evaporation space in the final effect is 55 kPa absolute. Heat-transfer coefficients in the effects are, from the first effect respectively, 600, 500 and 350 J m^{-2} s^{-1} °C^{-1}. Neglect specific heats and boiling-point elevation. Calculate also the quantity of input steam required per kg of water evaporated.

5. If in example 4 there were boiling point elevations of 0.6°, 1.5° and 4°C respectively in the effects starting from the first, what would be the change in the requirement of input steam required per kg water evaporated?

6. Estimate the quantity of 12°C cooling water requirement for a jet condenser to condense the 70°C vapours from an evaporator which concentrates 4000 kg h^{-1} of milk from 9% solids to 30% solids in one effect.
   Estimate the quantity of cooling water needed and the necessary heat-transfer area for a surface condenser if the cooling water leaves at a maximum of 25°C and the heat-transfer coefficient is 2200 J m^{-2} s^{-1} °C^{-1} in the condenser.

7. If in the evaporator of example 6 one-half of the evaporated vapour were mechanically recompressed with an energy expenditure of 160 kJ kg^{-1}, what effect would this have on the steam economy, assuming the steam supply was at 100 kPa absolute.

8. Estimate the rate of evaporation in the first effect of a standard calandria type of evaporator with 100 tubes, each 1 m long, evaporating fruit juice with approximately the same thermal properties as water with a pressure of 80 kPa absolute in the evaporator and 100 kPa absolute in the steam jacket. Take the tube diameter as 5 cm.

CHAPTER 9

CONTACT-EQUILIBRIUM SEPARATION PROCESSES

BIOLOGICAL raw materials are usually mixtures, and to prepare foodstuffs it may be necessary to separate some of the components of the mixtures. One method, by which this separation can be carried out, is by the introduction of a new phase to the system, allowing the components of the original raw material to distribute themselves between the phases. For example, freshly dug vegetables have another phase, water, added to remove unwanted earth; a mixture of alcohol and water is heated to produce another phase, vapour, which is richer in alcohol than the mixture. By choosing the conditions, one phase is enriched whilst the other is depleted in some components. The maximum separation is reached at the equilibrium distribution of the components. The components are distributed between the phases in accordance with equilibrium coefficients which give the relative concentrations in each phase when equilibrium has been reached. The two phases can then be separated by simple physical methods such as gravity settling. This process of contact, redistribution, and separation gives the name contact equilibrium separations. Successive stages can be used to enhance the separation.

An example is in the extraction of edible oil from soya beans. Beans containing oil are crushed, and then mixed with a solvent in which the oil, but not the other components of the beans themselves, is soluble. Initially, the oil will be distributed between the beans and the solvent but after efficient crushing and mixing, the oil will be dissolved in the solvent. In the separation, some solvent and oil will be retained by the mass of beans; these will constitute one stream and the bulk of the solvent and oil the other.

This process of contacting the two streams, of crushed beans and solvent, makes up one contact stage. To extract more oil from the beans, further contact stages can be provided by mixing the extracted beans with a fresh stream of solvent.

For economy and convenience, the solvent and oil stream from another extraction is often used instead of fresh solvent and so two streams, one containing beans and the other starting off as pure solvent, can move countercurrent to each other through a series of contact stages with progressive contacting followed by draining.

In order to effect the desired separation of oil from beans, the process itself has introduced a further separation problem – the separation of the oil from the solvent. However, the solvent is chosen so that this subsequent separation is simple, for example by distillation. In some cases, such as washing, further separation of dissolved material from wash water may not be necessary and one stream may be rejected as waste. In other cases, such as distillation, the two streams are generated from the mixture of original components by vaporization of part of the mixture.

In each stage of the process in which the streams come into contact, the material being transferred is distributed in equilibrium between the two streams. By removing the streams from the contact stage and contacting each with material of different composition, new equilibrium conditions are established and so separation proceeds.

The two features which are common to all equilibrium contact processes are the attainment of, or approach to, equilibrium and the provision of contact stages. Equilibrium is reached when a component is so distributed between the two streams that there is no tendency for its concentration in either stream to change. The opportunity to reach equilibrium is provided in each stage, and so with one or more stages the concentration of the transferred component changes progressively from one stream to the other, providing the desired separation.

Some examples of contact equilibrium separation processes are:

Gas absorption
Extraction and washing
Distillation
Crystallization
Membrane separations

In addition, drying and humidification and evaporation can be considered under this general heading for some purposes, but it seemed more appropriate in this book to take them separately.

For the analysis of these processes, there are two major sets of quantitative relationships; the equilibrium conditions which determine how the components are distributed between the phases, and the material flow balances which follow the progression of the components stage by stage.

confined by a partition in one region of a system. The partition is then removed. Random movement among the gas molecules will, in time, distribute component A through the mixture. The greater the concentration of A in the partitioned region the more rapidly will diffusion occur across the boundary once the partition is removed.

The relative proportions of the components in a mixture or a solution are expressed in terms of the concentrations. Any convenient units may be used for concentration, such as $g\,g^{-1}$, $g\,kg^{-1}$, $\mu g\,g^{-1}$ parts per million, and so on.

Because the gas laws are based on numbers of molecules, it is often convenient to express concentrations in terms of the relative numbers of molecules of the components. The unit in this case is called the molecular fraction, shortened to mole fraction, which has been introduced in Chapter 2. The mole fraction of a component in a mixture is the proportion of the number of molecules of the component present to the total number of the molecules of all the components.

In a mixture which contains w_A kg of component A of molecular weight M_A and w_B kg of component B of molecular weight M_B, the mole fraction:

$$x_A = \frac{\text{number of moles of } A}{\text{number of moles of } A + \text{number of moles of } B}$$

$$= \frac{w_A/M_A}{w_A/M_A + w_B/M_B} \tag{9.1}$$

PART 1. THEORY

CONCENTRATIONS

The driving force, which produces equilibrium distributions, is considered to be proportional at any time to the difference between the actual concentration and equilibrium concentration. Thus, concentrations in contact-equilibrium-separation processes are linked with the general driving force concept. Consider a case in which initially all of the molecules of some component A of a gas mixture are

and similarly,

$$x_B = \frac{w_B/M_B}{w_A/M_A + w_B/M_B}. \tag{9.2}$$

Notice that $(x_A + x_B) = 1$, and so, $x_B = (1 - x_A)$.

The definition of the mole fraction can be extended to any number of components in a multicomponent mixture and the mole fraction of any one component again expresses the relative number of molecules of that component to the total number of molecules of all the components in the mixture. Exactly the same method is followed if the weights of the components are expressed in grammes. The mole fraction is a ratio, and so has no dimensions.

EXAMPLE 9.1. A solution of ethanol in water contains 30% of ethanol by weight. Calculate the mole fractions of ethanol and water in the solution.

Molecular weight of ethanol, C_2H_5OH, is 46 and the molecular weight of water, H_2O, is 18.

Since, in 100 kg of the mixture there are 30 kg of ethanol and 70 kg of water,

the mole fraction of ethanol is

$$\frac{30/46}{30/46 + 70/18} = 0.144$$

and the mole fraction of water is

$$\frac{70/18}{30/46 + 70/18} = 0.856 = (1 - 0.144).$$

Concentrations of the components in gas mixtures can be expressed as weight fractions, mole fractions, and so on. When expressed as mole fractions, they can be related to the partial pressure of the components. The partial pressure of a component is that pressure which the component would exert if it alone occupied the whole volume of the mixture. Partial pressures of the components are additive, and their sum is equal to the total pressure of the mixture. The partial pressures and the mole fractions are proportional, so that the total pressure is made up from the sum of all the partial pressures, which are in the ratios of the mole fractions of the components.

If a mixture exists under a total pressure P and the mixture comprises a mole fraction x_A of component A, a mole fraction x_B of component B, a mole fraction x_C of component C and so on, then

$$P = Px_A + Px_B + Px_C + \cdots$$
$$= p_A + p_B + p_C + \cdots \qquad (9.3)$$

where p_A, p_B, p_C,... are the partial pressures of components A, B, C.....

In the case of gas mixtures, it is also possible to relate weight and volume proportions, as

Avogadro's Law states that under equal conditions of temperature and pressure, equal volumes of gases contain equal numbers of molecules. This can be put in another way by saying that in a gas mixture, volume fractions will be proportional to mole fractions.

EXAMPLE 9.2. Air is reported to contain 79 parts of nitrogen to 21 parts of oxygen, by volume. Calculate the mole fraction of oxygen and of nitrogen in the mixture and also the weight fractions and the mean molecular weight.

Since mole fractions are proportional to volume fractions,

the mole fraction of nitrogen $= \dfrac{79}{79 + 21}$

$$= 0.79$$

and the mole fraction of oxygen $= \dfrac{21}{79 + 21}$

$$= 0.21.$$

The molecular weight of nitrogen, N_2, is 28 and of oxygen, O_2, is 32. The weight fraction of nitrogen is given by:

$$\frac{\text{weight of nitrogen}}{\text{weight of nitrogen} + \text{weight of oxygen}} = \frac{79 \times 28}{79 \times 28 + 21 \times 32}$$

$$= 0.77.$$

Similarly, the weight fraction of oxygen $= \dfrac{21 \times 32}{79 \times 28 + 21 \times 32}$

$$= 0.23.$$

As the sum of the two weight fractions must add to 1, the weight fraction of the oxygen could have been found by the subtraction of $(1 - 0.77) = 0.23$.

To find the mean molecular weight, we must find the weight of one mole of the gas.

0.79 moles of N_2 weighing 0.79×28 kg = 22.1 kg plus 0.21 moles of O_2 weighing 0.21×32 kg = 6.7 kg make up 1 mole of air weighing 28.8 kg and so the mean molecular weight of air is 28.8, say 29.

GAS–LIQUID EQUILIBRIA

Molecules of the components in a liquid mixture or solution have a tendency to escape from the liquid surface into the gas above the solution. The escaping tendency sets up a pressure above the surface of the liquid owing to the concentration of the escaped molecules. This pressure is called the vapour pressure of the liquid.

The magnitude of the vapour pressure depends upon the liquid composition and upon the temperature. For pure liquids, vapour-pressure relationships have been tabulated and may be found in reference works such as Perry (1973) or the International Critical Tables. For a solution or a mixture, the various components in the liquid each exert their own partial vapour pressures.

When the liquid contains various components it has been found that, in many cases, the partial vapour pressure of any component is proportional to the mole fraction of that component in the liquid. That is,

$$p_A = H_A x_A \qquad (9.4)$$

where p_A is the partial vapour pressure of component A, H_A is a constant for component A at a given temperature and x_A is the mole fraction of component A in the liquid.

This relationship is approximately true for most systems and it is known as Henry's Law. The coefficient of proportionality H is known as the Henry's Law constant and has units of kPa mole fraction^{-1}. In reverse, Henry's Law can be used to predict the solubility of a gas in a liquid. If a gas exerts a given partial pressure above a liquid, then it will dissolve in the liquid until Henry's Law is satisfied and the mole fraction of the dissolved gas in the liquid is equal to the value appropriate to the partial pressure of that gas above the liquid.

EXAMPLE 9.3. Given that the Henry's Law constant for carbon dioxide in water at 25°C is 1.6×10^5 kPa per mole fraction, calculate the percentage solubility by weight of carbon dioxide in water under these conditions and at a partial pressure of carbon dioxide of 200 kPa above the water.

From Henry's Law $p = Hx$,

$$\therefore \quad 200 = 1.6 \times 10^5 x,$$

$$\therefore \quad x = 0.00125$$

$$= \frac{w_{CO_2}}{44} \Big/ \left(\frac{w_{H_2O}}{18} + \frac{w_{CO_2}}{44} \right).$$

But since $\dfrac{w_{H_2O}}{18} \gg \dfrac{w_{CO_2}}{44}$

$$1.25 \times 10^{-3} = \frac{w_{CO_2}}{44} \Big/ \frac{w_{H_2O}}{18},$$

$$\therefore \quad \frac{w_{CO_2}}{w_{H_2O}} = 1.25 \times 10^{-3} \times 44/18$$

$$= 3.1 \times 10^{-3} = 3.1 \times 10^{-1} \%.$$

SOLID–LIQUID EQUILIBRIA

Liquids have a capacity to dissolve solids up to an extent which is determined by the solubility of the particular solid material in that liquid. Solubility is a function of temperature and, in general, solubility increases with rising temperature. A solubility curve can be drawn to show this relationship, based on the equilibrium concentration in solution measured in convenient units, for example g kg^{-1}, as a function of temperature. Such a curve is illustrated in Fig. 9.1 for sodium nitrite in water. There are some relatively rare systems in which solubility decreases with temperature and they provide a reversed solubility curve. The equilibrium solution which is ultimately reached between solute and solvent is called a saturated solution, implying that no further solute can be taken into solution at that particular temperature.

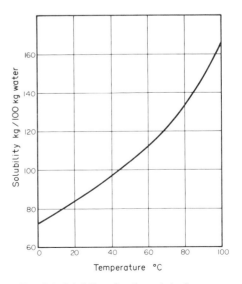

FIG. 9.1. Solubility of sodium nitrite in water.

An unsaturated solution plus solid solute is not in equilibrium as the solvent can dissolve more of the solid. When a saturated solution is heated, if it has a normal solubility curve, the solution then has a capacity to take up further solute material, and so it becomes unsaturated. Conversely when such a saturated solution is cooled it becomes super-saturated and at equilibrium that solute which is in excess of the solubility level at the particular temperature will come out of solution, normally as crystals. However, this may not occur quickly and in the interim the solution is spoken of as super-saturated and it is said to be in a metastable state.

EQUILIBRIUM-CONCENTRATION RELATIONSHIPS

A contact-equilibrium-separation process is de-signed to reduce the concentration of a component in one phase, or flowing stream in a continuing process, and increase it in another. Conventionally, and just to distinguish one stream from another, one is called the overflow and the other the underflow, the terms referred originally to a system of two liquids, one lighter (the overflow) and the other heavier (the underflow) than the other and between which the particular component was transferred. When there are several stages, the overflow and underflow streams then move off in opposite directions in a counterflow system.

Following standard chemical engineering nom-enclature, the concentration of the component in the lighter stream, that is the stream with the lower density, is denoted by y. For example, in a gas-absorption system, the light stream would be the gas; in a distillation column, it would be the vapour stream; in a liquid-extraction system, it would be the liquid overflow. The concentration of the com-ponent in the heavier stream is denoted by x. Thus we have two streams, in one of which the concentration of the component is y and in the other, the heavier stream, it is x. Then, for a given system, it is often convenient to plot corresponding values of y against x.

In the simple case of multistage oil extraction with a solvent, in which equilibrium is attained in each stage, the concentration of the oil is the same in the liquid solution spilling over or draining off in the overflow as it is in the liquid in the underflow containing the solids, so that in this case $y = x$ and the equilibrium concentration diagram is a straight line. In gas absorption, such relationships as Henry's Law relate the concentration in the light gas phase to that in the heavy liquid phase and so enable the equilibrium diagram to be plotted. In crystalli-zation, the equilibrium concentration corresponds to the solubility of the solute at the particular temperature. Across a membrane there is some equilibrium distribution of the particular com-ponent of interest. If the concentration in one stream is known, the equilibrium diagram allows us to read off the corresponding concentration in the other stream if equilibrium has been attained.

The attainment of equilibrium takes time and this has to be taken into account when considering contact stages. The usual type of rate equation applies, in which the rate is given by the driving force divided by a resistance term. The driving force is the extent of the departure from equilibrium and generally is measured by concentration differences. Resistances have been classified in different ways but they are generally assumed to be concentrated at the phase boundary.

Stage contact systems in which equilibrium has not been attained are beyond the scope of this book. In many practical cases, allowance can be made for non-attained equilibrium by assuming an efficiency for each stage.

OPERATING CONDITIONS

In a series of contact stages, in which the components counterflow from one stage to another, mass balances can be written around any stage, or any number of stages. This enables equations to be set down to connect the flow rates and the compositions of the streams. Consider the genera-lized system shown in Fig. 9.2, in which there is a stage contact process operating with a number of

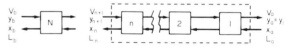

Fig. 9.2. Contact equilibrium stages.

stages and two contacting streams. By convention, the mass flow of the light stream is denoted by V and the flow of the heavy stream by L. Taking a balance over the first n stages we can write, for the total flow, mass entering must equal mass leaving, so:

$$V_{n+1} + L_a = L_n + V_a$$

and for the component being exchanged:

$$V_{n+1}y_{n+1} + L_a x_a = V_a y_a + L_n x_n$$

where V is the mass flow rate of the light stream, L is the flow rate of the heavy stream, y is the concentration of the component being exchanged in the light stream and x is the concentration of the component being exchanged in the heavy stream. In the case of the subscripts, n denotes conditions at equilibrium in the nth stage, $n+1$ denotes conditions at equilibrium in the $(n+1)$th stage and a denotes the conditions of the streams entering and leaving stage 1, one being raw material and one product.

Eliminating V_{n+1} between these equations, we have

$$V_{n+1} = L_n - L_a + V_a$$

and so,

$$y_{n+1}(L_n - L_a + V_a) = L_n x_n + V_a y_a - L_a x_a,$$

$$\therefore \quad y_{n+1} = x_n\left[\frac{L_n}{L_n - L_a + V_a}\right] + \left[\frac{V_a y_a - L_a x_a}{L_n - L_a + V_a}\right].$$

$$(9.5)$$

This is an important equation as it expresses the concentration in one stream in the $(n+1)$th stage in terms of the concentration in the other streams in the nth stage. In many practical cases in which equal quantities, or equal molal quantities, of the carrying streams move from one stage to another, that is where the flow rates are the same in all contact stages, then for the lighter phase $L_{n+1} = L_n = \ldots L_a$ and for the heavier phase $V_{n+1} = \cdots = V_a$. A simplified equation can be written for such cases:

$$y_{n+1} = x_n L/V + y_a - x_a L/V. \qquad (9.6)$$

CALCULATION OF SEPARATION IN CONTACT-EQUILIBRIUM PROCESSES

The separation which will be effected in a given series of contact stages can be calculated by combining the equilibrium and the operating relationships. Starting at one end of the process, the terminal separation can be calculated from the given set of conditions. Knowing, say, the x value in the first stage, x_1, the equilibrium condition gives the corresponding value of y in this stage, y_1. Then eqn. (9.5) or eqn. (9.6) can be used to obtain y_2, then the equilibrium conditions give the corresponding x_2, and so on … .

EXAMPLE 9.4. A continuous deodorizing system, involving a single-stage steam-stripping operation, is under consideration for the removal of a taint from cream. If the taint component is present in the cream to the extent of 8 parts per million (ppm) and if steam is to be passed through the contact stage in the proportions of 0.75 kg steam to every 1 kg cream, calculate the concentration of the taint in the leaving cream. The equilibrium concentration distribution of the taint has been found experimentally to be in the ratio of 1 in the cream to 10 in the steam and it is assumed that equilibrium is reached in the stage.

If the concentration of the taint in the cream is x and in the steam is y, both as mass fractions,

$\therefore$ from the condition that, at equilibrium, the concentration of the taint in the steam is 10 times that in the cream

$$10x = y$$

and in particular, $10x_1 = y_1$.

Now, y_1 the concentration of taint in the steam leaving the stage is also the concentration in the output steam

$$\therefore \quad y_1 = y_a = 10x_1.$$

The incoming steam concentration $= y_2 = 0$ as there is no taint in the entering steam.

The taint concentration in the entering cream is $x_a = 8$ ppm. These are shown diagrammatically in Fig. 9.3.

The problem is to determine x_1 the concentration of taint in the product cream.

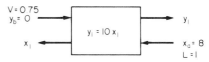

FIG. 9.3. Flows into and out from stage.

The mass ratio of stream flows is 1 of cream to 0.75 of steam and if no steam is condensed this ratio will be preserved through the stage.

$\therefore$ $1/0.75 = 1.33$ is the ratio of cream flow rate to steam flow rate $= L/V$.

Applying eqn. (9.6) to the one stage $n = 1$,

$$y_2 = x_1 \frac{L}{V} + y_a - x_a \frac{L}{V},$$

$$y_2 = 0 = x_1 1.33 + 10x_1 - 8 \times 1.33,$$

$$\therefore \quad x_1 = 10.64/11.33 = 0.94 \, \text{ppm}$$

which is the concentration of the taint in the leaving cream.

This simple example could have been solved directly without using the formula, but it shows the way in which the formula and the equilibrium conditions can be applied.

Based on the step-by-step method of calculation, it was suggested by McCabe and Thiele (1925) that the operating and equilibrium relationships could very conveniently be combined in a single graph.

The essential feature of their method is that whereas the equilibrium line is plotted directly, x_n against y_n, the operating relationships are plotted as x_n against y_{n+1}. Inspection of eqn. (9.5) shows that it gives y_{n+1} in terms of x_n and the graph of this is called the operating line. In the special case of eqn. (9.6), the operating line is a straight line whose slope is L/V and whose intercept on the y-axis is $(y_a - x_a L/V)$. Considering any stage in the process, it might be, for example, the first stage, we have the value of y from given or overall conditions. Proceeding at constant y to the equilibrium line we can then read off the corresponding value of x, which is x_1. From x_1 we proceed at constant x across to the operating line at which the intercept gives the value of y_2. Then the process can be repeated for y_2 to x_2, then to y_3 and so on. Drawing horizontal and vertical lines to show this, as in the illustration 9.4, a step pattern is traced out on the graph. Each step represents a stage in the process at which contact is provided between the streams, and the equilibrium attained. Proceeding step-by-step, it is simple to insert sufficient steps to move to a required final concentration in one of the streams, and so to be able to count the number of stages of contact to obtain this required separation. On the

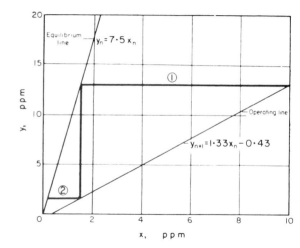

Fig. 9.4. Steam stripping: McCabe–Thiele plot.

graph of Fig. 9.4 is shown the operating line, plotting x_n against y_{n+1}, and the equilibrium line in which x_n is plotted against y_n. Starting from one terminal condition on the operating line the stage contact steps are drawn in until the desired other terminal concentrations are reached. This procedure is illustrated in Example 9.5.

PART 2　APPLICATIONS

GAS ABSORPTION

Gas absorption is a process in which a gaseous mixture is brought into contact with a liquid and during this contact a component is transferred between the gas stream and the liquid stream. The gas may be bubbled through the liquid, or it may pass over streams of the liquid, arranged to provide a large surface through which the mass transfer can occur. The liquid film in this latter case can flow down the sides of columns or over packing, or it can cascade from one tray to another with the liquid falling and the gas rising in the counterflow. The gas, or components of it, either dissolves in the liquid or extracts a volatile component from the liquid. An example of the first type is found in hydrogenation of oils, in which the hydrogen gas is bubbled through the oil with which it reacts. Generally, there is a catalyst present also to promote the reaction. The hydrogen is absorbed into the oil, reacting with the unsaturated bonds in the oil to harden it. Another example of gas absorption is in the carbonation of beverages. Carbon dioxide under pressure is dissolved in the liquid beverage, so that when the pressure is subsequently released on opening the container, effervescence occurs. An example of desorption is found in the steam stripping of fats and oils in which steam is brought into contact with the liquid fat or oil, and undesired components of the fat or oil pass out with the steam. This is used in the deodorizing of natural oils before blending them into food products such as margarine and in the stripping of unwanted flavours from cream before it is made into butter. The equilibrium conditions arise from the balance of concentrations of the gas or the volatile flavour, between the gas and the liquid streams.

In the gas-absorption process, sufficient time must be allowed for equilibrium to be attained so that the greatest possible transfer can occur and, also, opportunity must be provided for contacts between the streams to occur under favourable conditions.

Rate of Gas Absorption

The rates of mass transfer in gas absorption are controlled by the extent of the departure of the system from the equilibrium concentrations and by the resistance offered to the mass transfer by the streams of liquid and gas. Thus, we have the familiar expression:

rate of absorption = driving force/resistance,

The driving force is the extent of the difference between the actual concentrations and the equilibrium concentrations. This is represented in terms of concentration differences. For the resistance, the situation is complicated, but for practical purposes it is adequate to consider the whole of the resistance to be concentrated at the interface between the two streams. At the interface, two films are postulated, one in the liquid and one in the gas. The two-film theory of Lewis and Whitman defines these resistances separately, a gas film resistance and a liquid film resistance. They are treated very similarly to surface-heat coefficients and the resistances of the

two films can be combined in an overall resistance similar to an overall heat-transfer coefficient. The driving forces through each of the films are considered to be the concentration differences between the material in the bulk liquid or gas and the material in the liquid or gas at the interface. In practice, it is seldom possible to measure interfacial conditions and overall coefficients are used giving the equation

$$\mathrm{d}w/\mathrm{d}\theta = K_l A(x^* - x) = K_g A(y - y^*) \quad (9.7)$$

where $\mathrm{d}w/\mathrm{d}\theta$ is the quantity of gas passing across the interface in unit time, K_l is the overall liquid mass-transfer coefficient, K_g is the overall gas mass-transfer coefficient, A is the interfacial area and x, y are the concentrations of the gas being transferred, in the liquid and gas streams respectively. The quantities of x^* and y^* are introduced into the equation because it is usual to express concentrations in the liquid and in the gas in different units. With these, x^* represents the concentration in the liquid which would be in equilibrium with a concentration y in the gas and y^* the concentration in the gas stream which would be in equilibrium with a concentration x in the liquid.

Equation (9.7) can be integrated and used to calculate overall rates of gas absorption or desorption. For details of the procedure reference should be made to works such as Perry (1973), Charm (1963), Coulson and Richardson (1978) or McCabe and Smith (1975).

Stage-equilibrium Gas Absorption

The performance of countercurrent stage-contact gas-absorption equipment can be calculated if the operating and equilibrium conditions are known. The liquid stream and the gas stream are brought into contact in each stage and it is assumed that sufficient time is allowed for equilibrium to be reached. In cases where sufficient time is not allowed for equilibration, the rate equations have to be introduced and this complicates the analysis. However, in many cases of practical importance in the food industry, either the time is sufficient to reach equilibrium, or else the calculation can be carried out on the assumption that it is and a stage efficiency term introduced to allow for the actual conditions. Suitable efficiency values can sometimes be found experimentally, or estimated from published information.

After the streams in a contact stage have come to equilibrium, they are separated and then pass in opposite directions to the adjacent stages. The separation of the gas and the liquid does not generally present great difficulty and some form of cyclone separator is often used.

In order to calculate the equipment performance, operating conditions must be known or found from the mass balances. Very often the known factors are the gas and liquid rates of flow, the inlet conditions of gas and liquid, and one of the outlet conditions, in addition to the equilibrium relationship. The problem is to find how many contact stages are necessary to achieve the concentration change that is required. An overall mass balance will give the remaining outlet condition and then the operating line can be drawn. The equilibrium line is then plotted on the same diagram, and the McCabe–Thiele construction applied to solve the problem.

EXAMPLE 9.5. In Example 9.4, a calculation was made for a single-stage steam-stripping process to remove a taint from cream. The conditions were that stage-contact desorption was to be used to remove a taint, that was present at a concentration of 8 ppm in the cream, by contact with a counterflow current of steam. Consider, now, the case of a more difficult taint to remove in which the equilibrium concentration of the taint in the steam is only 7.5 times as great as that in the cream. If the relative flow rates of cream and steam are given in the ratio 1:0.75, how many contact stages would be required to reduce the taint concentration in the cream to 0.3 ppm assuming (a) 100% stage efficiency and (b) 70% stage efficiency? The initial concentration of the taint is 10 ppm, in this case.

Mass balance

Inlet cream taint concentration $= 10$ ppm
$$= x_a.$$
Outlet cream taint concentration $= 0.3$ ppm
$$= x_n.$$

Inlet steam taint concentration $= 0$ ppm
$$= y_{n+1}.$$

Assume a cream flow rate of 100 arbitrary units,
$$\therefore \quad \text{steam flow rate} = 75.$$

If y_1 is the outlet steam taint concentration,

total taint into equipment = total taint out of equipment.
$$100(10) = 75y_1 + 100(0.3),$$
$$\therefore \quad 100(10 - 0.3) = 75y_1,$$
$$\therefore \quad y_1 = 12.9 \text{ ppm} = y_a.$$

From eqn. (9.6)
$$y_{n+1} = x_n(L/V) + y_a + x_a(L/V),$$
$$\therefore \quad y_{n+1} = x_n(100/75) + 12.9 - 10(100/75)$$
$$= 1.33x_n - 0.43.$$

Equilibrium condition: $y_n = 7.5x_n.$

The operating and equilibrium lines have been plotted on Fig. 9.4 and it can be seen that two contact stages are sufficient to effect the required separation. The construction assumes 100% efficiency, so that, with a stage efficiency of 70%, the number of stages required would be 2(100/70) and this equals approximately three stages.

So the number of contact stages required assuming (a) 100% efficiency = 2, and (b) 70% efficiency = 3.

Notice that only a small number of stages are required for this operation, as the equilibrium condition is quite well removed from unity and the steam flow is of the same order as that of the cream. A smaller equilibrium constant, or a smaller relative steam-flow rate, would increase the required number of contact stages.

Gas-absorption Equipment

Good absorption equipment is designed to achieve the greatest practicable interfacial area between the gas and the liquid streams, so that liquid sprays and gas-bubbling devices are employed. In many cases, a vertical array of trays is so arranged that the liquid descends over a series of perforated trays, or flows down over ceramic packing which fills a tower. For the hydrogenation of oils, absorption is followed by reaction of the hydrogen with the oil and a nickel catalyst is used to speed up the reactions. Also, pressure is applied, to increase gas concentrations and so to speed up the reaction rates. The problems are concerned with arranging distribution of the catalyst, as well as of oil and hydrogen. Some designs spray oil and catalyst into hydrogen, others bubble hydrogen through a continuous oil phase in which catalyst particles are suspended.

For the stripping of volatile flavours and taints in deodorizing equipment, the steam phase is in general the continuous one and the liquid is sprayed into this and then separated. In one design of cream deodorizing plant, cream is sprayed into an atmosphere of steam and the two then pass on to the next stages or the steam may be condensed and fresh steam used in the next stage.

EXTRACTION AND WASHING

It is often convenient to use a liquid in order to carry out a separation process. The liquid is thoroughly mixed with the solids or other liquid from which the component is to be removed and then the two streams are separated. In the case of solids, the separation of the two streams is generally by simple settling. To separate liquid streams, the liquids must be immiscible, such as oil and water. Settling can be used for separation. In some cases, it is the solution in the introduced liquid which is required, such as in the extraction of coffee from coffee beans with water; in other cases, the washed solid may be the product as in the washing of butter.

The term washing is generally used where an unwanted constituent is removed in a stream of water. Liquid–liquid extraction is the name used when both streams in the extraction are liquid. Examples of extraction are found in the edible-oil industry in which oil is extracted from natural products such as peanuts, soya beans, rape seeds, sunflower seeds and so on. Liquid–liquid extraction is used in the extraction of fatty acids. Extraction is also an essential stage in the sugar industry when soluble sucrose is removed by water extraction from

sugar cane or beet. Washing occurs so frequently as to need no specific examples.

Factors controlling the operation are the area of contact between the streams, the time of contact, the properties of the materials so far as the equilibrium distribution of the transferred component is concerned, and the number of contact stages employed. In extraction from a solid, the solid matrix may hinder diffusion and so control the rate of extraction.

Rate of Extraction

The solution process can be considered in terms of the usual rate equation

rate of solution = driving force/resistance.

In this case, the driving force is the difference between the concentration of the component being transferred, the solute, at the solid interface and in the bulk of the solvent stream. For liquid–liquid extraction, a double film must be considered, at the interface and in the bulk of the other stream.

For solution from a solid component, the equation can be written

$$dw/d\theta = K_l A(y_s - y) \qquad (9.8)$$

where $dw/d\theta$ is the rate of solution, K_l is the mass-transfer coefficient, A is the interfacial area, and y, y_s are the concentrations of the soluble component in the bulk of the liquid and at the interface. It is usually assumed that a saturated solution is formed at the interface and so y_s is the concentration of a saturated solution at the temperature of the system.

Examination of eqn. (9.8) shows the effects of some of the factors which can be used to speed up rates of solution. Fine divisions of the solid component increases the interfacial area A. Good mixing ensures that the local concentration is equal to the mean bulk concentration. In other words, it means that there are no local higher concentrations, arising from bad stirring, increasing the value of y and so cutting down the rate of solution. An increase in the temperature of the system will, in general, increase rates of solution by not only increasing K_l, which is related to diffusion, but also by increasing the solubility of the solute and so increasing y_s.

In the simple case of extraction from a solid in a contact stage, a mass balance on the solute gives the equation

$$dw = V dy \qquad (9.9)$$

where V is the quantity of liquid in the liquid stream.

Substituting for dw in eqn. (9.8) we then have

$$V dy/d\theta = KA(y_s - y).$$

And this can be integrated over time θ during which time the concentration goes from an initial value of y_0, to a concentration y, giving

$$\log_e \frac{y_s - y_0}{y_s - y} = \theta KA/V. \qquad (9.10)$$

Equation (9.10) shows that the approach to equilibrium is exponential with time, but the equation cannot often be applied because of the difficulty of knowing or measuring the interfacial area A. In practice, suitable extraction times are generally arrived at by experimentation under the particular conditions that are anticipated for the plant.

Stage-equilibrium Extraction

Analysis of an extraction operation depends upon establishing the equilibrium and operating conditions. The equilibrium conditions are, in general, simple. Considering the extraction of a solute from a solid matrix, it is assumed that the whole of the solute is dissolved in one stage, which in effect accomplishes the desired separation. However, it is not possible then to separate all of the liquid from the solid because some solution is retained with the solid matrix and this solution contains solute. As the solid retains solution with it, the content of solute in this retained solution must be then progressively reduced by stage contacts. For example, in the extraction of oil from soya-bean seeds using hexane or other hydrocarbon solvents, the solid beans matrix retains its own weight, or more, of the solution after settling. This retained solution may contain a substantial proportion of the oil. The equilibrium conditions are simple because the concentration of the oil is the same in the solution that can be separated as it is in the solution that

remains with the seed matrix. Consequently, y, the concentration of oil in the "light" liquid stream, is equal to x, the concentration of oil in the solution in the "heavy" stream accompanying the seed matrix. The equilibrium line is, therefore, plotted from the relation $y = x$.

The operating conditions can be analysed by writing mass balances round the stages to give the eqn. (9.5). The plant is generally arranged in the form of a series of mixers, followed by settlers, in which the two streams are separated prior to passing to the next stage of mixers. For most purposes of analysis, the solid matrix need not be considered; the solids can be thought of as the means by which the two solution streams are separated after each stage. So long as the same quantity of solid material passes from stage to stage, and the same quantity of liquid is retained by the solids after each settling operation, the analysis is straightforward. In eqn. (9.5), V refers to the liquid overflow stream from the settlers, and L to the mixture of solid and solution that is settled out and passes on with the underflow.

If the underflow retains the same quantity of solution as it passes from stage to stage, eqn. (9.5) simplifies to eqn. (9.6). The extraction operation can then be analysed by application of step-by-step solution of the equations for each stage, or by the use of the McCabe–Thiele graphical method.

EXAMPLE 9.6. Oil is to be extracted from soya beans in a countercurrent stage-contact extraction apparatus, using hexane. If the initial oil content of the beans is 18%, the final extract solution is to contain 40% of oil, and if 90% of the total oil is to be extracted, calculate the number of contact stages that are necessary. Assume that the oil is extracted from the beans in the first mixer, that equilibrium is reached in each stage and the crushed bean solids in the underflow retain in addition half their weight of solution after each settling stage.

The extraction plant is illustrated diagrammatically in Fig. 9.5. Each box represents a

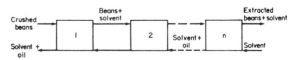

Fig. 9.5. Extraction stages.

mixing–settling stage and the stages are numbered from the stage at which the crushed beans enter.

The underflow will be constant from stage to stage (a constant proportion of solution is retained by the crushed beans) except for the first stage in which the entering crushed beans (bean matrix and oil) are accompanied by no solvent. After the first stage, the underflow is constant and so all stages but the first can be treated by the use of eqn. (9.6).

To illustrate the principles involved, the problem will be worked out from stage-by-stage mass balances, and using the McCabe–Thiele graphical method.

Basis for calculation: 100 kg raw material (beans and their associated oil) entering stage 1. Concentrations of oil will be expressed as weight fractions.

Overall mass balance

In 100 kg raw material there will be 18 % oil, that is 82 kg bean solids and 18 kg oil.

In the final underflow, 82 kg beans will retain 41 kg of solution, the solution will contain 10 % of the initial oil in the beans, that is, 1.8 kg so that there will be $(18 - 1.8) = 16.2$ kg of oil in the final overflow,

Analysis of stage 1

Oil concentration in underflow = product concentration = 0.4.

It is an equilibrium stage, so oil concentration in underflow equals oil concentration in overflow. Let y_2 represent the concentration of oil in the overflow from stage 2 passing in to stage 1, then, oil entering stage 1 equals oil leaving stage 1.

$$63.5y_2 + 18 = 41 \times 0.4 + 40.5 \times 0.4$$
$$\therefore \quad y_2 = 0.23.$$

Analysis of stage 2

$$x_2 = y_2 = 0.23,$$
$$\therefore \quad \text{balance on oil}$$
$$41 \times 0.4 + 63.5y_3 = 63.5 \times 0.23 + 41 \times 0.23,$$
$$\therefore \quad y_3 = 0.12.$$

Analysis of stage 3

$$x_3 = y_3 = 0.12,$$
$$\therefore \quad \text{balance on oil}$$
$$41 \times 0.23 + 63.5y_4 = 63.5 \times 0.12$$
$$+ 41 \times 0.12,$$
$$\therefore \quad y_4 = 0.049.$$

$\therefore$ extract contains $(16.2 \times 60/40) = 24.3$ kg of solvent,

$\therefore$ total volume of final overflow $= 16.2 + 24.3 = 40.5$ kg

and total solvent entering $= (39.2 + 24.3) = 63.5$ kg.

Note that the solution passing as overflow between the stages is the same weight as the solvent entering the whole system, i.e. 63.5 kg.

MASS BALANCE

Basis: 100 kg beans

Mass in (kg)		Mass out (kg)		
Underflow		Underflow		
Raw beans	100	Extracted beans + solution		123
Bean solids	82	Bean solids	82	
Oil	18	Oil	1.8	
		Solvent	39.2	
Overflow		Overflow		
Solvent	63.5	Total extract		40.5
		Solvent	24.3	
		Oil	16.2	
Total	163.5	Total		163.5

Analysis of stage 4

$$x_4 = y_4 = 0.049,$$

∴ balance on oil

$$41 \times 0.12 + 63.5y_5 = 63.5 \times 0.049$$
$$+ 41 \times 0.049,$$

∴ $y_5 = 0.00315.$

The required terminal condition is that the underflow from the final nth stage will have less than 1.8 kg of oil, that is, that x_n is less than $1.8/41 = 0.044$. Since $x_n = y_n$ and we have calculated that y_5 is 0.00315 which is less than 0.044, four stages of contact will be sufficient for the requirements of the process.

Using the graphical method, the general eqn. (9.6) can be applied to all stages after the first. From the calculations above for the first stage, we have $x_1 = 0.4$ and $y_2 = 0.23$ and these can be considered as the entry conditions x_a and y_a for the series of subsequent stages.

Applying eqn. (9.6) the operating line equation:

$$y_{n+1} = x_n L/V + y_a - x_a L/V.$$

Now $L = 41 \quad V = 63.5 \quad y_a = 0.23 \quad x_a = 0.4,$

∴ $y_{n+1} = 0.646 x_n - 0.028.$

The equilibrium line is:

$$y_n = x_n.$$

The operating line and the equilibrium line have been plotted on Fig. 9.6. The McCabe–Thiele construction has been applied, starting with the entry conditions to stage 2 on the operating line, and it can be seen that three steps are not sufficient for the required separation, but that four steps are. Since the initial stage is included but not shown on the diagram, four stages are necessary, which is the same result as was obtained from the step-by-step calculations.

The step construction on the McCabe–Thiele diagram can also be started from the nth stage, since we know that y_{n+1} which is the entering fresh solvent, equals 0. This will also give the same number of stages, but it will apparently show slightly different stage concentrations. The apparent discrepancy arises from the fact that in the overall balance, a final (given) concentration of oil in the overflow stream of 0.044 was used, and both the

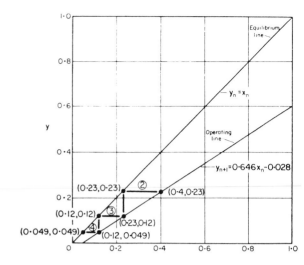

Fig. 9.6. Extraction: McCabe–Thiele plot.

step-by-step equations and the McCabe–Thiele operating line depend upon this. In fact, this concentration can never be reached using a whole number of steps under the conditions of the problem and to make the calculation precise it would be necessary to use trial-and-error methods. However, the above method is a sufficiently close approximation for most purposes.

In some practical extraction applications, the solids may retain different quantities of the solvent in some stages of the plant. For example, this might be due to rising concentrations of extract having higher viscosities. In this case, the operating line is not straight, but step-by-step methods can still be used. For some of the more complex situations other graphical methods using triangular diagrams can be employed and a discussion of their use may be found in Charm (1963), Coulson and Richardson (1978) or Treybal (1968).

It should be noted that in the chemical engineering literature what we have called extraction is more often called leaching, the term extraction being reserved for liquid–liquid contacting using immiscible liquids. "Extraction" is, however, in quite general use in the food industry to describe processes such as the one in the above example, whereas the term "leaching" would probably only cause confusion.

Washing

Washing is almost identical to extraction, the main distinction being one of the emphasis in that the inert material is the required product and the solvent used is water which is cheap and readily available.

Calculations on countercurrent washing can be carried out using the same methods as discussed under extraction, working from the operating and equilibrium conditions. In washing, fresh water is often used for each stage and the calculations for this are also straightforward.

In multiple washing, the water content of the material is x_w (weight fraction) and a fraction of this, x, is impurity, and to this is added yx_w of wash water, and after washing thoroughly, the material is allowed to drain. After draining it retains the same quantity, approximately, of water as before, x_w. The residual yx_w of wash liquid, now containing the same concentration of impurities as in the liquid remaining with the solid, runs to waste.

The impurity which was formerly contained in x_w of water is now in a mass $(x_w + yx_w)$: its concentration x has fallen by the ratio of these volumes, that is to $x[x_w/(x_w + yx_w)]$.

So the concentration remaining with the solid x_1 is given by:

$$x_1 = x[x_w/x_w(1 + y)] = x[1/(1 + y)],$$

after two washings

$$x_2 = x_1[1/(1 + y)] = x[1/(1 + y)]^2,$$

and so after n washings

$$x_n = x[1/(1 + y)]^n. \qquad (9.11)$$

If, on the other hand, the material is washed with the same total quantity of water as in the n washing stages, that is nyx_w, but all in one stage, the impurity content will be

$$x'_n = x[1/(ny + 1)] \qquad (9.12)$$

and it is clear that the multiple contact washing is very much more efficient in reducing the impurity content that is single contact washing using the same total quantity of water.

EXAMPLE 9.7. After precipitation and draining procedures, it is found that 100 kg of fresh casein

curd has a liquid content of 66% and this liquid contains 4.5% of lactose. Calculate the residual lactose in the casein after drying if the curd is washed three times with 194 kg of fresh water each time, and calculate the quantity of water that would have to be used in a single wash to attain the same lactose content in the curd as obtained after three washings. Assume perfect washing and draining of curd to 66% of moisture each time.

100 kg of curd contain 66 kg solution. The 66 kg of solution contain 4.5%, that is 3 kg of lactose.

In the first wash $(194 + 66) = 260$ kg of solution contain 3 kg lactose.

$\therefore$ In 66 kg of solution remaining there will be

$$(66/260) \times 3 = 0.76 \text{ kg of lactose.}$$

After the second wash the lactose remaining will be

$$(66/260) \times 0.76 = 0.19 \text{ kg.}$$

After the third wash the lactose remaining will be

$$(66/260) \times 0.19 = 0.048 \text{ kg.}$$

So, after washing and drying 0.048 kg of lactose will remain with 34 kg dry casein so that lactose content of the product is

$$0.048/34.05 = 0.14\%$$

requiring $3 \times 194 = 582$ kg of wash water.

To reduce the impurity content to 0.048 kg in one wash would require x kg of water, where

$$(3 \times 66)/(x + 66) = 0.048 \text{ kg,}$$

$$\therefore \quad x = 4060 \text{ kg.}$$

Alternatively using eqns. (9.11) and (9.12)

$$x_n = x[1/(1 + y)]^n$$

$$= 3\left[\frac{1}{1 + \dfrac{194}{66}}\right]^3 = 0.049,$$

$$x'_n = x[1/(ny + 1)],$$

$$0.049 = 3\left[\frac{1}{ny + 1}\right].$$

$$ny = 61.5.$$

$$\text{Total wash water} = ny\,x_w = 61.5 \times 66$$

$$= 4060 \text{ kg.}$$

Extraction and Washing Equipment

The first stage in an extraction process is generally mechanical grinding, in which the raw material is shredded, ground or pressed into suitably small pieces of flakes to give a large contact area for the extraction. In some instances, for example in sugar-cane processing and in the extraction of vegetable oils, a substantial proportion of the desired products can be removed directly by expression at this stage and then the remaining solids are passed to the extraction plant.

Fluid solvents are easy to pump and so overflows are often easier to handle than underflows and sometimes the solids may be left and solvent from successive stages brought to them. This is the case in the conventional extraction battery. In this a number of tanks, each suitable both for mixing and for settling, are arranged in a row or a ring. The solids remain in the one mixer–settler and the solvent is moved progressively round the ring of tanks, the number, n, often being about 12. At any time, two of the tanks are out of operation, one being emptied and the other being filled. In the remaining $(n - 2)$, tanks extraction is proceeding with the extracting liquid solvent, usually water, being passed through the tanks in sequence, the "oldest" (most highly extracted) tank receiving the fresh liquid and the "youngest" (newly filled with fresh raw material) tank receiving the most concentrated liquid. After this "youngest" tank, the liquid passes from the extraction battery to the next stage of the process. After a suitable interval, usually just a few minutes, the connections are altered so that the tank which has just been filled becomes the new "youngest" tank, the former "oldest" tank comes out of the sequence and is emptied, the one that was being emptied is filled and the remaining tanks retain their sequence each becoming one stage "older". This procedure which is illustrated in Fig. 9.7 in effect accomplishes countercurrent extraction, but with only the liquid physically having to be moved, apart from the emptying and filling. In the same way and for the same reasons as with counterflow heat exchangers, this countercurrent (or counterflow) extraction system provides the maximum mean driving force, the log mean concentration difference in this case in contrast to the log mean temperature difference in the heat

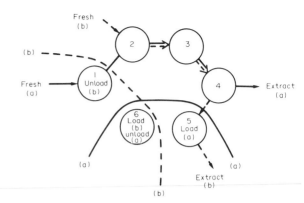

Phase (a)   Cells 5,6 out, 5 loading, 6 unloading
             1...4 extracting

Phase (b)   Cells 6,1 out, 6 loading, 1 unloading
             2...5 extracting

Thence to phase (c),(d) ..... etc.

Fig. 9.7. Extraction battery.

exchanger. This ensures that the equipment is used efficiently.

In some extractors, the solids are placed in a vertical bucket conveyor and moved up through a tower down which a stream of solvent flows. Other forms of conveyor may also be used, such as screws or metal bands, to move the solids against the solvent flow. Sometimes centrifugal forces are used for conveying, or for separating after contacting.

Washing is generally carried out in equipment which allows flushing of fresh water over the material to be washed. In some cases, the washing is carried out in a series of stages. Although water is cheap, in many cases very large quantities are used for washing so that attention paid to more efficient washing methods may well be worthwhile. Much mechanical ingenuity has been expended upon equipment for washing and many types of washers are described in the literature.

CRYSTALLIZATION

Crystallization is an example of a separation process in which mass is transferred from a liquid solution, whose composition is generally mixed, to a pure solid crystal. Soluble components are removed from solution by so adjusting the conditions that the solution becomes supersaturated and excess solute crystallizes out. This is generally accomplished by lowering the temperature, or by concentration of the solution. The equilibrium is established between the crystals and the surrounding solution, the mother liquor. The manufacture of sucrose, from sugar cane or sugar beet, is perhaps the most important example of crystallization in food technology, but crystallization is also used in the manufacture of other sugars, such as glucose and lactose, in the manufacture of food additives, such as salt, and in the processing of foodstuffs, such as ice cream. In the manufacture of sucrose from cane, the sugar is pressed out from the cane as a solution. This solution is purified and then concentrated to allow the sucrose to crystallize out from the solution.

Crystallization Equilibrium

Once crystallization is initiated, an equilibrium is set up between the crystals of pure solute and the residual mother liquor, the balance being determined by the solubility (concentration) and the temperature. The driving force making the crystals grow is the concentration excess (supersaturation) of the solution above the equilibrium (saturation) level and the resistances to growth are the resistance to mass transfer within the solution and the energy needed at the crystal surface for incoming molecules to orient themselves to the crystal lattice.

Solubility

Solubility is defined as the maximum weight of anhydrous solute that will dissolve in 100 g of solvent. In the food industry, the solvent is generally water.

Solubility is a function of temperature. For most food materials increase in temperature increases the solubility of the solute as shown for sucrose in Fig. 9.8. Pressure has very little effect on solubility.

During crystallization, the crystals are grown from solutions with higher concentrations than the saturation level in the solubility curves. Above the supersaturation line, crystals form spontaneously and rapidly, without external initiating action. This is called spontaneous nucleation. In the area of concentrations between the saturation and the

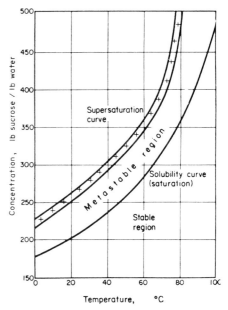

FIG. 9.8. Solubility and saturation curves for sucrose in water.

supersaturation curves, the metastable region, the rate of initiation of crystallization is slow; aggregates of molecules form but then disperse again and they will not grow unless seed crystals are added. Seed crystals are small crystals, generally of the solute, and they then grow by deposition of solute from the solution which continues until the solution concentration falls to the saturation line. Below the saturation curve there is no crystal growth.

EXAMPLE 9.8. If sodium chloride solution, at a temperature of 40°C, has a concentration of 50% when the solubility of sodium chloride at this temperature is 36.6 g/100 g water, calculate the quantity of sodium chloride crystals that will form once crystallization has been started.

Weight of salt in solution = 50 g/100 g solution
$$= 50 \text{ g}/50 \text{ g water.}$$

Saturation concentration = 36.6 g/100 g water,

∴ weight crystallized out = (100 − 36.6) g/100 g water
$$= 63.4 \text{ g}/100 \text{ g water.}$$

To remove more salt this solution would have to be concentrated by removal of water, or else cooled to a lower temperature.

Heat of crystallization

When a solution is cooled to produce a supersaturated solution and hence to cause crystallization, the heat which must be removed is the sum of the sensible heat necessary to cool the solution and the heat of crystallization. When using evaporation to achieve the supersaturation, the heat of vaporization must also be taken into account. Because few heats of crystallization are available, it is usual to take the heat of crystallization as equal to the heat of solution to form a saturated solution. Theoretically, it is equal to the heat of solution plus the heat of dilution, but the latter is small and can be ignored. For most food materials, the heat of crystallization is positive, i.e. heat is given out during crystallization. Note that heat of crystallization is the opposite of heat of solution. If a material takes in heat, i.e. has a negative heat of solution, then the heat of crystallization is positive. Heat balances can be calculated for crystallization.

EXAMPLE 9.9. Lactose syrup is concentrated to 8 g lactose per 10 g of water and then run into a crystallizing vat which contains 2500 kg of the syrup. In this vat, containing 2500 kg of syrup, it is cooled from 57°C to 10°C. Lactose crystallizes with one molecule of water of crystallization. The specific heat of the lactose solution is 3470 J kg^{-1} °C^{-1}. The heat of solution for lactose monohydrate is $-15,500$ kJ mol^{-1}. The molecular weight of lactose monohydrate is 360 and the solubility of lactose at 10°C is 1.5 g/10 g water. Assume that 1 % of the water evaporates and that the heat loss through the vat walls is 4×10^4 kJ. Calculate the heat to be removed in the cooling process.

Sensible heat lost from solution when cooled from 57°C to 10°C + heat of crystallization = Heat lost through walls + latent heat of evaporation + heat removed by cooling.

Sensible heat in solution when cooled from 57°C to 10°C

$$= 2500 \times 47 \times 3.470$$
$$= 40.8 \times 10^4 \text{ kJ.}$$

Heat of crystallization

$$= -15,500 \text{ kJ mole}^{-1}$$
$$= -15,500/360$$
$$= 43.1 \text{ kJ kg}^{-1}.$$

Solubility of lactose at 10°C, 1.5 g/10 g water,

∴ anhydrous lactose crystallized out
$$= (8 - 1.5) = 6.5 \text{ g/10 g water,}$$

∴ hydrated lactose crystallized
$$= 6.5 \times (342 + 18)/(342)$$
$$= 6.8 \text{ g/10 g water.}$$

Total water $= (10/18) \times 2500 \text{ kg}$
$$= 1390 \text{ kg,}$$

∴ total hydrated lactose crystallized out
$$= (6.8 \times 1390)/10$$
$$= 945 \text{ kg.}$$

Total heat of crystallization
$$= 945 \times 43.1$$
$$= 4.07 \times 10^4.$$

Heat removed by vat walls
$$= 4.0 \times 10^4 \text{ kJ.}$$

The latent heat of evaporation is, from Steam Tables, 2258 kJ kg^{-1},

∴ heat lost by evaporation
$$= 13.9 \times 2258 \text{ kJ}$$
$$= 3.14 \times 10^4 \text{ kJ.}$$

Heat balance

$$40.8 \times 10^4 + 4.07 \times 10^4 = 4 \times 10^4 + 3.14 \times 10^4$$
$$+ \text{ heat removed by}$$
$$\text{cooling.}$$

∴ Heat removed by cooling $= 37.73 \times 10^4$ kJ.

Rate of Crystal Growth

Once nucleii are formed, either spontaneously or by seeding, the crystals will continue to grow. The three main factors controlling the rates of both nucleation and of crystal growth are the temperature, the degree of supersaturation and the interfacial tension between the solute and the solvent. If supersaturation is maintained at a low level, nucleus formation is not encouraged but the available nucleii will continue to grow and large crystals will result. If supersaturation is high, there may be further nucleation and so the growth of existing crystals will not be so great. In practice, slow cooling maintaining a low level of super-saturation produces large crystals and fast cooling produces small crystals.

Nucleation rate is also increased by agitation. For example, in the preparation of fondant for cake decoration, the solution is cooled and stirred energetically. This causes fast formation of nucleii and a large crop of small crystals which give the smooth texture and the opaque appearance desired by the cake decorator.

Once nucleii have been formed the important fact in crystallization is the rate at which the crystals will grow. This rate is controlled by the diffusion of the solute through the solvent to the surface of the crystal and by the rate of the reaction at the crystal face when the solute molecules rearrange themselves into the crystal lattice.

These rates of crystal growth can be represented by the equations

$$dw/d\theta = K_d A(c - c_i), \tag{9.13}$$

$$dw/d\theta = K_s A(c_i - c_s) \tag{9.14}$$

where dw is the increase in weight of crystals in time $d\theta$, A is the surface area of the crystals, c is the solute concentration of the bulk solution, c_i is the solute concentration at the crystal–solution interface, c_s is the concentration of the saturated solution, K_d is the mass transfer coefficient to the interface and K_s is the rate constant for the surface reaction.

These equations are not easy to apply in practice because the parameters in the equations cannot be determined and so the equations are usually combined to give

$$dw/d\theta = K A(c - c_s) \tag{9.15}$$

where

$$1/K = 1/K_d + 1/K_s$$

or

$$dL/d\theta = K(c - c_s)/\rho_s \tag{9.16}$$

since

$$dw = A\rho_s dL$$

and $dL/d\theta$ is the rate of growth of the side of the crystal and ρ_s is the density of the crystal.

It has been shown that at low temperatures diffusion through the solution to the crystal surface requires only a small part of the total energy needed for crystal growth and, therefore, that diffusion at these temperatures has relatively little effect on the growth rate. At higher temperatures, diffusion energies are of the same order as growth energies, so that diffusion becomes much more important. Experimental results have shown that for sucrose the limiting temperature is about 45°C, above which diffusion becomes the controlling factor.

Impurities in the solution retard crystal growth; if the concentration of impurities is high enough, crystals will not grow.

Stage-equilibrium Crystallization

When the first crystals have been separated, the mother liquor can have its temperature and concentration changed to establish a new equilibrium and so a new harvest of crystals. The limit to successive crystallizations is the build up of impurities in the mother liquor which makes both crystallization and crystal separation slow and difficult. This is also the reason why multiple crystallizations are used, with the purest and best crystals coming from the early stages.

For example, in the manufacture of sugar, the concentration of the solution is increased and then seed crystals are added. The temperature is controlled until the crystal nucleii added have grown to the desired size, then the crystals are separated from the residual liquor by centrifuging. The liquor is next returned to a crystallizing evaporator, concentrated again to produce further supersaturation, seeded and a further crop of crystals of the desired size grown. By this method the crystal size of the sugar can be controlled. The final mother liquor, called molasses, can be held indefinitely without producing any crystallization of sugar.

EXAMPLE 9.10. The conditions in a series of sugar evaporators are:

First evaporator – temperature of liquor at 85°C, concentration of entering liquor 65%, weight of entering liquor 5000 kg h^{-1}, concentration of liquor at seeding, 82%.
Second evaporator – temperature of liquor 73°C, concentration of liquor at seeding 84%.
Third evaporator – temperature of liquor 60°C, concentration of liquor at seeding 86%.

Fourth evaporator – temperature of liquor 51°C, concentration of liquor at seeding 89%.

Calculate the yield of sugar in each evaporator and the concentration of the mother liquor leaving the final evaporator.

SUGAR CONCENTRATIONS (g/100 g water)

	On seeding	Solubility	Weight crystallized
First effect	456	385	71
Second effect	525	330	195
Third effect	614	287	327
Fourth effect	809	265	544

The sugar solubility figures are taken from the solubility curve, Fig. 9.7.

MASS BALANCE (weights in kg)
5000 kg sugar solution h^{-1}

	Into effect	At seeding	Sugar crystallized	Liquor from effect
First effect				
Water	1750	713	—	713
Sugar	3250	3250	506	2744
Second effect				
Water	713	522	—	522
Sugar	2744	2744	1018	1726
Third effect				
Water	522	279	—	279
Sugar	1726	1726	912	814
Fourth effect				
Water	279	99	—	99
Sugar	814	814	539	275

Yield in first effect
    506 kg h^{-1} 506/3250 = 15.6%.
Yield in second effect
    1018 kg h^{-1} 1018/3250 = 31.3%.
Yield in third effect
    912 kg h^{-1} 912/3250 = 28.1%.
Yield in fourth effect
    539 kg h^{-1} 539/3250 = 16.6%.
Lost in liquor
    275 kg h^{-1} 275/3250 = 8.4%.
Total yield 91.9%.

Quantity of sucrose in final syrup 275 kg/h^{-1}.

Concentration of final syrup 73.5%.

Crystallization Equipment

Crystallizers can be divided into two types: crystallizers and evaporators. A crystallizer may be a simple open tank or vat in which the solution loses heat to its surroundings. The solution cools slowly so that large crystals are generally produced. To increase the rate of cooling, agitation and cooling coils or jackets are introduced and these crystallizers can be made continuous. The simplest is an open horizontal trough with a spiral scraper. The trough is waterjacketed so that its temperature can be controlled.

An important crystallizer in the food industry is the cylindrical, scraped surface, heat exchanger which is used for plasticizing margarine and cooking fat, and for crystallizing ice cream. It is essentially a double-pipe heat exchanger fitted with an internal scraper, see Fig. 6.3(c). The material is pumped through the central pipe and agitated by the scraper, with the cooling medium flowing through the annulus between the outer pipes.

A crystallizer in which considerable control can be exercised is the Krystal or Oslo crystallizer. In this, a saturated solution is passed in a continuous cycle through a bed of crystals. Close control of crystal size can be obtained.

Evaporative crystallizers are common in the sugar and salt industries. They are generally of the calandria type. Vacuum evaporators are often used. Control of crystal size can be obtained by careful manipulation of the vacuum. The sugar solution is first concentrated by the evaporator and when seeding commences the vacuum is increased. This increase causes further evaporation of water which cools the solution and the crystals grow. Fresh saturated solution is added to the evaporator and evaporation continued until the crystals are of the correct size. In some cases, open pan steam-heated evaporators are still used, for example in making coarse salt for the fish industry. In some countries, crystallization of salt from sea water is effected by solar energy and this generally gives large crystals.

Crystals are regular in shape: cubic, rhombic, tetragonal and so on. The shape of the crystals forming may be influenced by the presence of other compounds in the solution, even in traces. The shape of the crystal is technologically important because such properties as the angle of repose of stacked crystals and rate of dissolving are related to the crystal shape. Another important property is the uniformity of size of the crystals in a product. In a product such as sucrose, a non-uniform crystalline mixture is unattractive in appearance, and difficult to handle in packing and storing as the different sizes tend to separate out. Also the important step of separating mother liquor from the crystals is more difficult.

MEMBRANE SEPARATIONS

Membranes can be used for separating constituents of foods on a molecular basis, where the foods are in solution and where a solution is separated from one less concentrated by a semi-permeable membrane. These membranes act somewhat as membranes do in natural biological systems. Water flows through the membrane from the dilute solution to the more concentrated one. The force producing this flow is called the osmotic pressure and to stop the flow a pressure, equal to the osmotic pressure, has to be exerted externally on the more concentrated solution. Osmotic pressures in liquids arise in the same way as partial pressures in gases: using the number of moles of the solute present and the volume of the whole solution, the osmotic pressure can be estimated using the gas laws. If pressures greater than the osmotic pressure are applied to the more concentrated solution, the flow will not only stop but will reverse so that water passes out through the membrane making the concentrated solution more concentrated. The flow will continue until the concentration rises to the point where its osmotic pressure equals the applied pressure. Such a process is called reverse osmosis and special artificial membranes have been made with the required "tight" structure to retain all but the smallest molecules such as those of water.

Also, "looser" membranes have been developed through which not only water, but also larger solute molecules can selectively pass if driven by imposed pressure. Membranes are available which can retain large molecules, such as proteins, while allowing through smaller molecules. Because the larger molecules are normally at low molar concentrations which exert very small osmotic pressures

which therefore enter hardly at all into the situation. Because of the resemblance to conventional filtration, this process is called ultrafiltration. In general, ultrafiltration needs relatively low differential pressures, up to a few atmospheres. If higher pressures are used, a protein or solute gel appears to form on the membrane, which resists flow, and so the increased pressure will not increase the transfer rate.

The main applications for ultrafiltration are for concentrating solutions of large polymeric molecules, such as milk and blood proteins. Another important application is to the concentration of whey proteins. Reverse osmosis, on the other hand, is concerned mainly with solutions containing smaller molecules such as simple sugars and salts at higher molar concentrations which exert higher osmotic pressures. To overcome these osmotic pressures, high external pressures have to be exerted, up to the order of 100 atmospheres. Limitations to increased flow rates arise in this case from the mechanical weaknesses of the membrane and from concentration of solutes which causes substantial osmotic "back" pressure. Applications in the food industry are in separating water from solutions such as fruit juices.

Rate of Flow Through Membranes

There are various equations to predict the osmotic pressures of solutions, perhaps the best known being the van't Hoff equation:

$$\Pi = MRT \qquad (9.17)$$

in which Π is the osmotic pressure (kPa), M the molar concentration (moles m^{-3}), T the absolute temperature ($^{\circ}$K), and R the universal gas a constant (kPa m^3 mole^{-1} $^{\circ}$K^{-1}). This equation is only strictly accurate when the dilution is infinitely great, but it can still be used as an approximation at higher concentrations. The net driving force for reverse osmosis is then the difference between the applied differential pressure ΔP, and this osmotic pressure which resists the flow in the desired "reverse" direction. Therefore it can be described by the standard rate equation, with the rate of mass transfer being equal to the driving force multiplied by the appropriate mass-transfer coefficient

$$dw/d\theta = KA[\Delta P - \Delta\Pi] \qquad (9.18)$$

where $dw/d\theta$ is the rate of mass transfer, K is the mass transfer coefficient, A the area through which the transfer is taking place, ΔP is the net applied pressure developed across the membrane and $\Delta\Pi$ is the net osmotic pressure across the membrane and resisting the flow. ΔP is therefore the difference in the applied pressure on the solutions at each side of the membrane and $\Delta\Pi$ is the difference in the osmotic pressures of the two solutions, as in Fig. 9.9. The gas constant is $8.314\,\text{kPa}\,\text{m}^3\,\text{mol}^{-1}\,{}^\circ\text{K}^{-1}$.

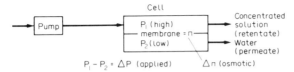

$$P_1 - P_2 = \Delta P \;(\text{applied}) \qquad \Delta\Pi \;(\text{osmotic})$$

FIG. 9.9. Reverse osmosis system.

EXAMPLE 9.11. A solution of sucrose in water at 25°C is to be concentrated by reverse osmosis. It is found that, with a differential applied pressure of 5000 kPa, the rate of movement of the water molecules through the membrane is $25\,\text{kg}\,\text{m}^{-2}\,\text{h}^{-1}$ for a 10% solution of sucrose. Estimate the flow rate through the membrane for a differential pressure of 10,000 kPa with the 10% sucrose solution, and also estimate the flow rate for a differential pressure of 10,000 kPa but with a sucrose concentration of 20%.

For sucrose, the molecular weight is 342 so for a 10% solution, molar concentration (from tables) is 0.304 moles m^{-3} and for 20%, 0.632 moles m^{-3}.

Applying eqn. (9.17)

for 10% solution, $\Pi = 0.304 \times 8.314 \times 298$

$$= 753\,\text{kPa}$$

and for 20% solution, $\Pi = 0.632 \times 8.314$

$$\times\, 298$$

$$= 1566\,\text{kPa}.$$

So we have for the first case, for $1\,\text{m}^2$ of membrane

$$dw/d\theta = 25 = K[5000 - 753]$$

$$\therefore \quad K = 5.9 \times 10^{-3}\,\text{kg}\,\text{m}^{-2}\,\text{h}^{-1}\,\text{kPa}^{-1}.$$

So for $\Delta P = 10,000\,\text{kPa}$,

$$dw/d\theta = 5.9 \times 10^{-3}[10,000 - 753]$$

$$= 55\,\text{kg}\,\text{m}^{-2}\,\text{h}^{-1}.$$

For $\Delta P = 10,000$ and 20% soln.

$$dw/d\theta = 5.9 \times 10^{-3}[10,000 - 1566]$$

$$= 50\,\text{kg}\,\text{m}^{-2}\,\text{h}^{-1}.$$

Experimental values of the osmotic pressure of the sucrose solutions at 10% and 20% are 820 and 1900 respectively, demonstrating the small error arising from applying the van't Hoff equation to these quite highly concentrated solutions. These experimental values slightly reduce the flow as can be seen by substituting in the equations.

In ultrafiltration practice, it is found that eqn. (9.18) applies only for a limited time and over a limited range of pressures. As pressure increases further, the flow ceases to rise or even falls. This appears to be caused, in the case of ultrafiltration, by increased mechanical resistance at the surface of the membrane due to the build-up of molecules forming a layer which is like a gel and which resists flow through it. Under these circumstances, flow is better described by diffusion equations through this resistant layer leading to equation

$$dw/d\theta = K'A \ln(c_i/c_b) \qquad (9.19)$$

where c_i and c_b are the solute concentrations at the interface and in the bulk solution respectively. The effect of the physical properties of the material can be predicted from known relationships for the mass transfer coefficient K' ($\text{m}\,\text{s}^{-1}$) which can be set equal to D/δ where D is the diffusivity of the solute ($\text{m}^2\,\text{s}^{-1}$), divided by δ, the thickness of the gel layer (m). This equation has been found to predict, with reasonable accuracy, the effect on the mass transfer of changes in the physicochemical properties of the solution. This is done through well-established relationships between the diffusivity D, the mass transfer coefficient K', and other properties such as density (ρ), viscosity (μ) and temperature (T) giving

$$\left(\frac{K'd}{D}\right) = a\left(\frac{dv\rho}{\mu}\right)^m\left(\frac{\mu}{\rho D}\right)^n$$

or $\qquad (\text{Sh}) = (K'd/D) = a\,(\text{Re})^m(\text{Sc})^n \qquad (9.20)$

where d is the hydraulic diameter, (Sh) the Sherwood number, (Sc) the Schmidt number

$(u/\rho D)$; and a, m, n are constants. Notice the similar form of eqn. (9.20) and the equation for heat transfer in forced convection, $(Nu) = a'(Re)^{m'}(Pr)^{n'}$, with (Sh) replacing (Nu) and (Sc) replacing (Pr). This is another aspect of the similarity between the various transport phenomena. These ideas, and the uses that can be made of them, are discussed in various books, such as Coulson and Richardson (1977) and McCabe and Smith (1975), and more comprehensively in Bird, Stewart and Lightfoot (1960).

In the case of reverse osmosis, the main resistance arises from increased concentrations and therefore increased back pressure from the osmotic forces. The flow rate cannot be increased by increasing the pressure because of the limited strength of membranes and their supports, and the difficulties of designing and operating pumps for very high pressures.

Membrane Equipment

The equipment for these membrane-separation processes consists of the necessary pumps, flow systems and membranes. In the case of ultrafiltration, the membranes are set up in a wide variety of geometrical arrangements, mostly tubular but sometimes in plates which can be mounted similarly to a filter press or plate heat exchanger. Flow rates are kept high over the surfaces and recirculation of the fluid on the high pressure, or retentate, side is often used; the fluid passing through, called the permeate, is usually collected in suitable troughs or tanks at atmospheric pressure.

In the case of reverse osmosis, the high pressures dictate mechanical strength, and stacks of flat disc membranes can be used one above the other. Another system uses very small diameter (around 0.04 mm) hollow filaments on plastic supports; the diameters are small to provide strength but preclude many food solutions because of this very small size. The main flow in reverse osmosis in the permeate.

The systems can be designed either as continuous or as batch operations. One limitation to extended operation arises from the need to control growth of bacteria. After a time bacterial concentrations in the system, for example in the gel at the surface of the ultrafiltration membranes, grow so high that

cleaning must be provided. This can be difficult as many of the membranes are not very robust either to mechanical disturbance or to the extremes of pH which could give quicker and better cleaning.

EXAMPLE 9.12. It is desired to increase the protein concentration in whey, from cheese manufacture, by a factor of 12 by the use of ultrafiltration to give an enriched fraction which can subsequently be dried and produce a 50% protein whey powder. The whey initially contains 6% of total solids, 12% of these being protein. Pilot scale measurements on this whey show that a permeate flow of $30 \, kg \, m^{-2} h^{-1}$ can be expected, so that if the plant requirement is to handle 30,000 kg in 6 hours, estimate the area of membrane needed. Assume that the membrane rejection of the protein is over 99%, and calculate the membrane rejection of the non-protein constituents.

Protein in initial whey $= 6 \times 0.12 = 0.7\%$.

Protein in retentate $= 12 \times$ concentration in whey

$$= 12 \times 6 \times 0.12$$
$$= 8.6\%.$$

Setting out a mass balance, basis 100 kg whey

	Water (kg)	Protein (kg)	Non-protein (kg)
Initial whey	94	0.7	5.3
Retentate	6.7	0.7	0.7
Permeate	87.3	0.0	4.6

$\therefore$ water removed per 100 kg whey = 87.3 kg.

The equipment has to process 30,000 kg in 6 h so the membrane has to pass the permeate at:

$$30,000 \times 91.9(100 \times 6) = 4595 \, kg \, h^{-1}$$

and permeate filtration rate is $30 \, kg \, m^{-2} h^{-1}$,

$$\therefore \quad \text{required area} = 4595/30$$
$$= 153 \, m^2,$$

Non-protein rejection rate $= 0.7/5.3$

$$= 13\%.$$

Membrane processes generally use only one apparent contact stage, but product accumulation with time, or with progression through a flow unit, gives situations which are equivalent to multistage units. Dialysis, which is a widely used laboratory membrane-processing technique, with applications in industry, sometimes is operated with multiple stages.

These membrane concentration and separation processes have great potential advantages in the simplicity of their operation and because drastic conditions, in particular the use of heat leading to thermal degradation, are not involved. Therefore more extensive application can be expected as membranes, flow systems and pumps are improved. Discussion of these processes can be found in papers by Thijssen, and Madsen, in Spicer (1974) and in Sourirajan (1977).

DISTILLATION

Distillation is a separation process, separating components in a mixture by making use of the fact that some components vaporize more readily than others. When vapours are produced from a mixture, they contain the components of the original mixture but in proportions which are determined by the relative volatilities of these components. The vapour is richer in some components, those that are more volatile, and so a separation occurs. In fractional distillation, the vapour is condensed and then re-evaporated when a further separation occurs. It is difficult and sometimes impossible to prepare pure components in this way, but a degree of separation can easily be attained if the volatilities are reasonably different. Where great purity is required, successive distillations may be used.

The main use of distillation in the food industry is for concentrating essential oils, flavours and alcoholic beverages, and in the deodorization of fats and oils.

The equilibrium relationships in distillation are governed by the relative vapour pressures of the mixture components, that is by their volatility relative to one another. The equilibrium curves for two-component vapour–liquid mixtures can conveniently be presented in two forms, as boiling temperature/concentration curves, or as vapour/liquid concentration distribution curves. Both forms are related and the concentration distribution

curves, which are much the same as the equilibrium curves used in extraction, can readily be obtained from the boiling point/concentration curves.

A boiling point/concentration diagram is shown in Fig. 9.10. Notice that there are two curves on the diagram, one giving the liquid concentrations and the other the vapour concentrations. If a horizontal

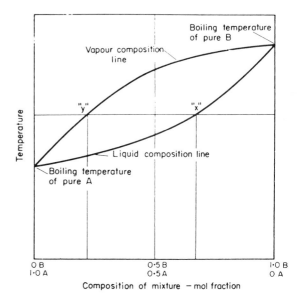

FIG. 9.10. Boiling point/concentration diagram.

line is drawn across the diagram within the limit temperatures of the two curves, it will cut the two lines. This horizontal line corresponds to a particular boiling temperature, the point at which it cuts the lower line gives the concentration of the liquid boiling at this temperature, the point at which it cuts the upper line gives the concentration of the vapour condensing at this temperature. Thus the two points give the two concentrations which are in equilibrium. They give in fact two corresponding values on the concentration distribution curves, the point on the liquid line corresponding to an x point (that is to the concentration in the heavier phase) and the point on the vapour line to a y point (concentration in the lighter phase). The diagram shows that the y value is richer in the more volatile component of the mixture than x, and this is the basis for separation by distillation.

It is found that some mixtures have boiling-point diagrams which are a different shape from that shown in Fig. 9.10. For these mixtures, as the temperature is increased the vapour and liquid composition lines come together. This means that, at this temperature, the liquid boils to give a vapour of the same composition as itself. Such mixtures constitute azeotropes and their formation limits the concentration attainable in a distillation column. The ethanol–water mixture, which is of great importance in the alcoholic beverage industry, has a minimum boiling-point azeotrope at composition 89.5 mole % (95.6% w/w) ethanol and 10.5 mole % (4.4% w/w) water, which boils at 78.15°C. In a distillation column, separating dilute ethyl alcohol and water, the limit concentrations of the streams are 100% water on the one hand in the "liquid" stream, and 95.6% ethyl alcohol 4.4% water by weight in the "vapour" stream, however many distillation stages are used.

A distillation column works by providing successive stages in which liquids boil and the vapours from the stage above condense and in which equilibrium between the two streams, liquid and vapour, is attained. Mass balances can be written for the whole column, and for parts of it, in the same way as with other contact equilibrium processes.

EXAMPLE 9.13. In a single-stage, continuous distillation column used for enriching alcohol–water mixtures, the feed contains 12% of alcohol, and 25% of the feed passes out with the top product (the "vapour" stream) from the still. Given that, at a boiling temperature of 95.5°C, 1.9 mole % of alcohol in the liquid is in equilibrium with 17 mole % of alcohol in the vapour, estimate the concentration of alcohol in the product from the still.

From the equilibrium data given and since the mole fraction of alcohol is small we may assume a linear equilibrium relationship. The equilibrium curve passes through $(0, 0)$ and $(1.9, 17)$ so that over this range we can say $y = x(17/1.9)$ or $x = y(1.9/17)$.

From the operating conditions given, as the feed is equal to $(L + V)$ we can write $F = L + V$ and also $V = F/4$ and so $F = 4V$ and $L = 3V$ and therefore, for the alcohol, if x_f is the concentration in the feed, we can write a mass balance across the distillation column, $4Vx_f = 3Vx + Vy$.

The concentration of alcohol in the feed is 12% which has to be expressed as a mole fraction to be in the same units as the equilibrium data. The molecular weight of alcohol is 46 (C_2H_5OH), and of water 18.

$$\therefore \quad x_f = (12/46)/(88/18 + 12/46)$$
$$= 0.05,$$
$$\therefore \quad \text{operating equation } 4 \times 0.05 = 3x + y$$
$$\text{equilibrium condition } x = (1.9/17)y,$$
$$y(3 \times 1.9/17) + y = 0.2$$

and so

$$\therefore \quad y = 0.15 \text{ mole } \%.$$

Letting the weight fraction of alcohol in the vapour stream be w we have

$$0.15 = (w/46)/(w/46 + (1 - w)/18)$$
$$\therefore \quad w = 31\%,$$
$$\therefore \quad \text{the concentration of alcohol in product from still} = 31\%.$$

Steam Distillation

In some circumstances in the food industry, distillation would appear to be a good separation method but it cannot be employed directly as the distilling temperatures would lead to breakdown of the materials. In cases in which volatile materials have to be removed from relatively non-volatile materials, steam distillation may sometimes be used to effect the separation at safe temperatures.

A liquid boils when the total vapour pressure of the liquid is equal to the external pressure on the system. Therefore, boiling temperatures can be reduced by reducing the pressure on the system; for example by boiling under a vacuum, or by adding an inert vapour which contributes to the vapour pressure, allowing the liquid to boil at a lower temperature. Such an addition must be easily removed from the distillate if the distillate is required and it must not react with any of the components which are required as products. The vapour which is added is generally steam and the distillation is then spoken of as steam distillation.

If the vapour pressure of the introduced steam is p_s and the total pressure is P, then the mixture will boil when the vapour pressure of the volatile component reaches a pressure of $(P - p_s)$, compared with the necessary pressure of P if there were no steam present. The distribution of steam and the volatile component being distilled, in the vapour, can be calculated. The ratio of the number of molecules of the steam to those of the volatile component will be equal to the ratio of their partial pressures

$$p_A/p_s = (P - p_s)/p_s = (w_A/M_A)/(w_s/M_s) \quad (9.21)$$

and so the weight ratios can be written

$$w_A/w_s = (P - p_s)/p_s \cdot (M_A/M_s) \quad (9.22)$$

where p_A is the partial pressure of the volatile component, p_s is the partial pressure of the steam, P is the total pressure on the system, w_A is the weight of component A in the vapour, w_s is the weight of steam in the vapour, M_A is the molecular weight of the volatile component and M_s is the molecular weight of steam.

Very often the molecular weight of the volatile component that is being distilled is much greater than that of the steam, so that the vapour may contain quite large proportions of the volatile component. Steam distillation is used in the food industry in the preparation of some volatile oils and in the removal of some taints and flavours, for example from edible fats and oils.

Vacuum Distillation

Reduction of the total pressure in the distillation column provides another means of distilling at lower temperatures. When the vapour pressure of the volatile substance reaches the system pressure, distillation occurs. With modern efficient vacuum-producing equipment, vacuum distillation is tending to supplant steam distillation. In some instances, the two methods are combined in vacuum steam distillation.

Batch Distillation

Batch distillation is the term applied to equipment into which the raw liquid mixture is admitted and then boiled for a time. The vapours are condensed, and at the end of the distillation time the liquid remaining in the still is withdrawn as the residue. In some cases the distillation is continued until the boiling point reaches some predetermined level, thus separating a volatile component from a less volatile residue. In other cases, two or more fractions can be withdrawn at different times and these will be of decreasing volatility. During batch distillation, the concentrations change both in the liquid and in the vapour.

Let L be the mols of material in the still and x be the concentration of the volatile component. Suppose an amount dL is vaporized, containing a fraction y of the volatile component. Then writing a material balance on component A, the volatile component,

$$y \, dL = d(Lx) = L \, dx + x \, dL,$$
$$\therefore \quad dL/L = dx/(y - x)$$

and this is to be integrated from L_0 mols of material of concentration x_0 up to L mole at concentration x. To evaluate this integral, the relationship between x and y, that is the equilibrium conditions, must be known. If the equilibrium relationship is a straight line, $y = mx + c$, then the integral can be evaluated,

$$\log_e L/L_0 = \frac{1}{m - 1} \mathrm{Log}_e \frac{(m - 1)x + c}{(m - 1)x_0 + c} \quad (9.21)$$

or

$$L/L_0 = \left(\frac{y - x}{y_0 - x_0}\right)^{1/(m-1)}$$

In general, the equilibrium relationship is not a straight line, and the integration has to be carried out graphically. A graph is plotted of x against $1/(y - x)$, and the area under the curve between values of x_0 and x is measured.

Distillation Equipment

The conventional distillation equipment for the continuous fractionation of liquids consists of three main items: a boiler in which the necessary heat to vaporize the liquid is supplied, a column in which the actual contact stages for the distillation separation are provided, and a condenser for condensation of the final top product. A typical column is illustrated in Fig. 9.11. The condenser and the boiler have no special features. The fractionation column is more complicated as it has to provide a series of contact stages for contacting the liquid and the vapour. The conventional arrangement is in the form of "bubble-cap" trays which are shown in Fig. 9.11(b). The vapours rise through the bubble caps.

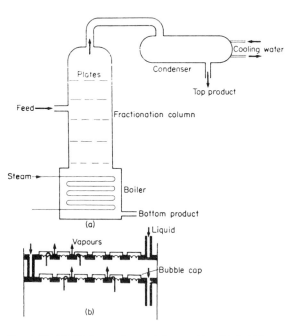

FIG. 9.11. Distillation column: (a) assembly, (b) bubble-cap plates.

The liquid flows across the trays past the bubble caps where it contacts the vapour and then over a weir and down to the next tray. Each tray represents a contact stage, or approximates to one as full equilibrium is not necessarily attained and a sufficient number of stages must be provided to reach the desired separation of the components.

In steam distillation, the steam is bubbled through the liquid and the vapours containing the volatile component and the steam are passed to the condenser. Heat may be provided by the condensation of the steam, or independently. In some cases the steam and the condensed volatile component are immiscible, so that separation in the condenser is simple.

SUMMARY

1. The equilibrium concentrations of components of mixtures often differ across the boundary between one phase and another, such as between liquid and solid, liquid and vapour, between immiscible liquids, and between liquids or gases separated by membranes.

2. These differences can be used to effect separations by the enrichment, of one phase relative to the other, by transfer of mass of particular components.

3. Rates of mass transfer across the phase boundaries are controlled by the differences between actual concentrations and equilibrium concentrations, which constitute the mass transfer driving force, and by the resistances which impede transfer. Therefore the rate of mass transfer is determined by a driving force and by a mass-transfer coefficient

$$\mathrm{d}w/\mathrm{d}\theta = kA(c - c_{\mathrm{equilibrium}}).$$

4. Analysis of mass-transfer-contact-equilibrium systems is carried out by comparing the equilibrium conditions to the actual conditions in the system and using the difference, together with material conservation relationships which describe the movements within and between the phases, to follow the transfer of mass.

5. The analysis can be carried out systematically, relating equilibrium conditions and material balance (or operating) conditions, and energy balances, over single and multistage systems.

PROBLEMS

1. If the composition of air is 23% nitrogen, 77% nitrogen by weight, and the Henry's Law constant for oxygen in water is 3.64×10^4 atm mole fraction^{-1} at 20°C, calculate the solubility of oxygen in water as a percentage by weight and as the mole fraction.

2. If in the deodorizer of worked Example 9.5, relative flow rates of cream and steam are altered to 1:1, what will be the final concentration of the taint in the cream coming from a plant with three contact stages?

3. Casein is to be washed, in a multistage system, by water. The casein curd has initially a water content of 60% and between stages it is drained on an inclined screen to 80% water (both on a wet basis). If the initial lactose content of the casein is

4.5%, and it is necessary to produce casein with a lactose content of less than 1% on a dry basis, how many washing steps would be needed if the wet casein is washed with twice its own weight of fresh water in each step?

4. Estimate the osmotic pressure of a solution of sucrose in water containing 20% by weight of sucrose. The density of this solution is $1081\,kg\,m^{-3}$.

5. In a six-step sugar-boiling crystallization process, the proportions of the sucrose present removed in the successive crystallizations are 66.7, 60%, 60%, 50%, 50% and 33%. If the original solution contained 0.3% of non-sucrose material in the solute, calculate the percentage of non-sucrose material in the final molasses and the proportion of the original sugar that remains in the molasses. Assume that after each crystallization all of the impurities remain with the mother liquor.

6. If for a particular ultrafiltration plant concentrating skim milk, for a concentration ratio of 7:1 of protein relative to lactose, the plant capacity is $570\,kg\,m^{-2}\,h^{-1}$ of skim milk, estimate the plant capacity at a concentration ratio of 2:1 and the percentage of the water in the skim milk removed by the ultrafiltration.

CHAPTER 10

MECHANICAL SEPARATIONS

MECHANICAL separations are divided into four groups – sedimentation, centrifugal separation, filtration and sieving. In sedimentation, two immiscible liquids, or a liquid and a solid, are separated by allowing them to come to equilibrium under the action of gravity, the heavier material falling with respect to the lighter. This may be a slow process and it is often speeded up by applying centrifugal forces to increase the rate of sedimentation; this is called centrifugal separation. Filtration is the separation of solids from liquids, by causing the mixture to flow through fine pores which are small enough to stop the solid particles but large enough to allow the liquid to pass. Classification of solid particles is often done by sieving.

Mechanical separation of particles from a fluid uses forces acting on these particles. The forces can be direct restraining forces such as in sieving and filtration, or indirect as in impingement filters. They can come from gravitational or centrifugal action, which can be thought of as negative restraining forces, moving the particles relative to the containing fluid. So the separating action depends on the character of the particle being separated and the forces on the particle which cause the separation. The important characteristics of the particles are size, shape and density. Those of the fluid are viscosity and density. The reactions of the different components to the forces set up relative motion between the fluid and the particles, and between particles of different character. Under these relative motions, particles and fluid accumulate in different regions and can be gathered as in the filter cake and the filtrate tank in the filter press, in the discharge valve in the base of the cyclone and the air outlet at the top, in the outlet streams of a centrifuge or on the various sized sieves of a sieve set.

In the mechanical separations studied, the forces considered are gravity, combinations of gravity with other forces, centrifugal forces, pressure forces in which the fluid is forced away from the particles, and finally total restraint of solid particles where normally the fluid is of little consequence. The velocities of particles moving in a fluid are important for several of these separations.

THE VELOCITY OF PARTICLES MOVING IN A FLUID

Particles in a liquid, under a constant force, for example the force of gravity, accelerate for a time and thereafter move at a uniform velocity. This maximum velocity which they reach is called their terminal velocity. The terminal velocity depends upon the size, density and shape of the particles, and upon the properties of the fluid.

When a particle moves steadily through a fluid, there are two principal forces acting upon it, the external force causing the motion and the drag force resisting motion which arises from the frictional action of the fluid. The net external force on the moving particle is applied force less the reaction force exerted on the particle by the surrounding fluid, which is also subject to the applied force, so that

$$F_s = Va(\rho_p - \rho_f)$$

where F_s is the net external accelerating force on the particle, V, is the volume of the particle, a is the

143

acceleration which results from the external force, ρ_p is the density of the particle and ρ_f is the density of the fluid.

The drag force on the particle (F_d) is obtained by multiplying the velocity pressure of the flowing fluid by the projected area of the particle

$$F_d = C\rho_f v^2 A/2$$

where C is the coefficient known as the drag coefficient, ρ_f the density of the fluid, v is the velocity of the particle and A the projected area of the particle at right angles to the direction of the motion.

If these forces are acting on a spherical particle so that $V = \pi D^3/6$ and $A = \pi D^2/4$, where D is the diameter of the particle, then equating F_s and F_d, in which case the velocity v becomes the terminal velocity v_m, we have

$$(\pi D^3/6) \times a(\rho_p - \rho_f) = C\rho_f v_m^2 \pi D^2/8.$$

It has been found, theoretically, that for the streamline motion of spheres, the coefficient of drag is given by the relationship

$$C = 24/(\text{Re}) = 24\mu/Dv_m\rho_f.$$

Substituting this value for C and rearranging, we arrive at the equation for the terminal velocity

$$v_m = D^2 a(\rho_p - \rho_f)/18\mu. \tag{10.1}$$

This is the fundamental equation for movement of particles in fluids.

SEDIMENTATION

Sedimentation uses gravitational forces to separate particulate material from fluid streams. The particles are usually solid, but they can be small liquid droplets, and the fluid can be either a liquid or a gas. Sedimentation is very often used in the food industry for separating dirt and debris from incoming raw material, crystals from their mother liquor and dust or product particles from air streams.

In sedimentation, particles are falling from rest under the force of gravity. Therefore in sedimentation, eqn. (10.1) takes the familiar form of Stokes' Law:

$$v_m = D^2 g(\rho_p - \rho_f)/18\mu. \tag{10.2}$$

Note that eqn. (10.2) is not dimensionless and so consistent units must be employed throughout. For example, in the SI system D would be m, g in $m\,\text{sec}^{-2}$, ρ in $kg\,m^{-3}$ and μ in $N\,s\,m^{-2}$, and then v_m would be in $m\,s^{-1}$. Particle diameters are usually very small and are measured in microns (micrometres) $= 10^{-6}\,m$ with the symbol μm.

Stoke's Law applies only in streamline flow and strictly only to spherical particles. In the case of spheres the criterion for streamline flow is that $(\text{Re}) \leq 2$, and many practical cases occur in the region of streamline flow, or at least where streamline flow is a reasonable approximation. Where higher values of the Reynolds number are encountered, more detailed references should be sought, such as Henderson and Perry (1955), Perry (1973) and Coulson and Richardson (1978).

EXAMPLE 10.1. Calculate the settling velocity of dust particles of 60 μm and 10 μm diameter in air at 21°C and 100 kPa pressure. Assume that the particles are spherical and of density 1280 kg m^{-3}, and that the viscosity of air $= 1.8 \times 10^{-5}\,N\,s\,m^{-2}$ and density of air $= 1.2\,kg\,m^{-3}$.

$\therefore$ for 60-μm particle

$$v_m = \frac{(60 \times 10^{-6})^2 \times 9.81 \times (1280 - 1.2)}{18 \times 1.8 \times 10^{-5})}$$

$$= 0.14\,m\,s^{-1}$$

and for 10 μm particles since v_m is proportional to the squares of the diameters,

$$v_m = 0.14 \times (10/60)^2 = 3.9 \times 10^{-3}\,m\,s^{-1}.$$

Checking the Reynolds number for the 60-μm particles,

$$(\text{Re}) = (Dv\rho/\mu) = (60 \times 10^{-6} \times 0.14 \times 1.2)/$$
$$(1.8 \times 10^{-5})$$
$$= 0.56.$$

Stokes' Law applies only to cases in which settling is free, that is where the motion of one particle is unaffected by the motion of other particles. Where particles are in concentrated suspensions, the motion of particles downward is accompanied by an appreciable upward motion of the fluid and so the particles interfere with the flow patterns round one another as they fall. Stokes' Law predicts velocities proportional to the square of the particle diameters. In concentrated suspensions, it is found that all particles appear to settle at a uniform velocity once a sufficiently high level of concentration has been reached. Where the size range of the particles is not much greater than 10:1, all the particles tend to settle at the same rate. This rate lies between the rates that would be expected from Stokes' Law for the largest and for the smallest particles. In practical cases, in which Stoke's Law or simple extensions of it cannot be applied, probably the only satisfactory method of obtaining settling rates is by experiment.

Gravitational Sedimentation of Particles in a Liquid

Solids will settle in a liquid whose density is less than their own. At low concentration, Stokes' Law will apply but in many practical instances the concentrations are too high.

In a cylinder in which a uniform suspension is allowed to settle, various quite well-defined zones appear as the settling proceeds. At the top is a zone of clear liquid. Below this is a zone of more or less constant composition, constant because of the uniform settling velocity of all sizes of particles. At the bottom of the cylinder is a zone of sediment. If the size range of the particles is wide, the zone of constant composition near the top will not occur and it will be replaced by an extended zone of variable composition.

In a continuous thickener, with settling proceeding as the material flows through, and in which clarified liquid is being taken from the top and sludge from the bottom, these same zones occur. The minimum area necessary for a continuous thickener can be calculated by equating the rate of sedimentation in a particular zone to the counter-flow velocity of the rising fluid. In this case we have

$$v_u = (F - L)(\mathrm{d}w/\mathrm{d}\theta)/A\rho$$

where v_u is the upward velocity of the flow of the liquid, F is the mass ratio of liquid to solid in the feed, L is the mass ratio of liquid to solid in the underflow liquid, $\mathrm{d}w/\mathrm{d}\theta$ is the mass rate of feed of the solids, ρ is the density of the liquid and A is the settling area in the tank.

If the settling velocity of the particles is v, then $v_u = v$ and, therefore

$$A = (F - L)(\mathrm{d}w/\mathrm{d}\theta)/v\rho. \qquad (10.3)$$

The same analysis applies to particles (droplets) of liquid as to solid particles. Motion between particles and fluid is relative, and some particles may in fact rise.

EXAMPLE 10.2. A continuous separating tank is to be designed to follow after a water washing plant for a liquid oil. Estimate the necessary area for the tank if the oil, on leaving the washer, is in the form of globules 5.1×10^{-5} m diameter, the feed concentration is 4 kg water to 1 kg oil, and the leaving water is effectively oil free. The feed rate is 1000 kg h^{-1}, the density of the oil is 894 kg m^{-3} and the temperature of the oil and of the water is 38°C. Assume Stokes' Law.

Viscosity of water $= 0.7 \times 10^{-3}$ N s m^{-2}.
Density of water $= 1000$ kg m^{-3}.
Diameter of globules $= 5.1 \times 10^{-5}$ m.

$\therefore$ from eqn. (10.2)

$$v_m = (5.1 \times 10^{-5})^2 \times 9.81 \times (1000 - 894)/$$
$$(18 \times 0.7 \times 10^{-3})$$
$$= 2.15 \times 10^{-4} \mathrm{m\,s}^{-1} = 0.77 \mathrm{m\,h}^{-1}$$

and since $F = 4$ and $L = 0$, and $\mathrm{d}w/\mathrm{d}\theta$ = flow of minor component $= 1000/5 = 200$ kg h^{-1}, we have from eqn. (10.3)

$$A = 4 \times 200/(0.77 \times 1000)$$
$$= 1.0 \mathrm{m}^2.$$

Equipment for separation of solid particles from liquids by gravitational sedimentation is designed to provide sufficient time for the sedimentation to occur and to permit the overflow and the sediment to be removed without disturbing the separation. Continuous flow through the equipment is generally desired, so the flow velocities have to be low enough to avoid disturbing the sediment. Various shaped vessels are used, with a sufficient cross-section to keep the velocities down and fitted with slow-speed scraper-conveyors and pumps to remove the settled solids. When vertical cylindrical tanks are used, the scrapers generally rotate about an axis in the centre of the tank and the overflow may be over a weir round the periphery of the tank, as shown diagrammatically in Fig. 10.1.

In some cases, where it is not practicable to settle out fine particles, these can sometimes be floated to the surface by the use of air bubbles. This technique

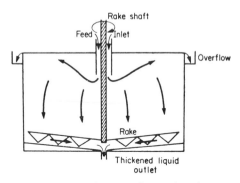

FIG. 10.1. Continuous-sedimentation plant.

is known as flotation and it depends upon the relative tendency of air and water to adhere to the particle surface. The water at the particle surface must be displaced by air, after which the buoyancy of the air is sufficient to carry both the particle and the air bubble up through the liquid.

Because it depends for its action upon surface forces, and surface forces can be greatly changed by the presence of even minute traces of surface active agents, flotation may be promoted by the use of suitable additives. In some instances, the air bubbles remain round the solid particles and cause froths. These are produced in vessels fitted with mechanical agitators, the agitators whip up the air–liquid mixture and overflow the froth into collecting troughs. The greatest application of froth flotation is in the concentration of minerals, but one use in the food industry is in the separation of small particles of fat from water. The froth is provided by dissolving air in water under pressure. On the pressure being released the air comes out of solution in the form of fine bubbles which rise and carry the fat with them to surface scrapers.

Sedimentation of Particles in a Gas

An important application, in the food industry, of sedimentation of solid particles occurs in spray dryers. In a spray dryer, the material to be dried is broken up into small droplets of about $100\,\mu$m diameter and these fall through heated air, drying as they do so. The necessary area so that the particles will settle can be calculated in the same way as for sedimentation. Two disadvantages arise from the slow rates of sedimentation: the large chamber areas required and the long contact times between particles and the heated air which may lead to deterioration of heat-sensitive products.

Settling Under Combined Forces

It is sometimes convenient to combine more than one force to effect a mechanical separation. In consequence of the low velocities, especially of very small particles, obtained when gravity is the only external force acting on the system, it is well worthwhile to also employ centrifugal forces. Probably the most common application of this is the cyclone separator. Combined forces are also used in some powder classifiers such as the rotary mechanical classifier and in ring dryers.

Cyclones

Cyclones are often used for the removal from air streams of particles of about $10\,\mu$m or more diameter. They are also used for separating particles from liquids and for separating liquid droplets from gases. The cyclone is a settling chamber in the form of a vertical cylinder, so arranged that the particle-laden air spirals round the cylinder to create centrifugal forces which throw the particles to the outside walls. Added to the gravitational forces, the centrifugal action provides reasonably rapid settlement rates. The spiral path, through the cyclone, provides sufficient separation time. A cyclone is illustrated in Fig. 10.2(a).

Stokes' Law shows that the terminal velocity of the particles is related to the force acting. In a centrifugal separator, such as a cyclone, for a particle, rotating round the periphery of the cyclone,

$$F_c = (mv^2)/r \qquad (10.4)$$

where F_c is the centrifugal force acting on the particle, m is the mass of the particle, v is the tangential velocity of the particle and r is the radius of the cyclone.

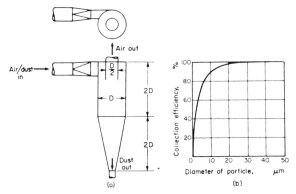

FIG. 10.2. Cyclone separator: (a) equipment, (b) efficiency of dust collection.

This equation shows that the force on the particle increases as the radius decreases, for a fixed velocity. Thus, the most efficient cyclones for removing small particles are those of smallest diameter. The limitations on the smallness of the diameter are the capital costs of small-diameter cyclones to provide sufficient output and the pressure drops.

The optimum shape for a cyclone has been evolved mainly from experience and proportions similar to those indicated in Fig. 10.4(a) have been found effective. The efficient operation of a cyclone depends very much on a smooth double helical flow being produced and anything which creates a flow disturbance or tends to make the flow depart from this pattern will have considerable and adverse effects upon efficiency. For example, it is important that the air enters tangentially at the top. Constricting baffles or lids should be avoided at the outlet for the air.

The efficiency of collection of dust in a cyclone is illustrated in Fig. 10.2(b). Because of the complex flow, the size cut of particles is not sharp and it can be seen that the percentage of entering particles which are retained in the cyclone falls off for particles below about 10 μm diameter. Cyclones can be used for separating particles from liquids as well as from gases and also for separating liquid droplets from gases.

Impingement separators

Other mechanical flow separators for particles in a gas use the principal of impingement in which deflector plates or rods, normal to the direction of flow of the stream, abruptly change the direction of flow. The gas recovers its direction of motion more rapidly than the particles because of its lower inertia. Suitably placed collectors can then be arranged to collect the particles as they are thrown out of the stream. This is the principle of operation of mesh and fibrous air filters. Various adaptations of impingement and settling separators can be adapted to remove particles from gases, but where the particle diameters fall below about 5 μm, cloth filters and packed tubular filters are about the only satisfactory equipment.

Classifiers

Classification implies the sorting of particulate material into size ranges. Use can be made of the different rates of movement of particles of different sizes and densities suspended in a fluid and differentially affected by imposed forces such as gravity and centrifugal fields, by making suitable arrangements to collect the different fractions as they move to different regions.

Rotary mechanical classifiers, combining differential settling with centrifugal action to augment the force of gravity and to channel the size fractions so that they can be collected, have come into increasing use in flour milling. One result of this is that because of small differences in sizes, shapes and densities between starch and protein-rich material after crushing, the flour can be classified into protein-rich and starch-rich fractions. Rotary mechanical classifiers can be used for other large particle separation in gases.

Classification is also employed in direct air dryers, in which use is made of the density decrease of material on drying. Dry material can be sorted out as a product and wet material returned for further drying. One such dryer uses a scroll casing through which the mixed material is passed, the wet particles pass to the outside of the casing and are recycled while the material in the centre is removed as dry product.

CENTRIFUGAL SEPARATIONS

The separation by sedimentation of two immiscible liquids, or of a liquid and a solid, depends on the effects of gravity on the components. Sometimes this separation may be very slow because the specific gravities of the components may not be very different, or because of forces holding the components in association, for example as occur in emulsions. Also, under circumstances when sedimentation does occur there may not be a clear demarcation between the components but rather a merging of the layers. For example, if whole milk is allowed to stand, the cream will rise to the top and there is eventually a clean separation between the cream and the skim milk. However, this takes a long time, of the order of one day, and so it is suitable, perhaps, for the farm kitchen but not for the factory. Much greater forces can be obtained by introducing centrifugal action, in a centrifuge. Gravity still acts and the net force is a combination of the centrifugal force with gravity as in the cyclone. Because in most industrial centrifuges, the centrifugal forces imposed are so much greater than gravity, the effects of gravity can usually be neglected in the analysis of the separation.

The centrifugal force on a particle which is constrained to rotate in a circular path is given by

$$F_c = mr\omega^2 \qquad (10.5)$$

where F_c is the centrifugal force acting on the particle to maintain it in the circular path, r is the radius of the path, m is the mass of the particle, and ω (omega) is the angular velocity of the particle.

Or, since $\omega = v/r$, where v is the tangential velocity of the particle

$$F_c = (mv^2)/r. \qquad (10.6)$$

Rotational speeds are normally expressed in revolutions per minute, so that eqn. (10.6) can also be written, as $\omega = 2\pi N/60$

$$F_c = mr(2\pi N/60)^2 = 0.011 \, mrN^2 \qquad (10.7)$$

where N is the rotational speed in revolutions per minute.

If this is compared with the force of gravity (F_g) on the particle, which is $F_g = mg$, it can be seen that the centrifugal acceleration, equal to $0.011 \, rN^2$, has replaced the gravitational acceleration, equal to g. The centrifugal force is often expressed for comparative purposes as so many "g".

EXAMPLE 10.3. How many "g" can be obtained in a centrifuge which can spin a liquid at 2000 rev/min at

a maximum radius of 10 cm?

$$F_c = 0.011 \, mrN^2,$$
$$F_g = mg,$$
$$\therefore \quad F_c/F_g = (0.011 \, rN^2)/g$$
$$= (0.011 \times 0.1 \times 2000^2)/9.81$$
$$= 450.$$

The centrifugal force depends upon the radius and speed of rotation and upon the mass of the particle. If the radius and the speed of rotation are fixed, then the controlling factor is the weight of the particle so that the heavier the particle the greater is the centrifugal force acting on it. Consequently, if two liquids, one of which is twice as dense as the other, are placed in a bowl and the bowl is rotated about a vertical axis at high speed, the centrifugal force per unit volume will be twice as great for the heavier liquid as for the lighter. The heavy liquid will occupy the annulus at the periphery of the bowl and it will displace the lighter liquid towards the centre. This is the principle of the centrifugal liquid separator, illustrated diagrammatically in Fig. 10.3.

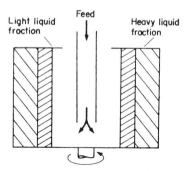

FIG. 10.3. Liquid separation in a centrifuge.

Rate of Separation

The steady-state velocity of particles moving in a streamline flow under the action of an accelerating force is, from eqn. (10.1),

$$v_m = D^2 a(\rho_p - \rho_f)/18\mu.$$

If a streamline flow occurs in a centrifuge we can write, from eqn. (10.7)

$$F_c = ma,$$

$$\therefore \quad F_c/m = a = r(2\pi N/60)^2,$$

so that

$$v_m = D^2 r(2\pi N/60)^2(\rho_p - \rho_f)/18\mu$$
$$= D^2 N^2 r(\rho_p - \rho_f)/1640\mu. \qquad (10.8)$$

EXAMPLE 10.4. A dispersion of oil in water is to be separated using a centrifuge. Assume that the oil is dispersed in the form of spherical globules 5.1×10^{-5} m diameter and that its density is $894 \, \text{kg m}^{-3}$. If the centrifuge rotates at 1500 rev/min and the effective radius at which the separation occurs is 3.8 cm calculate the velocity of the oil through the water. Take the density of water to be $1000 \, \text{kg m}^{-3}$ and its viscosity to be $7 \times 10^{-4} \, \text{N s m}^{-2}$. (The separation in this problem is the same as that in Example 10.3, in which the rate of settling under gravity was calculated.)

From eqn. (10.8)

$$v_m = (5.1 \times 10^{-5})^2 \times (1500)^2 \times 0.038 \times (1000 - 894)/(1.64 \times 10^3 \times 7 \times 10^{-4})$$
$$= 0.02 \, \text{m s}^{-1}.$$

Checking that it is reasonable to assume Stokes' Law

$$\text{Re} = (Dv\rho/\mu)$$
$$= (5.1 \times 10^{-5} \times 0.02 \times 1000)/(7.0 \times 10^{-4})$$
$$= 1.5$$

so that the flow is streamline and it should obey Stokes' Law.

Liquid Separation

The separation of one component of a liquid–liquid mixture, where the liquids are immiscible but finely dispersed, as in an emulsion, is a common operation in the food industry. It is particularly common in the dairy industry in which the emulsion, milk, is separated by a centrifuge into skim milk and cream. It seems worthwhile, on this account, to examine the position of the two phases in the centrifuge as it operates. The milk is fed continuously into the machine, which is generally a bowl rotating about a vertical axis, and cream and skim milk come from the respective discharges. At some point within the bowl there must be a surface of separation between cream and the skim milk.

Consider a thin differential cylinder, of thickness dr and height b as shown in Fig. 10.4(a):

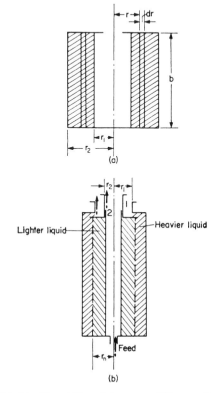

FIG. 10.4. Liquid centrifuge: (a) pressure difference, (b) neutral zone.

the differential centrifugal force across the thickness dr is given by

$$dF_c = (dm)r\omega^2$$

where dF_c is the differential force across the cylinder wall, dm is the mass of the differential cylinder, ω is the angular velocity of the cylinder and r is the radius of the cylinder. But, $dm = 2\pi\rho rb \, dr$, where ρ is the density of the liquid and b is the height of the cylinder. The area over which the force dF_c acts is $2\pi rb$, so that

$$dF_c/2\pi rb = dP = \rho\omega^2 r \, dr$$

where dP is the differential pressure across the wall of the differential cylinder.

To find the differential pressure in a centrifuge, between radius r_1 and r_2, the equation for dP can be integrated, letting the pressure at radius r_1 be P_1, and that at r_2, P_2 and so

$$P_2 - P_1 = \rho\omega^2(r_2^2 - r_1^2)/2. \qquad (10.9)$$

Equation (10.9) shows the radial variation in pressure across the centrifuge.

Consider now Fig. 10.4(b) which represents the bowl of a vertical continuous liquid centrifuge. The feed enters the centrifuge near to the axis, the heavier liquid A discharges through the top opening 1 and the lighter liquid B through the opening 2. Let r_1 be the radius at the discharge pipe for the heavier liquid and r_2 that for the lighter liquid. At some other radius r_n there will be a separation between the two phases, the heavier and the lighter. For the system to be in hydrostatic balance, the pressures of each component at radius r_n must be equal, so that applying eqn. (10.9) to find the pressures of each component at radius r_n, and equating these we have

$$\rho_A\omega^2(r_n^2 - r_1^2)/2 = \rho_B\omega^2(r_n^2 - r_2^2)/2,$$
$$\therefore \quad r_n^2 = (\rho_A r_1^2 - \rho_B r_2^2)/(\rho_A - \rho_B) \quad (10.10)$$

where ρ_A is the density of the heavier liquid and ρ_B is the density of the lighter liquid.

Equation (10.10) shows that as the discharge radius for the heavier liquid is made smaller, then the radius of the neutral zone must also decrease. When the neutral zone is nearer to the central axis, the lighter component is exposed only to a relatively small centrifugal force compared with the heavier liquid. This is applied where, as in the separation of cream from milk, as much cream as possible is to be removed and the neutral radius is therefore kept small. The feed to a centrifuge of this type should be as nearly as possible into the neutral zone so that it will enter with the least disturbance of the system. This relationship can, therefore, be used to place the feed inlet and the product outlets in the centrifuge to get maximum separation.

EXAMPLE 10.5. If a cream separator has discharge radii of 5 cm and 7.5 cm and if the density of skim milk is $1032\ \mathrm{kg\,m^{-3}}$ and that of cream is $865\ \mathrm{kg\,m^{-3}}$, calculate the radius of the neutral zone so that the feed inlet can be designed.

From eqn. (10.10)

$$r_n^2 = [1032 \times (0.075)^2 - 865 \times (0.05)^2]/$$
$$(1032 - 865)$$
$$= 0.022\ \mathrm{m^2},$$
$$\therefore r_n = 0.15\ \mathrm{m}.$$

Centrifuge Equipment

The simplest form of centrifuge consists of a bowl spinning about a vertical axis, as shown in Fig. 10.4(a). Liquids, or liquids and solids, are introduced into this and under centrifugal force the heavier liquid or particles pass to the outermost regions of the bowl, whilst the lighter components move towards the centre. If the feed is all liquid, then suitable collection pipes can be arranged to allow separation of the heavier and the lighter components. Various arrangements are used to accomplish this collection effectively and with a minimum of disturbance to the flow pattern in the machine. To understand the function of these collection arrangements, it is very often helpful to think of the centrifuge action as analogous to gravity settling, with the various weirs and overflows acting in just the same way as in a settling tank even though the centrifugal forces are very much greater than gravity.

In liquid-separation centrifuges, conical plates are arranged as illustrated in Fig. 10.5(a) and these give smoother flow and better separation.

Whereas liquid phases can easily be removed from a centrifuge, solids present much more of a problem. Stationary ploughs cannot be used as these create too much disturbance of the flow

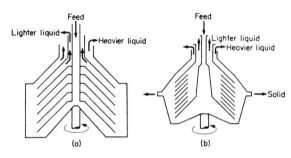

FIG. 10.5. Liquid centrifuges: (a) conical bowl, (b) nozzle.

pattern on which the centrifuge depends for its separation. One method of handling solids is to provide nozzles on the circumference of the centrifuge bowl as illustrated in Fig. 10.5(b). These nozzles may be opened at intervals to discharge accumulated solids together with some of the heavy liquid. Alternatively, the nozzles may be open continuously relying on their size and position to discharge the solids with as little as possible of the heavier liquid. These machines thus separate the feed into three streams, light liquid, heavy liquid and solids, the solids carrying with them some of the heavy liquid as well. Another method of handling solids from continuous feed is to employ telescoping action in the bowl, sections of the bowl moving over one another and conveying the solids that have accumulated towards the outlet, as illustrated in Fig. 10.6(a).

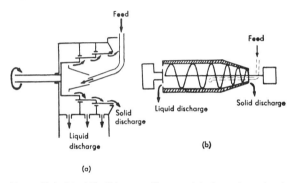

Fig. 10.6. Liquid/solid centrifuges: (a) telescoping bowl, (b) horizontal bowl-scroll discharge.

The horizontal bowl, scroll discharge, centrifuge, as illustrated in Fig. 10.6(b) can discharge continuously. In this machine, the horizontal collection scroll (or screw) rotates inside the conical-ended bowl of the machine and conveys the solids with it, whilst the liquid discharges over an overflow towards the centre of the machine and at the opposite end to the solid discharge. The essential feature of these machines is that the speed of the scroll, relative to the bowl, must not be great. For example, if the bowl speed is 2000 rev/min a suitable speed for the scroll might be 25 rev/min relative to the bowl which would mean a scroll speed of 2025 or 1975 rev/min. These differential speeds are maintained by gearing between the driving shafts for the bowl and the scroll. These machines can continuously handle feeds with solid contents of up to

30%. A discussion of the action of centrifuges is given by Trowbridge (1962) and they are also treated in McCabe and Smith (1975) and Coulson and Richardson (1977).

FILTRATION

In another class of mechanical separations virtually total restraint is imposed on the particles above a given size by imposing a screen in the flow, through which they cannot pass. The fluid in this case is subject to a force which moves it past the particles. This is called filtration. The particles suspended in the fluid, which will not pass through the apertures, are retained and build up into what is called a filter cake. Sometimes it is the fluid, the filtrate, that is the product, in other cases the filter cake.

The fine apertures necessary for filtration are provided by fabric filter cloths, by meshes and screens of plastics or metals, or by beds of solid particles. In some cases, a thin preliminary coat of cake, or of other fine particles, is put on the cloth prior to the main filtration process. This preliminary coating is put on in order to have sufficiently fine pores on the filter and it is known as a pre-coat.

The analysis of filtration is largely a question of studying the flow system. The fluid passes through the filter medium, which offers resistance to its passage, under the influence of a force which is the pressure differential across the filter. Thus, we can write the familiar equation:

$$\text{rate of filtration} = \text{driving force}/\text{resistance}.$$

Resistance arises from the filter cloth, mesh, or bed, and to this is added the resistance of the filter cake as it accumulates. The filter-cake resistance is obtained by multiplying the specific resistance of the filter cake, that is its resistance per unit thickness, by the thickness of the cake. The resistances of the filter material and pre-coat are combined into a single resistance called the filter resistance. It is convenient to express the filter resistance in terms of a fictitious thickness of filter cake. This thickness is multiplied by the specific resistance of the filter cake to give the filter resistance. Thus the overall equation giving the volumetric rate of flow $dV/d\theta$ is

$$\frac{dV}{d\theta} = \frac{A\,\Delta P}{R}.$$

As the total resistance is proportional to the viscosity of the fluid, we can write

$$R = \mu r(L_c + L)$$

where R is the resistance to flow through the filter, μ is the viscosity of the fluid, r is the specific resistance of the filter cake, L_c is the thickness of the filter cake and L is the fictitious equivalent thickness of the filter cloth and pre-coat, A is the filter area, and ΔP is the pressure drop across the filter.

If the rate of flow of the liquid and its solid content are known and assuming that all solids are retained on the filter, the thickness of the filter cake can be expressed by

$$L_c = wV/A$$

where w is the fractional solid content per unit volume of liquid, V is the volume of fluid that has passed through the filter and A is the area of filter surface on which the cake forms.

The resistance can then be written

$$R = \mu r(wV/A + L) \qquad (10.11)$$

and the equation for flow through the filter, under the driving force of the pressure drop is then

$$dV/d\theta = A\,\Delta P/\mu r\,[w(V/A) + L]. \qquad (10.12)$$

Equation (10.12) may be regarded as the fundamental equation for filtration. It expresses the rate of filtration in terms of quantities which can be measured, found from tables, or in some cases estimated. It can be used to predict the performance of large-scale filters on the basis of laboratory or pilot scale tests. Two applications of eqn. (10.12) are filtration at a constant flow rate and filtration under constant pressure.

Constant-rate Filtration

In the early stages of a filtration cycle, it frequently happens that the filter resistance is large relative to the resistance of the filter cake because the cake is thin. Under these circumstances, the resistance offered to the flow is virtually constant and so filtration proceeds at a more or less constant rate. Equation (10.12) can then be integrated to give the quantity of liquid passed through the filter in a given time. The terms on the right-hand side of eqn. (10.12) are constant so that integration is very simple:

$$dV/A\,d\theta = V/A\theta = \Delta P/\mu r(wV/A + L)$$

or

$$\Delta P = V/A\theta \times \mu r(wV/A + L). \qquad (10.13)$$

From eqn. (10.13) the pressure drop required for any desired flow rate can be found. Also, if a series of runs is carried out under different pressures, the results can be used to determine the resistance of the filter cake.

Constant-pressure Filtration

Once the initial cake has been built up, and this is true of the greater part of many practical filtration operations, flow occurs under a constant-pressure differential. Under these conditions, the term ΔP in eqn. (10.12) is constant and so

$$\mu r(w/V/A + L)\,dV = A\,\Delta P\,d\theta$$

and integration from $V = 0$ at $\theta = 0$, to $V = V$ at $\theta = \theta$

$$\mu r(wV^2/2A + LV) = A\,\Delta P\theta$$

and rewriting this

$$\theta A/V = (\mu rw/2\,\Delta P)(V/A) + \mu rL/\Delta P. \,(10.14)$$

Equation (10.14) is useful because it covers a situation which is frequently found in a practical filtration plant. It can be used to predict the performance of filtration plant on the basis of experimental results. If a test is carried out using constant pressure, collecting and measuring the filtrate at measured time intervals, a graph can be plotted of $\theta/(V/A)$ against (V/A) and from the statement of eqn. (10.14) it can be seen that this graph should be a straight line. The slope of this line will correspond to $\mu rw/2\,\Delta P$ and the intercept on the $\theta/(V/A)$ axis will give the value of $\mu rL/\Delta P$. Since, in general, μ, w, ΔP and A are known or can be measured, the values of the slope and intercept on this graph enable L and r to be calculated.

EXAMPLE 10.6. A filtration test was carried out on a laboratory filter press under a constant pressure of 340 kPa and volumes of filtrate were collected as follows:

Filtrate volume (kg)	20	40	60	80
Time (min)	8	26	54.5	93

The area of the laboratory filter was 0.186 m². If in a plant scale filter, it is desired to filter a slurry containing the same material, but at 50% greater concentration than that used for the test, and under a pressure of 270 kPa, estimate the quantity of filtrate that would pass through in 1 h if the area of the filter is 9.3 m².

From the experimental data:

V (kg)	20	40	60	80
θ (s)	480	1560	3270	5580
V/A (kg/m²)	107.5	215	323	430
$\theta/(V/A)$ (s m² kg⁻¹)	4.47	7.26	10.12	12.98

These values of $\theta(V/A)$ are plotted against the corresponding values of V/A in Fig. 10.7. From the graph, we find that the slope of the line is 0.0265, and the intercept 1.6.

Then substituting in eqn. (10.14) we have

$$\theta/(V/A) = 0.0265(V/A) + 1.6.$$

To fit the desired conditions for the plant filter, the constants in this equation will have to be modified. If all of the factors in eqn. (10.14) except those which are varied in the problem are combined into constants, K and K', we can write

$$\theta/(V/A) = (w/\Delta P)K(V/A) + K'/\Delta P. \qquad (a)$$

In the laboratory experiment $w = w_1$, and $\Delta P = \Delta P_1$.

$$\therefore \quad K = (0.0265\,\Delta P_1/w_1) \text{ and } K' = 1.6\,\Delta P.$$

For the new plant condition, $w = w_2$ and $P = P_2$, so that, substituting in the eqn. (a) above, we then have for the plant filter, under the given conditions

$$\theta/(V/A) = (0.0265\,\Delta P_1/w_1)(w_2/\Delta P_2)(V/A)$$
$$+ (1.6\,\Delta P_1)(1/\Delta P_2)$$

and since from these conditions

$$\Delta P_1/\Delta P_2 = 340/270$$

and $$w_2/w_1 = 150/100,$$

$$\therefore \quad \theta/(V/A) = 0.0265(340/270)(150/100)(V/A)$$
$$+ 1.6(340/270)$$
$$= 0.05(V/A) + 2.0,$$

$$\therefore \quad \theta = 0.5(V/A)^2 + 2.0(V/A).$$

We have to find the volume that passes the filter in 1 h which is 3600 s, that is to find V for $\theta = 3600$. And so

$$3600 = 0.05(V/A)^2 + 2.0(V/A)$$

and solving this quadratic equation we find that

$$V/A = 250\,\text{kg m}^{-2}$$

and so the slurry passing through 9.3 m² in 1 h would be

$$250 \times 9.3 = 2325\,\text{kg}.$$

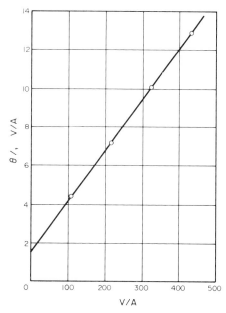

FIG. 10.7. Filtration graph.

Filter-cake Compressibility

With some filter cakes, the specific resistance varies with the pressure drop across it. This is because the cake becomes more dense under the higher pressure and so provides fewer and smaller passages for flow. The effect is spoken of as the compressibility of the cake. Soft and flocculent materials provide highly compressible filter cakes, whereas hard granular materials, such as sugar and salt crystals, are little affected by pressure. To allow for cake compressibility the empirical relationship has been proposed:

$$r = r' \Delta P^s$$

where r is the specific resistance of the cake under pressure P, ΔP is the pressure drop across the filter, r' is the specific resistance of the cake under a pressure drop of 1 atm and s is a constant for the material, called its compressibility

This expression for r can be inserted into the filtration equations, such as eqn. (10.14), and values for r' and s can be determined by carrying out experimental runs under various pressures.

Filtration Equipment

The basic requirements for filtration equipment are: mechanical support for the filter medium, flow access to and from the filter medium and provision for removing the filter cake. In some instances, washing of the filter cake to remove traces of the solution may be necessary. Pressure can be provided on the upstream side of the filter, or a vacuum can be drawn downstream, or both can be used to drive the fluid through.

Plate and frame filter press

In the plate and frame filter press, a cloth or mesh is spread out over plates which support the cloth along ridges but at the same time leave a free area, as large as possible, below the cloth for flow of the filtrate. This is illustrated in Fig. 10.8(a). The plates with their filter cloths may be horizontal, but they are more usually hung vertically with a number of plates operated in parallel to give sufficient area.

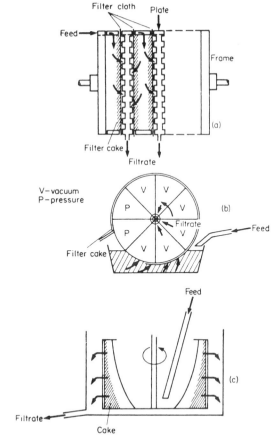

FIG. 10.8. Filtration equipment: (a) plate and frame press, (b) rotary vacuum filter, (c) centrifugal filter.

Filter cake builds up on the upstream side of the cloth, that is the side remote from the plate. In the early stages of the filtration cycle, the pressure drop across the cloth is small and filtration proceeds at more or less a constant rate. As the cake increases, the process becomes more and more a constant-pressure one and this is the case throughout most of the cycle. When the available space between successive frames is filled with cake, the press has to be dismantled and the cake scraped off and cleaned, after which a further cycle can be initiated. The plate and frame filter press is cheap but it is difficult to mechanize to any great extent.

Variants of the plate and frame press have been developed which allow easier discharging of the filter cake. For example, the plates, which may be rectangular or circular, are supported on a central hollow shaft for the filtrate and the whole assembly enclosed in a pressure tank containing the slurry. Filtration can be done under pressure or vacuum. The advantage of vacuum filtration is that the pressure drop can be maintained whilst the cake is still under atmospheric pressure and so can be removed easily. The disadvantages are the greater cost of maintaining a given pressure drop by applying a vacuum and the limitation on the vacuum to about 80 kPa maximum. In pressure filtration, the pressure driving force is limited only by the economics of attaining the pressure and by the mechanical strength of the equipment.

Rotary filters

In rotary filters, the flow passes through a rotating cylindrical cloth from which the filter cake can be continuously scraped. Either pressure or vacuum can provide the driving force, but a particularly useful form is the rotary vacuum filter. In this, the cloth is supported on the periphery of a horizontal cylindrical drum which dips into a bath of the slurry. Vacuum is drawn in those segments of the drum surface on which the cake is building up. A suitable bearing applies the vacuum at the stage where the actual filtration commences and breaks the vacuum at the stage where the cake is being scraped off after filtration. Filtrate is removed through trunnion bearings. Rotary vacuum filters are expensive, but they do provide a considerable degree of mechanization and convenience. A rotary vacuum filter is illustrated diagrammatically in Fig. 10.8(b).

Centrifugal filters

Centrifugal force is used to provide the driving force in some filters. These machines are really centrifuges fitted with a perforated bowl which may also have filter cloth on it. Liquid is fed into the interior of the bowl and under the centrifugal forces, it passes out through the filter material. This is illustrated in Fig. 10.8(c).

Air filters

Filters are used quite extensively to remove suspended dust or particles from air streams. The air or gas moves through a fabric and the dust is left behind. These filters are particularly useful for the removal of fine particles. One type of bag filter consists of a number of vertical cylindrical cloth bags 15–30 cm diameter, the air passing through the bags in parallel. Air bearing the dust enters the bags, usually at the bottom and the air passes through the cloth. A familiar example of a bag filter for dust is to be found in the domestic vacuum cleaner. Some designs of bag filters provide for the mechanical removal of the accumulated dust. For removal of particles less than 5 μm diameter in modern sterilization units, paper filters and packed tubular filters are used. These cover the range of sizes of bacterial cells and spores.

SIEVING

In the final separation operation in this group, restraint is imposed on some of the particles by mechanical screens which prevent their passage. This is done successively, using increasingly smaller screens, to give a series of particles classified into size ranges. The fluid, usually air, can effectively be ignored in this operation which is called sieving. The material is shaken or agitated above a mesh or cloth screen, so that particles of smaller size than the mesh openings can pass through under the force of gravity. Rates of throughput of sieves are dependent upon a number of factors, chiefly the nature and the shape of the particles, the frequency and the amplitude of the shaking, the methods used to prevent sticking or bridging of particles in the apertures of the sieve and the tension and physical nature of the sieve material.

Standard sieve sizes have been evolved, covering a range from 25 mm aperture down to about 0.6 mm aperture. The mesh was originally the number of apertures per inch. A logical base for a sieve series would be that each sieve size have some fixed relation to the next larger and to the next smaller. A convenient ratio is 2:1 and this has been chosen for the standard series of sieves in use in the United States, the Tyler sieve series. The mesh numbers are expressed in terms of the numbers of opening to the inch (= 2.54 cm). By suitable choice of sizes for the wire from which the sieves are woven, the ratio of opening sizes has been kept approximately constant in moving from one sieve to the next. Actually, the ratio of 2:1 is rather large so that the normal series progresses in the ratio of $\sqrt{2}:1$ and if still closer ratios are required intermediate sieves are available to make the ratio between adjacent sieves in the complete set $\sqrt[4]{2}:1$. The standard British series of sieves has been based on the available standard wire sizes, so that, although apertures are generally of the same order as the Tyler series, aperture ratios are not constant. In the SI system, apertures are measured in mm. A table of sieve sizes has been included in Appendix 10.

In order to get reproducible results in accurate sieving work, it is necessary to standardize the procedure. The analysis reports either the percentage of material which is retained on each sieve, or the cumulative percentage of the material larger than a given sieve size.

The results of a sieve analysis can be presented in various forms, perhaps the best being the cumulative analysis giving, as a function of the sieve aperture (D), the weight fraction of the powder $F(D)$ which passes through that and larger sieves, irrespective of what happens on the smaller ones. That is the cumulative fraction sums all particles smaller than the particular sieve of interest.

Thus $F = F(D)$,

$$\mathrm{d}F/\mathrm{d}D = F'(D)$$

where $F'(D)$ is the derivative of $F(D)$ with respect to D.

$$\text{So } \int_{D_1}^{D_2} \mathrm{d}F = \int_{D_1}^{D_2} F'(D)\mathrm{d}D \qquad (10.15)$$

and this gives the cumulative fraction between two sizes D_2 (larger) and D_1 which is also that fraction passing through sieve of aperture D_2 and caught on that of aperture D_1. The $F'(D)$ graph gives a size distribution analysis.

EXAMPLE 10.7. Given the following sieve analysis:

Sieve size mm	% Retained
1.00	0
0.50	11
0.25	49
0.125	28
0.063	8
Through 0.063	4

plot a cumulative sieve analysis and estimate the weight fraction of particles of sizes between 0.300 and 0.350 mm and 0.350 and 0.400 mm.

From the above table:

Less than aperture (mm)	0.063	0.125	0.250	0.500	1.00
Percentage (cumulative)	4	12	40	89	100

This has been plotted on Fig. 10.9 and the graph $F(D)$ has been smoothed. From this the graph of $F'(D)$ has been plotted, working from that slope of $F(D)$, to give the particle size distribution.

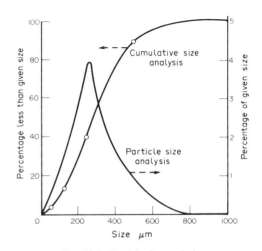

FIG. 10.9. Particle-size analysis.

To find the fraction between the specified sizes, eqn. (10.15) indicates that this will be given directly by the fraction that the area under the $F'(D)$ graph and between the sizes of interest is to the total area under the $F'(D)$ curve. Counting squares, on Fig. 10.9, gives

between 0.300 and 0.350 mm as 13%
and 0.350 and 0.400 mm as 9%.

For industrial sieving, it is seldom worthwhile to continue until equilibrium is reached. In effect, a sieving-efficiency term is introduced, as a proportion only of the particles smaller than a given size actually get through. The sieves of a series are often mounted one above the other, and a mechanical shaker used.

Sieve analysis for particle-size determination should be treated with some caution especially for particles deviating radically from spherical shape, and needs to be supplemented with microscopical examination of the powders. The size distribution of powders can be useful to estimate parameters of technological importance such as the surface area available for a reaction, the ease of dispersion in water of a dried milk powder, or the performance characteristics of a spray dryer or a separating cyclone.

Industrial sieves include rotary screens, which are horizontal cylinders either perforated or covered with a screen, into which the material is fed. The smaller particles pass through as they tumble around in the rotating screens. Other industrial sieves are vibrating screens, generally vibrated by an eccentric weight; and multi-deck screens on which the particles fall through from one screen to another until they reach one which is too fine for them to pass. With vibrating screens, the frequency and amplitude of the vibrations can significantly affect the separation achieved. Screen capacities are usually rated in terms of the quantity passed through per unit area in unit time. Particles that can conveniently be screened industrially range from $50\,\mu m$ diameter, upwards.

Continuous vibrating sieves used in the flour-milling industry employ a sieve with increasing apertures so that the fine fraction at any stage is being removed as the flour particles are being moved along. The shaking action of the sieve provides the necessary motion to make the particles fall through and also conveys the oversize particles on to the next section. Below the sieves, in some cases, air classification may be used to remove bran.

SUMMARY

1. Particles can be separated from fluids, or particles of different sizes from each other, making use of forces which have different effects depending on particle size.
2. Flow forces in fluids give rise to velocities of particles relative to the fluid of

$$v = D^2 a(\rho_p - \rho_f)/18\mu$$

and where the particle is falling under gravity $a = g$ giving Stokes' Law

$$v = D^2 g(\rho_p - \rho_f)/18\mu.$$

3. Thickeners can be used to settle out solids, and the minimum area of a continuous thickener can be calculated from

$$v = (F - L)(dw/d\theta)/A\rho.$$

4. Gravitational and centrifugal forces can be combined in a cyclone separator.
5. In a centrifuge, the force relative to the force of gravity is given by $(0.011rN^2)/g$.
6. In a filter, the particles are retained and the fluid passes at a rate given by

$$dV/d\theta = A\,\Delta P/\mu r\,[w(V/A) + L].$$

7. Sieve analysis can be used to estimate particle size distributions.

PROBLEMS

1. A test was carried out on a wine filter. It was found that under a pressure of 350 kPa gauge, the rate of flow was $450\,\mathrm{kg\,h^{-1}}$ from a total filter area of $0.82\,\mathrm{m^2}$. Assuming that the quantity of cake is insignificant in changing the resistance of the filter, if another filter of $6.5\,\mathrm{m^2}$ area is added, what pressure would be required for a throughput of 500 hectolitres per 8-hour shift from the combined plant?
2. In the filter system of problem 1, if the viscosity of the wine was $1.8 \times 10^{-3}\,\mathrm{N\,s\,m^{-2}}$, calculate the value of the specific cake resistance and the equivalent thickness of the filter cloth for the system with the pressure of 350 kPa in the test if the slurry concentration is 4 kg solid in 100 kg of water.
3. If in the system of problem 1, the plant-scale operations produce a throughput in 1 hour of 2800 kg estimate the compressibility of the filter cake.
4. Calculate the settling velocity of sand particles 0.2 mm diameter in 22% salt solution of density $1240\,\mathrm{kg\,m^{-3}}$ at 20°C. Take the density of sand as $2010\,\mathrm{kg\,m^{-3}}$.
5. If in a trough of slowly $(0.01\,\mathrm{m\,s^{-1}})$ flowing 22% salt solution 0.8 m long, it was desired to settle out sand particles, with which the solution had become contaminated, estimate the smallest diameter of sand particle which would be removed.
6. It is desired to establish a centrifugal force of 6000g in a small centrifuge with an effective working radius of 9 cm. At what speed would the centrifuge have to rotate? If the actual centrifuge bowl has a radius of 8 cm minimum and 9 cm maximum what is the difference in the centrifugal force between the minimum and the maximum radii?
7. In a centrifuge separating oil (of density $900\,\mathrm{kg\,m^{-3}}$) from brine (of density $1070\,\mathrm{kg\,m^{-3}}$) the discharge radius for the oil is 5 cm. Calculate a suitable radius for the brine

discharge and for the feed intake so that the machine will work smoothly assuming that the volumes of oil and of brine are approximately equal.

8. If a centrifuge is regarded as similar to a gravity settler but with gravity replaced by the centrifugal field, calculate the area of a centrifuge of working radius r and speed of rotation N revolutions m^{-1} which would have the same throughput as a gravity settling tank of area 100 m^2.

9. If an olive-oil emulsion of 5 μm droplets is to be separated in a centrifuge, from water, what speed would be necessary if the radial travel of the particles is 3 cm and the effective radius of the centrifuge is 5 cm?

10. A sieve analysis gives the following results:

Sieve size mm	Wt. retained g
1.00	0
0.500	64
0.250	324
0.125	240
0.063	48
Through 0.063	24

Plot a cumulative size analysis and a size-distribution analysis, and estimate the weights, per 1000 kg of powder, which would lie in the size ranges 0.150 to 0.200 mm and 0.250 to 0.350 mm.

11. If a dust, whose particle size distribution is as in the table below, is passed through a cyclone with a collection efficiency as shown in Fig. 10.2 estimate the size distribution of the dust passing out.

Particle diameter

<0.5 μm	3 μm	6 μm	10 μm	15 μm	25 μm

Wt. of particles kg

0.2	0.7	0.4	0.2	0.1	0

CHAPTER 11

SIZE REDUCTION

Raw materials often occur in sizes that are too large to be used and, therefore, they must be reduced in size. This size-reduction operation can be divided into two major categories depending on whether the material is a solid or a liquid. If it is solid, the operations are called grinding and cutting, if it is liquid, emulsification or atomization. All depend on the reaction to shearing forces within solids and liquids.

GRINDING AND CUTTING

Grinding and cutting reduce the size of solid materials by mechanical action, dividing them into smaller particles. Perhaps the most extensive application of grinding in the food industry is in the milling of grains to flour, but it is used on many other occasions, such as in the grinding of corn for manufacture of corn starch, the grinding of sugar and the milling of dried foods, such as vegetables. Cutting is used to break down large pieces of food into smaller pieces suitable for further processing, such as in the preparation of meat for retail sales and in the preparation of processed meats, and processed vegetables.

In the grinding process, materials are reduced in size by fracturing them. The mechanism of fracture is not fully understood, but in the process the material is stressed by the action of mechanical members of the grinding machine and initially the stress is absorbed internally by the material as strain energy. When the local strain energy exceeds a critical level, which is a function of the material, fracture occurs along lines of weakness and the stored energy is released. Some of the energy is taken up in the creation of new surface, but the greater part of it is dissipated as heat. Time also plays a part in the fracturing process and it appears that material will fracture at lower stress concentrations if these can be maintained for longer periods. Grinding is, therefore, achieved by mechanical stress followed by rupture and the energy required depends upon the hardness of the material and also upon the tendency of the material to crack – its friability.

The force applied may be compression, impact, or shear, and both the magnitude of the force and the time of application affect the extent of grinding achieved. For efficient grinding, the energy applied to the material should exceed the minimum energy needed to rupture the material by as small a margin as possible. Excess energy is lost as heat and this loss should be kept as low as practicable.

The important factors to be studied in the grinding process are the amount of energy used and the amount of new surface formed by grinding.

Energy Used in Grinding

Grinding is a very inefficient process and it is important to use energy as efficiently as possible. Unfortunately, it is not easy to calculate the minimum energy required for a given reduction process, but some theories have been advanced which are useful.

These theories depend upon the basic assumption that the energy required to produce a change dL in a particle of a typical size dimension L is a simple power function of L:

$$dE/dL = KL^n \qquad (11.1)$$

159

where dE is the differential energy required, dL is the change in a typical dimension, L is the magnitude of a typical length dimension and K, n are constants.

Kick assumed that the energy required to reduce a material in size was directly proportional to the size reduction ratio dL/L. This implies that n in eqn. (11.1) is equal to -1. If

$$K = K_K f_c$$

where K_K is called Kick's constant and f_c is called the crushing strength of the material, we have

$$dE/dL = K_K f_c L^{-1}$$

which, on integration gives

$$E = K_K f_c \log_e(L_1/L_2). \qquad (11.2)$$

Equation (11.2) is a statement of Kick's Law. It implies that the specific energy required to crush a material, for example from 10 cm down to 5 cm, is the same as the energy required to crush the same material from 5 mm to 2.5 mm.

Rittinger, on the other hand, assumed that the energy required for size reduction is directly proportional, not to the change in length dimensions, but to the change in surface area. This leads to a value of -2 for n in eqn. (11.1) as area is proportional to length squared. If we again put

$$K = K_R f_c$$

where K_R is called Rittinger's constant, and integrate the resulting form of eqn. (11.1), we obtain

$$E = K_R f_c(1/L_2 - 1/L_1). \qquad (11.3)$$

Equation (11.3) is known as Rittinger's Law. As the specific surface of a particle, the surface area per unit mass, is proportional to $1/L$, eqn. (11.3) postulates that the energy required to reduce L for a mass of particles from 10 cm to 5 cm would be the same as that required to reduce, for example, the same mass of 5-mm particles down to 4.7 mm. This is a very much smaller reduction, for that quantity of energy per unit mass but on the smaller particles,

then that predicted by Kick's Law.

It has been found, experimentally, that for the grinding of coarse particles in which the increase in surface area per unit mass is relatively small, Kick's Law is a reasonable approximation. For the size reduction of fine powders, on the other hand, in which large areas of new surface are being created, Rittinger's Law fits the experimental data better.

Bond has suggested an intermediate course, in which he postulates that n is $-3/2$ and this leads to

$$E = E_i(100/L_2)^{1/2}(1 - 1/q^{1/2}). \qquad (11.4)$$

Bond defines the quantity E_i by this equation: L is measured in microns in eqn. (11.4) and so E_i is the amount of energy required to reduce unit mass of the material from an infinitely large particle size down to a particle size of 100 μm. It is expressed in terms of q, the reduction ratio where $q = L_1/L_2$.

Note that all of these equations [eqns. (11.2), (11.3), (11.4)] are dimensional equations and so if quoted values are to be used for the various constants, the dimensions must be expressed in appropriate units. In Bond's equation, if L is expressed in microns, this defines E_i and Bond calls this the Work Index.

The greatest use of these equations is in making comparisons between power requirements for various degrees of reduction.

EXAMPLE 11.1. Sugar is ground from crystals of which 80% pass a 500-μm sieve, down to a size in which 80% passes a 88-μm sieve and a 5-horsepower motor is found just sufficient for the required throughput. If the requirements are changed such that the grinding is only down to 80% through a 125-μm sieve but the throughput is to be increased by 50% would the existing motor have sufficient power to operate the grinder? Assume Bond's equation.

Using the subscripts 1 for the first condition and 2 for the second, and letting W kg.h^{-1} be the initial throughput, then if x is the required power

$$E_1 = 5/W = E_i(100/88 \times 10^{-6})^{1/2}\left[1 - \left(\frac{88}{500}\right)^{1/2}\right].$$

$$E_2 = x/1.5W = E_i(100/125 \times 10^{-6})^{1/2}\left[1 - \left(\frac{125}{500}\right)^{1/2}\right],$$

$$\frac{E_2}{E_1} = x/(1.5 \times 5) = \frac{(88 \times 10^{-6})^{1/2}\left[1 - \left(\frac{125}{500}\right)^{1/2}\right]}{(125 \times 10^{-6})^{1/2}\left[1 - \left(\frac{88}{500}\right)^{1/2}\right]},$$

$$\therefore \quad \frac{x}{7.5} = 0.84 \times \frac{0.500}{0.58} = 0.72,$$

$$\therefore \quad x = 5.4 \text{ horsepower.}$$

So the motor would have insufficient power to pass the 50% increased throughput though it should be able to handle an increase of 40%.

New Surface Formed by Grinding

When a uniform particle is crushed, after the first crushing the size of the particles produced will vary a great deal from relatively coarse to fine and even to dust. As the grinding continues, the coarser particles will be further reduced but there will be less change in the size of the fine particles. Careful analysis has shown that there tends to be a certain size which increases in its relative proportions in the mixture and which soon becomes the predominant size fraction. For example, wheat after first crushing gives a wide range of particle sizes in the coarse flour, but after further grinding the predominant fraction soon becomes that passing a 250-μm sieve and being retained on a 125-μm sieve. This fraction tends to build up, however long the grinding continues, so long as the same type of machinery, rolls in this case, is employed.

The surface area of a fine particulate material is large and can be important. Most reactions are related to the surface area available, so the surface area can have a considerable bearing on the properties of the material. For example, wheat in the form of grains is relatively stable so long as it is kept dry, but if ground to a fine flour has such a large surface per unit mass that it becomes liable to explosive oxidation, as is all too well known in the milling industry.

The surface area per unit mass is called the specific surface. To calculate this in a known mass of material it is necessary to know the particle-size distribution and, also, the shape factor of the

particles. The particle size gives one dimension which can be called the typical dimension, D_p, of a particle. This has now to be related to the surface area.

We can write, arbitrarily,

$$V_p = pD_p^3$$

and

$$A_p = 6qD_p^2$$

where V_p is the volume of the particle, A_p is the area of the particle surface, D_p is the typical dimension of the particle and p, q are factors which connect the particle geometries.

For example, for a cube, the volume is D_p^3 and the surface area is $6D_p^2$; for a sphere the volume is $(\pi/6)D_p^3$ and the surface area is πD_p^2. In each case the ratio of surface area to volume is $6/D_p$.

A shape factor is now defined as $q/p = \lambda$, so that for a cube or a sphere $\lambda = 1$. It has been found, experimentally, that for many materials when ground, the shape factor of the resulting particles is approximately 1.75, which means that their surface area to volume ratio is nearly twice that for a cube or a sphere.

The ratio of surface area to volume is

$$A_p/V_p = 6q/pD_p = 6\lambda/D_p \tag{11.5}$$

so that if there is a mass w of particles of density ρ_p the number of particles is $w/\rho_p v_p$, each of area A_p, and so

$$A_t = (w/\rho_p pD_p^3)(6qD_p^2)$$
$$= 6\lambda w/\rho_p D_p \tag{11.6}$$

where A_t is the total area of the mass of particles.

Equation (11.6) can be combined with the results of sieve analysis to estimate the total surface area of a powder.

EXAMPLE 11.2. In an analysis of ground salt using Tyler sieves, it was found that 38% of the total salt passed through a 7-mesh sieve but was caught on a 9-mesh sieve. For one of the finer fractions, 5% passed an 80-mesh sieve but was retained on a 115-mesh sieve. Estimate the surface areas of these two fractions in a 5-kg sample of the salt, if the density of salt is $1050\ kg\,m^{-3}$ and the shape factor is 1.75.

Aperture of Tyler sieves, 7 mesh = 2.83 mm, 9 mesh = 2.00 mm, 80 mesh = 0.177, 115 mesh = 0.125 mm.
Mean aperture 7 and 9 mesh = 2.41 mm.
Mean aperture 80 and 115 mesh = 0.151 mm.

$$\therefore \quad A_1 = (6 \times 1.75 \times 0.38 \times 5)/(1050 \times 2.41 \times -10^3) = 7.88\ m^2,$$
$$A_2 = (6 \times 1.75 \times 0.05 \times 5)/(1050 \times 1.51 \times 10^{-4}) = 16.6\ m^2$$

Grinding Equipment

Grinding equipment can be divided into two classes – crushers and grinders. In the first class the major action is compressive, whereas grinders combine shear and impact with compressive forces.

Crushers

Jaw and gyratory crushers are heavy equipment and are not used extensively in the food industry. In a jaw crusher, the material is fed in between two heavy jaws, one fixed and the other reciprocating, so as to work the material down into a narrower and narrower space, crushing it as it goes. The gyratory crusher consists of a truncated conical casing, inside which a crushing head rotates eccentrically. The crushing head is shaped as an inverted cone and the material being crushed is trapped between the outer fixed, and the inner gyrating, cones, and it is again forced into a narrower and narrower space during which time it is crushed. Jaw and gyratory crusher actions are illustrated in Fig. 11.1(a) and (b).

Crushing rolls consist of two heavy cylinders, mounted parallel to each other and close together. They rotate in the same direction and the material to be crushed is trapped and nipped between them, being crushed as it passes through. In some cases, the rolls are both driven at the same speed. In other cases, they may be driven at differential speeds, or only one roll is driven. A major application is in the cane-sugar industry, where several stages of rolls are used to crush the cane.

Hammer mills

In a hammer mill, swinging hammer heads are attached to a rotor which rotates at high speed inside a hardened casing. The principle is illustrated in Fig. 11.2(a). The material is crushed and pulverized between the hammers and the casing, and remains in the mill until it is fine enough to pass

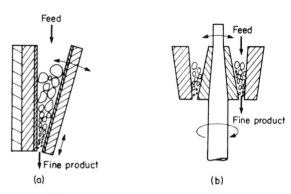

FIG. 11.1. Crushers: (a) jaw, (b) gyratory.

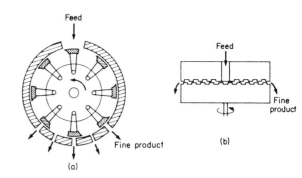

FIG. 11.2. Grinders: (a) hammer mill, (b) plate mill.

through a screen which forms the bottom of the casing. Both brittle and fibrous materials can be handled in hammer mills, though with fibrous material, projecting sections on the casing may be used to give a cutting action.

Fixed-head mills

Various forms of mills are used in which the material is sheared between a fixed casing and a rotating head, often with only fine clearances between them. One type is a pin mill in which both the static and the moving plates have pins attached on the surface and the powder is sheared between the pins.

Plate mills

In plate mills the material is fed between two circular plates, one of them fixed and the other rotating. The feed comes in near the axis of rotation and is sheared and crushed as it makes its way to the edge of the plates, see Fig. 11.2(b). The plates can be mounted horizontally as in the traditional Buhr stone used for grinding corn, which has a fluted surface on the plates. The plates can be mounted vertically also. Developments of the plate mill have led to the colloid mill, which uses very fine clearances and very high speeds to produce particles of colloidal dimensions.

Roller mills

Roller mills are similar to roller crushers, but they have smooth or finely fluted rolls, and rotate at differential speeds. They are used very widely to grind flour. Because of their simple geometry, the maximum size of the particle that can pass between the rolls can be regulated. If the friction coefficient between the rolls and the feed material is known the largest particle that will be nipped between the rolls can be calculated, knowing the geometry of the particles.

Miscellaneous milling equipment

The range of milling equipment is very wide. It includes ball mills, in which the material to be ground is enclosed in a horizontal cylinder or a cone and tumbled with a large number of steel balls, natural pebbles or artificial stones, which crush and break the material. Ball mills have limited applications in the food industry, but they are used for grinding food-colouring materials. The edge-runner mill, which is basically a heavy broad wheel running round a circular trough, is used for grinding chocolate and confectionery. Many types of milling equipment have come to be traditional in various industries and it is often claimed that they provide characteristic actions which are peculiarly suited to, and necessary for, the product.

Cutters

Cutting machinery is generally simple, consisting of rotating knives in various arrangements. A major problem often is to keep the knives sharp so that they cut rather than tear. An example is the bowl chopper in which a flat bowl containing the material revolves beneath a vertical rotating cutting knife.

EMULSIFICATION

Emulsions are stable suspensions of one liquid in another, the liquids being immiscible. Stability of the emulsion is obtained by dispersion of very fine droplets of one liquid, called the disperse phase, through the other liquid which is called the continuous phase. The emulsion is stable when it can persist without change, for long periods of time, without the droplets of the disperse phase coalescing with each other, or rising or settling. The stability of an emulsion is controlled by interfacial surface forces, by the size of the disperse phase droplets, by the viscous properties of the continuous phase and by the density difference between the two phases. The dispersed particles in the emulsion have a very large surface area, which is created in the process of emulsification.

Surface effects depend upon the properties of the materials of the two phases, but very often a third component is added which is absorbed at the interface and which helps to prevent the droplets from coalescing. These added materials are called emulsifying agents and examples are phosphates and glycerol monostearate.

The size of the disperse phase droplets is important and these are commonly of the order $1-10\,\mu m$ diameter. Below $0.1\,\mu m$ droplet diameter, the dispersion is often spoken of as colloidal. Coalescence of the disperse phase droplets is hindered by increased viscosity in the continuous liquid phase. The nearer the densities of the components are to each other, the less will be the separating effect of gravitational forces. Stokes' Law gives a qualitative indication of the physical factors which influence the stability of an emulsion. This is because the relative flow of the particles under gravitational forces may break the emulsion, so stability is enhanced by small settling velocities. From eqn. (10.2)

$$v = D^2 g(\rho_p - \rho_f)/18\mu$$

the critical importance of particle size, occurring as a squared term, can be seen. Also it shows why emulsions are more stable when density differences are small and when the viscosity of the continuous phase is high.

Preparation of Emulsions

The essential feature of an emulsion is the small size of the disperse phase droplets. This can be achieved by imposing very high shearing stresses upon the liquid that is to be dispersed and the shearing forces break the material into the multitude of fine particles.

Shearing is, generally, attained by passing the liquid through a high-pressure pump, to bring it up to pressures of the order of 7×10^3 kPa, and then discharging this pressure suddenly by expansion of the liquid through a small gap or nozzle; the equipment is often called a homogenizer. In passing through the nozzle, very large shear forces are exerted on the liquid, dispersing it into the small particles.

Centrifugal orifices may also be used to obtain the shearing action. Discs spinning at high velocities give rise to high shearing forces in liquids flowing over them. Flow between contra-rotating discs, which may have pegs on the disc faces, can be used to produce emulsions. Designs in which small clearances are used between a stationary disc and high-speed flat or conical rotating disc are called colloid mills. Another source of energy for shearing is from ultrasonic vibrations induced in the liquid.

Existing emulsions can be given increased stability by decreasing the size of the droplets by impact or by shearing the emulsion still further, and the process is called homogenizing. Homogenizing results in smaller and more uniform droplet sizes and a practical example is the homogenizing of milk.

Examples of emulsions met with frequently in the food industry are – milk (fat dispersed in water), butter (water dispersed in fat), mayonnaise (fat in water) and ice cream (fat in water which is then frozen).

Milk is an emulsion of fat in water which is not stable indefinitely as it separates, on standing, into skim milk and cream. This is caused by the density differences between the fat and the water, the globules rising as predicted by Stokes' Law and coalescing at the surface to form a layer of cream. After homogenizing, this separation does not occur as the globules are much reduced in size. Homogenizing is also used with ice-cream mixes which are dispersions of fat and air in sugar solutions and in the manufacture of margarine.

The same surface effects which govern liquid emulsions also apply to dispersions of solids in liquids and of liquids or solids in gases. Colloidal solutions of solids can be produced if the particle size is of the necessary order, below about 0.1 μm, and again stability depends upon the surface properties of the materials. Aerosols, for example fine mists in the atmosphere, can also be quite stable.

SUMMARY

1. Size reduction is accomplished by shearing forces which cause the material to fracture releasing most of the applied energy as heat.
2. A general equation giving the power required for size reduction is:

$$dE/dL = KL^n$$

and from this can be derived
   (a) Kick's Law in which $n = 1$ and which may be integrated to give:

   $$E = K_K f_c \log_e(L_1/L_2).$$

   (b) Rittinger's Law in which $n = -2$, integrated to give:

   $$E = K_R f_c(1/L_2 - 1/L_1).$$

   (c) Bond's equation in which $n = -3/2$, integrated to give:

   $$E = E_i(100/L_2)^{1/2}(1 - 1/q^{1/2}).$$

It appears that Kick's results apply better to coarser particles, Rittinger's to fine ones with Bond's being intermediate.

3. The total surface area of a powder is important and can be estimated from

$$A = 6\lambda w / \rho_p D_p.$$

4. An emulsion is produced by shearing forces which reduces the size of droplets of the dispersed phase to diameters of the order of $0.1-10\,\mu m$, with a large specific surface area. Application of Stokes' Law gives an indication of emulsion stability.

PROBLEMS

1. From measurements on a uniformly sized material from a dryer, it is inferred that the surface area of the material is $12\,m^2$. If the density of the material is $1450\,kg\,m^{-3}$ and the total weight is 360 kg calculate the number and the equivalent diameter of the particles if their value of λ is 1.75.

2. Calculate the shape factors λ for model systems in which the particles are:
   (a) cylinders with $L = 2D$,
   (b) tetrahedra with their sides being equilateral triangles.
   Estimate the specific surface area of a powder consisting of equal numbers of the above two shapes in which there are 4×10^3 particles kg^{-1} the cylinders having a density of $1330\,kg\,m^{-3}$ and the tetrahedra a density of $1500\,kg\,m^{-3}$.

3. It is found that the energy required to reduce particles from a mean diameter of 1 cm to 0.3 cm is $11\,kJ\,kg^{-1}$. Estimate the energy requirement to reduce the same particles from a diameter of 0.1 cm to 0.01 cm assuming:
   (a) Kick's Law,
   (b) Rittinger's Law,
   (c) Bond's Law.

4. If it is suspected that the oxidation reactions which create off-flavours are surface reactions which proceed at a rate which is uniform with time, and if the shelf life of the product is directly related to the percentage of the off-flavours which have been produced, estimate the percentage reduction in shelf life consequent upon the size reductions of example 3, that is from 1 cm to 0.3 cm and from 0.1 cm to 0.01 cm in diameter, assuming $\lambda = 1.5$.

5. If it is desired to reduce the separation time for milk to at least one week (before cream will rise to the top), what diameter of cream droplet would Stokes' Law predict to be necessary for the homogenization to achieve?

CHAPTER 12

MIXING

MIXING is the dispersing of components, one throughout the other. It occurs in innumerable instances in the food industry and is probably the most commonly encountered of all process operations. Unfortunately, it is also one of the least understood. There are, however, some aspects of mixing which can be measured and which can be of help in the planning and designing of mixing operations.

CHARACTERISTICS OF MIXTURES

Ideally, a mixing process begins with the components, grouped together in some container, but still separate as pure components. Thus, if small samples are taken throughout the container, they will almost all consist of one pure component, the frequency of occurrence of the components being proportional to the fractions of these components in the whole container. As mixing then proceeds, samples will increasingly contain more of the components, in proportions approximating to the overall proportions of the components in the whole container. Complete mixing could then be defined as that state in which all samples are found to contain the components in the same proportions as in the whole mixture. Actually, this state of affairs would only be attained by some ordered grouping of the components and would be a most improbable result from any practical mixing process. Another approach can then be made, defining the perfect mixture as one in which the components in samples occur in proportions whose statistical chance of occurrence is the same as that of a statistically random dispersion of the original components. Such a dispersion represents the best that random mixing processes can do.

MEASUREMENT OF MIXING

The production of fully mixed small volumes, which can be taken or sampled for measurement, is what mixing is all about. Sample compositions move from the initial state to the mixed state, and measurements of mixing must reflect this.

The problem at once arises, what size of sample should be chosen? To take extreme cases, if the sample is so large that it includes the whole mixture, then the sample composition is at once mean composition and there remains no mixing to be done. At the other end of the scale, if it were possible to take samples of molecular size, then every sample would contain only one or other of the components in the pure state and no amount of mixing would make any difference. Between these lie all of the practical sample sizes, but the important point is that the results will depend upon sample size.

In many practical mixing applications, suitable sample sizes are prescribed by process conditions or product requirements. For example, if table salt is to contain 1 % magnesium carbonate, the addition of 10 kg of magnesium carbonate to 990 kg of salt ensures, overall, that this requirement has been met. However, if the salt is to be sold in 2-kg packets, the practical requirement might well be that each packet contains 20 g of magnesium carbonate with some specified tolerance, and adequate mixing would have to be provided. A realistic sample size to take from this mixture, containing 1000 kg of mixture, would be 2 kg. As mixing proceeds, greater numbers of samples containing both components appear and their composition tends towards 99% salt and 1% magnesium carbonate.

It can be seen from this discussion that the deviation of the sample compositions from the mean composition of the overall mixture represents a measure of the mixing process. This deviation decreases as mixing progresses. A satisfactory way of measuring the deviation is to use the statistical term called the standard deviation. This is the mean of the sum of the squares of the deviations from the mean, and so it gives equal value to negative and positive deviation and increasingly greater weight to larger deviations because of the squaring. It is given by:

$$s^2 = 1/n[(x_1 - \bar{x})^2 + (x_2 - \bar{x})^2 + \cdots (x_n - \bar{x})^2]$$

(12.1)

where s is the standard deviation, n is the number of samples taken, x_1, x_2,... are the fractional compositions of component X in the 1, 2...n, samples and $\bar{x}$ is the mean fractional composition of component X in the whole mixture.

Using eqn. (12.1) values of s can be calculated from the measured sample compositions, taking the n samples at some stage of the mixing operation. Often it is convenient to use s^2 rather than s, and s^2 is known as the variance of the fractional sample compositions from the mean composition.

EXAMPLE 12.1. After a mixer mixing 99 kg of salt with 1 kg of magnesium carbonate had been working for some time, ten samples, each weighing 20 g, were taken and analysed for magnesium carbonate. The weights of magnesium carbonate in the samples were 0.230, 0.172, 0.163, 0.173, 0.210, 0.182, 0.232, 0.220, 0.210, 0.213 g. Calculate the standard deviation of the sample compositions from the mean composition.

Fractional compositions of samples, that is the fraction of magnesium carbonate in the sample, are respectively:

0.0115, 0.0086, 0.0082, 0.0087, 0.0105, 0.0091, 0.0116, 0.0110, 0.0105, 0.0107.

Mean composition of samples, overall $= 1/100$
$= 0.01$.

Deviation of samples from mean, (0.0115 − 0.01), (0.0086 − 0.01), etc.

$$\therefore \quad s^2 = 1/10[(0.0115 - 0.01)^2$$
$$+ (0.0086 - 0.01)^2 + \cdots]$$
$$= 2.250 \times 10^{-6},$$
$$\therefore \quad s = 1.5 \times 10^{-3}.$$

At some later time samples were found to be of composition: 0.0113, 0.0092, 0.0097, 0.0108, 0.0104, 0.0098, 0.0104, 0.0101, 0.0094, 0.0098, giving $s^2 = 3.7 \times 10^{-7}$ and showing the reducing standard deviation. With continued mixing the standard deviation diminishes further.

The process of working out the differences can be laborious, and often the standard deviation can be obtained more quickly by making use of the mathematical relationship, proof of which will be found in any textbook on statistics:

$$s^2 = 1/n\left[\sum(x_1^2) - \sum(\bar{x})^2\right]$$
$$= 1/n\left[\sum(x_1^2) - n(\bar{x})^2\right]$$
$$= 1/n\left[\sum(x_1^2)\right] - (\bar{x})^2.$$

PARTICLE MIXING

If particles are to be mixed, starting out from segregated groups and ending up with the components randomly distributed, the expected variances (s^2) of the sample compositions from the mean sample composition can be calculated.

Consider a two-component mixture, consisting of a fraction p of component P and a fraction q of component Q. In the unmixed state virtually all small samples taken will consist either of pure P or of pure Q. From the overall proportions, if a large number of samples are taken, it would be expected that a proportion p of the samples would contain pure component P; that is their deviation from the mean composition would be $(1 - p)$, as the sample containing pure P has a fractional composition 1 of component P. Similarly, a proportion q of the samples would contain pure Q, that is, a fractional composition 0 in terms of component P and a deviation $(0 - p)$ from the mean. Summing these in terms of fractional composition of component P and remembering that $p + q = 1$

$$s_0^2 = 1/n[pn(1 - p)^2 + (1 - p)n(0 - p)^2]$$

$$\text{(for } n \text{ samples)}$$

$$= p(1 - p). \tag{12.2}$$

When the mixture has been thoroughly dispersed, it is assumed that the components are distributed through the volume in accordance with their overall proportions. The probability that any particle picked at random will be component Q will be q, and $(1 - q)$ that it is not Q. Extending this to samples containing N particles, it can be shown, using probability theory, that

$$s_r^2 = p(1 - p)/N = s_0^2/N. \tag{12.3}$$

This assumes that all the particles are equally sized and that each particle is either pure P or pure Q. For example, this might be the mixing of equal-sized particles of sugar and milk powder. The subscripts o and r have been used to denote the initial and the random values of s^2, and inspection of the formulae, eqn. (12.2) and eqn. (12.3), shows that in the mixing process the value of s^2 has decreased from $p(1 - p)$ to $1/N$th of this value. It has been suggested that intermediate values between s_0^2 and s_r^2 could be used to show the progress of mixing. Suggestions have been made for a mixing index, based on this, for example

$$(M) = (s_0^2 - s^2)/(s_0^2 - s_r^2) \tag{12.4}$$

which is so designed that (M) goes from 0 to 1 during the course of the mixing process. This measure can be used for mixtures of particles and also for the mixing of heavy pastes.

EXAMPLE 12.2. For a particular bakery operation it was desired to mix dough in 95-kg batches and then at a later time to blend in 5 kg of yeast. For product uniformity it is important that the yeast be well distributed and so an experiment was set up to follow the course of the mixing. It was desired to calculate the mixing index after 5 and 10 min mixing.

Sample yeast compositions, expressed as the percentage of yeast in 100-g samples were found to be:

After 5 min
   0.0 16.5 3.2 2.2 12.6 9.6 0.2 4.6 0.5 8.5

After 10 min
   3.4 8.3 7.2 6.0 4.3 5.2 6.7 2.6 4.3 2.0

Calculating $s_5^2 = 3.0 \times 10^{-3}$

$$s_{10}^2 = 3.8 \times 10^{-4}.$$

The value of $s_0^2 = 0.05 \times 0.95 = 4.8 \times 10^{-2}$ and $s_r^2 \doteq 0$ as the number of "particles" in a sample is very large,

$$\therefore \quad (M)_5 = (4.8 - 0.3)/4.8 = 0.93$$

and $\quad (M)_{10} = (4.8 - 0.04)/4.8 = 0.99.$

Mixing of Widely Different Quantities

The mixing of particles varying substantially in size or in density presents special problems, as there will be gravitational forces acting in the mixer which will tend to segregate the particles into size and density ranges. In such a case, initial mixing in a mixer may then be followed by un-mixing and so the time of mixing may be quite critical.

Mixing is simplest when the quantities that are to be mixed are roughly in the same proportions. In cases where very small quantities of one component have to be blended uniformly into much larger quantities of other components, the mixing is best split into stages, keeping the proportions not too far different in each stage. For example, if it is required to add a component such that its final proportions in the product are 50 parts per million it would be hopeless to attempt to mix this in a single stage. A possible method might be to use four mixing stages, each with the proportions about 30:1. In planning the mixing process it would be necessary to take analyses through each stage of mixing, but once mixing times had been established it should only be necessary to make check analyses on the final product.

EXAMPLE 12.3. It is desired to mix vitamin powder at the level of $10^{-3}\%$ by weight into a 1 tonne batch of powdered cereal. Two double-cone blenders are available, one (L) with a capacity of 100 to 500 kg powder and another (S) with a capacity of 10 to 50 kg. Both will mix adequately in 10 min so long as the minor constituent constitutes not less than 10%. Suggest a procedure for the mixing.

Total weight vitamin needed

$$= 1000 \times 10^{-5} \, \text{kg}$$
$$= 10 \, \text{g},$$

$\therefore$ divide into two, $2 \times 5 \, \text{g}$ as two final 500-kg batches will be needed. Then:

(1) Hand blend 5 g and 50 g → mixture (1), and then (1) and 945 g → mixture (2). This may need analytical checking to set up a suitable hand-mixing procedure.
(2) Take (2) + 9 kg cereal and mix in (S) → mixture (3).
(3) Take (3) + 90 kg cereal and mix in (L) → mixture (4).
(4) Take (4) + 400 kg cereal and mix in (L) → mixture (5) – product.
(5) Repeat, with other 5-g vitamin and 500 kg cereal, steps (1) to (4).

Rates of Mixing

Once a suitable measure of mixing has been found, it becomes possible to discuss rates of accomplishing mixing. It has been assumed that the mixing index ought to be such that the rate of mixing at any time, under constant working conditions, such as in a mixer working at constant speed, ought to be proportional to the extent of mixing remaining to be done at that time. That is,

$$\mathrm{d}M/\mathrm{d}\theta = K\,[(1 - (M))] \qquad (12.5)$$

where (M) is the mixing index and K is a constant, and on integrating from $\theta = 0$ to $\theta = \theta$ during which (M) goes from 0 to (M),

$$[(1 - (M))] = e^{-K\theta}$$

or

$$(M) = 1 - e^{-K\theta} \qquad (12.6)$$

This exponential relationship, using (M) as the mixing index, has been found to apply in many experimental investigations at least over two or three orders of magnitude of (M). In such cases, the constant K can be related to the mixing machine and to the conditions and it can be used to predict,

for example, the times required to attain a given degree of mixing.

EXAMPLE 12.4. In a batch mixer, blending starch and dried-powdered vegetables for a soup mixture, the initial proportions of dried vegetable to starch were 40:60. If the variance of the sample compositions measured in terms of fractional compositions of starch was found to be 0.0823 after 300 s of mixing, for how much longer should the mixing continue to reach the specified maximum sample composition variance of 0.02?

Assume that the starch and the vegetable particles are of approximately the same physical size and that a sample contains 24 particles.

Then taking the fractional content of dried vegetables to be $p = 0.4$,

$$\therefore \quad (1 - p) = (1 - 0.4) = 0.6,$$
$$\therefore \quad s_o^2 = 0.4 \times 0.6 = 0.24,$$
$$s_r^2 = s_o^2/N = 0.24/24 \text{ from eqn. (12.5)}$$
$$= 0.01,$$

$\therefore$ substituting in eqn. (12.6) we have

$$(M) = (s_o^2 - s^2)/(s_o^2 - s_r^2)$$
$$= (0.24 - 0.0823)/(0.24 - 0.01)$$
$$= 0.685$$

Substituting in eqn.

$$\therefore \quad e^{-300K} = 1 - 0.685 = 0.315,$$
$$\therefore \quad 300\,K = 1.55,$$
$$\therefore \quad K = 5.2 \times 10^{-3}.$$

For $s^2 = 0.02$,

then $(M) = (0.24 - 0.02)/(0.24 - 0.01)$
$$= 0.957,$$
$$\therefore \quad 0.957 = 1 - e^{-5.2 \times 10^{-3}\theta},$$
$$\therefore \quad \theta = 603 \text{ s, say } 600 \text{ s},$$

$\therefore$ the additional mixing time would be 600 s − 300 s = 300 s.

Energy Input in Mixing

Quite substantial quantities of energy can be consumed in some types of mixing, such as in the mixing of plastic solids. There is no necessary connection between energy consumed and the progress of mixing — to take an extreme example there could be shearing along one plane, then recombining to restore the original arrangement, then repeating which would consume energy but accomplish no mixing at all. However, in well-designed mixers energy input does relate to mixing progress, though the actual relationship has normally to be determined experimentally. In the mixing of flour doughs using high-speed mixers, the energy consumed, or the power input at any particular time, can be used to determine the necessary mixing time. This is a combination of mixing with chemical reaction as the flour oxidizes during mixing which leads to increasing resistance to shearing and so to increased power being required to operate the mixer.

EXAMPLE 12.5. In a particular mixer used for mixing flour doughs for breadmaking, it has been found that mixing can be characterized by the total energy consumed in the mixing process and that sufficient mixing has been accomplished when 8 watt hours of energy have been consumed by each kg of dough.

Such a mixer, handling 2000 kg of dough, is observed just after starting to be consuming 80 amperes per phase, which rises steadily over 10 s to 400 amperes at which level it then remains effectively constant. The mixer is driven by a 440-volt, 3-phase electric motor with a power factor $(\cos \phi)$ of 0.89, and the overall mechanical efficiency between motor and mixing blades is 75%. Estimate the necessary mixing time.

Power to the motor $= \sqrt{3}EI \cos \phi$ where I is the current per phase and E and $\cos \phi$ in this case are 440 volts and 0.89, respectively. In first 10 s, $I_{average} = \frac{1}{2}(80 + 400) = 240$ amperes.

$\therefore$ Energy consumed in first 10 s

$= \text{power} \times \text{time}$

$= 240 \times \sqrt{3} \times 0.89 \times 0.75 \times 10/3600$

$= 130.5$ watt h

$= 130.5/2000 = 0.06$ Wh kg^{-1}.

Energy still needed after first 10 s

$= (8 - 0.06) = 7.94$ Wh kg^{-1}.

$\therefore$ Additional time needed, at steady 400 ampere current

$= (7.94 \times 2000 \times 3600)/$
$\qquad (1.73 \times 400 \times 440 \times 0.75 \times 0.89)$

$= 281$ s.

$\therefore$ Total time $= 281 + 10$ s $= \underline{4.9 \min}$.

In actual mixing of doughs the power consumed would decrease slowly and more or less uniformly, but only by around 10–15% over the mixing process.

LIQUID MIXING

Food liquid mixtures can be sampled and analysed in the same way as solid mixtures but little investigational work has been published on this, or on the mixing performance of fluid mixers. Most of the information that is available concerns the power requirements for the most commonly used liquid mixer—some form of paddle or propeller stirrer. In these mixers, the fluids to be mixed are placed in containers and the stirrer is rotated. Measurements have been made in terms of dimensionless ratios involving all of the physical factors which influence power consumptions. The results have been correlated in an equation of the form

$$(Po) = K(Re)^n(Fr)^m \qquad (12.7)$$

where $(Re) = D^2 N \rho / \mu$, $(Po) = (P/D^5 N^3 \rho)$ and this is called the Power number, $(Fr) = (DN^2/g)$ and this is called the Froude number; D is the diameter of the propeller, N is the rotational frequency of the propeller (rev/min), ρ is the density of the liquid, μ is the viscosity of the liquid and P is the power consumed by the propeller.

Notice that the Reynolds number uses the product DN for the velocity which differs by a factor of π from the actual velocity at the tip of the propeller.

The Froude number correlates the effects of gravitational forces and it only becomes significant when the liquid surface is disturbed by the propeller. Below Reynolds numbers of about 300 the Froude number is found to have little or no effect, so that eqn. (12.7) becomes

$$(Po) = K(Re)^n. \qquad (12.8)$$

Experimental results from the work of Rushton are shown plotted in Fig. 12.1. Unfortunately, general formulae have not been obtained, so that the results are confined to the particular experimental propeller configurations which were used. If experimental curves are available, then they can be used to give values for n and K in eqn. (12.8) and the equation then used to predict power consumption. For example, for a propeller, with a pitch equal to the diameter, Rushton gives $n = -1$ and $K = 41$. In cases in which experimental results are not already available, the best approach to the prediction of power consumption in propeller mixers is to use physical models, measure the factors, and then use eqn. (12.7) or eqn. (12.8) for scaling up the experimental results.

EXAMPLE 12.6. Vitamin concentrate is being blended into molasses and it has been found that satisfactory mixing rates can be obtained in a small tank 0.67 m diameter with a propeller rotating at 450 rev min^{-1}. If a large-scale plant is to be designed which will require a tank 2 m diameter, what will be suitable values to choose for tank depth, propeller diameter and rotational speed, if it is desired to preserve the same mixing conditions as in the smaller plant? What would be the power requirement for the motor driving the propeller? Assume that the viscosity of molasses is 6.6 N s m^{-2} and its density is 1520 kg m^{-3}.

Use the subscripts S for the small tank and L for the larger one. To preserve geometric similarity the dimensional ratios should be the same in the large tank as in the small.

Given that the full-scale tank is three times larger than the model,

$$\therefore \quad D_L = 3D_S,$$
$$\therefore \quad H_L = 3H_S = 3 \times 0.75 = 2.25\,\text{m}$$
$$= \text{depth of large tank}$$

and

$$D_L = 3D_S = 3 \times 0.33 = 1\,\text{m}$$
$$= \text{propeller diameter in the large tank.}$$

For dynamic similarity, $(\text{Re})_L = (\text{Re})_S$.

$$\therefore \quad D_L^2 N_L = D_S^2 N_S,$$
$$\therefore \quad N_L = (1/3)^2 \times 450$$
$$= 50\,\text{rev min}^{-1}$$
$$= 0.83\,\text{rev sec}^{-1}$$
$$= \text{speed of propeller in the large tank.}$$

Now

$$(\text{Re}) = (D_L^2 N_L \rho / \mu)$$
$$\therefore \quad (\text{Re}) = (1^2 \times 0.83 \times 1520)/6.6$$
$$= 191,$$

$$\therefore \quad \text{eqn. (12.8) is applicable, and assuming that}$$
$$K = 41 \text{ and } n = -1, \text{ we have}$$

$$(\text{Po}) = 41(\text{Re})^{-1} = P/D^5 N^3 \rho,$$
$$P = (41 \times 1^5 \times (0.83)^3 \times 1520)/(191)$$
$$= 186\,\text{J s}^{-1}$$

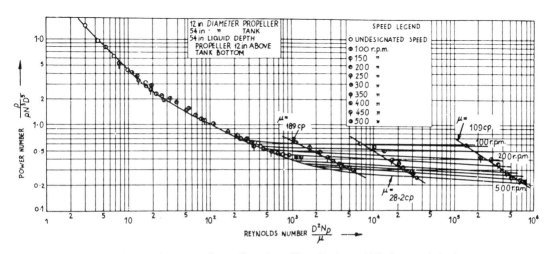

FIG. 12.1. Performance of propeller mixers [from Rushton (1950) by permission].

and since 1 horsepower $= 746\,\mathrm{J\,s^{-1}}$,

∴   required motor $= 186/746$, say 1/4
horsepower.

Apart from deliberate mixing, liquids in turbulent flow or passing through equipment such as pumps are being vigorously mixed. By planning such equipment in flow lines, or by ensuring turbulent flow in pipe lines, liquid mixing may in many instances be satisfactorily accomplished as a by-product of fluid transport.

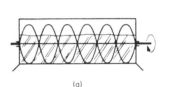 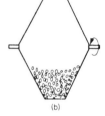

FIG. 12.2. Mixers: (a) ribbon blender, (b) double-cone mixer.

MIXING EQUIPMENT

Many forms of mixers have been produced from time to time but over the years a considerable degree of standardization of mixing equipment has been reached in different branches of the food industry. Possibly the easiest way in which to classify mixers is to divide them according to whether they mix liquids, dry powders, or thick pastes.

Liquid Mixers

For the deliberate mixing of liquids, the propeller mixer is probably the most common and the most satisfactory. In using propeller mixers, it is important to avoid regular flow patterns such as an even swirl round a cylindrical tank which may accomplish very little mixing. To break up these streamline patterns, baffles are often fitted, or the propeller may be mounted asymmetrically. Various baffles can be used and the placing of these can make very considerable differences to the mixing performances. It is tempting to relate the amount of power consumed by a mixer to the amount of mixing produced, but there is no necessary connection and very inefficient mixers can consume large amounts of power.

Powder and Particle Mixers

The essential feature in these mixers is to displace parts of the mixture with respect to other parts. The ribbon blender, for example, shown in Fig. 12.2(a) consists of a trough in which rotates a shaft with two open helical screws attached to it, one screw being right-handed and the other left-handed. As the shaft rotates sections of the powder move in opposite directions and so particles are vigorously displaced relative to each other. A commonly used blender for powders is the double-cone blender in which two cones are mounted with their open ends fastened together and they are rotated about an axis through their common base. This mixer is shown in Fig. 12.2(b).

Dough and Paste Mixers

Dough and pastes are mixed in machines which have, of necessity, to be heavy and powerful. Because of the large power requirements, it is particularly desirable that these machines mix with reasonable efficiency, as the power is dissipated in the form of heat which may cause substantial heating of the product. Such machines may require jacketing of the mixer to remove as much heat as possible with cooling water.

Perhaps the most commonly used mixer for these very heavy materials is the kneader which employs two contra-rotating arms of special shape, which fold and shear the material across a cusp, or division, in the bottom of the mixer. The arms are of so-called sigmoid shape as indicated in Fig. 12.3.

They rotate at differential speeds, often in the ratio of nearly 3:2. Developments of this machine include types with multiple sigmoid blades along extended troughs, in which the blades are given a set and the material makes its way continuously through the machine.

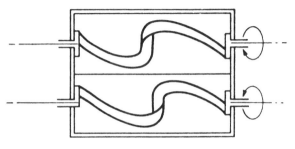

Fig. 12.3. Kneader.

Another type of machine employs very heavy contra-rotating paddles, whilst a modern continuous mixer consists of an interrupted screw which oscillates with both rotary and reciprocating motion between pegs in an enclosing cylinder. The important principle in these machines is that the material has to be divided and folded and also displaced so that fresh surfaces recombine as often as possible.

SUMMARY

1. Mixing can be characterized by analysis of sample compositions and then calculation of the standard deviation, s, of these from the mean composition of the whole mixture,

where

$$s^2 = 1/n[(x_1 - \bar{x})^2 + (x_2 - \bar{x})^2 + \cdots + (x_n - \bar{x})^2].$$

2. An index of mixing is given by:

$$(M) = (s_o^2 - s^2)/(s_o^2 - s_r^2).$$

3. The mixing index M can often be related to the time of mixing by

$$[1 - (M)] = e^{-K\theta}.$$

4. The power consumed in liquid mixing can be expressed by a relationship of the form

$$Po = K(Re)^n(Fr)^m.$$

PROBLEMS

1. Analysis of the fat content of samples from a chopped-meat mixture in which the overall fat content was 15% gave the following results, expressed as percentages:

$$23.4 \quad 10.4 \quad 16.4 \quad 19.6 \quad 30.4 \quad 7.6$$

For this mixture, estimate the value of s^2, s_o^2, and s_r^2, if the samples are 5 g and the particle sizes in the mixture are 0.1 g.

2. If it is found that the mixture in problem 1 is formed from the initial separate ingredients of fat and lean meat after mixing for 10 min estimate the value of the mixing index after a further 5 min of mixing.

3. For a liquid mixer in which a propeller stirrer, 0.3 m in diameter, is rotating at 300 rev/min in water estimate the power required to operate the stirrer. The tank is 0.6 m in diameter.

4. If the same assembly as in problem 3 is to be used to stir olive oil estimate the power needed.

5. A blended infant feed powder is to include a nutrient supplement, supplied as a powder similar to the bulk feed, incorporated at 15 parts per million. The plant is to produce 50 tonnes per day and has powder mixers with capacities of 3, 0.5 and 0.05 tonnes, which will mix efficiently down to one-sixth of their nominal capacity. Suggest a mixing schedule which should lead to the required dispersion of the supplement.

CHAPTER 13

SOME ENGINEERING APPLICATIONS OF PROCESS ENGINEERING IN THE FOOD INDUSTRY

In order to provide a perspective for food-process engineering, applications in two important food industries will be explored briefly. The two chosen are the meat and the dairy industries, both of which have provided man with food over the ages. Until the beginning of the present century, these industries had grown in size and scope from farm and cottage units up to substantial factories but their methods were still the traditional ones. Virtually the only factor that had changed is size. Today, we find that these industries are being greatly reorganized and changed almost beyond recognition and this is largely owing to the impact of modern technology and process engineering. Not only are the old operations being carried out more efficiently, but new products are being developed. Animals and plants and their products are now seen as raw materials, as protein, carbohydrate, fat, minerals, hormones, enzymes and vitamins and the possibilities for development are limitless.

THE MEAT INDUSTRY

The meat industry begins with the live animal and after slaughter the first operation is dis-assembly. Component parts of the animal are dismembered and the initial products are carcass meat, blood, offals, glands, pelts, wool, hair, hides, feathers, bristles, bones and hooves. The meat may be used directly or after chilling or freezing or it may be processed. Blood may go to human or animal food, to glues, fertilizers or to blood albumin. Some offals are used directly as food, others are processed for food or rendered to give high-protein material to feed animals or plants. From glands and other organs come preparations of hormones and enzymes. Pelts, wool, hair, hides, bones, bristles and feathers have limited application as human foods, though gelatin has long been regarded as edible.

It is interesting and illustrative to trace some of the applications of process engineering to the processing of foods.

Material and Energy Balances

Material balances are essential control tools for the processing plants, especially as the values of the products rise, to ensure that all economic products are recovered and used and that as much of the material as possible is sold to gain the highest returns such as in the more expensive cuts of meat. Balances can also be used for day-to-day controls and costing and to indicate where technological developments might be worthwhile. Material and energy balances can be applied to services, such as steam and hot-water supplies whose relative importance is increasing as energy costs rise.

Fluid Flow

Fluid flow enters into freezing and chilling where cooling media, generally air but sometimes water or radiant panels, remove heat from the product, into washing of meat and the by-products, into the flow of refrigerants and steam and water and in air-conditioning plant. A large meat-processing plant may use thousands of cubic metres of water every day. A modern use of fluid flow is the pumping of waste materials to the rendering plant.

Heat Transfer

Heat transfer is the unit operation which includes chilling and freezing, the major modern method of meat preservation. Heat is transferred either in heating or in cooling in virtually every process: sterilization, canning, tempering, cooking and a multitude of others.

Evaporation

Evaporation is used to concentrate cooking liquors from meat-canning operations and from rendering plants. Single and multiple effect evaporators are used.

Drying

Drying is one method of preserving meat, which may be air dried, roller dried and freeze dried. The almost unavoidable drying of meat in cold stores is a considerable economic problem in the industry where shrinkage may easily amount to several percent of the initial weight: in this case the mechanisms of drying need to be understood so that drying can be minimized. Fertilizers, stock foods, meat extract, gelatin, intestines and blood may all be dried, and the equipment used includes roller dryers, rotary dryers, vacuum dryers and numerous types of air dryers.

Equilibrium Contact Separations

Gas absorption occurs in the chlorination of process water, deaeration of boiler waters, froth flotation for fat separation, removal of odours from air and in aeration of waste waters. Extraction is used in solvent removal of fats and to obtain soluble proteins by heating in water to dissolve the proteins. Washing is applied extensively to fats and to such products as sausage casings from intestines, as well as to meat itself. Distillation occurs in the recovery of solvents in solvent rendering. It is also the basis for the deodorization of fats and is used in the separation of fatty acids and to prepare pharmaceutical products. Fats crystallize to a greater or lesser extent depending on the conditions of their preparation and treatment and control of this crystallization is very important in products such as lard and margarine. Membranes are used in the separation of blood protein fractions by ultrafiltration.

Mechanical Separations

Fats and water can be removed from the residual solids from the rendering process by filtration, although modern plants use other types of mechanical separation such as continuous horizontal-bowl centrifuges. Filtration can also be used to remove some of the water from coagulated blood and in the bleaching of fats. Sedimentation finds application in the clarification of fats and in the removal of solids from waste waters. Cyclones are found in connection with grinding operations and for fine products. Bag filters are also used, for example in bone flour production. Continuous centrifuges are coming into prominence for separation of solids from liquids, separating immiscible liquids from each other and in rendering processes and they are tending to displace batch centrifuges, filters and sedimentation.

Size Reductions

Many of the by-products of the meat industry are sold in powder form and so grinding may be necessary. In many forms of processed meat, grinding is required to produce, for example, such things as sausages and minced meat. Extrusion is used to prepare processed meat products as sausages. Very fine grinding and emulsification is used prior to separating protein from bones.

Mixing

Mixing enters into the preparation of processed meats. It is important also for the preparation of feeding meals. Efficient mixing is also important in rendering cookers to give good and even heat transfer.

THE DAIRY INDUSTRY

The dairy industry takes whole milk from the cow as its raw material. Milk contains protein, carbohydrate, fat, minerals and water. The simplest final milk product is milk itself, but even this requires chilling, heat processing and pasteurization to make it safe, and often homogenization and fat removal to meet consumer needs. Other common dairy products are cream, butter, cheese, casein, lactose, lactalbumin, dried whole or skim milk and evaporated milk and cream. Food-process engineering has become very important in the efficient production of these materials, especially in factories that may handle hundreds and even thousands of cubic metres of milk per day. As in the meat industry, almost the total range of available unit operations is applied in milk processing.

Material and Energy Balances

The total amount of material coming into a factory in the raw milk must pass out in products or in wastes. As the wastes are valueless, or may even have a negative value in that they have to be processed to meet the environmental requirements of the community, it is of importance that they be minimized and material balances have to be carried out to check this. Material balances working from

the waste streams have proved a valuable management tool in the dairy industry. Other balances can keep account of valuable products such as milk fat, and can indicate needs for better housekeeping or recovery technology.

Energy is a major cost in operations such as drying and methods such as product heat recovery, vapour compression and total energy systems in which electrical or mechanical energy is generated, have been used in dairy factories.

Fluid Flow

As the raw material and many of the products of the dairy industry are fluids, many applications of fluid flow occur in every factory as the milk is pumped from process to process. Some of the products have quite complex rheological characteristics so that non-Newtonian aspects become important.

Heat Transfer

Heat transfer is of importance in the initial handling of the raw milk to minimize deterioration and then to destroy any pathogenic organisms that may be present. Most milk is pasteurized and some is processed at higher temperatures to give almost sterile milk that will keep for long periods. Heating and cooling also enter into most other processes in the dairy industry and plate heat exchangers are very widely encountered and also scraped surface exchangers and shell and tube units in evaporators. Heating is needed in the various stages of the removal of water to produce dried products such as milk powder, casein, lactalbumin and lactose. Cooling and chilling enter into the manufacture of butter and cheese and into their storage to minimize deteriorative changes.

Drying

Many dairy products are powders where a drying process is essential. In some cases powders are dried in air dryers such as with casein and drying rooms for cheese. In other cases drying is from liquids such as in the spray drying or roller drying of milk. Drying is even applied to butter to produce anhydrous milk fat. Drying on storage is important with products such as cheese, and equilibrium moisture contents with powder products.

Evaporation

Prior to drying of liquids, it is almost always economic to remove a substantial proportion of the water by evaporation and this is extensively done in the dairy industry. Evaporators have become large and elaborate with up to seven or more effects and with complex heat-economy systems including vapour recompression, by steam jet ejectors, and feed pre-heaters.

Equilibrium Contact Separations

Washing is used to remove impurities and residues from butter and casein. Distillation and steam stripping are used in the removal of taints and odours from cream before it is made into butter. Crystallization has an important bearing on the properties of butter, and of milk powders, evaporated milk and ice cream, and is an essential step in the manufacture of lactose. The constituent fats of butter can be separated by fractional crystallization from solvents. Membranes, particularly ultrafiltration, are used in the treatment of whey to separate protein and carbohydrate constituents with their different molecular weights.

Mechanical Separations

Water is removed from cheese curd by filtration. Filters are also used to remove foreign matter from milk and cream and to remove powder particles from air streams in dryers of products such as casein and lactose. Rotary vacuum filters are used to recover fine precipitates such as those of lactalbumin. Sedimentation is used with curds such as cheese and casein and can be supplemented by centrifuges. Classification and sieving enable the various size fractions of dried-powder products to be separated and if necessary particular fractions to be recycled for further processing. Centrifuges find very extensive uses for the separation of cream from milk and to remove precipitates of casein and lactose from water.

Size Reduction

Many of the products are ground to produce fine powders; casein, lactalbumin, milk powders and dried whey may all be ground. Homogenization of milk is a well-established practice to prevent phase separation of the cream. Butter and cheese may be extruded and cut to produce consumer-sized quantities.

Mixing

Mixing and blending are used to ensure uniform products both with liquids, an example being the blending of milk after arrival at the factory, and with solids such as dried-milk powders to blend out variations in raw materials or process conditions. Powders can also segregate during transport and therefore require remixing.

These examples show how the processes used in two separate food industries can be broken down into the same unit operations. This applies equally to the processes in other food industries. Thus the fundamental principles described in this book can be applied to processing operations throughout the food industry.

APPENDIX 1

SYMBOLS, UNITS AND DIMENSIONS

a acceleration m s^{-2}; $[L][\theta]^{-2}$

       thickness m; $[L]$

a_w water activity; dimensionless

A area m^2; $[L]^{-2}$

b height of liquid in a centrifuge m; $[L]$

(Bi)   Biot number $h_s L/k$; dimensionless

c specific heat capacity J kg^{-1} °C^{-1}; $[F][L][M]^{-1}[T]^{-1}$,

       c_p specific heat capacity at constant pressure, c_s humid heat

C heat conductance J m^{-2} s^{-1} °C^{-1}; $[F][L]^{-1}[\theta]^{-1}[T]^{-1}$

       coefficients—discharge, drag, geometric; dimensionless

d differential operator; diameter

D diameter m; $[L]$

       diffusivity m^2 s^{-1}; $[L]^2[\theta]^{-1}$

e small temperature difference °C; $[T]$

       roughness factor m; $[L]$

E energy J; $[F][L]$

       E_c pump energy, E_f friction energy, E_h heat energy, E_i work index in grinding, E_k kinetic energy, E_p potential energy, E_r pressure energy

f friction factor; dimensionless

f_c crushing strength kg m^{-1} s^{-2}; $[M][L]^{-1}[\theta]^{-2}$

F force N; $[F]$

       F_c centrifugal force, F_d drag force, F_e external force, F_f friction force, F_g gravitational force

       ratio of liquid to solid in thickener feed; dimensionless time to sterilize at 121°C min; $[\theta]$

(Fo)   Fourier number $(k\theta/c\rho L^2)$; dimensionless

(Fr)   Froude number (DN^2/g); dimensionless

$F(D)$ Cumulative particle size distribution, $F'(D)$ particle size distribution; dimensionless

g acceleration due to gravity m s^{-2}; $[L][\theta]^{-2}$

G mass rate of flow kg m^{-2} s^{-1}; $[M][L]^{-2}[\theta]^{-1}$

(Gr)   Grashof number $(D^3\rho^2\beta g\,\Delta t/\mu^2)$; dimensionless

h heat transfer coefficient J m^{-2} s^{-1}; $[F][L]^{-1}[\theta]^{-1}[T]^{-1}$

       h_c convection, h_h condensing vapours on horizontal surfaces, h_r radiation, h_s surface, h_v condensing vapours on vertical surface

H enthalpy J; $[F][L]$

       head of a fluid m; $[L]$

       Henry's Law constant atm mole fraction^{-1} kPa mole fraction^{-1}; $[F][L]^{-2}$

k constant

constant of proportionality

friction loss factor; dimensionless

thermal conductivity J m^{-1} s^{-1} °C^{-1}; $[F][\theta]^{-1}[T]^{-1}$

mass-transfer coefficient

k_g gas mass-transfer coefficient s m^{-1}; $[\theta][L]^{-1}$

k_g' mass-transfer coefficient based on humidity difference kg m^{-2} s^{-1}; $[M][L]^{-2}[\theta]^{-1}$

k_l liquid mass transfer coefficient kg m^{-2} s^{-1}; $[M][L]^{-2}[\theta]^{-1}$

K constant, K', K'', etc.

mass-transfer coefficient kg m^{-2} h^{-1}; $[M][L]^{-2}[\theta]^{-1}$

K_x crystal interface

K_K Kick's constant m^3 kg^{-1}; $[L]^3[M]^{-1}$

K_R Rittinger's constant m^4 kg^{-1}; $[L]^4[M]^{-1}$

K_s rate constant for crystal surface reactions m s^{-1}; $[L][\theta]^{-1}$

K_D rate constant for crystal surface reactions m s^{-1}; $[L][\theta]^{-1}$

L flow rate of heavy phase kg h^{-1}; $[M][\theta]^{-1}$

half thickness of slab for Fourier and Biot numbers m; $[L]$

length m; $[L]$

ratio of liquid to solid in thickener underflow; dimensionless thickness of filter cake m; $[L]$

(Le) Lewis number $(h_c/k_g'C_p)$; dimensionless

m mass kg; $[M]$

number, general

(M) mixing index, dimensionless

M molecular weight; dimensionless

molal concentration (kg) moles m^{-3}; $[M][L]^{-3}$

n number, general

N number of particles in sample; rotational frequency, revolutions/minute; $[\theta]^{-1}$

(Nu) Nusselt number $(h_c D/k)$; dimensionless

p partial pressure Pa; $[F][L]^{-2}$

p_a partial pressure of vapour in air, p_s saturation partial pressure;

ratio in mixing and grinding; dimensionless

P constant in freezing formula; dimensionless; power N m s^{-1}; $[F][L][\theta]^{-1}$

pressure Pa; $[F][L]^{-2}$

P_a pressure on surface Pa; $[F][L]^{-2}$

(Po) Power number $(P/D^5N^3\rho)$; dimensionless

(Pr) Prandtl number $(c_p\mu/k)$; dimensionless

q heat flow rate J s^{-1}; $[F][L][\theta]^{-1}$

fluid flow rate m^3 s^{-1}; $[L]^3[\theta]^{-1}$

ratio in grinding and mixing; dimensionless

Q quantity of heat J; $[F][L]$

r radius m; $[L]$

r_n neutral radius in centrifuge

specific resistance of filter cake kg m^{-1}; $[M][L]^{-1}$

R constant in freezing formulae; dimensionless

Universal gas constant 8.314 kJ mole^{-1} °K^{-1}; $[L]^2[\theta]^{-2}[T]^{-1}$

(Re) Reynolds number $(Dv\rho/\mu)$ and $(D^2N\rho/\mu)$; dimensionless

s compressibility of filter cake; dimensionless

distance m; $[L]$

standard deviation of sample compositions from the mean in mixing; dimensionless

s_o and s_r initial and random values of s in mixing; dimensionless
S_c Schmidt number $(\mu/\rho D)$; dimensionless
S_h Sherwood number (kd/D); dimensionless
SG   specific gravity; dimensionless
t temperature °C; $[T]$
             t_a air, t_s surface, t_c centre
T temperature absolute K; $[T]$
             T_{av} mean temperature
             T_m mean temperature in radiation
U overall heat-transfer coefficient $J\,m^{-2}\,s^{-1}\,°C^{-1}$; $[F][L]^{-1}[\theta]^{-1}[T]^{-1}$
v velocity $m\,s^{-1}$; $[L][\theta]^{-1}$
V flow rate of light phase $kg\,h^{-1}$; $[M][\theta]^{-1}$
             volume m^3; $[L]^3$
             volume flow rate $m^3\,s^{-1}$; $[L]^3[\theta]^{-1}$
w solid content per unit volume $kg\,m^{-3}$; $[M][L]^{-3}$
             weight kg; $[F]$
W work $N\,m$; $[F][L]$
x concentration in heavy phase $kg\,m^{-3}$; $[M][L]^{-3}$
             distance m; $[L]$
             fraction, mole or weight; dimensionless
$\bar{x}$ mean
X moisture content; dimensionless
             X_c critical moisture content, X_f final moisture content
             thickness of slab m; $[L]$
y concentration in light phase $kg\,m^{-3}$; $[M][L]^{-3}$
             fraction, mole or weight, dimensionless
Y humidity, absolute; dimensionless
z height m; $[L]$
             temperature difference for 10-fold change in thermal death time °C, $[T]$
Z depth of fluid m; $[L]$

α absorbtivity; dimensionless
β coefficient of thermal expansion $m\,m^{-1}\,°C^{-1}$; $[T]^{-1}$
             β_1, β_2 length ratios in freezing formula; dimensionless
δ thickness of layer for diffusion m; $[L]$
Δ difference
             Δt_m logarithmic mean temperature difference °C; $[T]^{-1}$
ε emissivity; dimensionless
             roughness factor; dimensionless
η efficiency of coupling
θ time h, min., s; $[\theta]$
             θ_f freezing time
λ latent heat $J\,kg^{-1}$; $[F][M]^{-1}$
             shape factor for particles; dimensionless
μ viscosity $N\,s^{-1}\,m^{-1}$; $[M][L]^{-1}[\theta]^{-1}$
π 3.1416
Π total pressure Pa; $[M][L]^{-1}[\theta]^{-2}$
             osmotic pressure kPa; $[F][L]^{-2}$
ρ density $kg\,m^{-3}$; $[M][L]^{-3}$

σ Stefan–Boltzman constant $\mathrm{kg\,m^{-1}\,s^{-1}\,^{\circ}C^{-4}}$; $[M][\theta]^{-3}[T]^{-4}$ or $[F][L]^{-1}[\theta]^{-1}[T]^{-4}$

τ shear stress in a fluid Pa; $[F][L]^{-2}$

ϕ fin efficiency; dimensionless

ω angular velocity radians $\mathrm{s^{-1}}$, $[\theta]^{-1}$

APPENDIX 2

UNITS AND CONVERSION FACTORS

Length	1 inch	$= 0.0254\,\text{m}$
	1 ft	$= 0.3048\,\text{m}$
Area	1 ft^2	$= 0.0929\,\text{m}^2$
	1 ft^3	$= 0.0283\,\text{m}^3$
Volume	1 gal Imp	$= 0.004546\ \text{m}^3$
	1 gal US	$= 0.003785\ \text{m}^3$
	1 litre	$= 0.001$
Mass	1 lb	$= 0.4536\ \text{kg}$
Density	1 lb/ft^3	$= 16.01\ \text{kg m}^{-3}$
Velocity	1 ft/sec	$= 0.3048\ \text{m s}^{-1}$
Pressure	1 lb/m^2	$= 6894\ \text{Pa}$
	1 torr	$= 133.3\ \text{Pa}$
	1 atm	$= 1.013 \times 10^5\ \text{Pa}$
Viscosity	1 cP	$= 0.001\ \text{N s m}^{-2}$
	1 lb/ft sec	$= 1.488\ \text{N s m}^{-2}$
Energy	1 Btu	$= 1055\,\text{J}$
	1 cal	$= 4.186\ \text{J}$
Power	1 kW	$= 1\ \text{kJ s}^{-1}$
	1 horsepower	$= 745.7\,\text{kW}$
	1 ton refrigeration	$= 3.519\,\text{kW}$

Heat-transfer coefficient $1\ \text{Btu ft}^{-2}\ \text{h}^{-1}\ °\text{F}^{-1} = 5.678\,\text{J m}^{-2}\,\text{s}^{-1}\,°\text{C}$

Thermal conductivity $1\ \text{Btu ft}^{-1}\ \text{h}^{-1}\ °\text{F}^{-1} = 1.731\,\text{J m}^{-1}\,\text{s}^{-1}\,°\text{C}^{-1}$

Constants π 3.1416

   σ $1.380 \times 10^{-23}\ \text{J K}^{-1}$

   e 2.7183

   R $8.314\ \text{m}^3\ \text{kPa mole}^{-1}\ \text{K}^{-1}$ or $\text{J K}^{-1}\text{mole}^{-1}$

(M) Mega $= 10^6$, (k) kilo $= 10^3$, (m) milli $= 10^{-3}$, (μ) micro $= 10^{-6}$

Temperature unit $°\text{F} = 5/9\ (°\text{C})$

APPENDIX 3

SOME PROPERTIES OF GASES

Some Properties of Gases
(Atmospheric pressure)

	Thermal conductivity ($J\ m^{-1}\ s^{-1}\ °C^{-1}$)	Specific heat ($kJ\ kg^{-1}\ °C^{-1}$)	Density ($kg\ m^{-3}$)	Temperature ($°C$)
Air	0.024	1.005	1.29	0
	0.031	1.005	0.94	100
Carbon dioxide	0.015	0.80	1.98	0
	0.022	0.92	1.46	100
Refrigerant 12	0.0083	0.92	0	
(dichlorodifluoromethane)	0.014			100
Nitrogen	0.024	1.05	1.3	0
	0.031			100

SOME PROPERTIES OF LIQUIDS

	Thermal conductivity ($J\ m^{-1}\ s^{-1}\ °C^{-1}$)	Specific heat ($kJ\ kg^{-1}\ °C^{-1}$)	Density ($kg\ m^{-3}$)	Viscosity ($N\ s\ m^{-2}$)	Temperature (°C)
Water	0.57	4.21	1000	1.79×10^{-3}	0
		4.18	987	0.56×10^{-3}	50
	0.68	4.21	958	0.28×10^{-3}	100
Sucrose 20 % soln.	0.54	3.8	1070	1.92×10^{-3}	20
				0.59×10^{-3}	80
60 % soln.				60.2×10^{-3}	20
				5.4×10^{-3}	80
				3.7×10^{-3}	95
Sodium chloride 22 % soln.	0.54	3.4	1240	2.7×10^{-3}	2
Acetic acid	0.17	2.2	1050	1.2×10^{-3}	20
Ethyl alcohol	0.18	2.3	790	1.2×10^{-3}	20
Glycerine	0.28	2.4	1250	830×10^{-3}	20
Olive oil	0.17	2.0	910	84×10^{-3}	20
Rape-seed oil			900	118×10^{-3}	20
Soya-bean oil			910	40×10^{-3}	30
Tallow			900	18×10^{-3}	65
Milk (whole)	0.56	3.9	1030	2.12×10^{-3}	20
Milk (skim)			1040	1.4×10^{-3}	25
Cream: 20 % fat			1010	6.2×10^{-3}	3
30 % fat			1000	13.8×10^{-3}	3

APPENDIX 5

SOME PROPERTIES OF SOLIDS

	Thermal conductivity ($J\ m^{-1}\ s^{-1}\ °C^{-1}$)	Specific heat ($kJ\ kg^{-1}\ °C^{-1}$)	Density ($kg\ m^{-3}$)	Temperature (°C)
1. Metals				
Aluminium	220	0.87	2640	0
Brass	97	0.38	8650	0
Cast iron	55	0.42	7210	0
Copper	388	0.38	8900	0
Steel, mild	45	0.47	7840	18
Steel, stainless	21	0.48	7950	20
2. Non-metals				
Asbestos sheet	0.17	0.84	890	51
Brick	0.7	0.92	1760	20
Cardboard	0.07	1.26	640	20
Concrete	0.87	1.05	2000	20
Celluloid	0.21	1.55	1400	30
Cotton wool	0.04	1.26	80	30
Cork	0.043	1.55	160	30
Expanded rubber	0.04		72	0
Fibreboard insulation	0.052		240	21
Glass, soda	0.52	0.84	2240	20
Ice	2.25	2.10	920	0
Mineral wool	0.04		145	30
Polyethylene	0.55	2.30	950	20
Polystyrene foam	0.036		24	0
Polyurethane foam	0.026		32	0
Polyvinyl chloride	0.29	1.30	1400	20
Wood shavings	0.09	2.5	150	0
Wood	0.28	2.5	700	30

SOME PROPERTIES OF AIR AND OF WATER

Temperature (°C)	Thermal conductivity ($J\ m^{-1}\ s^{-1}\ °C^{-1}$)	Viscosity ($N\ s\ m^{-2}$)	Specific heat ($kJ\ kg^{-1}\ °C^{-1}$)	Density ($kg\ m^{-3}$)
		AIR		
-73	0.0189	1.36×10^{-5}	0.996	1.76
-18	0.0230	1.65×10^{-5}	1.00	1.38
0	0.0242	1.73×10^{-5}	1.005	1.29
38	0.0267	1.91×10^{-5}	1.005	1.14
93	0.0301	2.15×10^{-5}	1.009	0.96
149	0.0334	2.40×10^{-5}	1.017	0.83
204	0.0367	2.60×10^{-5}	1.026	0.74
		WATER		
0	0.57	1.87×10^{-3}	4.23	1000
4	0.57	1.53×10^{-3}	4.23	1000
16	0.59	1.16×10^{-3}	4.19	1000
27	0.61	0.87×10^{-3}	4.19	998
38	0.62	0.68×10^{-3}	4.19	992
66	0.66	0.43×10^{-3}	4.19	977
93	0.68	0.30×10^{-3}	4.19	965

Extracted from *An Introduction to Heat Transfer*, Fishenden, M. and Saunders, O. A., by permission of the Clarendon Press, Oxford.

THERMAL DATA FOR SOME FOOD PRODUCTS

	Freezing point (°C)	Percent water	Specific heat		Latent heat of fusion (kJ kg^{-1})
			above freezing	below freezing (kJ kg^{-1} °C^{-1})	
Fruit					
Apples	−2	84	3.60	1.88	280
Bananas	−2	75	3.35	1.76	255
Grapefruit	−2	89	3.81	1.93	293
Peaches	−2	87	3.78	1.93	289
Pineapples	−2	85	3.68	1.88	285
Watermelons	−2	92	4.06	2.01	306
Vegetables					
Asparagus	−1	93	3.93	2.01	310
Beans (green)	−1	89	3.81	1.97	297
Cabbage	−1	92	3.93	1.97	306
Carrots	−1	88	3.60	1.88	293
Corn	−1	76	3.35	1.80	251
Peas	−1	74	3.31	1.76	247
Tomatoes	−1	95	3.98	2.01	310
Meat					
Bacon		20	2.09	1.26	71
Beef	−2	75	3.22	1.67	255
Fish	−2	70	3.18	1.67	276
Lamb	−2	70	3.18	1.67	276
Pork	−2	60	2.85	1.59	197
Veal	−2	63	2.97	1.67	209
Miscellaneous					
Beer	−2	92	4.19	2.01	301
Bread	−2	32–37	2.93	1.42	109–121
Eggs	−3		3.2	1.67	276
Ice cream	−3 to −18	58–66	3.3	1.88	222
Milk	−1	87.5	3.9	2.05	289
Water	0	100	4.19	2.05	335

Based on extracts, by permission, from *ASHRAE Guide and Data Books*.

Specific heats, latent heats of freezing and thermal conductivities of foodstuffs can be estimated if the percentage of water in the foodstuff is known. If this percentage is p then:

region between $0°C$ and $-18°C$. Freezing of foodstuffs occurs over a range of temperatures and not at any fixed point. For complete data the only really satisfactory source is a thermodynamic chart such as those prepared by Riedel (for example, in

(a) Specific heat $= 4.19p/100 + 0.84(100 - p)/100\,kJ\,kg^{-1}\,°C^{-1}$ above freezing

$\qquad\qquad\quad = 2.1p/100 + 0.84(100 - p)/100\,kJ\,kg^{-1}\,°C^{-1}$ below freezing.

(b) Latent heat $= 335p/100\,kJ\,kg^{-1}$

(c) Thermal conductivity $= 0.55p/100 + 0.26(100 - p)/100\,J\,m^{-1}\,s^{-1}\,°C^{-1}$ above freezing

$\qquad\qquad\qquad\qquad\quad = 2.4p/100 + 0.26(100 - p)/100\,J\,m^{-1}\,s^{-1}\,°C^{-1}$ below freezing.

These equations represent a considerable over-simplification so they, and also the tabulated data, should be used with caution, particularly in the

DKV Arbeitsblatt 8-11, 1957 C. F. Muller, Karlsruhe) for lean beef, and also for egg yolk, potato and fish.

STEAM TABLE — SATURATED STEAM

(Temperature Table)

Temperature (°C)	Pressure (kPa)	Enthalpy (sat. vap.) (kJ kg^{-1})	Latent heat (kJ kg^{-1})	Specific volume (m^3 kg^{-1})
0	0.611	2501	2501	206
1	0.66	2503	2499	193
2	0.71	2505	2497	180
4	0.81	2509	2492	157
6	0.93	2512	2487	138
8	1.07	2516	2483	121
10	1.23	2520	2478	106
12	1.40	2523	2473	93.8
14	1.60	2527	2468	82.8
16	1.82	2531	2464	73.3
18	2.06	2534	2459	65.0
20	2.34	2538	2454	57.8
22	2.65	2542	2449	51.4
24	2.99	2545	2445	45.9
26	3.36	2549	2440	40.0
28	3.78	2553	2435	36.7
30	4.25	2556	2431	32.9
40	7.38	2574	2407	19.5
50	12.3	2592	2383	12.0
60	19.9	2610	2359	7.67
70	31.2	2627	2334	5.04
80	47.4	2644	2309	3.41
90	70.1	2660	2283	2.36
100	101.35	2676	2257	1.673
105	120.8	2684	2244	1.42
110	143.3	2692	2230	1.21
115	169.1	2699	2217	1.04
120	198.5	2706	2203	0.892
125	232.1	2714	2189	0.771

* Reproduced with permission from J. H. Keenan *et al.*, *Steam Tables—International Edition in Metric Units*, John Wiley, New York, 1969

Appendix 8 (*continued*)

Temperature (°C)	Pressure (kPa)	Enthalpy sat. vap.) (kJ kg^{-1})	Latent heat (kJ kg^{-1})	Specific volume (m^3 kg^{-1})
130	270.1	2721	2174	0.669
135	313.0	2727	2160	0.582
140	361.3	2734	2145	0.509
150	475.8	2747	2114	0.393
160	617.8	2758	2083	0.307
180	1002	2778	2015	0.194
200	1554	2793	1941	0.127

(Pressure Table)

Temperature (°C)	Pressure (kPa)	Enthalpy sat. vap.) (kJ kg^{-1})	Latent heat (kJ kg^{-1})	Specific volume (m^3 kg^{-1})
7.0	1.0	2514	2485	129
9.7	1.2	2519	2479	109
12.0	1.4	2523	2473	93.9
14.0	1.6	2527	2468	82.8
15.8	1.8	2531	2464	74.0
17.5	2.0	2534	2460	67.0
21.1	2.5	2540	2452	54.3
24.1	3.0	2546	2445	45.7
29.0	4.0	2554	2433	34.8
32.9	5.0	2562	2424	28.2
40.3	7.5	2575	2406	19.2
45.8	10.0	2585	2393	14.7
60.1	20.0	2610	2358	7.65
75.9	40.0	2637	2319	3.99
93.5	80.0	2666	2274	2.09
99.6	100	2676	2258	1.69
102.3	110	2680	2251	1.55
104.8	120	2684	2244	1.43
107.1	130	2687	2238	1.33
109.3	140	2690	2232	1.24
111.4	150	2694	2227	1.16
113.3	160	2696	2221	1.09
115.2	170	2699	2216	1.03
116.9	180	2702	2211	0.978
118.6	190	2704	2207	0.929
120.2	200	2707	2202	0.886
127.4	250	2717	2182	0.719
133.6	300	2725	2164	0.606
138.9	350	2732	2148	0.524
143.6	400	2739	2134	0.463
147.9	450	2744	2121	0.414
151.9	500	2749	2109	0.375
167.8	750	2766	2057	0.256
179.9	1000	2778	2015	0.194

APPENDIX 9(a)

PSYCHROMETRIC CHART

Normal temperatures 1013.25 millibars

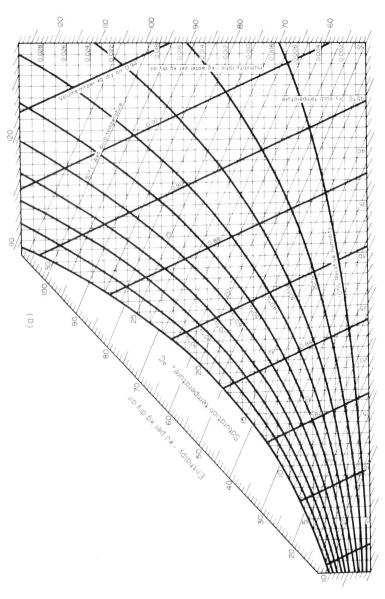

PSYCHROMETRIC CHART

High temperatures 1013.25 millibars

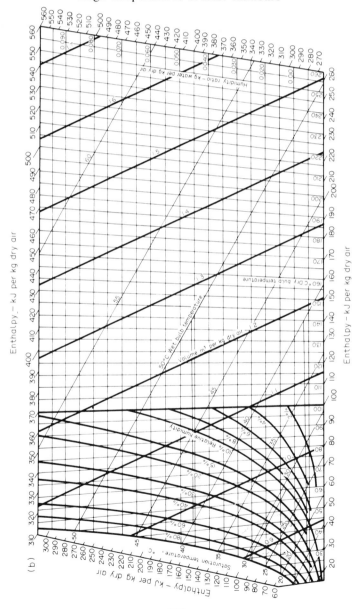

APPENDIX 10

STANDARD SIEVES

Aperture $(m \times 10^{-3})$	ISO nominal aperture $(m \times 10^{-3})$	U.S. no.	Tyler no.
22.6		$\frac{7}{8}$ in.	0.883 in.
16.0	16	$\frac{5}{8}$ in.	0.624 in.
11.2	11.2	$\frac{7}{16}$ in.	0.441 in.
8.0	8.00	$\frac{5}{16}$ in.	$2\frac{1}{2}$ mesh
5.66	5.60	No. $3\frac{1}{2}$	$3\frac{1}{2}$ mesh
4.00	4.00	5	5 mesh
2.83	2.80	7	7 mesh
2.00	2.00	10	9 mesh
1.41	1.41	14	12 mesh
1.00	1.00	18	16 mesh
0.707	0.710	25	24 mesh
0.50	0.500	35	32 mesh
0.354	0.355	45	42 mesh
0.250	0.250	60	60 mesh
0.177	0.180	80	80 mesh
0.125	0.125	120	115 mesh
0.088	0.090	170	170 mesh
0.063	0.063	230	250 mesh
0.044	0.045	325	325 mesh

PRESSURE/ENTHALPY CHARTS FOR REFRIGERANTS

(a) Dichlorodifluoromethane (refrigerant 12 — "freon")
(b) Ammonia (refrigerant 717)

* Reproduced with permission:
For ammonia (NH$_3$) at 0°C from *Kaltermachinen Regeln*, 5th edition, Verlag, C. F. Muller, Karlsrube.
For refrigerant 12 from the U.K. *Institution of Heating and Ventilating Engineers Guide*, fig. B14-11.

(a)

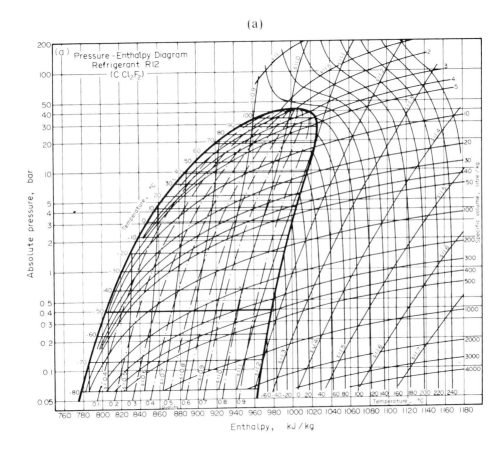

(b)

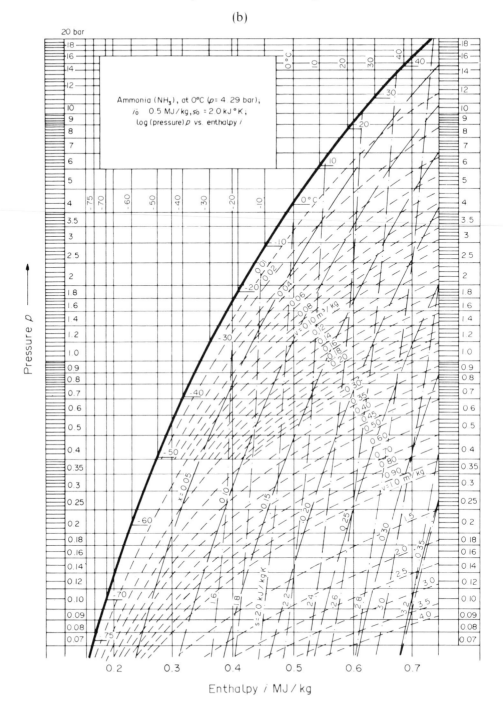

Enthalpy i MJ/kg

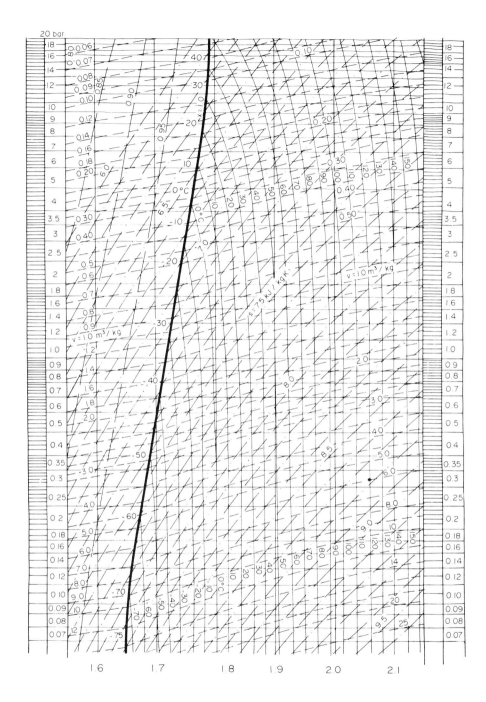

REFERENCES

ASHRAE Guide and Data Books, American Society of Heating, Refrigerating and Air Conditioning Engineers, New York.

BIRD, R. B., STEWART, W. E. and LIGHTFOOT, E. N. (1960) *Transport Phenomena*, Wiley, New York.

BOND, F. C. (1952) *Min. Engng.* **4**, 484; *Chem. Engng.* **59**, 169.

CHARM, S. E. (1970) *The Fundamentals of Food Engineering*, 2nd Edition, AVI, Westport.

CLELAND, A. C. and EARLE, R. L. (1982) *Int. J. Refrig.* **5**, 134.

COULSON, J. M. and RICHARDSON, J. F. (1977, 1978) *Chemical Engineering*, **Vol. 1**, 3rd Edition. **Vol. 2**, 3rd Edition, Pergamon, Oxford.

DKV Arbeitsblatt 2-02 (1950), C. F. Muller, Karlsruhe.

EDE, A. J. (1949) *Mod. Refrig.* **52**, 52.

ESTY, J. R. and MEYER, K. F. (1922) *J. Infect. Dis.* **31**, 650.

FISHENDEN, M. D. and SAUNDERS, O. A. (1950) *An Introduction to Heat Transfer*, Oxford University Press.

GROSSE, J. W. and DUFFIELD, G. M. (1954) *Chem. Ind.* 1464.

HENDERSON, S. M. and PERRY, R. L. (1955) *Agricultural Process Engineering*, Wiley, New York.

International Critical Tables (1930), McGraw-Hill, New York.

JASON, A. C. (1958) in *Fundamental Aspects of the Dehydration of Foodstuffs*, Society of Chemical Industry, London.

MCADAMS, W. H. (1954) *Heat Transmission*, 3rd Edition, McGraw-Hill, New York.

MCCABE, W. L. and SMITH, J. C. (1975) *Unit Operations of Chemical Engineering*, McGraw-Hill, New York.

MCCABE, W. L. and THIELE, E. W. (1925) *Industr. Eng. Chem.* **17**, 605.

MANHEIM, H. C., STEINBERG, M. P., NELSON, A. I. and KENDALL, T. W. (1957) *Food Technol.* **11**, 384.

MOODY, L. F. (1944) *Trans. Am. Soc. Mech. Engrs.* **66**, 671.

PERRY, J. H. (1973) *Chemical Engineers Handbook*, 5th Edition, McGraw-Hill, New York.

PLANK, R. (1913) *Z. Ges Kälteind*, **20**, S.109; (1941) *Ibid.*, Beih. Reihe 3, H.10.

RUSHTON, J. N., COSTICH, E. W. and EVERETT, H. S. (1950) *Chem. Engng. Prog.* **46**, 395.

SOURIRAJAN, S. (ed.) (1977) *Reverse Osmosis and Synthetic Membranes; Theory, Technology and Engineering*, Nat. Res. Council of Canada, Ottawa.

SPICER, A. (1974) *Advances in Preconcentration and Dehydration of Foods*, Applied Science, London.

STUMBO, C. R. (1973) *Thermobacteriology*, 2nd Edition, Academic, New York.

THIJSSEN, H. A. C. (1974) in *Advances in Preconcentration and Dehydration of Foods*, A. Spicer (ed.), Applied Science, London.

TREYBAL, R. E. (1968) *Mass Transfer*, 2nd Edition, McGraw-Hill, New York.

TROWBRIDGE, M. E. O'K. (1962) *Chem. Engng.* (U.K.) No. 162, A.73.

WHITMAN, W. G. (1923) *Chem. and Met. Engng.* **29**, 147.

BIBLIOGRAPHY

General Data

Handbook of Chemistry and Physics, Chemical Rubber Publishing, Sandusky.

International Critical Table (1932) McGraw-Hill, New York.

KEENAN, J. H., KEYES, F. G., HILL, P. G. and MOORE, J. G. (1969) *Steam Tables*, Wiley, New York.

PERRY, R. H. and CHILTON, C. H. (1973) *Chemical Engineers Handbook*, 5th Edition, McGraw-Hill, New York.

Fluid Flow

STREETER, V. L. and WILEY, V. (1979) *Fluid Mechanics*, 6th Edition, McGraw-Hill, New York.

Heat Transfer

EDE, A. J. (1967) *An Introduction to Heat Transfer*, Pergamon, Oxford.

FISHENDEN, M. and SAUNDERS, O. A. (1950) *An Introduction to Heat Transfer*, Oxford University Press, Oxford.

KERN, D. Q. (1950) *Process Heat Transfer*, McGraw-Hill, New York.

MCADAMS, W. H. (1954) *Heat Transmission*, 3rd Edition, McGraw-Hill, New York.

Sterilization by Heat

STUMBO, C. R. (1973) *Thermobacteriology in Food Processing*, 3rd Edition, Academic, New York.

Refrigeration

ASHRAE Guide and Data Books, American Society of Heating, Refrigerating, and Air Conditioning Engineers, New York.

ANDERSEN, S. A. (1959) *Automatic Refrigeration*, McLaren, Glasgow.

JORDAN, R. C. and PRIESTER, G. B. (1956) *Refrigeration and Air Conditioning*, Prentice Hall, Englewood Cliffs.

VENEMANN, H. G. (1946) *Refrigeration Theory and Applications*, 2nd Edition, Nickerson and Collins, Chicago.

Dehydration

Fundamental Aspects of the Dehydration of Foodstuffs (1958) The Society of Chemical Industry, London.

KEEY, R. B. (1978) *Introduction to Industrial Drying Operations*, Pergamon, Oxford.

VAN ARSEL, W. B., COPLEY, M. J. and MORGAN, A. I. (1973) (eds.) *Food Dehydration*, 2nd Edition, **Vol. 1,** Principles, AVI, Westport.

SPICER, A. (1974) (ed.) *Advances in Preconcentration and Dehydration of Foods*, Applied Science, London.

Food Engineering

BRENNAN, J. G., BUTTERS, J. R., COWELL, N. D. and LILLY, A. E. (1976) *Food Engineering Operations* (2nd Edition), Applied Science, London.

CHARM, S. E. (1971) *The Fundamentals of Food Engineering* (2nd Edition), AVI, Westport.

HARPER, J. C. (1976) *Elements of Food Engineering*, AVI, Westport.

HELDMAN, D. R. (1975) *Food Process Engineering*, AVI, Westport.

LENIGER, H. A. and BEVERLOO, W. A. (1975) *Food Process Engineering*, Reidel, Dordrecht.

LONCIN, M. and MERSON, R. L. (1979) *Food Engineering: Principles and Selected Applications*, Academic, New York.

Chemical Engineering Unit Operations

BEEK, W. J. and MUTTZALL, K. M. K. (1975) *Transport Phenomena*, Wiley, London.

BLACKADDER, D. A. and NEDDERMAN, R. M. (1971) *A Handbook of Unit Operations*, Academic, London.

COULSON, J. M. and RICHARDSON, J. F. (1977, 1978) *Chemical Engineering*, 3rd Edition, **Vols. 1, 2,** Pergamon, Oxford.

FOUST, A. S., WENZEL, L. A., CLUMP, C. W., MAUS, L. and ANDERSEN, L. B. (1980) *Principles of Unit Operations*, 2nd Edition, Wiley, New York.

HENDERSON, S. M. and PERRY, R. L. (1955) *Agricultural Process Engineering*, Wiley, New York.

MCCABE, W. L. and SMITH, J. C. (1975) *Unit Operations of Chemical Engineering*, 3rd Edition, McGraw-Hill, New York.

TREYBAL, R. E. (1968) *Mass Transfer*, 2nd Edition, McGraw-Hill, New York.

INDEX